BRITISH INSTITUTE AT ANKARA
Monograph 44

AT EMPIRES' EDGE: PROJECT PAPHLAGONIA

REGIONAL SURVEY IN NORTH-CENTRAL TURKEY

Edited by
Roger Matthews and Claudia Glatz

Published by
BRITISH INSTITUTE AT ANKARA
10 Carlton House Terrace, London SW1Y 5AH

© British Institute of Archaeology at Ankara 2009
ISBN 978 1 898249 23 8

All rights reserved. No parts of this publication may be reproduced, stored in a retrieval system, or transmitted, in any form or by any means, electronic, mechanical, photocopying, recording, or otherwise, without the prior permission of the British Institute of Archaeology at Ankara.

Typeset by Gina Coulthard
Printed by Stephen Austin & Sons Ltd, Hertford

Published with the assistance of financial contributions from the Anglo-Turkish Society
and members of the British Institute at Ankara

This volume is designed to be read and consulted alongside the associated Project Paphlagonia electronic archive and web resource (http://www.ucl.ac.uk/paphlagonia/). There, amongst other features, can be found photographs and drawings of all diagnostic sherds recovered in the course of the project, as well as detailed site catalogues, numerous colour figures and other relevant materials.

Cover illustrations: front, Ilgaz mountains behind PS016, Salman West; back, a Paphlagonian village view, Karaören

Preface and Acknowledgements

This volume is the final publication of a fieldwork programme conducted between 1997 and 2001 under the title of Project Paphlagonia. The project was directed by Roger Matthews in post as Director of the British Institute of Archaeology at Ankara (as it then was, hereafter BIAA). Almost all funding toward the fieldwork was generously provided by the BIAA, for which I am extremely grateful. Financial support from the Society for the Promotion of Hellenic Studies in the 2001 season was also greatly appreciated. Post-fieldwork processing, analysis and publication preparation have been kindly supported by grants from the BIAA, the Mediterranean Archaeological Trust, the Graduate School of UCL and the Institute of Archaeology UCL, to all of whom sincere thanks are here given. The sections of Chapter Two reported on by Vedat Toprak, Arda Arcasoy and M. Lütfi Süzen constitute the final report of the project ODTÜ-AGÜDOS 98.03.09.01.06 prepared in the Geological Engineering Department of the Middle East Technical University (Ankara, Turkey) for the BIAA.

Sincere and heartfelt gratitude is due to the many individuals who provided assistance to the project at some stage through its life. In particular, I wish to thank all staff at the Directorate-General of Monuments and Museums of the Republic of Turkey, including successive Directors-General (Engin Özgen, Mehmet Akif Işık, Ender Varinlioğlu, Alpay Pasinli) and especially our official Turkish government representatives (1997 Cevdet Sevinç, 1998 Gülay Aslan, 1999 Zehra Taşkıran, 2000 Gülcan Demir, 2001 Nilgün Sinan), all of whom played integral and much appreciated roles within the execution of the project. In the field we received friendly advice and assistance from all officials of the Governorates of Çankırı and Karabük and especially from successive Directors of Çankırı Museum (Erol Özen, Yücel Kiper and, for the 2005 study season, Yusuf Demirci), as well as from other staff of the museum, the cultural directorate, the *jandarma* and the villagers of the region. Staff of the BIAA were tremendously helpful in a broad range of ways, in particular in London Gina Coulthard and in Ankara Gülgün Girdivan, Yaprak Eran, Yiğit Erbil, and Zeynep and Ali Koç. At the initiation of the project, discussions with Jim Coulton, Jim Crow, Wendy Matthews, Stephen Mitchell, Neil Roberts and Mark Whittow were especially helpful. Sincere thanks also to David French for a memorable day investigating ancient routes and roads of the region.

I am above all grateful to members of the Project Paphlagonia field teams, who shared the journey of fieldwork with me and whose company made the experience all the more rewarding and stimulating:

1997 season: Andrew Goldman, Wendy Matthews, Penny McParlin, Tom Pollard, Michael Ramage;
1998 season: Raoul Bull, Wendy Matthews, Tom Pollard;
1999 season: Arda Arcasoy, Peter Boyer, Daniela Cottica, Gareth Darbyshire, Warren Eastwood, Michael Given, Elizabeth Hunt, Wendy Matthews, Neil Roberts, Caroline Steele, M. Lütfi Süzen, Vedat Toprak, Mark Whittow;

2000 season: Gareth Darbyshire, Kevan Edinborough, Sandrine Hourcade-Lamarque, Kate O'Brien, Caroline Steele, Jed Stevenson, Zuzanna Stroynowski, Richard Wilkinson;

2001 season: Daniela Cottica, Gareth Darbyshire, Naomi Hollis, Susan Holmes, Mehdi İlhan, Ben Marsh, Wendy Matthews, Michael Metcalfe, Caroline Steele, Michael Tabona, Joanna Taylor, Burcu Tung, Emma Twigger, Helen Wickstead, Richard Wilkinson;

2005 Çankırı Museum study season: Daniela Cottica, Claudia Glatz.

For assistance and advice regarding the lengthy and difficult task of producing this final publication I owe deep gratitude to the following people: Gina Coulthard, Jim Coulton, Varina Delrieu, Çiğdem Eissenstadt, Birger Helgestad, Rebekah Miracle, Andrew Peacock, Tom Pollard, Matthew Reynolds, Alessandra Salvin, Emma Twigger and Helen Wickstead, as well as two anonymous referees. Michael Metcalfe wishes to thank the following for their help with his contribution: Simona Todaro, Santo Privitera, Ben Millis, Jonathan Prag and Peter Thonemann. He is also grateful to Christian Marek for reading and improving his section of Chapter Six.

Previous reports and syntheses on Project Paphlagonia include: Glatz, Matthews 2005; Matthews 1997; 1998; 1999a; 1999b; 1999c; 2000a; 2000b; 2000c; 2000d; 2001a; 2001b; 2002; 2003; 2004a; 2004b; 2007; Matthews, Glatz forthcoming; Matthews et al. 1998). The site catalogue includes XY coordinates in WGS-1984 (Datum), UTM zone 36N (Geographic Coordinate System) projection format. Sincere thanks to Varina Delrieu, Birger Helgestad, Jon Reades, Ash Rennie and Helen Taylor for assistance with the web resource elements of the project. I close by expressing gratitude to my co-editor, Claudia Glatz, without whose input of time and expertise this volume would have taken much longer to appear.

Roger Matthews
London, February 2009

Contributors

Arda Arcasoy	Department of Geological Engineering, Middle East Technical University, Ankara
Julian Carolan	School of Geography, Archaeology and Palaeoecology, Queen's University, Belfast
Daniela Cottica	Department of Sciences of Antiquity and the Near East, Venice International University
Warren Eastwood	School of Geography, Earth and Environmental Sciences, The University of Birmingham
Claudia Glatz	Institute of Archaeology, University College London
M. Mehdi İlhan	Centre for Arab and Islamic Studies, The Australian National University, Canberra
Ben Marsh	Department of Geography and Program in Environmental Studies, Bucknell University
Roger Matthews	Institute of Archaeology, University College London
Michael Metcalfe	Mediterranean Center for Arts and Sciences, University of Siracusa
Neil Roberts	School of Geography, Plymouth University
Andreas Schachner	German Archaeological Institute, Istanbul
M. Lütfi Süzen	Department of Geological Engineering, Middle East Technical University, Ankara
Vedat Toprak	Department of Geological Engineering, Middle East Technical University, Ankara

List of figures
Chapter One
1.1 Map of Turkey to show Project Paphlagonia survey region
1.2 Çankırı town, with citadel centre right, in trees in distance
1.3 North Anatolian Fault Zone at Kızıllar village, sites PS064–PS067
1.4 Kızılırmak river at the town of Kızılırmak
1.5 Çankırı town viewed from the citadel
1.6 Anatolian plateau near Işık Dağı in southwest of Çankırı province
1.7 View looking north towards Ilgaz from İnköy. The two mounds of Salman West (PS016) and Salman East (PS015), bisected by the modern road, are visible in left middle distance
1.8 Ilgaz mountains under snow
1.9 Ilgaz mountains in summer
1.10 The Devrez river near Orta
1.11 Abandoned field systems on the Köroğlu mountains
1.12 Landscape in the region of Eskipazar
1.13 A Paphlagonian village view, Karaören
1.14 Map of Çankırı and southeast Karabük provinces to show *ilçe*
1.15 Paphlagonian villagers
1.16 Extensive survey by vehicle
1.17 Extensive survey on foot
1.18 Extensive survey: completing site and landscape forms
1.19 Ancient cemetery uncovered by illicit activity
1.20 View of Salman East (PS015)
1.21 Extensive and intensive survey: map of all located sites
1.22 Distribution of intensive survey sample blocks
1.23 Intensive survey: walking the line
1.24 Intensive survey: lunch break
1.25 Intensive survey: plan of Çivi sample block
1.26 Intensive survey: plan of Ilgaz sample block
1.27 Intensive survey: plan of Eldivan sample block
1.28 Intensive survey: plan of Dumanlı sample block
1.29 Intensive survey: plan of Salur sample block
1.30 Intensive survey: plan of Bölükören sample block
1.31 Intensive survey: plan of Dağtarla sample block
1.32 Intensive survey: plan of Çerkeş sample block
1.33 Intensive survey: plan of Kızılırmak sample block
1.34 Intensive survey: plan of Mart sample block
1.35 Intensive survey: extreme field-walking
1.36 Manuring of fields with village debris

Chapter Two
2.1 Cattle in Kızılırmak region
2.2 Water buffalo in Orta region
2.3 Topography and drainage of the Paphlagonia survey region. Elevations from NASA Shuttle-borne radar data
2.4 Generalised geology of parts of the survey region. Derived from MTA n.d. Incomplete coverage is a result of limited geological map coverage
2.5 Roman and modern routes of communication in Inner Paphlagonia (after Talbert 2000)
2.6 Landscape capability mapping from spring 1998 Thematic Mapper imagery, derived by identifying and mapping contemporary vegetation classes. Incomplete coverage is a result of imagery limitations. Lowest class (forest and scrub) includes bare rock and water. The analysis tended to over-populate the poorer classes. Imagery acquired courtesy D. Griffin
2.7 Landslide in Ilgaz mountain range, exposing buried Byzantine site
2.8 Map to show location of 1:100,000 and 1:25,000 scale map sheets

2.9   Simplified geological map showing tectonic units of Turkey
2.10   Schematic maps of the areas of Çerkeş, Kurşunlu and Ilgaz (simplified from Barka 1984)
2.11   Map of north-central Turkey, showing epicentres of earthquakes AD 1900–2000
2.12   Earthquake damage in region of Orta, June 2000
2.13   Distribution of rock categories across the survey region
2.14   Distribution of individual rock categories across the survey region
2.15   Relief map of survey region
2.16   Histograms relating to morphological features of the survey region
2.17   Slope map of survey region
2.18   Aspect map of survey region
2.19   Rose diagram showing aspect topography of survey region
2.20   Map showing general topography of survey region
2.21   Distribution of settlement in Çankırı province, AD 1950
2.22   Intensive survey blocks: Çerkeş, Çivi, Bölükören
2.23   Intensive survey blocks: Dağtarla, Salur, Ilgaz
2.24   Intensive survey blocks: Dumanlı, Mart, Eldivan
2.25   Intensive survey block: Kızılırmak
2.26   General view of Çerkeş survey block
2.27   General view of Çerkeş survey block
2.28   General view of Çivi survey block
2.29   General view of Çivi survey block
2.30   General view of Bölükören survey block
2.31   General view of Bölükören survey block
2.32   General view of Dağtarla survey block
2.33   General view of Dağtarla survey block
2.34   General view of Salur survey block
2.35   General view of Salur survey block
2.36   General view of Ilgaz survey block
2.37   General view of Ilgaz survey block
2.38   General view of Dumanlı survey block
2.39   General view of Dumanlı survey block
2.40   General view of Mart survey block
2.41   General view of Mart survey block
2.42   General view of Eldivan survey block
2.43   General view of Eldivan survey block
2.44   General view of Kızılırmak survey block
2.45   General view of Kızılırmak survey block
2.46   Map of survey region showing location of visited lakes
2.47   Inflatable boat on Paphlagonian lake
2.48   Extrusion of core into piping tubes
2.49   Çöl Göl age depth curve
2.50   Lithology, loss-on-ignition, magnetic susceptibility and grain-size analyses for COL99
2.51   Selected geochemical and mineralogical data for COL99
2.52   Summary percentage pollen diagram for COL99
2.53   Sr-Ca ratio for COL99 compared to $\delta^{18}O$ record for Nar Gölü (Jones et al. 2006) on common timescale

Chapter Three
3.1   Palaeolithic sites located in Project Paphlagonia
3.2   Possible Lower Palaeolithic implement from PS058
3.3   Possible Lower Palaeolithic implements from Dumanlı 03S03
3.4   Sites Eldivan 02S03 and Eldivan 02S04, on foreground slopes
3.5   Middle Palaeolithic implements from sites Eldivan 02S03 and Eldivan 02S04
3.6   Middle Palaeolithic implements from sites Eldivan 02S03 and Eldivan 02S04

3.7 Chalcolithic sites located in Project Paphlagonia
3.8 Obsidian strata in layers of volcanic ash near PS050 Salur Höyük
3.9 PS050 Salur Höyük
3.10 Early Chalcolithic painted sherd from PS050 Salur Höyük (top right)
3.11 Chalcolithic and Early Bronze Age sherds from PS005
3.12 Site Çivi 05S01, Sariçi Höyük
3.13 Site PS005, atop flat summit
3.14 Early Bronze Age sites located in Project Paphlagonia
3.15 Selected sherds from site PS187
3.16 Selected sherds from site PS174
3.17 PS111, Yazıboy, view: the site sits atop the small flat promontory in the mid-left of the image, directly above foreground trees
3.18 Sherds from PS111, Yazıboy
3.19 Sherds from PS111, Yazıboy
3.20 Sherds from PS111, Yazıboy
3.21 Sherds from PS111, Yazıboy
3.22 Sherds from PS111, Yazıboy
3.23 Sherds from PS111, Yazıboy
3.24 Sherds from PS111, Yazıboy
3.25 Sherds from PS111, Yazıboy
3.26 Dumanlı 03S04, atop summit in mid-distance
3.27 PS219, Salur North, in foreground with PS050, Salur Höyük, beyond
3.28 Selected sherds from PS219, Salur North
3.29 Selected sherds from PS219, Salur North
3.30 Selected sherds from PS219, Salur North
3.31 Selected sherds from PS219, Salur North
3.32 Metal objects from PS219, Salur North
3.33 Pottery from sites PS005, PS013, PS015, PS016, PS050
3.34 Pottery from sites PS057, PS111
3.35 Pottery from sites PS122, PS155, PS174, PS187, PS198, PS218
3.36 Pottery from site PS219
3.37 Pottery from site PS219
3.38 Pottery from site PS219
3.39 Objects and pottery from sites PS219, Çivi 05S01, Dumanlı 03S04

Chapter Four
4.1 Second-millennium BC sites located in Project Paphlagonia
4.2 PS183, Maltepe
4.3 PS016, Salman West, and PS015, Salman East, looking north from İnköy
4.4 Ilgaz mountains behind PS016, Salman West
4.5 Ramps of PS016, Salman West
4.6 Plan of PS016, Salman West
4.7 PS057, Dumanlı. The main wall runs across the centre of the image in the middle distance
4.8 PS057, Dumanlı, main wall
4.9 PS057, Dumanlı, detail of main wall showing stepped alignment
4.10 PS057, Dumanlı, access ramp at south end of main wall
4.11 Plan of PS057, Dumanlı
4.12 Ancient tracks in the region of PS218, Kanlıgöl
4.13 PS218, Kanlıgöl, located on the flat promontory on the horizon
4.14 PS218, Kanlıgöl, with figures ascending the access ramp
4.15 PS218, Kanlıgöl, collapsed stone circumvallation
4.16 Plan of PS218, Kanlıgöl
4.17 PS122, İnceboğaz. To the left an Iron Age tumulus sits atop the Bronze Age access ramp

4.18   Look-out site Eldivan 04S01
4.19   Looking east across the Eldivan plain. In the centre Eldivan Höyük (PS178) stands out amongst the vegetation, with the look-out site, Eldivan 04S01, located on the centre of the high ridge beyond
4.20   The Devrez Çay near Sakaeli, Orta
4.21   Pottery from site PS015, Salman East
4.22   Pottery from site PS015, Salman East
4.23   Pottery from site PS016, Salman West
4.24   Pottery from site PS016, Salman West
4.25   Pottery from site PS016, Salman West
4.26   Pottery from site PS016, Salman West
4.27   Pottery from site PS057, Dumanlı
4.28   Pottery from site PS057, Dumanlı
4.29   Pottery from site PS170, İnandık
4.30   Pottery from site PS170, İnandık
4.31   Pottery from site PS183, Maltepe
4.32   Pottery from site PS122, İnceboğaz
4.33   Pottery from site Mart 01S01
4.34   Pottery from site Mart 01S01
4.35   Pottery from site Mart 01S01
4.36   Pottery from site Mart 01S01
4.37   Copper alloy projectile point from site PS169, Kara Mustafa Höyük
4.38   Copper alloy projectile point from site Çivi 05S01
4.39   Pottery from sites PS005, PS013, PS015
4.40   Pottery from site PS016
4.41   Pottery from sites PS033a, PS040, PS050, PS052
4.42   Pottery from sites PS057, PS113, PS122, PS154
4.43   Pottery from sites PS155, PS156, PS169, PS170
4.44   Pottery from sites PS171, PS176, PS178
4.45   Pottery from sites PS183, PS198, PS218, PS219
4.46   Pottery from sites Çivi 05S01, Eldivan 04S01, Dumanlı 02C28, Dumanlı 02S05, Mart 01S02
4.47   Pottery from site Mart 01S01

Chapter Five
5.1   Iron Age sites located in Project Paphlagonia
5.2   Pottery from PS156
5.3   Phrygian grey ware sherds from PS178
5.4   PS052, Kızılca Tepe
5.5   Pottery from PS052, Kızılca Tepe
5.6   Stone-lined burial chamber at tumulus PS061
5.7   Architectural tile from PS015, Salman East
5.8   Burial tumuli and rock-cut tombs located in Project Paphlagonia
5.9   Illicitly excavated tumulus PS129
5.10   Tumulus PS017 on high spur
5.11   Lowland tumulus PS021
5.12   Rock-cut tomb PS211, Deliklikaya
5.13   Rock-cut tomb PS142, Karakoyunlu
5.14   Pottery from sites PS003, PS015
5.15   Pottery from sites PS016, PS050, PS052, PS057
5.16   Pottery from sites PS122, PS154, PS170, PS172
5.17   Pottery from site PS178
5.18   Pottery from sites PS211, PS218, Eldivan 03S01, Ilgaz 02S01, Mart 01S01

Chapter Six

6.1 View from summit of Asar Tepe, PS096, facing northwest, with extensive platform in the foreground and traces of illicit digging
6.2 Site PS003, Kurmalar
6.3 Architectural element illicitly excavated at Asar Tepe, PS096
6.4 Architectural element illicitly excavated at Asar Tepe, PS096. Parts of an eagle in relief can be discerned at the right
6.5 Architectural element, said originally to have had a depiction of an elephant, at Asar Tepe, PS096
6.6 Hellenistic and Hellenistic–Roman sites located in Project Paphlagonia
6.7 Tumulus with adjacent earthen platform, PS128
6.8 Stone lion at the *kaymakamlık* of Ilgaz, PS022
6.9 Stone lion at the *kaymakamlık* of Ilgaz, PS022
6.10 Site PS168, Çankırı citadel, in distance with goat in foreground
6.11 The Tatlı Çay as it enters Çankırı town
6.12 The Acı Çay to the south of Çankırı town
6.13 Construction work on ancient site of Çankırı in 1997
6.14 Kaisareia Hadrianopolis, PS098, mosaic floor in illicit excavations
6.15 Kaisareia Hadrianopolis, PS098, architectural element
6.16 Kaisareia Hadrianopolis, PS099, group of rock-cut graves
6.17 Kaisareia Hadrianopolis, PS100, stone-clad entrance to the city
6.18 Kaisareia Hadrianopolis, PS101, broken column
6.19 Kaisareia Hadrianopolis, PS105, brick dome or vault, largely underground
6.20 Kaisareia Hadrianopolis, PS109, architectural element now in Eskipazar *belediye* garden
6.21 Inscriptions located in Project Paphlagonia
6.22 Antoninopolis, PS063, remains at Bedil village
6.23 Antoninopolis, PS064, located across the fields to the west of the modern village of Kızıllar
6.24 Main east-west route in region of Ilgaz, looking north, mounds of Salman East and Salman West visible in centre
6.25 Robbed-out stretch of Roman road on west side of Eldivan Dağı, Eldivan 02S02, 05S02
6.26 Robbed-out stretch of Roman road on west side of Eldivan Dağı, Eldivan 02S02, 05S02
6.27 Stretch of Roman road near Kisecik, south of Ilgaz
6.28 Traces of roads and tracks west of Korgun
6.29 Roman and Roman–Byzantine sites located in Project Paphlagonia
6.30 Çankırı citadel, PS168 general view
6.31 Çankırı citadel, PS168 multi-phase tower
6.32 Çankırı citadel, PS168 multi-phase tower
6.33 Çankırı citadel, PS168 cistern in interior
6.34 Pottery from PS168, Çankırı citadel
6.35 Byzantine sites located in Project Paphlagonia
6.36 Monastery/chapel site at İnköy, PS010
6.37 Monastery/chapel site at İnköy, PS010
6.38 Monastery/chapel site at Salur 03S01
6.39 Monastery/chapel site at Salur 03S01
6.40 Site PS196, Zırçalı Mevkii, with illicit excavation in foreground
6.41 Site PS196, Zırçalı Mevkii, moulded tile with cross motif
6.42 Site PS196, Zırçalı Mevkii, moulded tile fragments
6.43 Pottery from site PS196, Zırçalı Mevkii
6.44 Tile with triple impressed lines, PS115
6.45 Tile with triple impressed lines, PS064
6.46 Fortified hilltop sites located in Project Paphlagonia
6.47 Fortified hilltop site, PS029, Gökçeören
6.48 Fortified hilltop site, PS029, Gökçeören, plan
6.49 Fortified hilltop site, PS043, Gavur

6.50	Fortified hilltop site, PS043, Gavur
6.51	Fortified hilltop site, PS043, Gavur, plan
6.52	Fortified hilltop site, PS074, Bozoğlu, plan
6.53	Fortified hilltop site, PS085, Yalakçukurören
6.54	Fortified hilltop site, PS085, Yalakçukurören, plan
6.55	Pottery from site PS074, Bozoğlu
6.56	Pottery from site PS043, Gavur
6.57	Fortified hilltop site, PS051, Kurşunlu
6.58	Fortified hilltop site, PS051, Kurşunlu
6.59	Fortified hilltop site, PS051, Kurşunlu
6.60	Fortified hilltop site, PS051, Kurşunlu, plan
6.61	PPI.1, site PS003a, inscription
6.62	PPI.1, site PS003a, inscription
6.63	PPI.2, site PS028, inscription
6.64	PPI.3, site PS042a, inscription
6.65	PPI.3, site PS042a, inscription
6.66	PPI.4, site PS062, inscription
6.67	PPI.4, site PS062, inscription
6.68	PPI.5, site PS062, inscription, left section
6.69	PPI.5, site PS062, inscription, middle section
6.70	PPI.5, site PS062, inscription, right section
6.71	PPI.6, site PS067, inscription
6.72	PPI.6, site PS067, squeeze of inscription
6.73	PPI.7, site PS070, inscription
6.74	PPI.8, site PS070, inscription
6.75	PPI.9, site PS071, inscription
6.76	PPI.9, site PS071, inscription
6.77	PPI.10, site PS092a, inscription, left section
6.78	PPI.10, site PS092a, inscription, right section
6.79	PPI.11, site PS092a, inscription
6.80	PPI.11, site PS092a, inscription
6.81	PPI.12, site PS096, inscription
6.82	PPI.13, site PS096, inscription
6.83	PPI.13, site PS096, inscription
6.84	PPI.14, site PS096, inscription
6.85	PPI.15, site PS097, inscription, left section
6.86	PPI.15, site PS097, inscription, right section
6.87	PPI.16, site PS098, inscribed fragment
6.88	PPI.16, site PS098, inscription
6.89	PPI.17, site PS109, inscription
6.90	PPI.18, site PS109, inscription
6.91	PPI.19, site PS117, inscription
6.92	PPI.20, site PS117, inscription
6.93	PPI.20, site PS117, inscription, left section
6.94	PPI.20, site PS117, inscription, right section
6.95	PPI.21, site PS119, inscription, left section
6.96	PPI.21, site PS119, inscription, right section
6.97	PPI.22, site PS120, inscription
6.98	PPI.23, site PS124, inscription, contrast enhanced
6.99	PPI.24, site PS141, inscription, left section
6.100	PPI.24, site PS141, inscription, middle section
6.101	PPI.24, site PS141, inscription, right section
6.102	Pottery from sites PS003, PS004, PS007, PS029, PS032, PS048, PS064

6.103   Pottery from sites PS066, PS074, PS089, PS115
6.104   Pottery from sites PS118, PS157, PS167, PS168
6.105   Pottery from site PS196
6.106   Pottery from sites PS204, PS227, Dağtarla 02S01
6.107   Pottery from sites Eldivan 01 (PS178), Ilgaz 01S03, Ilgaz 03S04, Mart 01S02

Chapter Seven
7.1   Population shifts by quarter AD 1521–1578
7.2   View of Taş Mescid
7.3   View of Taş Mescid
7.4   Gravestone inscription dated AH 1277/AD 1860–1861
7.5   Population of Çankırı town at intervals from AD 1521–1990
7.6   Total population of the villages of Çankırı, Koçhisar and Çerkeş through the 16th century AD

Chapter Eight
8.1   Summary chart of settlement count, weighted count (sites per century) and aggregate settlement areas, in hectares, per period
8.2   Site-size distributions period by period
8.3   Settlement continuity and abandonment
8.4   Settlement count, weighted count (sites per century) and aggregate settlement areas, in hectares, for the second millennium BC. OH = Old Hittite; EEM = Early Empire; LEM = Late Empire
8.5   Settlement count, weighted count (sites per century) and aggregate settlement areas, in hectares, for the Iron Age
8.6   Settlement count, weighted count (sites per century) and aggregate settlement areas, in hectares, for the first millennium AD

All photographs in this volume were taken by Roger Matthews.

List of tables

Chapter One
1.1 Periods of the Paphlagonian past: material culture and textual sources
1.2 Size categories of sites in Project Paphlagonia
1.3 Typology of sites in Project Paphlagonia

Chapter Two
2.1 Modern climate data for Çankırı city (after Alex 1985: 58)
2.2 Contemporary land-use patterns in Çankırı province (after http://www.cankiri.gov.tr/ana/tarim/tarim.htm)
2.3 Use of arable land in Çankırı province (after http://www.cankiri.gov.tr/ana/tarim/tarim.htm)
2.4 Contemporary farm animals of Çankırı province (after http://www.cankiri.gov.tr/ana/tarim/tarim.htm)
2.5 Properties of the rock types of the area
2.6 Some properties of the nine rock categories
2.7 Elevation, slope and aspect data of the study area. Histograms in fig. 2.16 are drawn according to the % column in this table
2.8 Landscape capabilities of intensive survey units, derived from satellite mapping as described for fig. 2.6
2.9 Lakes sampled in Çankırı province during 1999 field season, and modern water chemistry
2.10 ^{14}C dates for COL99
2.11 COL99 core description

Chapter Four
4.1 Schematic overview of historical and archaeological chronologies
4.2 Sites of second-millennium BC date and their attributes. Sites marked * have occupation principally of Roman–Byzantine date and are not included in the spatial and settlement analyses for the second millennium BC

Chapter Five
5.1 Iron Age chronology, based on Gordion/Yassıhöyuk sequence
5.2 Iron Age sites and their attributes
5.3 Sites with material of Early Iron Age date
5.4 Tumuli and rock-cut sites

Chapter Seven
7.1 The quarters of Çankırı town in AD 1521 and AD 1578

Abbreviations used in the pottery and object figure catalogues

h	high
m	medium
l	low
min	mineral
veg	vegetal
inc	inclusions
v	very
f	fine
c	coarse
ext	exterior
int	interior
brn	burnished
smoo	smoothed

Contents

Chapter One   1
Project Paphlagonia: Research Issues, Approaches and Methods
Roger Matthews

Chapter Two   27
Contexts of Human Interaction: Geology, Geography, Geomorphology and Environment
*Ben Marsh, Neil Roberts, Vedat Toprak, Roger Matthews, Warren Eastwood,
Julian Carolan, Arda Arcasoy and M. Lütfi Süzen*

Chapter Three   75
Silent Centuries: Paphlagonia from the Palaeolithic to the Early Bronze Age, 200,000–2000 BC
Roger Matthews

Chapter Four   107
A Landscape of Conflict and Control: Paphlagonia during the Second Millennium BC
Claudia Glatz, Roger Matthews and Andreas Schachner

Chapter Five   149
A Dark Age, Grey Ware and Elusive Empires: Paphlagonia through the Iron Age, 1200–330 BC
Roger Matthews

Chapter Six   173
Landscapes with Figures: Paphlagonia through the Hellenistic, Roman and Byzantine Periods, 330 BC–AD 1453
Roger Matthews, Michael Metcalfe and Daniela Cottica

Chapter Seven   227
Çankırı in History: Insights from Ottoman Documents
M. Mehdi İlhan

Chapter Eight   239
People and Place in Paphlagonia: Trends and Patterns in Settlement through Time
Roger Matthews and Claudia Glatz

Site Catalogue   251

Bibliography   261

Chapter One

Project Paphlagonia:
Research Issues, Approaches and Methods

Roger Matthews

Birth of a project

All archaeological projects have a historical context. In the interests of transparency, historical curiosity and because it is impossible to separate Project Paphlagonia from the contingencies of its context, this final publication commences with an outline of the history of its origins. Project Paphlagonia was born and blossomed within the context of my spell as Director of the British Institute of Archaeology at Ankara from 1996 to 2001. In the light of the five-year term of tenure and the challenge to devise a field project that could be executed within that time-span, several important factors came to the fore. Firstly, it appeared that the most exciting opportunities to make a major contribution to the history and archaeology of Turkey might eventuate from investigation of a relatively unexplored region of the country. Secondly, the sorts of issues and approaches that I had in mind, considered below, would require survey on a grand scale, with large area coverage as well as scope for more detailed work. Thirdly, I was eager to study long-term trends, patterns, processes and interactions between human communities and their landscapes, rather than focusing on a specific period. Fourthly, the special potential within the study of ancient Turkey for combining archaeological and textual evidence could be maximised by a concern with certain issues that in turn might point to the choice of a specific geographical region for survey. Finally, our Institute had recently received a directive from the Turkish General Directorate of Monuments and Museums encouraging us to invest efforts in parts of Turkey not traditionally favoured by archaeologists and historians, including the north-central region.

With these and doubtless other, less articulated, factors in mind and taking advice from a host of colleagues, I decided on a project that would take the form of a multi-period survey somewhere in north-central Turkey. An initial choice of the modern province of Tokat for the survey region had to be abandoned once it became clear that a Turkish colleague was about to start work there. I am grateful to him for what at the time was a disappointment, for it steered my attention westwards to the province of Çankırı and led to the passing of five blissful summers working and walking in the beautiful landscapes of this little-known part of Turkey.

The province of Çankırı lies directly north of Ankara province, Çankırı town, Roman Gangra/Germanikopolis, being at a distance of 130km from Ankara city (fig. 1.1). Despite its proximity to the Turkish capital and to Istanbul, Çankırı is today little visited by either foreigners or Turks, and through its history there runs a theme of isolation and exile (fig. 1.2). In the Byzantine period religious dissidents were exiled to Gangra, including Dioskoros of Ephesos in AD 452 and Timothy the Cat a few years later (Mango, Scott 1997: 163, 172). In more recent times the great Turkish poet Nazim Hikmet served much of his prison exile in Çankırı jail, where several of his most famous poems were composed, before his release in 1950 and a long external exile in Bulgaria, Poland and the Soviet Union where he died in 1963 (Fuat 1985; Fergar 1992). Attitudes towards the place as somewhat remote and isolated have percolated into modern academia, so that statements such as 'even in Paphlagonia early urbanisation is attested' or 'thirty-four cities in Asia Minor are known to have celebrated Augustus' cult, including even such remote places as Gangra' are not uncommon (Levick 1996: 662–63, 658).

Strabo, a native of the nearby town of Amaseia, modern Amasya, defined Paphlagonia thus:

On the east, then, the Paphlagonians are bounded by the Halys river; on the south by Phrygians and the Galatians who settled among them; on the west by the Bithynians and Mariandyni, and on the north by the

Chapter One

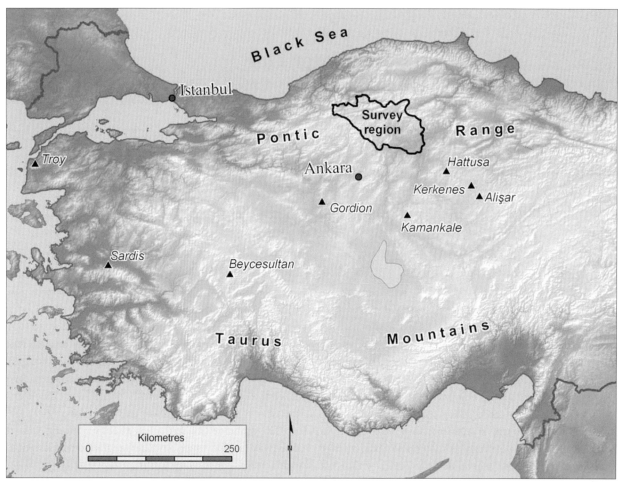

Fig. 1.1. Map of Turkey to show Project Paphlagonia survey region

Fig. 1.2. Çankırı town, with citadel centre right, in trees in distance

Euxine. Now this country was divided into two parts, the interior and the part on the sea, each stretching from the Halys river to Bithynia (*Geography* 12.3.9).

The designated survey region for Project Paphlagonia was that part of the Roman province that straddled the transition from upland plateau to highland zone, or the interior half of the province as delimited in the lines above from Strabo. In effect, this area is Inner Paphlagonia, a term already used by Ramsay in his classic study of 1890, *The Historical Geography of Asia Minor* (Ramsay 1890: 191–92). In modern political terms the survey area comprises the entirety of the province of Çankırı, plus two sub-provinces (Eskipazar and Ovacık) that in 1995 were taken from Çankırı and incorporated into the newly-created province of Karabük (see fig. 1.14).

Research issues: general and specific

There were essentially two interconnected types of research issue in Project Paphlagonia, the general and the specific. Among the general issues were broad questions concerning the ways in which people and landscapes interact. Why do people settle in certain places, in certain types of settlement, with certain sorts of land around them at certain times? What are the factors that shape the ways in which people live in their landscapes, how they farm, how they herd their flocks, how they travel across the land? How do those factors develop through time and thus differentially affect the shape and structure of settlement, and how might we detect such factors through application of the methods of regional survey? How do we distinguish and define the factors – geological, topographical, environmental, economic, social, cultural, political – that might be in play at any time?

The most promising possibilities in this regard seem to be provided by border zones. Borders are often unsettled places where the potential for dramatic change is sharpest, where small alterations in certain critical factors, spatially or through time, can have broad and far-reaching consequences (Lightfoot, Martinez 1995). By definition borders are meeting places where at least two different entities abut or collide. Those entities might take many forms, ranging from geological landforms to political states. The scope for study of border zones is immense within Turkey, and especially so in north-central Anatolia where many border issues are open to investigation, as we shall see in the course of this volume. These border issues relate not solely to tangible and physical frontiers, but also to such concerns as the limits of particular types of evidential source. Most significantly, if we track the story of human occupation in north-central Turkey, we immediately notice how it dips in and out of the written historical record, so that we attain tantalisingly rich glimpses of life ways at certain periods – the Late Bronze Age, the Roman–Byzantine, the Ottoman – while in others we must rely solely on archaeological evidence (table 1.1). The region teeters through time on the borders of history.

Set within the context of these general concerns, specific research issues in Project Paphlagonia relate to the particularities of the region itself and its known history, to which we now turn. As explored in Chapter Two, the very land forms of northern Turkey constitute a border zone. In the most basic of senses, that of tectonics, the region is traversed by the great North Anatolian Fault Zone, one of the major and most active fault areas in Turkey (fig. 1.3). This zone is created by the northward drift of the Arabian plate, pushing up the Taurus mountains of south Turkey while squeezing the central part of the country westwards into the Aegean. Ongoing slippage along this fault zone means land to the south of the fault zone is sliding westwards in a series of violent jolts, while land to the north stays relatively in place.

A major attraction of Çankırı province is the great variety of its landforms. Here there is endless scope for the exploration of how human settlement and landforms might be intertwined through history. A two-hour drive through the province takes in a wide range of landscapes. As we enter the province from the south we near the Kızılırmak river, steadily making its way from central Anatolia to the Black Sea coast (fig. 1.4). In its short stretch through Çankırı province it dissects a Miocene gypsum plateau whose rock-salt content prevents the growth of trees or any but the most salt-tolerant scrub. Settlement here is thin and scattered. Sweeter water around Çankırı town, by contrast, permits the blossoming of both plant life and human settlement in an oasis of green (fig. 1.5). To the west lie the rolling northern fringes of the Anatolian plateau, hills and plains with often good soils for farming and stock-raising (fig. 1.6). Heading north from Çankırı town, we reach the edge of the plateau, the road making a steep drop to Ilgaz in a series of hair-pin bends (fig. 1.7). Here we are again at a border, that between the rolling uplands of the Anatolian plateau, to the south behind us as we look northwards, and the daunting mountains of the Pontic region, running east-west across our field of view and stretching in a series of parallel chains up to the Black Sea coast, some 200km to the north. Dominating the scene is the bulk of the Ilgaz mountains, attaining 2,400m at this point and forming a considerable obstacle, though not insurmountable, to communication and transport. These mountains are covered in snow for several months of the winter (fig. 1.8), while in spring and summer they display an Alpine range of flora and fauna (fig. 1.9).

Period	Material culture	Text	Text source
Palaeolithic	Yes	No	
Neolithic	No?	No	
Chalcolithic	Yes	No	
Early Bronze Age	Yes	No	
Middle Bronze Age	Yes	?	Assyrian
Late Bronze Age – Hittite	Yes	Yes	Hittite
Late Bronze Age – Kaska	?	Yes	Hittite
Phrygian	Yes	?	?Phrygian
Achaemenid	?	Yes	Persian
Mithridatic	?	Yes	Roman
Galatian	?	Yes	Roman
Roman	Yes	Yes	Roman
Byzantine	Yes	Yes	Byzantine
Early Turkish	Yes	Yes	Byzantine/Turkish
Ottoman Turkish	Yes	Yes	Ottoman
Modern Turkish	Yes	Yes	Turkish

Table 1.1. Periods of the Paphlagonian past: material culture and textual sources

Fig. 1.3. North Anatolian Fault Zone at Kızıllar village, sites PS064–PS067

Project Paphlagonia: Research Issues, Approaches and Methods

Fig. 1.4. Kızılırmak river at the town of Kızılırmak

Fig. 1.5. Çankırı town viewed from the citadel

Fig. 1.6. Anatolian plateau near Işık Dağı in southwest of Çankırı province

Fig. 1.7. View looking north towards Ilgaz from İnköy. The two mounds of Salman West (PS016) and Salman East (PS015), bisected by the modern road, are visible in left middle distance

Fig. 1.8. Ilgaz mountains under snow

Fig. 1.9. Ilgaz mountains in summer

Chapter One

As we look downwards we discern the line of the Devrez Çay, a tributary of the Kızılırmak, flowing across the scene from west to east (fig. 1.10). Along the valley of this river and its neighbours runs the modern road cutting across north Turkey, today carrying traffic from Iran to Europe and back. Moving westwards, the river valleys open out into broad rolling expanses, largely treeless, immediately to the south of the fault zone. Further south still we encounter the bleak massif of Köroğlu, harsh and exposed terrain where eagles soar and freshly abandoned field systems bear witness to the end, for now at least, of a long struggle to make the land yield its guarded riches (fig. 1.11). But as we descend from the massif and continue westwards we notice a marked increase in the fertility of the land and in the density and spread of modern human settlement (fig. 1.12). There are more trees, more fields under cultivation and more villages. This western part of Çankırı and Karabük provinces looks more towards Istanbul than to either Ankara or the Pontic zone and once more here is a border issue, in terms of cultural alignments, that may be traceable in the past of the region.

Today, viewed at the human scale, these distinct environmental eco-zones within Paphlagonia seem rather solid and permanent, but were they always so? In order to explore issues of continuity and change in the environment, in its geography, geomorphology and climate, and so to be able to consider how these factors may have impacted on human settlement and land use, the project involved the expertise of geologists, geomorphologists and environmentalists, and results of their studies are presented in Chapter Two.

Turning to specific archaeological research issues, let us begin with prehistory. The prehistory of northern Anatolia is poorly developed, at least partly due to the paucity of fieldwork in the region. A major aim was therefore to attempt to locate sites of early date and to see how they might relate to already known prehistoric patterns elsewhere in Anatolia, as discussed in Chapter Three. Looking at the larger picture in the Palaeolithic period, it is well established that Neandertals evolved in the cold climates of Europe before migrating eastwards into Western Asia, where their remains have been recovered from excavations at sites such as Dederiyeh in Syria and Shanidar Cave in north Iraq. The most direct route from Europe to Syria and Iraq is through Turkey and so Neandertals must have traversed this land. Evidence for that traverse is indeed already considerable from numerous stray finds and a few excavations within Turkey (Kuhn 2002), although virtually no fossilised bones have been found. Did northern Anatolia feature as a significant route for Neandertals moving from Europe to Western Asia? Recovery of their stone tools and implements might help answer this question.

Fig. 1.10. The Devrez river near Orta

Fig. 1.11. Abandoned field systems on the Köroğlu mountains

Fig. 1.12. Landscape in the region of Eskipazar

Sites of the Upper Palaeolithic period (ca. 40,000–12,000 BP), by which time anatomically modern humans were the sole surviving hominid, are much scarcer in Turkey, particularly on the plateau (Kuhn 2002). There are almost certainly climatic factors behind the dearth of Upper Palaeolithic sites as compared to Middle Palaeolithic ones, associated with the peak of the Last Glacial and the preference of hunting groups for lowland zones, but how might the north Anatolian evidence bear on this issue?

Another highly significant prehistoric issue is that of the Neolithic period, through which hunting communities adopted settled life as full-time farmers and stock-raisers. Before 1997 no convincing Neolithic sites had been found in northern Anatolia and extremely few Chalcolithic ones also. Was this a genuine absence or an artefact of the sparseness of fieldwork in the region? Only further fieldwork could tell. And if such fieldwork failed to locate Neolithic and Chalcolithic sites then potential explanations for this apparent lack of settlement would need to be considered.

Moving onto the Early Bronze Age, through the third millennium BC, again our knowledge of this part of Turkey is minimal. In one of the few excavations in the region, a cemetery of this period had been excavated at Balıbağı near Çankırı town (Süel 1989), yielding numerous burials in pithos vessels and a few scraps of metalwork that hinted at connections with the spectacular Early Bronze Age tombs of Alaca Hüyük, not far to the east. Indeed much of our knowledge of north Anatolia in the Early Bronze Age stemmed from excavation of cemeteries, as at Alaca, Horoztepe and Eskiyapar. But what of settlement patterns, location preferences, proximity to natural resources during this period? And, given the broad east-west scope of the chosen survey region, what might be the picture in the Early Bronze Age of the western part of Çankırı and Karabük provinces? Might communities here look more to the west, towards Istanbul and even southeast Europe, than south and east into Anatolia?

With the second millennium BC, especially its later centuries, we enter an era when for the first time written records can be brought to bear on the Paphlagonian past. These documents come in the form of cuneiform texts of the Hittite empire, whose capital, Boğazköy-Hattusa, is located only 100km to the southeast of Çankırı town. Many texts tell of the Kaska, a transhumant, loosely-federated group of tribes who dwelt in the mountain zones across northern Turkey, and who constituted a major thorn in the side of the imperial presence (Glatz, Matthews 2005). Texts tell of Kaska raids on Hittite towns and temples, and of campaigns by Hittite armies, led by the Great King, into the mountains. There are also attempts to sign treaties with the Kaska and to bribe them into submission. From these assorted texts, found principally at Boğazköy-Hattusa itself, we gain a vivid picture of northern Anatolia as a contested frontier zone, at the edge of an empire, and in a perpetual state of military alert or activity. What might these attributes mean for the ways in which the landscape was settled in this period? In Chapter Four we explore how these textually-attested factors can be related to the striking settlement patterns recovered on the ground.

After the collapse of the Hittite empire, around 1180 BC, the region once more entered an episode of darkness without writing for several centuries. Recent excavations at nearby Boğazköy-Hattusa have recovered evidence for Early Iron Age occupation immediately succeeding the destruction of the great city, and it is conceivable that these remains indicate an intrusion by Kaska peoples into the Hittite heartland at this time, first to destroy and then to settle. Could we identify a Kaska material culture in Paphlagonia that matched with, or diverged from, the new Boğazköy-Hattusa evidence, and thus provide some pointers to possible origins of the Kaska at Boğazköy-Hattusa?

During the early first millennium BC, newcomers swept into Anatolia from southeast Europe, bringing new traditions and material culture traits with them. Among these people were the Phrygians and among their traditions was the use of large mounds, or tumuli, for burying the dead. Their capital city at Gordion, only 85km southwest of Ankara and 190km southwest of Çankırı town, is one of the few excavated sites within reasonable distance of the Project Paphlagonia survey area, and has yielded extensive material remains not only of the Phrygian period but also of other episodes, including the Bronze Age and Roman period (Kealhofer 2005). Gordion is therefore a key comparative site for any project in north Anatolia. What kind and degree of impact did the Phrygian incursion have on Paphlagonia, in terms of burial practices and settlement? Was Paphlagonia within the remit of Phrygian control during this part of the Iron Age?

For the later Iron Age a host of historical and archaeological issues were in need of attention in northern Anatolia, as discussed in Chapter Five. What was the impact of the absorption of the region into the Achaemenid empire, a political entity notoriously difficult to detect in the archaeological record, particularly given the geographic location of Paphlagonia at the edge of the empire? How was settlement affected by the drawn-out conflict between Rome and the Mithridatic Pontic kingdoms (Erciyas 2006a) when, once more, Inner Paphlagonia served as a contested frontier zone between two competing powers? How, if at all, was Paphlagonia affected by the Galatian incursions of the third century BC, when tribes of newcomers again arrived from southeast Europe and settled in parts of western and central Anatolia? Ongoing work in Ankara province was revealing much new information on alleged Galatian hilltop sites (Darbyshire et al. 2000), but did such sites exist further north, into Çankırı province?

With the dominance of Rome in much of Asia Minor and the creation of Paphlagonia as a Roman province in 6 BC a whole new set of research issues comes to the fore, as reviewed in Chapter Six. What impact on the nature and distribution of settlement might the imposition of the *pax Romana* have had? With the region now secure, arguably for the first time, as an integrated province of a great empire, and no longer an active frontier zone, what might the impact be on settlement and land use through the early centuries of Roman domination? More specifically could we identify, or confirm, on the ground traces of Roman towns attested in written sources, and already provisionally located in pioneering work by David Wilson (1960)?

Byzantine Paphlagonia features often in written texts, but archaeologically is little known (Belke 1996). As the Byzantine empire began to crumble, Paphlagonia and other parts of central Anatolia found themselves once more on the front line, active frontier zones again. How did this dramatic, but familiar, shift in political and military circumstances affect the nature of settlement through the long, steady decline in Byzantine occupation in the region? With the rise to supremacy of the Ottoman state, we see north Anatolia once more secured within an established imperial format, and no longer a contested border zone. How did this renewed stability show itself in the settlement record? For this period the written documentation is both rich and unusually focused on the minutiae of daily village life, in the form of tax registers providing highly detailed information on the capacity of villages and villagers to provide tax to the state authorities. These documents enable the historical exploration of many aspects of village life, including demography, subsistence, economy, and agricultural and social practices, as explored in Chapter Seven.

The final chronological episode worthy of consideration in a long-term study of settlement and society in Paphlagonia is of course that of the present. Today is a time of dramatic and far-reaching change in Paphlagonia, as elsewhere in rural Turkey. Age-old agricultural practices, and their attendant social and economic aspects, are rapidly changing, partly as a result of technological impositions and imports from outside – the tractor, the diesel engine, electricity – and partly due to mass migration of young elements of the population away from rural areas and into large conurbations, such as Ankara, Istanbul or further afield (Aydın 1990). These trends are having an immense impact on the nature and structure of human settlement in contemporary Paphlagonia (fig. 1.13).

Fig. 1.13. A Paphlagonian village view, Karaören

Summary of research issues

In sum, there are numerous general and specific research issues to be addressed within the framework of Project Paphlagonia, as treated in the chapters that follow. While many of these issues pertain to specific periods, it is fair to say that many of them also belong to a restricted range of key questions that we can now summarise.

Key issue 1: Within the context of Inner Paphlagonia, what are the factors that shape the ways in which people live in their landscapes, how they farm, how they herd their flocks, how they travel across the land, how they bury their dead, and how do those factors change in structure and impact through time?

Key issue 2: How does the border zone, and sometimes marginal, nature of Inner Paphlagonia affect the structure of settlement as we can study it from period to period?

Key issue 3: How do the various imperial entities, already known to us through written documents and other evidence, affect settlement and life ways through history in Inner Paphlagonia, particularly given its geographical location at the edge of empires?

Key issue 4: How might archaeological and textual evidence best be combined and integrated in approaching the past of Inner Paphlagonia?

Previous research in the region

Before proceeding to a consideration of field methods, it will be helpful to place Project Paphlagonia in the broader context of previous and ongoing archaeological investigation in northern and central Anatolia. Here we provide a brief summary of the explorations and projects that have a major bearing on the substantive results from Project Paphlagonia, and that help to construct a framework on which to situate both the research issues outlined above and the results as presented throughout the volume.

North-central Anatolia does not feature prominently in the itineraries of early explorers in Turkey. The major east-west route running through Gerede, Çerkeş and Ilgaz was used by several travellers of Ottoman times, heading from Istanbul towards Erzurum and beyond (Yerasimos 1991: 60–61). Nineteenth-century visitors included Ainsworth (1842) and von Flottwell (1895) who produced a sketch-plan of Çankırı citadel. This phase of initial exploration culminated in the three expeditions (1899, 1900, 1903) of Richard Leonhard, mapped by Richard Kiepert and published in Leonhard's sumptuous volume *Paphlagonia* (1915). Modern archaeological exploration of the region, and particularly its pre-Classical past, can be said to begin with the survey of Charles Burney in 1954–1955, during which a few sites were located in Çankırı province as well as many others over a vast area of north Anatolia (Burney 1956). Earlier surveys by Kökten had covered stretches of north Anatolia to the east of the Kızılırmak river (Kökten 1944).

Turning next to recent and ongoing excavations, within Çankırı province itself, extremely few legal investigations had, still have, taken place. Many Iron Age burial tumuli have been excavated, most of them illicitly but some under the careful supervision of officials from Çankırı Museum, especially in recent years. As mentioned above, there had been a series of excavations at the Early Bronze Age cemetery of Balıbağı and adjacent Late Bronze Age settlement, near Çankırı town (Süel 1989), where numerous graves were excavated. To the south, near the border with Ankara province, road-widening operations revealed sherds of a spectacular relief vase and subsequent excavations at the site of İnandık uncovered structures of the Hittite period in the Late Bronze Age (Özgüç 1988). The İnandık vase is now one of the centrepieces of the Museum of Anatolian Civilisations in Ankara.

Beyond Çankırı province, excavations at a range of important sites provided much-needed comparative material within which to situate our always fragmentary surface finds. These excavations and their results are referred to in detail at the relevant points in the chapters that follow and so only brief mention is made here. On the Black Sea coast to the north the multi-period mound of İkiztepe is uniquely informative (Bilgi 2001). For the Chalcolithic, Bronze Age and Iron Age, excavations at the Hittite capital of Boğazköy-Hattusa are of great value in the study of Paphlagonia pottery (Müller-Karpe 1988; Partzinger, Sanz 1992; Schoop 2003a; 2005a; 2006; Genz 2004a), while long-standing fieldwork at Gordion is of equal value for much of the time-span between the Early Bronze Age and Roman period, with useful material from Galatian and Hellenistic levels (Kealhofer 2005). For Roman, Byzantine and Turkish materials, assorted work in and around Ankara provides a degree of comparative background. As we shall see, points of comparison can be found with many other sites, near and far, but the few mentioned here provide the essence of a frame of reference.

In addition to excavations, there have been several archaeological surveys in north and central Anatolia, whose results significantly intertwine with our own at various points. Principal projects include a prehistoric survey of parts of Kastamonu (Marro 2000), a Bronze Age survey of Çorum province (Yıldırım, Sipahi 2004), an Iron Age Galatian survey of Ankara province (Vardar, Vardar 2001), a prehistoric survey of Amasya and Tokat provinces (Özsait 1994; Özsait, Koçak 1996), as well as surveys further afield to the north in Samsun (Dönmez 1999) and Sinop (Işın 1998), to the east in Sivas (Ökse 1999) and to the south in central Anatolia (Omura 2002). Marek's (1993; 2003) superb epigraphic surveys of the region provide a host of valuable data for the Roman and Byzantine periods. Results from these surveys, most of which were designed to investigate specific periods or issues, as well as from other relevant projects, are considered at the appropriate points in the chapters that follow.

Approaches and methods

We have reviewed the research issues that stimulated and shaped the academic structure of the project, as well as the backdrop of previous work in and around the region. It is now time to consider how a desire to pursue this research agenda was operationalised by means of a practical and effective field methodology. In recent decades archaeological survey has progressed immensely from its early status as handmaiden to excavation. As elsewhere in the world, surveys have become common practice in the lands around the Mediterranean, in Greece, Italy, North Africa, the Levant, and their results recognised as having a validity and worth in their own right. The methodology of survey has become a well-trodden arena of debate, with much detailed consideration of the intricacies of sampling, field-walking, site identification and categorisation, off-site activity areas and a host of related issues (succinctly summarised in Mattingly 2000; see also Alcock, Cherry 2004; Kowaleski 2008).

The methods employed in Project Paphlagonia were devised and adapted through the course of fieldwork to balance two overriding factors. On the one hand, I wanted to work in a large geographical area, as only so could the broad historical and archaeological questions, outlined above, on topics such as scale and hierarchy of settlement be addressed. The magnitude and diachronic nature of the research questions demanded work on a grand scale. The survey region of Project Paphlagonia comprises 8,454km², about the same area as the entire island of Crete (at 8,305km² – Cunningham, Driessen 2004: 102). Clearly, special survey approaches, combining extensive and intensive methods, would be needed to deal with a more or less totally unexplored landscape on this scale. In this respect, the survey methods adopted in Project Paphlagonia have more in common with other large-scale, diachronic regional investigations, such as the exploration of 5,500km² of diverse territory in Aetolia in western Greece (Bommeljé et al. 1987), rather than with the high-intensity focus on often tightly restricted geographical sections of landscape that characterises many modern survey projects in the Mediterranean region.

Nevertheless, results achieved through extensive survey in Project Paphlagonia would need verification and checking by more high-resolution methods, or they would remain forever questionable in their validity and applicability. If we found no Neolithic sites through extensive survey, no-one would be very surprised, given that such sites might be little more than small scatters of lithics or potsherds on the flat surface of the land. Again, if we found only large Roman settlements we would have little idea of the true settlement patterns and hierarchy of the region. We needed then to apply intensive survey methods to sample areas of the survey region, and these methods are discussed below, after a section on extensive survey and before a final section on the GIS analyses, and interpretation and publication of survey results.

Extensive survey
The approaches and methods of extensive survey in the context of Project Paphlagonia were designed to retrieve a maximum spread of information from a large region that had received minimal previous archaeological investigation. This phase of the fieldwork was intended to provide a basic framework of occupational history, which would be of interest and value in its own right, but which would also steer the research towards more focused and intensive issues for the second phase of the project. Extensive survey was conducted during the 1997–1999 seasons, while intensive survey occupied the 2000–2001 field seasons.

How, then, to tackle a highly diverse and unexplored region covering 8,454km²? Researches prior to fieldwork established a hit-list of fewer than 20 probable sites of archaeological or historical interest, identified by previous travellers and researchers in the region. These sites formed a core of places to be visited early on, but we still needed a more systematic way of dealing with the enormity of the landscape. The modern administrative structure of the area provided the framework. The constitution of each modern Turkish province as a series of sub-provinces, or *ilçe*, gave a ready-made and highly convenient division of the territory into manageable pieces (fig. 1.14). Çankırı province today contains a total of 12 *ilçe*, as follows: Atkaracalar, Bayramören, Çankırı, Çerkeş, Eldivan, Ilgaz, Kızılırmak, Korgun, Kurşunlu, Orta, Şabanözü and Yapraklı. The two *ilçe* of Karabük province, previously belonging to Çankırı province and contained within the scope of Project Paphlagonia, are Eskipazar and Ovacık. We decided to treat each *ilçe* in turn, conducting extensive survey in all of them in succession.

Each *ilçe* has a main centre, usually a small town, and that is where we started our enquiries. The first port of call in each *ilçe* was the headquarters of the *jandarma*, the authority responsible for rural security. Here we not only registered our presence as a matter of formality with the authorities, but also gleaned a wealth of insights into the local scene, including details of possible sites, lists of locations where illicit digging was known to have taken place and other highly useful practical information. From the *jandarma*, the next step was to call on all the principal modern settlements of that *ilçe*. It was impossible to visit every village in every *ilçe*, but all towns and all major villages were visited, plus a very large number of small villages. In each settlement we addressed ourselves to the most senior local authority, either the *belediye başkanı* (municipal mayor) or the *muhtar* (village headman) depending on the administrative status of the settlement. Again, this call was partly to register our presence and partly in order to gather local information. Strong reliance on local information as a guide to the location of archaeological sites is also a feature of survey conducted in the neighbouring province to the north, Kastamonu, where difficulties of terrain and site visibility are more extreme than in Project Paphlagonia (Marro 2000: 947).

From many conversations with officials and with the hundreds of villagers whom we encountered in the course of fieldwork we steadily built up a web of local information about sites and possible site locations (fig. 1.15). All these leads were followed up, which generally involved a great deal of driving, frequently over rough ground (fig. 1.16), followed by long walks through the

Chapter One

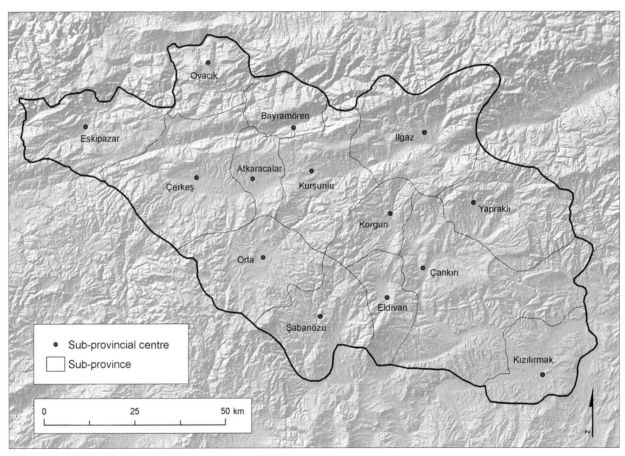

Fig. 1.14. Map of Çankırı and southeast Karabük provinces to show ilçe

Fig. 1.15. Paphlagonian villagers

often breathtaking scenery of Inner Paphlagonia (fig. 1.17). Once a site had been reached and located, its details were recorded on two set forms (fig. 1.18). One form contained information on the site itself – its extent, nature and density of surface material, evidence of structures and so on – while a second form related to the geographical environs of the site – geology, geomorphology, local land use, nearby routes and other pertinent information. The details entered into these forms provide the basis of the site catalogue published here. All sites were photographed and some were planned and sketched where relevant. Contour plans were made of a few more significant mounds. Sites were located on copies of maps of the region at 1:25,000 scale.

A range of types of archaeological site was encountered, as categorised in the site catalogue. Most commonly, sites take the form of spreads of material, chiefly potsherds, across the flat surface of the land. Such sites vary in extent from extremely small, a few dozen square metres, to quite large, many hectares, and are often first encountered by villagers in the course of ploughing their fields. The vast majority of these flat sites date to the Hellenistic, Roman and Byzantine periods. Cemeteries belonging mainly to these periods were also located, all of them detectable only by virtue of the fact that illicit excavation had thrown up visible evidence in the form of bones, tomb fittings or other debris (fig. 1.19). Some numbers of mounds, or *höyüks*, were located, ranging in size from fractions of a hectare to several hectares, but never approaching the massive size of mounds elsewhere in Turkey and Western Asia. Even long-occupied, multi-period mounds such as Salman Höyük near Ilgaz (Chapter Four), one of the most

Project Paphlagonia: Research Issues, Approaches and Methods

Fig. 1.16. Extensive survey by vehicle

Fig. 1.17. Extensive survey on foot

Fig. 1.19. Ancient cemetery uncovered by illicit activity

Fig. 1.18. Extensive survey: completing site and landscape forms

Fig. 1.20. View of Salman East (PS015)

important Bronze Age and Iron Age sites of Inner Paphlagonia, cover less than a single hectare in extent (fig. 1.20). Other types of site include burial tumuli, rock-cut features, field systems, rare caves, standing buildings, architectural fragments re-used in modern settings and inscribed material in the form of stone columns or pedestals.

Collections of surface material were carried out at all sites where material was present. In the vast majority of cases all visible surface artefacts were collected from a particular site, as most sites were both small in extent and yielded relatively meagre quantities of objects. Sites with large quantities of pottery were rare and usually took the form of larger *höyüks*, often with multi-period occupation. In these cases, only diagnostic sherds were collected, and in a few instances sites were deemed large and complex enough to benefit from gridded collection of surface objects, as noted in the site catalogue. Perhaps in keeping with its often marginal nature, Inner Paphlagonia is never rich in ceramic or other material, the quantities recovered from each site being generally quite low. The most frequent category of collected material was pottery, followed by ceramic tile, lithics, ground stone, glass, spindle whorls and a very few coins. Collected items were conveyed each day to the project accommodation (local hotels in Ilgaz, Eskipazar and Çankırı) where they were sorted, washed, drawn, photographed, catalogued and studied. All collected material from Project Paphlagonia is now stored in Çankırı Museum.

Through all seasons of extensive survey, 261 archaeological sites in all were detected and recorded in Inner Paphlagonia (fig. 1.21: see site catalogue). It is important to stress that no attempt was made at exhaustive recovery of sites during the programme of extensive survey. There are certainly hundreds, possibly thousands, of sites still to be found within the survey region. The intention was to recover a sample sufficient to enable the construction of a basic framework of settlement history that could be further explored through the conduct of intensive survey. The nature of that framework, and its implications for intensive work, are considered period by period in the chapters that follow.

Intensive survey

In order to explore some of the finer-scale details of settlement and landscape use in Paphlagonia, a programme of intensive survey was pursued during field seasons 2000–2001. Intensive survey is demanding of three related commodities: time, labour and money. It was unarguably necessary to conduct intensive survey within the remit of Project Paphlagonia for, as mentioned, only so could we gain a degree of security and confidence in the results obtained from extensive survey, but in terms of cost effectiveness there is a case to be made for systematic and careful extensive survey, as carried out here from 1997–1999, as a stand-alone methodology for treating *de novo* a large and diverse tract of territory, and for recovering from that landscape a wealth of pertinent and often highly detailed information, provided of course that the questions and objectives are framed so as to suit an extensive approach.

With the benefit of hindsight it is now possible to state that in no specific case in Project Paphlagonia did the results gleaned from intensive survey overthrow, and only rarely significantly modify, interpretations previously arrived at from the programme of systematic extensive survey. All our major conclusions about settlement history were reached on the basis of extensive survey and then verified through intensive survey. Of course, without the intensive survey there would have been no convincing verification of preliminary interpretations, but on the basis of experience gained from Project Paphlagonia it is encouraging to note that it is feasible to conduct low-budget extensive surveys of large regions with meaningful results, provided that sufficient attention is given to the aims, approaches, methods and execution of extensive survey. That said, the programme of intensive survey in Project Paphlagonia did yield a great deal of fine detail on many issues of settlement history, and these results are integrated with those of extensive survey in the following chapters. Methodologically, we strongly agree with the statement of Kowalewski (2008: 251) that, 'It is better to begin with regional coverage and in later field seasons sample areas, sites, or topics more intelligently from the known regional universe' rather than pursue uncontextualised and too tightly focused 'surface artefact surveys' that produce 'well-executed color maps [that] still look like the world as seen through prison bars'.

The methods of intensive survey employed in 2000–2001 were developed to address the principal concern of sampling and representation. Over the two seasons a total of ten sample areas were treated by intensive survey (fig. 1.22). These areas took the form of sample rectangles, each measuring 10km by 4km, thus 40km^2 in area. The sample blocks were not randomly distributed throughout the survey region, but rather their distribution took into account several factors. Firstly, an attempt was made to cover the full range of landscape forms within Inner Paphlagonia, including river valleys, upland plateaux, foothills, mountains and steppe. Most sample blocks included more than one such landscape element. Secondly, extensive survey had thrown up some striking settlement issues that called out sharply for exploration through intensive work. These included the paucity of early prehistoric sites, especially of the Neolithic and Chalcolithic periods, an apparent absence of small Late Bronze Age sites and an apparent wealth of sites of all sizes of Roman and early Byzantine date. Focus on these issues helped direct the location of intensive sample blocks, for example, ensuring that they each contained at least one already known Late Bronze Age site so that exploration of site hinterlands could be made.

The methods of intensive survey used in Project Paphlagonia were as follows. Topographic maps for each sample block were produced by electronically blowing up 1:25,000 maps to 1:10,000 scale to be used in the field. The required sample block was located on the ground, usually not difficult with the maps and GPS readings, and

Project Paphlagonia: Research Issues, Approaches and Methods

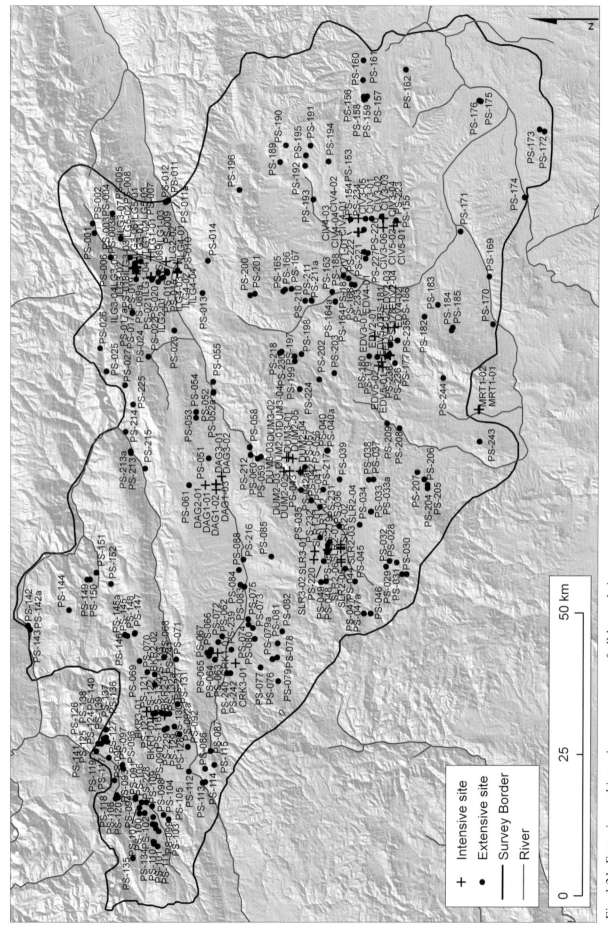

Fig. 1.21. Extensive and intensive survey: map of all located sites

Chapter One

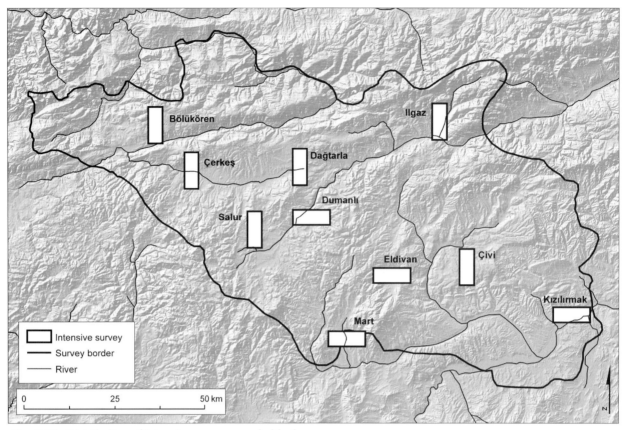

Fig. 1.22. Distribution of intensive survey sample blocks

sample transects were more specifically located. The choice of transects within sample blocks was again dependent on a range of non-random factors, including pressures of time, suitability of the terrain for fieldwalking (much of the terrain being impassable on foot), proximity to known sites and the desire to cover as far as possible a representative sample of landscape types within each sample block. We then drove as close as possible to the mid-point of the intended transect and parked the vehicles wherever convenient. The exact mid-point of the transect was located and from there we walked in a set direction either east-west or north-south depending on the alignment of the sample block, walking across the short dimension of the block. Through the two seasons there were between six and nine walkers in a line, spaced so that the total length of walkers equalled 100m (fig. 1.23). Walking proceeded in this way until the edge of the sample block was encountered, as defined by the maps and GPS readings. The line of walkers then pivoted about one of its end members and returned in the same fashion to the mid-point of the transect, having so far walked a total of 4km. At this point it would usually be lunch-time, served as a picnic from the vehicles (fig. 1.24). Thereafter, the second half of the transect was walked in the opposite direction, the other edge of the block reached, the line pivoted and the transect completed by a return to

Fig. 1.23. Intensive survey: walking the line

Fig. 1.24. Intensive survey: lunch break

18

the mid-point. A single transect thus occupied the space of 4km by 200m, covered by a line of walkers 100m long walking a total of 8km in two adjacent strips of 4km. Each transect thus covered an area of 0.8km². Initially we walked five transects in each sample block, making a total of 4km², or 10% of the total sample block area of 40km². Due to pressures of time, later blocks were sampled by three transects, totalling 2.4km², or 6% of the block area. The location of each transect within all sample blocks is shown in the GIS maps below (figs 1.25–1.34). In all, over two intensive field seasons, 36 transects were walked across the often highly undulating Paphlagonian landscape (fig. 1.35), giving a total of 288km. As project director I felt obliged, indeed honoured, to walk every one of those 288km, on top of several hundred kilometres walked in extensive survey, and I am grateful to all who joined me for at least some of the way.

During walking of transects a considerable amount of activity and recording was underway. Firstly, a team leader was striving to keep us all in line, properly spaced and heading in the correct direction. Secondly, a team member was recording on the 1:10,000 map copy the modern land-use practices of the transect, defining them in categories such as stubble, fallow, newly-ploughed, orchard and so on. The window of opportunity for carrying out intensive field-walking in northern Turkey is quite small. The cereal crops have to be harvested and the land ploughed, but the next crop not sown. August and early September were the

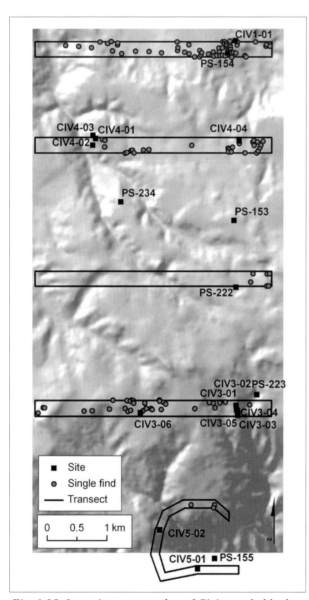

Fig. 1.25. Intensive survey: plan of Çivi sample block

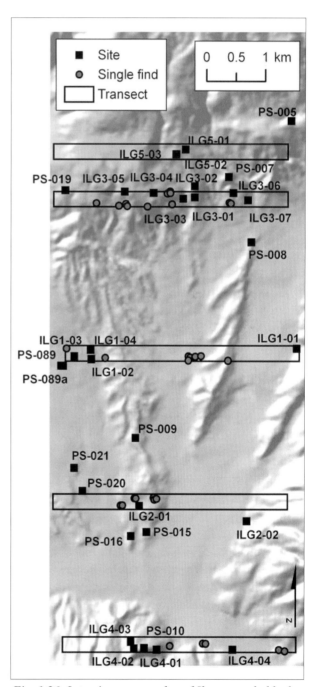

Fig. 1.26. Intensive survey: plan of Ilgaz sample block

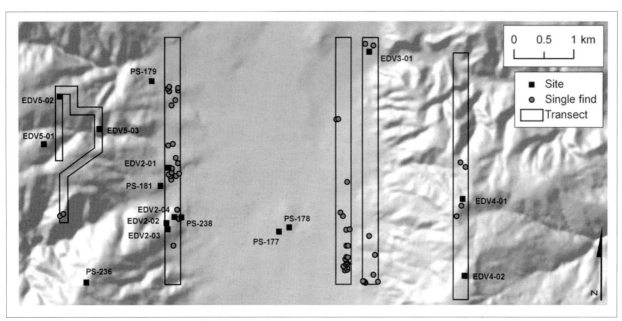

Fig. 1.27. Intensive survey: plan of Eldivan sample block

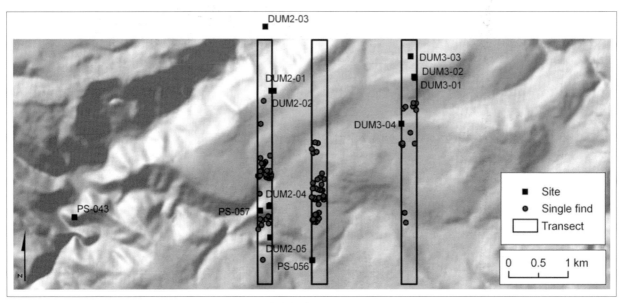

Fig. 1.28. Intensive survey: plan of Dumanlı sample block

ideal time. Modes of modern land use are of interest in themselves, but for our purposes here the major consideration was how they affected the visibility of surface objects. As it happens, there appear to be no dramatic correlations in our results between recoverable object density and type of modern land use, doubtless partly due to the generally low levels of artefact frequency.

All team members were constantly on the look out for artefacts. Within intensive transects, all finds, whether or not diagnostic, were collected and retained. Running lists of numbers were assigned to finds in categories of pottery, tile, lithics, glass and miscellaneous. At several points during the average transect walk there would be decisions to be made about whether or not 'a site' had been encountered, and this issue usually involved a group discussion about the density and nature of surface finds. In practice, there was consistently high agreement among the team over the identification of sites in terms of surface densities of finds. Sites were almost always highly discrete entities, with sharply defined borders beyond which artefacts were found in negligible or no quantities. A similarly high resolution of sites with little evidence for off-site material was encountered in approximately comparable terrain during survey in Rough Cilicia (Blanton 2000: 3). While the practice of field manuring (conducted today in the region: fig. 1.36) does produce the well-known halo of debris around settlements (Wilkinson 1989), the evidence for this practice in the past of Paphlagonia, even in the Roman and Byzantine periods, appears to be weak unless it be argued that survivable cultural material was somehow not included in manure deposits.

Through the walking of the 36 transects in ten different sample blocks, in all 76 further archaeological sites were encountered and recorded, in the same manner as those found in extensive survey, making a total of 337 sites of all periods found in Project Paphlagonia by both extensive and intensive methods. Again, we stress that this number certainly represents only a proportion, though undoubtedly a significant one, of the totality of archaeological sites located within the survey region.

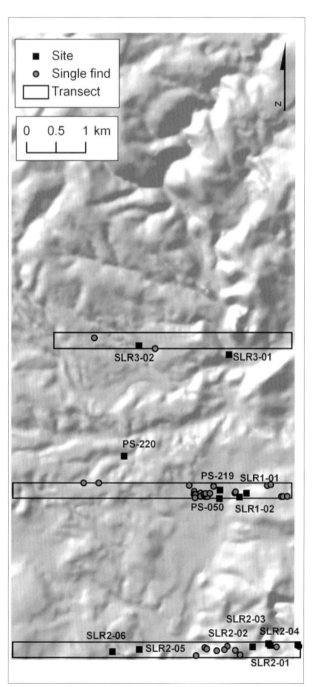

Fig. 1.29. Intensive survey: plan of Salur sample block

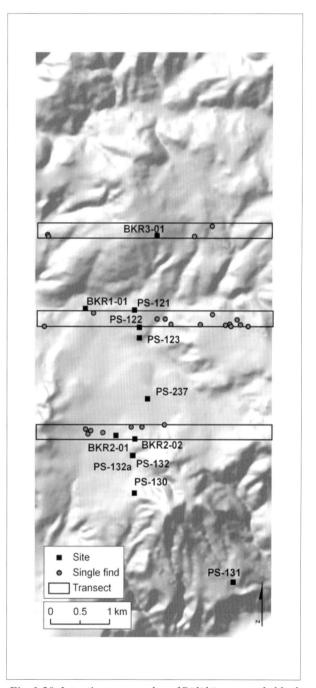

Fig. 1.30. Intensive survey: plan of Bölükören sample block

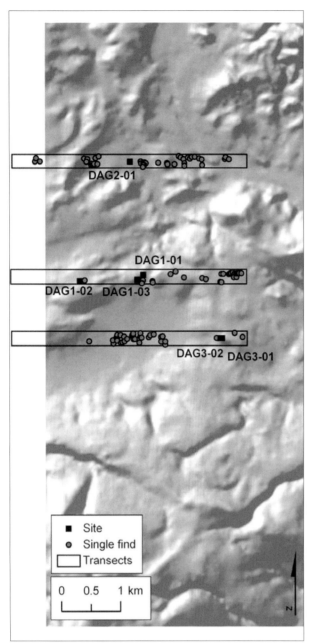

Fig. 1.31. Intensive survey: plan of Dağtarla sample block

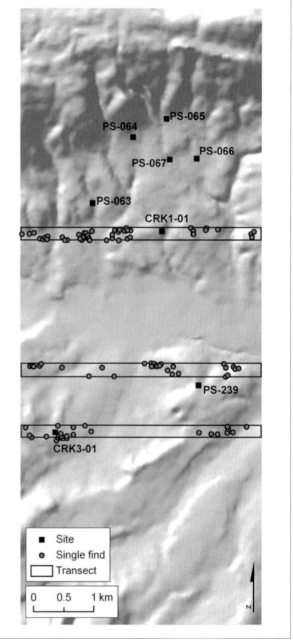

Fig. 1.32. Intensive survey: plan of Çerkeş sample block

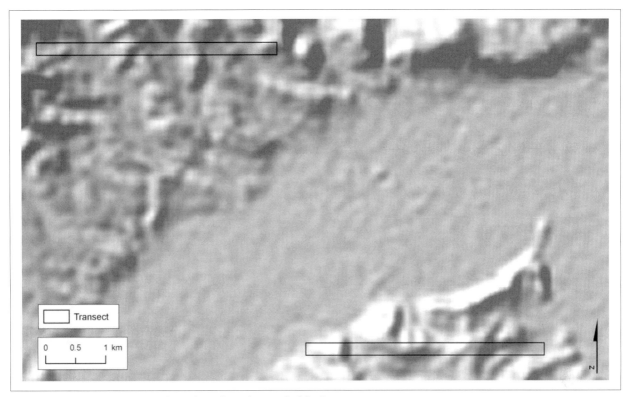

Fig. 1.33. Intensive survey: plan of Kızılırmak sample block

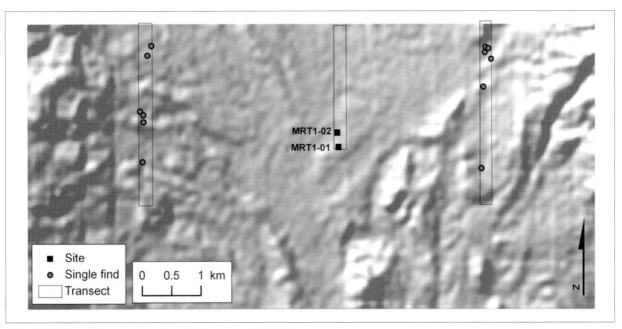

Fig. 1.34. Intensive survey: plan of Mart sample block

Chapter One

Fig. 1.35. Intensive survey: extreme field-walking

Fig. 1.36. Manuring of fields with village debris

Interpretations
Once fieldwork had been completed, all data on intensive survey were input into a GIS application, as illustrated in the accompanying figures. The methods employed in this process involved the digitisation of the field maps and all data upon them, including topographic data, land-use patterns, isolated find locations and numbers, and site locations. Along with the distribution maps produced through extensive means, these maps provide the basis for the period by period analysis of subsequent chapters. In Chapter Eight an attempt is made to explore diachronic change and continuity through analysis of trends and patterns in settlement distribution, site size, hierarchy and other factors, many of which are addressed in the period-specific chapters that follow.

An initial interpretive device is to categorise located sites by size or extent (Jameson et al. 1994: 248–53). There are numerous possible ways in which to divide a corpus of sites into size groupings, and the one chosen here is intended to provide the maximum interpretive facility while suiting the range of site sizes detectable in the specific context of Project Paphlagonia. As already mentioned, there are extremely few very large archaeological sites in Inner Paphlagonia, only a handful of Romano-Byzantine towns breaking this rule, and so a division of sites into size categories needs to focus on the lower end of the size scale. In the end, taking into account the distribution of Paphlagonian sites across the small end of the spectrum, seven size divisions were decided upon (table 1.2).

A further interpretive approach is to categorise sites by type and/or by function, wherever possible. Such categories may relate to site morphology (*höyük*, surface scatter, rock-cut site, cave, hilltop site) and/or to site attributes (fortification walls, human remains, craft production debris, architectural fragments). For the purposes of this project sites were divided into the following functional categories (table 1.3), some of which may of course include sites of other categories within them.

Thus farmsteads are understood to take up to 1ha in area, a compromise between the various figures suggested by researchers working in the Greek and Roman worlds (summarised in Blanton 2000: 64). On the basis of these two classes of categorisation, every site found within Project Paphlagonia can be assigned an alpha-numeric code that defines it in terms of its areal extent and its putative function. It should be stressed that the size and functional attributions of sites are highly provisional and not to be taken too rigidly. In many cases it is not possible to determine a site's size, especially if multi-period, within specific time-spans and most sites are likely to span more than one functional category. The classification is to be regarded as a convenient analytical tool, certainly to be subject to rigorous modification in the light of further fieldwork.

Category 1	Isolated small feature (e.g., inscribed pillar, architectural fragment, pithos)
Category 2	Site covering up to 0.1ha
Category 3	Site covering 0.1–0.25ha
Category 4	Site covering 0.26–1ha
Category 5	Site covering 1.01–4ha
Category 6	Site covering 4.01–10ha
Category 7	Site covering more than 10ha

Table 1.2. Size categories of sites in Project Paphlagonia

Category A	Town/large village (including sites of Categories 6–7 in table 1.2)
Category B	Village (including sites of Category 5 in table 1.2)
Category C	Farmstead (including sites of Categories 2–4 in table 1.2)
Category D	Lowland fortified site
Category E	Hilltop fortified site
Category F	Rock-cut tomb/chapel/cistern
Category G	Flat inhumation cemetery
Category H	Tumulus
Category I	Quarry
Category J	Lithic scatter
Category K	Inscription on discrete stone element
Category L	Inscription on rock-face
Category M	*Höyük* (settlement mound)
Category N	Standing building
Category O	Natural cave
Category P	Field systems
Category Q	Sherd scatter
Category R	Road or path
Category S	Pile of stones
Category T	Isolated, not *in situ*, stone element or pithos
Category U	Church

Table 1.3. Typology of sites in Project Paphlagonia

Chapter Two

Contexts of Human Interaction: Geology, Geography, Geomorphology and Environment

Ben Marsh, Neil Roberts, Vedat Toprak, Roger Matthews, Warren Eastwood, Julian Carolan, Arda Arcasoy and M. Lütfi Süzen

Introduction
By Roger Matthews
Inner Paphlagonia contains a broad variety of landscapes, as briefly reviewed in the previous chapter. Few regions of Turkey contain so much diversity within a single province: from mountain peaks to rolling steppe, from lush open valley to vertiginous gorge and from barren salt plateau to thickly forested upland. Additionally, a strong border aspect to the region, at the most basic level, is generated by the fact that a major tectonic feature, the North Anatolian Fault Zone (hereafter NAFZ: Brinkmann 1976; Bingöl 1989), cuts across the province from east to west, delineating the transition between the elevated Anatolian plateau to the south and the Pontic mountain zone to the north. How was human settlement and land use affected by the land and landforms of the region? What role did the availability, or absence, of specific natural resources play through time? How were aspects of the landscape employed or shaped by human communities in order to further their desires and needs for protection, communication, isolation or agricultural productivity? In order to address these and many other questions, the studies reported on in this chapter were conducted within the framework of Project Paphlagonia. There are here four main aims, each treated in a distinct section.

> To consider some general aspects of the physical environment of Inner Paphlagonia.
> To discuss specific aspects of the geology and topography of Inner Paphlagonia, and to provide an account of procedures and methods employed in approaching, categorising and graphically representing key features of the Paphlagonian landscape.
> To consider the geomorphology of the ten sample blocks where intensive survey was conducted.
> To consider environmental issues as approached through a programme of coring of lake bed deposits.

Modern climate
The modern climate of Çankırı town is summarised in the following table (table 2.1; see also Mason 1942: 195–229; Alex 1985: 58). The region's climate is characteristic of its situation between the Anatolian plateau, to the south, and the Pontic mountains and Black Sea region, to the north, with mild, wet springs, warm long summers and quite severe winters with over three months each year below freezing. Rainfall averages over 400mm per year, largely falling between December and May. The northern parts of the province, especially around the heights of Ilgaz, endure much more severe winters than parts to the south.

Modern land use
The variable landscapes of Çankırı province today support a wide variety of agricultural and farming activities, which may best be summarised in a series of tables based on information gleaned from the Turkish government web-site for Çankırı province (http://www.cankiri.gov.tr/ana/tarim/tarim.htm: accessed 21 June 2008) (tables 2.2–2.4; figs 2.1, 2.2). It is interesting to compare these proportions of known land use with those determined by Ben Marsh from Thematic Mapper satellite imagery and described in the section below relating to the intensive survey blocks. Much detail on modern land-use practices, climate, demography and many other aspects of village life in the region of Ilgaz can be found in Alexandre 1994.

	Jan	Feb	Mar	Apr	May	Jun	Jul	Aug	Sep	Oct	Nov	Dec	Year
Absolute max. temp °C	14.3	22.0	29.0	31.0	33.4	37.0	41.7	41.8	36.7	33.6	23.1	18.2	41.8
Average max. temp °C	3.8	5.8	11.6	18.0	22.6	26.9	30.5	30.7	25.7	19.8	12.8	6.0	17.9
Average min. temp °C	-3.1	-2.4	0.4	4.8	9.0	11.9	13.9	13.6	9.5	4.8	1.2	-1.3	5.2
Absolute min. temp °C	-25.0	-24.0	-15.5	-5.6	0.6	1.6	6.7	4.6	-2.0	-6.0	-15.1	-17.7	-25.0
Number of frosty days	22	20	15	4	0	0	0	0	0	4	11	17	93
Average rainfall in mm	45.8	49.8	48.5	36.9	55.8	39.4	10.5	16.7	23.3	15.5	22.2	55.2	419.6
Relative rainfall as %	10.9	11.9	11.6	8.8	13.3	9.4	2.5	4.0	5.5	3.7	5.3	13.2	100.0
Number of days with snow	5	5	2	1	0	0	0	0	0	0	1	3	17
Average rel. humidity %	78	75	66	61	61	56	51	52	59	65	72	80	65
Hours of sunshine	74	81	133	195	254	288	344	313	255	214	117	53	2,321

Table 2.1. Modern climate data for Çankırı city (after Alex 1985: 58)

Land use type	Hectares	Percentage
Arable	236,000	31.9
Forest	204,393	27.6
Meadow/pasture	279,154	37.9
Unusable/populated land	19,253	2.6
Total	738,800	100.0

Table 2.2. Contemporary land-use patterns in Çankırı province (after http://www.cankiri.gov.tr/ana/tarim/tarim.htm)

Arable type	Hectares	Percentage
Cereals (wheat, barley, corn, rice)	111,365	47.2
Fallow	68,581	29.1
Animal fodder (clover, rapeseed, vetch)	14,493	6.1
Legumes (lentil, chickpea, bean)	2,432	1.0
Fruit, vegetables, orchards (melon, watermelon, assorted others)	8,983	3.8
Industrial cultivation (sugarbeet, sunflower, potato)	5,202	2.2
Fields currently not profitable to farm	24,944	10.6
Total	236,000	100.0

Table 2.3. Use of arable land in Çankırı province (after http://www.cankiri.gov.tr/ana/tarim/tarim.htm)

Animal	Quantity
Cattle	112,885
Water Buffalo	2,234
Sheep	121,345
Goat	22,277
Turkey	20,940
Chicken	1,604,300
Bee (hives)	44,723

Table 2.4. Contemporary farm animals of Çankırı province (after http://www.cankiri.gov.tr/ana/tarim/tarim.htm)

Fig. 2.1. Cattle in Kızılırmak region

Fig. 2.2. Water buffalo in Orta region

The physical environment of Inner Paphlagonia
By Ben Marsh
Basic geology

The physical landscape of Inner Paphlagonia provides the framework upon which all human occupation is constructed. The resources, habitations, agriculture and transportation networks of the occupants are conditional upon the rock, soil and topography of the region. In a continuous dialectic, humans in turn have altered the land, soil and hydrology through their use and abuse of those resources. The physical framework provides a crucial element of the analysis of the archaeological patterns of the region. The Paphlagonia region represents a typical Anatolian upland landscape in many ways (fig. 2.3). Vigorous tectonic activity built, and continues to build, a region of high relief from diverse earth materials. Lying within a broad-scale convergence zone, Anatolia is underlain predominantly by rocks brought to the surface, often from great depths beneath a now-closed sea, by large and long-lasting compressional forces (MTA n.d.). The rocks are typical ocean floor lithologies: especially limestones and mafic crystallines. Shallow lakebed deposits – marl, siltstone and salts – overlie the harder rocks, particularly in the southeast of the study region.

The general geological arrangement of the region can be described as controlled by four generalised geologic units, as shown on the geologic map of the central study area (fig. 2.4) (see also below).

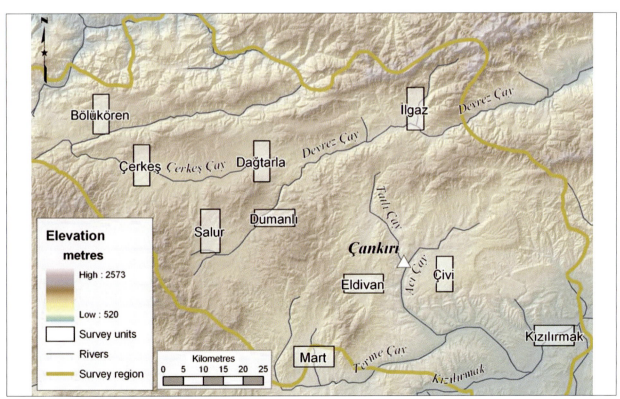

Fig. 2.3. Topography and drainage of the Paphlagonia survey region. Elevations from NASA Shuttle-borne radar data

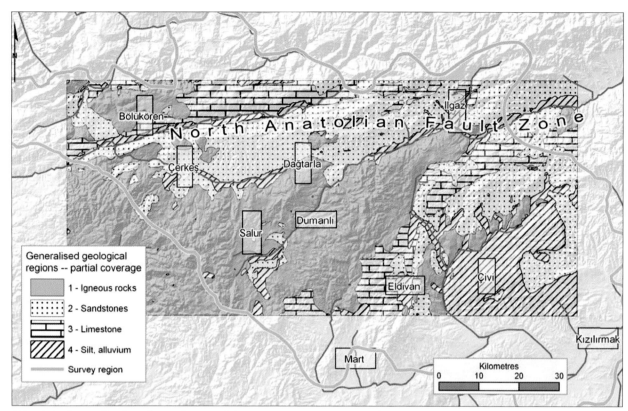

Fig. 2.4. Generalised geology of parts of the survey region. Derived from MTA n.d. Incomplete coverage is a result of limited geological map coverage

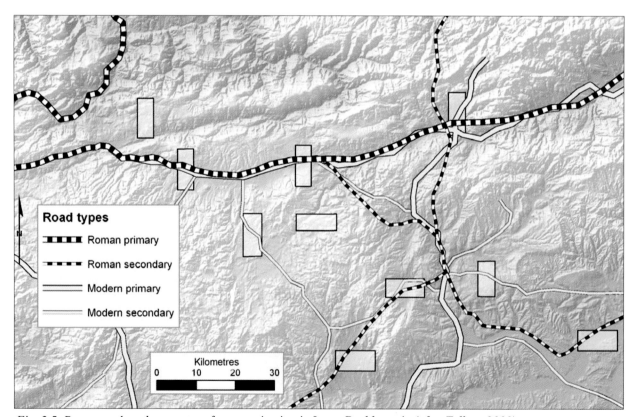

Fig. 2.5. Roman and modern routes of communication in Inner Paphlagonia (after Talbert 2000)

Region 1 is a triangle of resistant igneous rocks, anchored in the southwest corner of the study area pointing toward the northeast corner. These are areas of high relief and yield the poorest soils in the region.

Region 2 is composed of fractured, linear sandstone bodies that form elongate hills of intermediate relief. Sandstone soils are of low quality and usually only support grazing.

Region 3 is composed of two discontinuous zones of marble and limestone. The region comprises two belts, one on either side of region 2. Limestone/marble soils are often very heavily eroded, but patchy rich limestone clay soils also derive from these rocks.

Region 4 is composed of several relatively recent, silty sedimentary sources, covering the southeast of the study region and additional scattered valleys. A thick section of Tertiary-age gypsum and marl (interbedded with red, weakly consolidated volcanics) drapes over the older geology in the southeast of the area, and narrow, but important, alluvial valley fills are contained in the larger stream valleys, including the Kızılırmak. These landscapes are generally of low relief, and carry the best soils in the area, except where at this point in its trajectory the Kızılırmak flows through a salty Miocene plateau in the southeastern corner of the survey region, which severely degrades the fertility of the soils here. Steep portions, such as those along river valleys, carry thin and degraded versions of these soils.

Streams and communications
The stream pattern in Paphlagonia has long been important to its human use, both as a control on the location of travel routes through the region and because valley bottoms are optimal sites for towns and for supported agriculture in alluvial environments (fig. 2.3). Geology and rock structure control the stream patterns thoroughly in this region. Major drainage is consistently east-west, parallel to the NAFZ, except for the largest stream of the Kızılırmak river that diagonally cuts the southeast corner of the region within the wide lowland of weak sedimentary rocks. A few major streams, and much secondary drainage, run north-south, connecting the interior of the region with the largest streams.

Easiest transportation access through the region follows drainage and therefore basic structure. Fig. 2.5, of the Roman road pattern (modified slightly from Talbert 2000), shows a pre-modern transportation system, and modern Turkish routes are also shown in order to illustrate the persistence of the communication texture (Kümmerly, Frey 1985). Generally the map shows that earlier communications avoided stream valleys and very steep slopes more than do modern roads constructed and maintained by large-scale machinery.

Railways, more constrained by contours, more closely follow the lines of pre-modern routes, as in the case of the Çankırı-Kurşunlu railroad which cuts across the barren tract of land west of Korgun, as did the major Roman road (see Chapter Six), in order to avoid the steep contours of the drop to Ilgaz that pose no problem to the modern road.

The major through-route in the region, which was a branch of the Silk Road from early times and now still important as a Turkish national route, follows the east-west alignment of the NAFZ, now occupied by the Devrez Çay and the Çerkeş Çay (Mason 1943: 383 gives a good description of this and other routes of the region). The clearest north-south route through the central region runs up the Acı Çay, following the Tatlı Çay above Çankırı, and cresting the upland south of Ilgaz, although the route via Korgun to Kurşunlu appears to have been the main south-north route in Roman–Byzantine times. From Ilgaz, this route continues over the Ilgaz mountain range and on to the Gök Çay at the north of the study area, into a sparsely occupied mountain zone stretching to Kastamonu and the Black Sea coast. The main route from Ankara entered the region from the southwest, crossing the Eldivan plain before arriving at Çankırı, always the major urban focus of the entire region (see Chapter Six).

Resources and land use
Inner Paphlagonia hosts a range of natural resources that have been exploited through many periods of the past (Mason 1943: 109–30 provides a still useful overview of the mineral resources of Turkey). Soil is the premier resource for most pre-modern societies, as it underlies the capacity of societies to produce food either directly for subsistence or for the accumulation of surpluses that might enable trade and exchange near and far. The soil resource in the study region reflects the impact of geology and topography, and is therefore highly patterned and closely follows the landform regions seen in fig. 2.4. The pre-agricultural soil depth was greatest on weak rock, such as the silty rocks in the southeast, and least on hard rocks like the igneous rocks in the southwest. Soils are also thinnest on steep slopes, again as in the southwest and northwest, and thickest on flat land. Similarly, the texture of the soils is usually finest, and therefore best for plants, on weak rocks.

Fig. 2.6 is a landscape vegetation capacity map, derived from Thematic Mapper satellite imagery. Contemporary vegetation was modelled from the imagery spectral signatures and then converted into an ordinal scale of human vegetative land-use intensity. Judging from relict stands and from analogous situations in nearby regions, pre-agricultural vegetation of this

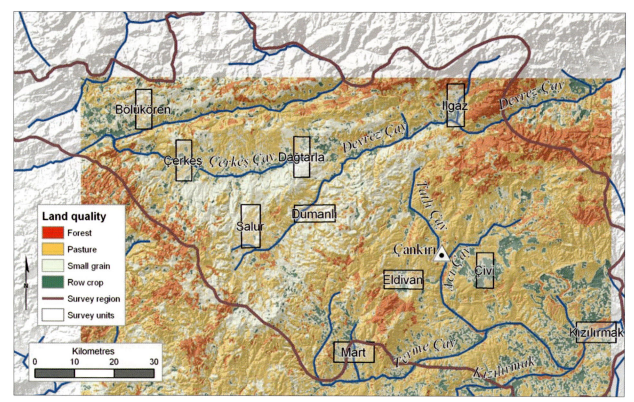

Fig. 2.6. Landscape capability mapping from spring 1998 Thematic Mapper imagery, derived by identifying and mapping contemporary vegetation classes. Incomplete coverage is a result of imagery limitations. Lowest class (forest and scrub) includes bare rock and water. The analysis tended to over-populate the poorer classes. Imagery acquired courtesy D. Griffin

region was vertically banded according to the moisture regime, from steppe at the lowest elevations, through open hardwood parkland in the middle elevations, to forest with a full canopy at the higher elevations. Contemporary vegetation is more controlled by human choices about vegetation resource value, which is in turn a product of soil quality.

Soil quality is the primary control on the land capability, along with accessibility, irrigation water, high water table and slope. The map in fig. 2.6 can be taken as a first approximation of a soil quality map. The pattern is emphatic and mirrors the geologic map quite closely. The local lowland soils are predominately mollisols of various thicknesses, with dark, humic-rich surface horizons still preserved in stable parts of the landscape. Mollisols are classic grassland soils, the basis of the great small-grain agricultural regions the world over. It is certain that higher quality land covered much more of the region in antiquity than today, especially in the steeper parts, which have eroded, and the stream valleys, which have been heavily silted in. A discussion of human impact will follow in this chapter (see below).

The highest capability class, soils that support row crops, is concentrated in the flat parts of the weak rock region in the southeast third of the map and a few valleys in the north. The very best soils, capable of supporting row crops in the absence of irrigation, are rare, located only on a few flat, silty uplands, most notably the Çivi upland southeast of Çankırı. The second class, suitable for small-grain crops, is spread widely on the sandstone landscape. Pasture-quality land dominates most of the dissected middle-elevation land across the entire region. The poorest land, suitable only for unmanaged forest, is found on the peaks of the hard-rock mountains of the igneous rocks, in steep valley-sides and along wet floodplains.

Water is the second most important surface resource controlling land use in the region. An important factor in the survey area is the high salinity of much of the water resource, particularly around the gypsum plateau to the east of Çankırı town, through which the Kızılırmak flows. The minimal water requirement for a grazing economy is the presence of springs for stock, which is rarely a limiting factor in a hilly landscape like this one, since springs will form below mountains in all but the driest climates. Sufficient spring or stream water for the domestic uses of a town is also not usually a limiting factor. Water supplies suitable for pre-mechanised irrigation are much more limited. Valley flats along major streams or at the foot of large uplands are among the few places that combine abundant, controllable surface water with productive soils. Most of the highest capability class on the vegetation map is of this landscape type. The flat valley bottom of the Eldivan survey unit illustrates an excellent landscape situation for simple irrigation, with moderate-sized streams disgorging onto an alluvial plain.

Building stone was an important resource for the construction of defended sites or large ceremonial structures, such as the wall complex at site PS057, Dumanlı (see Chapter Four). A central contradiction in the Paphlagonian landscape, as in many ancient situations, is that the best building stone is found in the area with the worst soils, and vice versa. This is because soil-forming processes act quickly on weak rock and make deep soils, but resistant rocks that make good building stones do not weather quickly. Much of the best building stone is basalt, from the region of basic volcanics. Basalt tends to fracture along its jointing planes into coherent, rectilinear blocks. The most productive landscape, alluvium and siltstone, provided very little solid rock.

By contrast, clay for tile and mud for mud-brick are most prevalent in the regions of good soils, since clay and mud are soil components. Clay of appropriate quality for ceramics is rarely in limited supply, since the small quantities that are needed can be carried significant distances. Generally these materials will not be from basaltic landscapes, as the resultant clays shrink excessively on drying and crack the wares that are made from them.

Certain other minerals were likely provided by the landscape. Salt was certainly abundant in the siltstone/ gypsum plateau southeast of Çankırı, and perhaps elsewhere. Gypsum itself is a good source of lime, for plaster and cement. Besides the siltstone region and the limestone uplands, lime can be collected from caliche soil nodules found in alluvial deposits downstream from basic rocks, and iron ore also found as 'bog iron' occurs in such deposits. It would be difficult to map such resources reliably; as these alluvial sections are often eroded away or not presently visible at the surface because of the human-induced burial that has affected most stream valleys. Although rare to absent in Çankırı itself, deposits of copper and lead ores do occur in adjacent parts of the southern Black Sea region (Koçak 2006) and have clearly had some impact on human occupation and exploitation of the region at large.

Human impact

The present landscape of the Paphlagonian region is quite different from the landscapes of antiquity, largely as a result of human-induced alterations. Evidence for the changes comes from observation of soil profiles and sedimentary sections in the region, from lake coring within the area (see Roberts, this chapter) and from detailed research in adjacent parts of Anatolia (Marsh 1999; 2005).

Soil erosion is the predominant human influence, along with its related effects on streams, groundwater, alluvial deposits and flood-plains. Evidence for soil loss is always somewhat indirect. The area from which the soil has been removed is often altered in subtle ways and the main evidence is necessarily an absence, and hard to record. Nevertheless, the evidence in this region is compelling. Steep-sided gullies cut into rounded hillsides are often indicators of vigorous erosion, and such features are common in this region. Such gullies, to the depth of tens of metres, are widespread in this area. In many cases, the gullies have coalesced to the extent that the previous rounded hill slopes are obliterated. In certain areas the gullies are undercutting ancient structures, as at site Çivi 05S01 for example, giving a good general marker of the timing of erosion. Large slumps and related landslides are also visible in many parts of the region, suggesting the influence of stream undercutting on hill slopes as well as of earthquake shakes (fig. 2.7). Conventional agronomic analysis indicates that more soil erosion occurs through the effect of dispersed 'sheetwash' of broad hillsides than by the acute impact of gullying. In the Paphlagonia region there is good evidence of extensive sheetwash, which has revealed blocks and stones in fields. Many fields are presently too rocky to farm, yet are surrounded by old stone walls that separate them into farm-plot sized units. Elsewhere fields are piled high with pyramids of blocks that were collected from the agricultural surface, yet the surface is now nearly covered by rocks and blocks.

Fig. 2.7. Landslide in Ilgaz mountain range, exposing buried Byzantine site

Judging from current land-use patterns, and from evidence elsewhere in Anatolia, it is probable that excessive sheep/goat grazing is the landscape impact with the most widespread influence on soil stability. Deep erosion has occurred on hills much steeper than any that are now farmed, for instance, and the effect of sheep/goat grazing continues after flatter lands are too eroded to be farmed.

Contemporary farm practices are clearly evolving rapidly in this region. The general trend is toward an agricultural retreat from steep, high or rocky land. Numerous relict field systems are visible on marginal land, characterised by walls, water retention weirs or fieldstone cairns. In some cases, these field systems are in use in one area and abandoned nearby, but in other cases the time of most recent use is unclear. Recently abandoned *yaylas* (summer pasture camps) can be dated in the near past by their modest state of disrepair and by historical and ethnographic evidence. Most villages are being depopulated, on the evidence both of the abandoned buildings and the report of local inhabitants. Mechanisation accounts for some of the labour shift, but a net effect of mechanisation is abandonment of small, steep or rocky plots not suitable for farming with tractors as opposed to animal traction.

Overall, it is probable that the effect of soil erosion on the agricultural landscape of this region has been substantial and locally catastrophic, leaving only a small fraction of the high-quality pre-agricultural soil resource, and degrading most of the rest. The present agricultural landscape is a relict, preserved on the flattest land. This land, however, was always very good land, and the current map pattern does tell of the soil quality present in earlier times. The major alteration of the soil resource since ancient times is probably the degradation of unwatered upland soils suitable for small-grain agriculture to a quality only suitable for grazing, that is, the ancient version of the vegetation potential map would have had much more of the 'small grain' category, extending over land now in the 'grazing' category.

The impact of soil erosion extends to the lowlands into which the soil is washed. No systematic effort was made in this project to measure or date stream sedimentary impacts in the region, but simple observation and analogies to nearby landscapes give a picture of what is most likely to have happened here. It is clear that massive stream deposition has affected the study region. A single dramatic exposure on the stream draining the Eldivan valley shows 8–10m of coarse cobble and sand sediment atop a relatively fresh soil horizon. The buried soil was a vertic mollisol, with some organic material and calcium carbonate deposits preserved in it. Although precise dating was not attempted, both of these materials are unstable over geological time and suggest a Holocene age. Simple visual analysis suggests that the level of preservation was equivalent to Bronze Age profiles elsewhere. Deep, fresh-looking coarse alluvial deposits are widespread along major streams in the region, but even less is known about their ages. In other parts of Anatolia streams have aggraded significantly since the intensification of human land use during the Bronze Age (Marsh 1999). This stream transition, a widespread increase in fine-grain sedimentation, is presumed to be indicative of an early human landscape disturbance between about 1500 BC and AD 600. The transition is called the Beyşehir Occupation phase, first described from southwest Turkey (Bottema, Woldring 1990).

The impacts to be expected in the lowlands from human-induced alluviation include boulder fans covering lowlands (as seen in the Eldivan unit and the southern end of the Salur unit), expansion of wetlands on floodplains and alluvial surfaces (as seen in the Eldivan and Kızılırmak units) and burial of archaeological materials (as can be seen around the base of the Bronze Age mound in Eldivan, site PS178). The amount of arable land may increase in places in the lowlands from alluviation, as rocky stream valleys are blanketed, but it is more likely that valuable farmland will be covered in coarse gravel or waterlogged by siltation.

An important secondary change from soil erosion is the degradation of water resources. The major impact is the decrease in groundwater recharge that occurs in upland regions after human disturbance. Because vegetation slows the surface runoff enough to provide much higher infiltration compared to unvegetated levels, farming and grazing lower the groundwater directly. Soil erosion prevents future vegetation and thus permanently degrades the groundwater resource. Lack of vegetation also increases surface runoff, which increases erosion and thus accelerates itself in a positive feedback loop. Furthermore, the high surface flows mobilise large-sized stream bedloads, which get spread across productive lands downstream.

Decreased groundwater storage damages or destroys springs. With a low groundwater level, springs will flow less vigorously and will stop earlier in the dry season. Some springs may be directly damaged by the transported sediment, as it fills the depressions in which they lie and diverts water from reaching the surface. Wells will similarly be lower and are more likely to get depleted. Groundwater feeds all dry-season stream flow in Anatolia, and the decline in groundwater will decrease that flow, thus increasing the relative number of intermittent streams that are dry in the summer. Because of these decreases in summer stream flow, salty or alkaline surface waters are less diluted than they would have been previously.

Aspects of geology and topography
By Vedat Toprak, Arda Arcasoy and M. Lütfi Süzen

Representations of landscapes and sites: maps, software and databases

A basic requirement of all such studies is the availability of suitable maps. For Project Paphlagonia, access to 1:25,000 scale colour topographic maps was provided through a specific project (ODTÜ-AGÜDOS 98.03.09.01.06), as a collaboration between the Geological Engineering Department of the Middle East Technical University, Ankara (METU) and the British Institute of Archaeology at Ankara (BIAA). Additionally, key 1:100,000 scale topographic maps for the survey region were obtained, a total of 13 such sheets covering the entire survey area of Çankırı province and the relevant parts of Karabük province. The location of these sheets is depicted in fig. 2.8.

A key resource is the geological mapping at 1:100,000 scale obtained from MTA (Maden Tetkik ve Arama Genel Müdürlüğü = General Directorate of Mineral Research and Exploration). These maps were purchased as hardcopies and digitised on an A1 tablet in the laboratory at METU in order to convert the data into a workable digital format. The rock units used in the geological maps were reorganised and grouped into nine categories that form the basis for the analyses here (see below). In the reorganisation of the rock units the only criterion considered is the type of rock unit, and therefore rock units of the same material, but formed in different geological time intervals and/or environments, are assigned to the same category.

Local morphological data are gleaned from the 1:25,000 topographic maps of the area. These maps are used to extract the following information:

> UTM coordinates (metres)
> Landform (pattern based on 10m contour interval)
> Elevation (metres above sea level)
> Aspect (azimuth 0°–359°)
> Slope (0°–90°)

The 1:25,000 scale maps have a 10m contour interval, which is the best available resolution for most rural areas of Turkey. These maps are hardcopy and were not digitised, except for those sample blocks where intensive survey was conducted (see below). All readings on the 1:25,000 scale maps were therefore made manually. At the regional scale, topographic data are based on a 500m grid elevation map of Turkey. Relief, slope and aspect maps of the whole survey region were prepared from these data, as considered below.

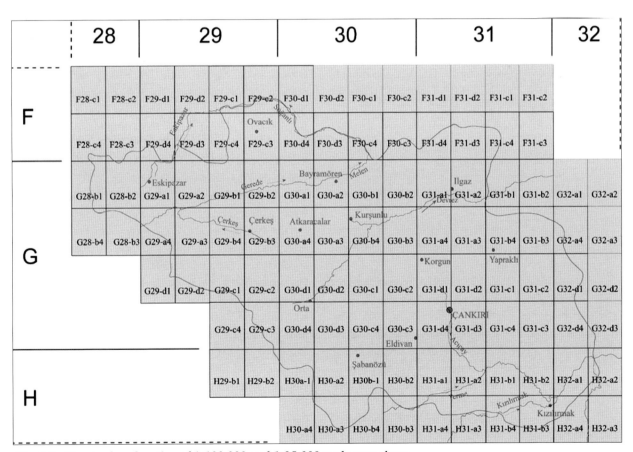

Fig. 2.8. Map to show location of 1:100,000 and 1:25,000 scale map sheets

The following software applications were employed in these studies:

> ArcInfo – for digitising topographic maps
> TntMips – for processing various geo-referenced spatial data and GIS applications
> RockWorks99 – for the preparation of rose diagrams
> Aldus Freehand – for drawing maps and preparing composite figures
> Surfer – for plotting site density and population density of modern settlements
> Excel – for producing histograms

In the context of the METU-BIAA joint project, two databases were constructed and employed. The first database comprises a list of archaeological and historical sites, based on the Project Paphlagonia site catalogue, but adding a considerable amount of information. The second database concerns 902 modern settlements of the survey region and forms the basis for analyses to be presented elsewhere. These databases contain all the vital statistics on sites featured in the studies in this volume, including:

> Site number
> Site name
> Site coordinates – seven-digit Y (northing) and six-digit X (easting) coordinates of the site in the UTM system in metres, read from the 1:25,000 topographic maps. In most cases, the maximum amount of error is 25m (= 1mm on the map)
> Topographic map sheet number (for key, see fig. 2.8)
> Site type (for categorisation of sites by type, see Chapter One)
> Site size (for categorisation of sites by size, see Chapter One)
> Site morphology, including;
  ~ landform type
  ~ elevation in metres above sea level (maximum error of 5m)
  ~ aspect of the surface where site is located (measured as an angle/azimuth read clockwise from direction north)
  ~ slope, measured as the vertical difference between a point above and a point below the site
> Rock properties – basic properties of rock units associated with sites within the study area, based on the 1:100,000 scale geological maps of the area, including;
  ~ name of the rock, as assigned by MTA geologists
  ~ category of the rock, according to simplified nine-fold division (see above)
  ~ age of the rock, as assigned by MTA geologists
  ~ MTA code, as used in original 1:100,000 MTA maps

Geology of Inner Paphlagonia

Geological aspects of the investigation area are here discussed in two sections. In the first section, the North Anatolian Fault Zone (NAFZ) is considered. The second section covers the rock types that have been mapped in the survey area, based on the 1:100,000 scale geological maps of MTA. As mentioned, these rocks are grouped into nine categories for the purposes of this research. Also in this section morphological characteristics – elevation, slope and aspect – of the nine rock categories will be presented.

The North Anatolian Fault Zone and seismicity of the area

The survey area is located in a region where intensive geological processes occurred, and continue to occur, in both the palaeo-tectonic and neo-tectonic periods. During the palaeo-tectonic period, the most significant geological event is the convergence and subsequent collision between the Eurasian plate to the north and the African plate to the south (Şengör, Yılmaz 1981). The product of this collision, which terminated the Tethys Ocean, was the formation of four major rock associations, namely Pontides, Anatolides, Taurides and the Folded Belt (fig. 2.9). The study area is located at the boundary of two of these associations, Anatolides to the south and Pontides to the north, and one of the rock types exposed in this area, the melange, defines the boundary between the two rock formations.

The neo-tectonic period in the region was initiated approximately five million years ago by a collision between the Arabian and Anatolian plates, and the current major active faults of Turkey are the direct outcome of this collision. The NAFZ (Ambraseys 1970; Şengör 1979) and the East Anatolian Fault Zone (Arpat, Şaroğlu 1972; 1975) are the most prominent instances of these faults. The NAFZ has a length of more than 1,200km, extending throughout Anatolia from Iran in the east to the Aegean Sea in the west (fig. 2.9). Rather than a single rupture, the fault is composed of a zone 3–60km wide, with several parallel to sub-parallel faults.

The NAFZ cuts across the survey area in an east-west direction. Intensive studies of the NAFZ have been conducted by several researchers (Tokay 1973; 1982; Hancock, Barka 1983; Barka 1984). Geological maps showing different segments of the NAFZ around Çerkeş, Kurşunlu and Ilgaz are presented in fig. 2.10. The index map in fig. 2.10 shows the traces of ground ruptures caused by the major earthquakes of 1944 and 1951. The distribution of modern villages directly over or close to still active, and therefore highly dangerous, fault lines (see fig. 1.3) is explained by the occurrence of water sources, in the form of springs, formed in association with these faults. Extensive talus deposits, fault-associated landslides (fig. 2.7), linear stream channels and perpendicular tribu-

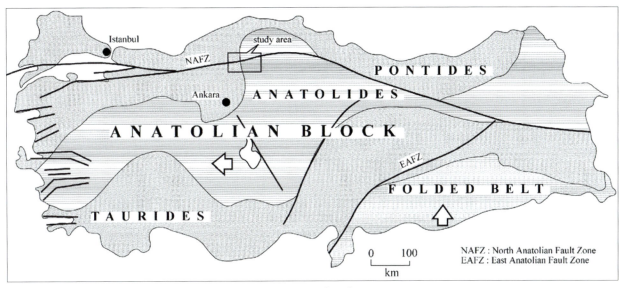

Fig. 2.9. Simplified geological map showing tectonic units of Turkey

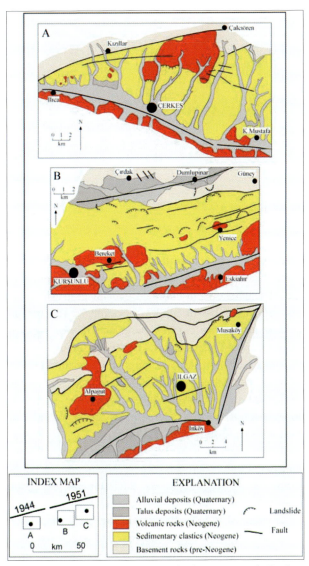

Fig. 2.10. Schematic maps of the areas of Çerkeş, Kurşunlu and Ilgaz (simplified from Barka 1984)

taries are some of the striking features that stem from recent faulting in the region. There are further traits visible in the field that indicate recent fault activity, including:

> Intensely crushed rock belts trending parallel to the faults
> Linear boundaries between different rock units of different ages
> Alignment of springs that use the fault planes as pathways to reach the surface
> Presence of hot springs
> Presence of travertine deposited by chemical precipitation of hot springs – some of these travertines may not be associated with hot springs today, indicating a shift in the location of the spring
> Deposition of alluvial fans at the mouths of streams, where streams are elevated by fault activity
> Typical fault controlled landform (linear valleys and ridges, fault scarps, triangular facets)
> Drainage pattern formed under the control of fault activity (particularly in the northern part of the area)
> Mass-movements (landslides, rock falls)

These traits are sharply underlined by the seismic history of the region in recent times. Epicentres of earthquakes occurring AD 1900–2000 are shown in fig. 2.11. A total of 1,348 earthquakes are recorded for this period, and there have been more since 2000. The most forceful earthquake recorded in the region during the 20th century, with a magnitude of 7.2, occurred in 1944 in the north of the survey area near Ilgaz. The two next strongest earthquakes were 6.9 in 1951 and 6.4 in 1953. An earthquake of magnitude 6.0 struck in the Orta region on 6 June 2000 (Koçyiğit et al. 2001) (fig. 2.12).

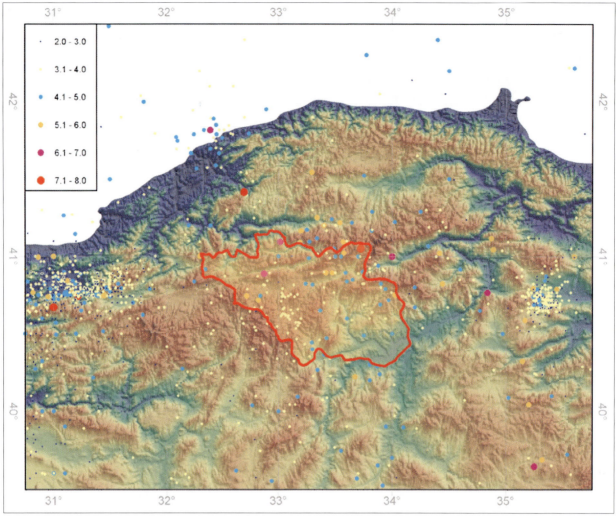

Fig. 2.11. Map of north-central Turkey, showing epicentres of earthquakes AD 1900–2000

Fig. 2.12. Earthquake damage in region of Orta, June 2000

Rock types, categories and characteristics

The geological maps prepared by MTA form the basis for analyses carried out in this study. These maps are used only to distinguish the rock units exposed in the investigated area. The total number of rock units having distinct lithological characteristics and different ages of formation is 97. All these units are mapped separately in the area and shown in the MTA geological maps. Table 2.5 presents a list of all 97 rock units. The second column of the table gives the name of the rock as assigned by MTA geologists. The third column displays the modification of the rock units into a smaller number of rock categories. The fourth column shows the geological time intervals during which the rock was formed, while the last column gives the MTA codes of rock units as featured on MTA maps.

Rocks exposed in the area belong to a variety of lithological units and geological times. Almost all rock types, formed in different geological environments, exist side by side in the study area because of the intense tectonic deformation that has occurred during both the palaeotectonic and neo-tectonic periods. Ninety seven rock classes are reduced to nine categories, considering their lithological characteristics and ages. Table 2.6 shows the summary of this categorisation. The distribution of the

No	Rock type	Rock category	Age	MTA code
1	Alluvium	Alluvium	Quaternary	Q-22-K
2	Travertine	Carbonate	Quaternary	Q-29-K
3	Clastic	Soft clastics	Pliocene	PL-18-K
4	Clastic	Soft clastics	Pliocene	PL-19-K
5	Basalt	Volcanic	Pliocene	PLB-K
6	Basalt	Volcanic	Early Pliocene	PL1B-K
7	Vocaniclastic	Volcanic	Late Miocene	M3-10-K
8	Evaporate	Evaporate	Late Miocene	M3-12-K
9	Clastic	Layered clastics	Late Miocene	M3-18-K
10	Clastic	Layered clastics	Late Miocene	M3-19-K
11	Limestone	Carbonate	Late Miocene	M3-8-K
12	Andesite-Basalt	Volcanic	Late Miocene	M3-AB-K
13	Basalt	Volcanic	Late Miocene	M3B-K
14	Agglomerate-Tuff-Andesite	Volcanic	Late Miocene	M3P1P2A-K
15	Andesite-Dacite-Tuff	Volcanic	Middle–Late Miocene	M2ADP-K
16	Clastic	Layered clastics	Middle–Late Miocene	M2M3-18-K
17	Limestone	Carbonate	Middle–Late Miocene	M2M3-7-K
18	Andesite-Basalt-Dacite	Volcanic	Middle–Late Miocene	M2M3ABD-K
19	Basalt-Andesite	Volcanic	Middle–Late Miocene	M2M3BA-K
20	Basalt-Andesite-Tuff	Volcanic	Middle–Late Miocene	M2M3BAP2-K
21	Pyroclastic-Andesite-Basalt	Volcanic	Middle–Late Miocene	M2M3PAB-K
22	Clastic	Layered clastics	Middle Miocene	M2-19-K
23	Clastic	Layered clastics	Middle Miocene	M2-20-K
24	Shale	Layered clastics	Middle Miocene	M2-3-K
25	Pyroclastic	Volcanic	Early–Middle Miocene	M1M2P-K
26	Andesite-Tuff-Agglomerate	Volcanic	Early Miocene	M1AP2P2-K
27	Dacite-Rhyolite	Volcanic	Early Miocene	M1DP-K
28	Rhyolite-Dacite-Tuff	Volcanic	Early Miocene	M1PDP2-K
29	Pyroclastic	Volcanic	Early Miocene	M1P-K
30	Clastic	Layered clastics	Miocene	M1M3-20-K
31	Limestone	Carbonate	Miocene	M-8-K
32	Andesite-Basalt	Volcanic	Miocene	MAB-K
33	Clastic	Layered clastics	Oligocene–Early Miocene	OLM1-18-K
34	Clastic	Layered clastics	Oligocene–Miocene	OLM-18-K
35	Clastic	Layered clastics	Oligocene–Middle Miocene	OLM2-18-K
36	Clastic	Hard clastics	Late Eocene–Oligocene	E3OL1-18-S
37	Evaporate	Evaporate	Late Eocene–Oligocene	E3OL-12-K
38	Clastic	Hard clastics	Late Eocene–Oligocene	E3OL-18-K
39	Clastic	Hard clastics	Middle Eocene	E2-18-K
40	Clastic	Hard clastics	Middle Eocene	EB-18-K
41	Clastic	Hard clastics	Middle Eocene	EB-18-KS
42	Clastic	Hard clastics	Middle Eocene	EB-18-S
43	Clastic	Hard clastics	Middle Eocene	EB-1-S
44	Clastic	Hard clastics	Early–Middle Eocene	E1E2-18-K
45	Clastic	Hard clastics	Early–Middle Eocene	E1E2-18-KS
46	Clastic	Hard clastics	Early–Middle Eocene	E1E2-1-SK
47	Limestone	Carbonate	Early–Middle Eocene	E1E2-8-S
48	Andesite-Dacite-Agglomerate	Volcanic	Early Eocene	E1ADP1-SK

Table 2.5. Properties of the rock types of the area

49	Shale	Hard clastics	Early Eocene	ES-3-S
50	Clastic	Hard clastics	Eocene	E-18-S
51	Clastic	Hard clastics	Late Paleocene–Lutetian	PN2EB-19-YS
52	Clastic	Hard clastics	Paleocene	PN-18-S
53	Granodiorite	Volcanic	Paleocene	Y1J2Q-PN
54	Olistostrome	Melange	Late Cretaceous–Early Eocene	K2E1-15-SY
55	Limestone	Carbonate	Maastrichtian–Early Eocene	KME1-7-SY
56	Limestone	Carbonate	Maastrichtian–Paleocene	KMPN-8-S
57	Limestone	Carbonate	Maastrichtian–Paleocene	KMPN-8-SY
58	Flysch	Hard clastics	Albian–Paleocene	KFPN-20-YS
59	Limestone	Carbonate	Late Cretaceous–Paleocene	KMPN-8-S
60	Volcaniclastic	Volcanic	Campanian–Paleocene	KLPN-10-S
61	Volcaniclastic	Volcanic	Maastrichtian	KM-10-SY
62	Flysch	Hard clastics	Maastrichtian	KM-20-S
63	Volcaniclastic	Volcanic	Late Cretaceous	K2-10-SY
64	Volcaniclastic	Volcanic	Late Cretaceous	K2-10-Y
65	Granite	Volcanic	Late Cretaceous	Y1J2Q-J2
66	Volcaniclastic	Volcanic	Senonian	K2S-10Y
67	Flysch	Hard clastics	Campanian–Maastrichtian	KLKM-20-S
68	Clastic	Hard clastics	Cenomanian–Campanian	KGKL-19-Y
69	Volcaniclastic	Volcanic	Cenomanian–Turonian	KGKH-10-Y
70	Clastic	Hard clastics	Cenomanian–Turonian	KGKH-19-Y
71	Flysch	Hard clastics	Cenomanian–Turonian	KGKH-20-Y
72	Limestone	Carbonate	Cenomanian–Turonian	KGKH-7-Y
73	Ophiolite	Melange	Santonian–Campanian	MMZ-KKKL
74	Clastic	Hard clastics	Berriasian–Cenomanian	KAKG-19-Y
75	Limestone	Carbonate	Berriasian–Santonian	KAKK-8-S
76	Limestone	Carbonate	Early Cretaceous	K1-8-SA
77	Ophiolite	Melange	Cretaceous	MMZ-K
78	Chert	Carbonate	Callovian–Aptian	JHKS-17-Y
79	Flysch	Hard clastics	Portlandian–Senonian	JLK2S-20-S
80	Clastic	Hard clastics	Portlandian–Berriasian	JLKA-20-SY
81	Andesite-Basalt-Tuff	Volcanic	Jurassic–Cretaceous	JKABP2-Y
82	Limestone	Carbonate	Late Jurassic–Early Cretaceous	J3K1-8-S
83	Flysch	Hard clastics	Malm–Neocomian	J3K1N-20-SY
84	Chert-Basalt-Shale-Ophiolite	Melange	Jurassic–Cretaceous	VMZ-JK
85	Gabbro,Ophiolite	Melange	Jurassic–Cretaceous	WMZ-JK
86	Limestone	Carbonate	Middle–Late Triassic	T2T3-8-S
87	Meta-olistostrome	Metamorphic	Middle–Late Triassic	T2T3OLM
88	Meta-olistostrome	Metamorphic	Liassic	J1OLM
89	Marble	Metamorphic	Late Triassic–Liassic	T3J1MR
90	Phyllite	Metamorphic	Late Triassic–Liassic	T3J1SF
91	Schist-Calcschist	Metamorphic	Late Triassic–Liassic	T3SK
92	Schist	Metamorphic	Triassic–Early Jurassic	TJ1S
93	Meta-clastic	Metamorphic	Triassic	TDM
94	Olistostrome	Melange	Permian	P-15-Y
95	Limestone	Carbonate	Middle Devonian–Early Carboniferous	D2C1-8-S
96	Clastic	Hard clastics	Ordovician–Early Devonian	OD1-20-S
97	Meta-granitoid	Metamorphic	Precambrian	PEYM

Table 2.5 (continued). Properties of the rock types of the area

Contexts of Human Interaction: Geology, Geography, Geomorphology and Environment

Category	Number of classes in the original data	Area covered (%)	Age range
Alluvium	1	9.52	Quaternary
Soft clastics	2	8.97	Pliocene
Layered clastics	10	20.21	Oligocene-Miocene
Volcanics	27	28.28	Jurassic–Pliocene
Evaporates	2	2.56	Eocene–Miocene
Carbonates	16	4.85	Devonian–Quaternary
Melange	6	10.79	Permian–Early Eocene
Hard clastics	25	13.19	Ordovician–Oligocene
Metamorphics	8	1.63	Precambrian–Triassic

Table 2.6. Some properties of the nine rock categories

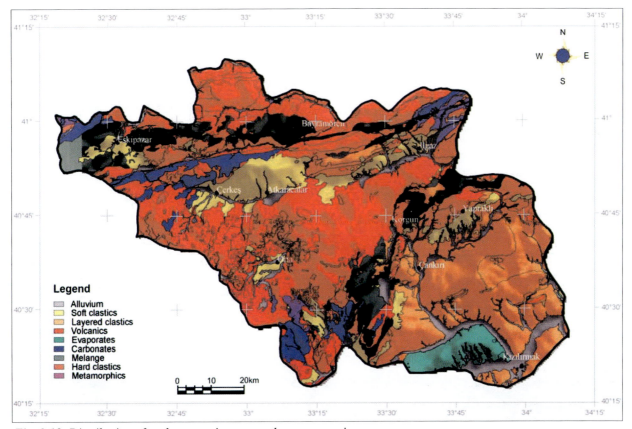

Fig. 2.13. Distribution of rock categories across the survey region

nine categories is illustrated in the geological map given in fig. 2.13, while the distribution of individual classes is illustrated in fig. 2.14. The basic properties of the nine rock categories are as follows.

Alluvium: this type corresponds to one class in the original MTA data. It is the youngest unit exposed (Quaternary) and covers an area of 9.52% of the survey region. It is generally deposited at gently sloping to horizontal surfaces. The distribution of alluvium in the area indicates a close association with the main streams and their tributaries.

Soft clastics: this category is formed by two rock types of Pliocene age. They are composed of unconsolidated continental clastics that cover an area of 8.97%. They are deposited in the north-central part of the area along the depressions formed by the NAFZ and in the upper parts of the drainage basin of the Kızılırmak river. They provide a gentle topography suitable for agricultural activities.

Layered clastics: these are sedimentary rocks with a medium to high degree of consolidation. They correspond to ten different MTA rock classes and cover an area of 20.21%. They are mostly exposed within the drainage basin of the Kızılırmak river. They produce, in general, a gentle and smooth topography locally dissected by minor tributaries.

Volcanics: volcanic rocks are the most common rocks in the survey area. Twenty seven classes of volcanic rocks ranging in age from Jurassic to Pliocene are distinguished in the region. They cover 28.28% of the area, the highest percentage of all nine categories. Dominant lithologies of this category are basalt, andesite, rhyolite, dacite and other volcaniclastics such as tuff, agglomerate and pyroclastic. The distribution of the volcanics in the area suggests that they mostly belong to the Galatean volcanic province of Miocene age. Older volcanics are exposed as belts along the NAFZ in the northern parts of the area.

Evaporates: evaporates are composed of two rock classes of Eocene–Miocene interval and they cover 2.56% of the area. They are exposed only in the southeast part of the area and are characterised by a high content of salt that is also present in water springs in this part of the survey region.

Carbonates: carbonates are composed of 16 rock classes, 14 of which are limestone, one cherty limestone and one travertine. The ages of these classes have a wide range from Devonian to Quaternary (Quaternary carbonate is travertine). They cover 4.85% of the area and are made up of four main masses scattered over the region.

Melange: melange is a chaotic mixture of rock masses usually formed in continental collision areas. The melange in the area is composed of six different rock classes, which cover 10.79% of the region. Dominant lithologies are ophiolites and olistostromes with the blocks of other rock bodies. The spatial distribution of melange in the area forms two distinct belts. One of the belts has an arced shape that defines the north boundary of the Kızılırmak drainage basin, while the second belt is exposed in the vicinity of the NAFZ and extends in an east-west direction.

Hard clastics: this category is composed of 25 different sedimentary rock classes and covers 13.19% of the area. Dominant lithologies are shale, siltstone, sandstone, conglomerate and flysch. They are concentrated as discontinuous scattered masses in the central and continuous masses in the northern parts of the area, and are formed in Ordovician to Oligocene eras. Older

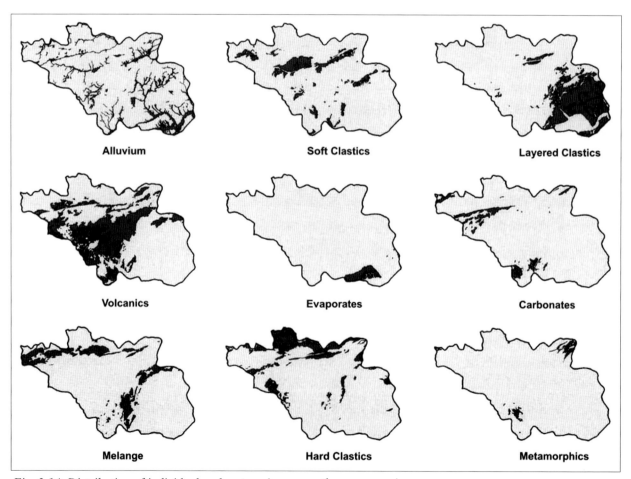

Fig. 2.14. Distribution of individual rock categories across the survey region

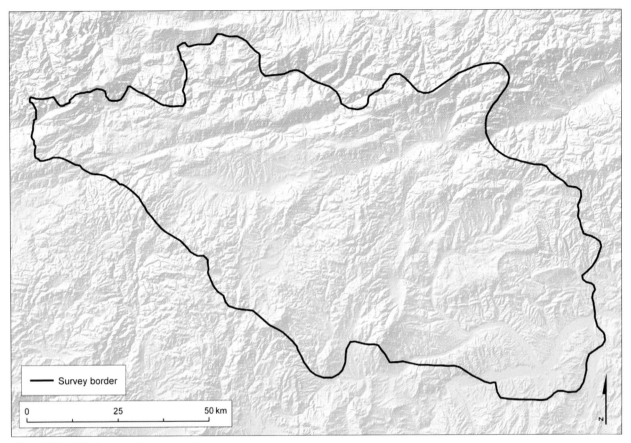

Fig. 2.15. Relief map of survey region

classes of this category are characterised by very hard, moderately to steeply inclined sedimentary strata.

Metamorphics: metamorphic rocks are the oldest rocks in the area (Precambrian to Triassic). This category is composed of eight rock classes and covers an area of 1.63%, which is the lowest percentage of all categories. Dominant lithologies of metamorphic rocks are schist, phyllite, marble, meta-granitoids, meta-olistostrome and meta-clastics. Two large exposures in the area are located in the southwest and northeast parts.

Topography of Inner Paphlagonia
Topographic characteristics of the area are considered using the elevation data of Turkey at 500m grid spacing. Three outputs produced from these data and explained below are relief, slope and aspect maps of the study area. The reliability of these maps can be questioned due to the wide grid spacing that may miss some of the details of the topography. The best solution to this problem would be to use digital maps at 1:25,000 scale, but such an exercise would require a much greater time investment than was available, including digitisation of hardcopy maps. Nevertheless, considering the size of the area, important information can be extracted from 500m grid data used as a basis for some generalisations.

Relief topography
A relief map of the area is given in fig. 2.15. The southeast and northwest parts of the area have the lowest elevations. The northern half of the area is characterised by generally east-west trending depressions and ridges formed in the context of the NAFZ. The river valleys of Çerkeş, Gerede, Devrez and Soğanlı are the products of this tectonic impact. The southern half of the area, on the other hand, particularly towards the southeast, is represented by an arcuate topographic high, a result of the Kızılırmak river and its tributaries that form an inward radial drainage pattern suggesting no or significantly less tectonic influence.

A histogram is depicted using 35,487 pixels (grid cells) from the 500m grid elevation data of the area (table 2.7; fig. 2.16A). The lowest and the highest elevations are recorded as 428m and 2,112m, respectively. Elevation values are plotted as 50m intervals versus percentage. The most concentrated elevation is about 1,300m with a density of 6.5%. The density of elevations below 550m and above 1,750m is less than 1%.

Slope topography
A slope map of the area was prepared from the same 500m spacing grid data (fig. 2.17). The slope amount in

Elevation		
Interval	Freq.	%
401–450	2	0.01
451–500	5	0.01
501–550	225	0.63
551–600	1,059	2.99
601–650	1,080	3.04
651–700	918	2.57
701–750	962	2.71
751–800	1,004	2.83
801–850	1,124	3.17
851–900	1,555	4.38
901–950	1,546	4.36
951–1,000	1,516	4.27
1,001–1,050	1,774	5.00
1,051–1,100	1,728	4.87
1,101–1,150	1,756	4.95
1,151–1,200	1,831	5.16
1,201–1,250	2,079	5.86
1,251–1,300	2,347	6.61
1,301–1,350	2,331	6.57
1,351–1,400	2,102	5.92
1,401–1,450	1,871	5.27
1,451–1,500	1,633	4.60
1,501–1,550	1,275	3.59
1,551–1,600	988	2.78
1,601–1,650	932	2.63
1,651–1,700	730	2.06
1,701–1,750	447	1.26
1,751–1,800	262	0.74
1,801–1,850	168	0.47
1,851–1,900	100	0.28
1,901–1,950	50	0.14
1,951–2,000	41	0.12
2,001–2,050	34	0.10
2,051–2,100	10	0.03
2,101–2,150	2	0.01
Total	**35,487**	

Slope		
Degree	Freq.	%
0–1	579	1.63
1–2	1,439	4.05
2–3	2,044	5.76
3–4	2,404	6.77
4–5	2,774	7.82
5–6	2,878	8.11
6–7	2,878	8.11
7–8	2,647	7.46
8–9	2,342	7.00
9–10	2,035	5.73
10–11	1,953	5.50
11–12	1,402	3.95
12–13	1,332	3.75
13–14	1,164	3.28
14–15	1,017	2.86
15–16	918	2.59
16–17	806	2.27
17–18	705	1.99
18–19	610	1.72
19–20	515	1.45
20–21	488	1.38
21–22	399	1.12
22–23	312	0.88
23–24	298	0.84
24–25	270	0.76
25–26	186	0.52
26–27	160	0.45
27–28	161	0.45
28–29	148	0.42
29–30	120	0.34
30–31	105	0.30
31–32	81	0.23
32–33	59	0.17
33–34	52	0.15
34–35	43	0.12
35–36	24	0.07
36–37	19	0.05
37–38	23	0.06
38–39	24	0.07
39–40	18	0.05
40–41	13	0.04
41–42	15	0.04
42–43	7	0.02
43–44	13	0.04
44–45	3	0.01
45–46	3	0.01
46–47	1	0.00
Total	**35,487**	

Aspect		
Azimuth	Freq.	%
00–09	1,125	3.21
10–19	837	2.39
20–29	780	2.23
30–39	657	1.88
40–49	759	2.17
50–59	738	2.11
60–69	723	2.06
70–79	786	2.24
80–89	966	2.76
90–99	1,170	3.34
100–109	1,059	3.02
110–119	981	2.80
120–129	1,035	2.96
130–139	1,359	3.88
140–149	1,464	4.18
150–159	1,725	4.92
160–169	1,656	4.73
170–179	1,545	4.41
180–189	1,536	4.38
190–199	1,077	3.06
200–209	807	2.30
210–219	687	1.96
220–229	630	1.80
230–239	486	1.39
240–249	483	1.38
250–259	534	1.52
260–269	558	1.59
270–279	744	2.12
280–289	702	2.00
290–299	822	2.35
300–309	837	2.39
310–319	858	2.45
320–329	1,053	3.01
330–339	1,290	3.68
340–349	1,314	3.75
350–359	1,239	3.54
Total	**35,022**	

Table 2.7. Elevation, slope and aspect data of the study area. Histograms in fig. 2.16 are drawn according to the % column in this table

Contexts of Human Interaction: Geology, Geography, Geomorphology and Environment

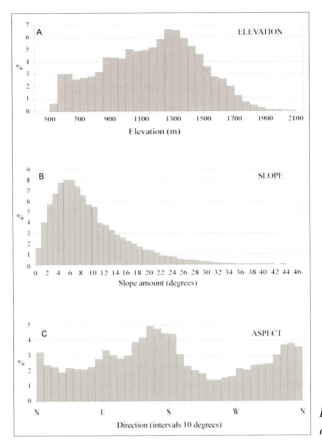

Fig. 2.16. Histograms relating to morphological features of the survey region

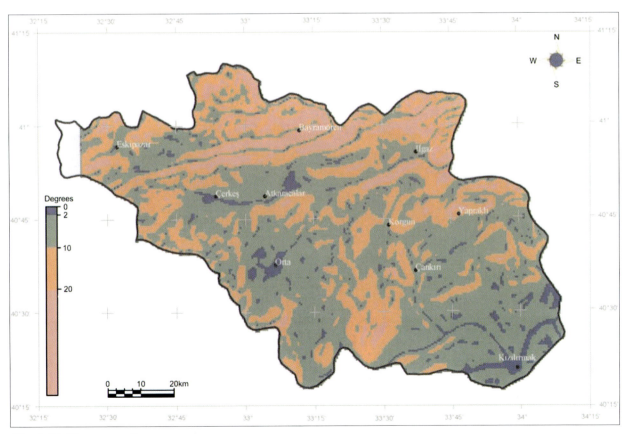

Fig. 2.17. Slope map of survey region

this map is shown in four intervals, namely 0°–2°, 2°–10°, 10°–20° and >20°. These intervals are selected arbitrarily; and the data could of course be processed using different intervals.

The first interval (0°–2°) indicates horizontal to sub-horizontal areas. These areas are dominantly observed in the drainage basin of the Kızılırmak river, between Çerkeş and Kurşunlu, and around Orta. Other areas of this interval are observed as thin belts, linear or curvilinear, along the major streams. The second interval (2°–10°) covers much of the area, particularly in the central and southeast parts. Most of the major streams and their tributaries are located in the regions of this interval. The third interval (10°–20°) areas have two major distributions, in the north and south parts of the area. In the north parts, these regions are exposed as narrow and long zones extending in approximate east-west directions parallel to the strike of the faults within the NAFZ. In the south part, on the other hand, they represent scattered elliptical or irregular regions. The last interval of slope (>20°) is represented by the higher altitudes of elevated regions. They are mostly confined to the north part of the area forming east-west extending ridges. Here we are truly into the steep territory of the Pontic zone.

A histogram from the slope data is given at 1° intervals (table 2.7; fig. 2.16B). The most frequent slope amounts in the area are between 2° and 11°, with a density of more than 5%. Maximum concentration is at 5°–7° at about 8%. Small concentrations of gentle, or horizontal, slopes in both the slope map and the histogram may be due to the large grid spacing of the original data.

Aspect topography

An aspect map of the area was prepared from elevation data with 500m grid spacing (fig. 2.18), which shows the direction of slope of unit pixels. The number of the pixels in this data set is smaller than as used in the relief and slope maps because horizontal pixels were not assigned an aspect value. Densities of aspect values at 10° intervals are shown in a histogram (table 2.7; fig. 2.16C) and a rose diagram, which gives a more immediately comprehensible idea of the aspect pattern (fig. 2.19).

The colour scale used in fig. 2.18 shows the direction of the aspect for each corresponding pixel. Although the scale is gradational from one colour to another, the four dominant directions are shown in blue (north), yellow (east), red (south) and green (west). Transitional colours indicate the aspect directions other than the four cardinal directions. The dominance of the red and blue colours is the most striking feature of the map. This means that the area is dominated by south-facing and north-facing slopes.

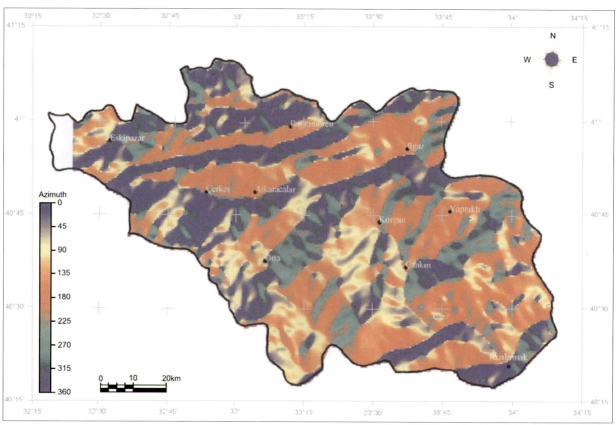

Fig. 2.18. Aspect map of survey region

Contexts of Human Interaction: Geology, Geography, Geomorphology and Environment

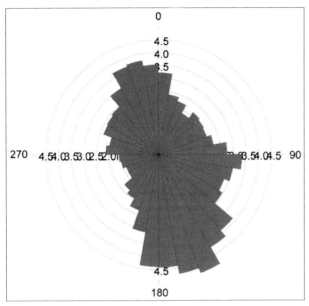

Fig. 2.19. Rose diagram showing aspect topography of survey region

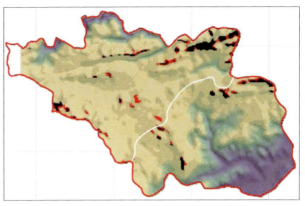

Fig. 2.20. Map showing general topography of survey region

The distribution pattern of these colours suggests that the area is characterised by parallel belts of ridges and valleys trending in approximately east-west directions. The orientation of the belts is northeast/southwest in the southern parts of the area. The asymmetry of the ridges can be recognised from the differential widths of these belts, as can also be confirmed by the information provided from the relief map. Thus, the difference in the widths of the blue and red bands to the north and south of the Gerede river, for example, suggests that the south-facing slope of the ridge to the north of the river is steeper than the north-facing slope. The opposite observation can be made for the ridge located to the south of the river.

General comments on topography

The general morphology of the area is well illustrated by the data considered here. The survey area can be divided into two sub-areas with diverse morphological characteristics (fig. 2.20). The first sub-area covers the southeast region, drained by the Kızılırmak river and its tributaries. The second sub-area covers the north and west parts of the region and is drained by the Devrez, Çerkeş and Gerede (Melen) rivers. The boundary of these two sub-areas is defined by a topographic high made up of melange rock units passing south of Orta and occurring around Korgun and Yapraklı.

The southeast sub-area is characterised by low internal relief, relatively less dissection, low elevation and gentle topography. Slopes are usually less than 10° and the prevailing aspect direction is south-southeast (figs 2.17, 2.18). Rock units exposed in this part are alluvium, layered clastics and evaporates (fig. 2.14). Analysis of modern settlement densities suggests that this area has the lowest population frequency as well as the lowest population density, except for large settlements such as Çankırı town (fig. 2.21). Settlements are located relatively far from each other, but are more populated compared with those in the northwest sub-area.

The northwest sub-area is characterised by approximately east-west extending ridges formed by tectonic activity of the NAFZ. This sub-area is more dissected and with higher internal relief. Slopes are more severe in this sub-area and surfaces face generally north or south. Almost all rock units, except evaporates, are exposed here. Alluvium, soft clastics and layered clastics are observed at low, others at high elevations (fig. 2.14). Frequency of modern settlements per unit area is high, particularly in the northwest section of the sub-area.

Goemorphology of intensive survey sample blocks
By Ben Marsh
Introduction
This section provides detailed descriptions of the ten survey blocks within which the intensive transects were walked (fig. 2.6). Survey blocks are compact landscape regions (ca. 10km by 4km) with broadly comparable landscape characteristics. In a general sense the survey blocks should represent a small suite of potential land-use choices, so that the transects are sampling variations on a single land-use theme. Descriptions of the blocks give a sense of the larger landscape that the transects sample, and the nearby resources available to the occupants. Subsequent quantitative analyses of the survey transect yields may be based on the soil resource characteristics of the blocks that they are in. Fig. 2.6 locates the ten survey blocks within the landscape and table 2.8 summarises the landscape quality of each

Chapter Two

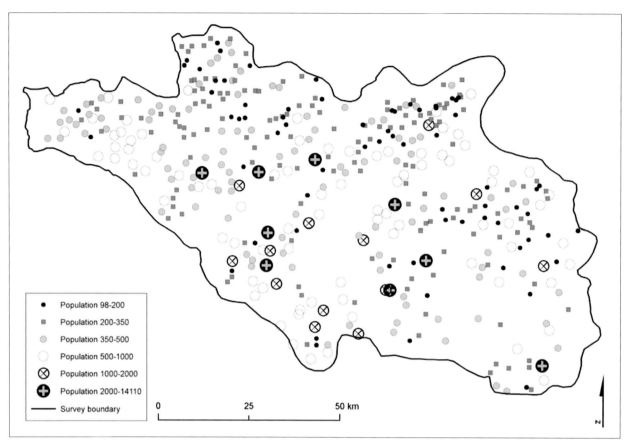

Fig. 2.21. Distribution of settlement in Çankırı province, AD 1950

intensive survey block as depicted in figs 2.22–2.25). These figures stand good comparison with those obtained from current official Turkish government sources (see above, tables 2.2–2.4).

Çerkeş (figs 2.22A, 2.26, 2.27)
The Çerkeş block, just west of the modern town of Çerkeş, spans the broad valley of the Çerkeş Çay, crossing about 5km of lowland, low slopes and dissected piedmont. Like the Ilgaz and Dağtarla blocks, the Çerkeş block is crossed by the major east-west route across Anatolia, part of the Silk Road.

Bedrock underlying the Çerkeş block is sandstone, which supports low-quality soils, and thus the bedrock uplands, composing about half the block, support only grazing. The central valley, as well as the lateral feeder valleys in the south, carry rich alluvial soils. Patches of rich soil also rise up the slope to the north and the plateau upland in the extreme north (Kabalı Dağı) is topped by small-grain soils. Presently the survey block maps as 28% excellent farmland and 14% small-grain agriculture.

Abundant water is available in the several stream valleys, and springs line the valley edge. Typified by the town of Çerkeş, and by its Roman predecessor Antoninopolis (see Chapter Six), good settlement sites lie along the valley floor. Post-agricultural land changes in this unit have been less than in most units, because the slopes are relatively slight. Some thinning of upland soils and some siltation of the lowlands may be expected, along with diminution of dry-season water supplies.

Çivi (figs 2.22B, 2.28, 2.29)
The Çivi survey block is the richest of all in agricultural terms. The survey block spans a broad marl plateau which is surrounded on three sides by wide stream valleys. The plateau lies about 200m above the surrounding streams. The plateau surface in the general area of the survey block is punctured in several places by sizable collapse basins caused by solution of the gypsum and salt layers of the bedrock; several of these basins hold lakes (see below). Elsewhere on the plateau the collapse process created deep, fertile, flat-bottomed, well-watered valleys extending northward. To the south the plateau ends abruptly in a cliff of deformed, salt-rich sedimentary rocks. Access to the region is generally good, but most through-routes skirt the region and take the valley to the west to approach Çankırı directly.

Contexts of Human Interaction: Geology, Geography, Geomorphology and Environment

Survey unit	Forest & scrub	Pasture & grazing	Small grain	Row crop	Highest-quality soils
Çerkeş	4%	55%	14%	25%	2%
Çivi	5%	30%	1%	50%	13%
Bölükören	15%	35%	35%	11%	5%
Dağtarla	5%	24%	54%	16%	2%
Salur	2%	54%	42%	2%	1%
Ilgaz	21%	27%	28%	22%	2%
Dumanlı	11%	45%	42%	1%	0%
Mart	6%	64%	1%	22%	8%
Eldivan	17%	51%	14%	15%	2%
Kızılırmak	31%	43%	1%	23%	2%

Table 2.8. Landscape capabilities of intensive survey units, derived from satellite mapping as described for fig. 2.6

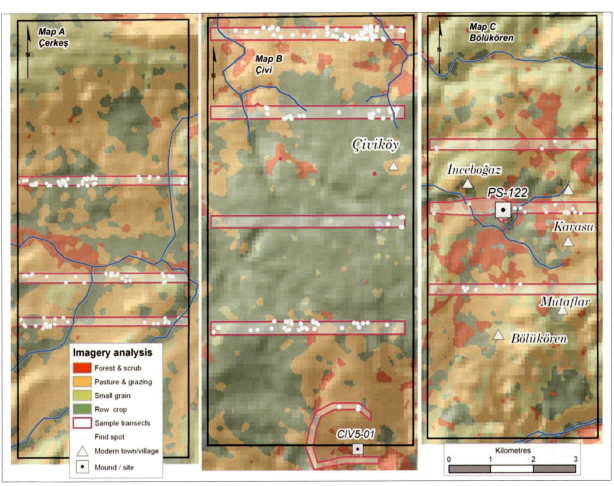

Fig. 2.22. Intensive survey blocks: Çerkeş, Çivi, Bölükören

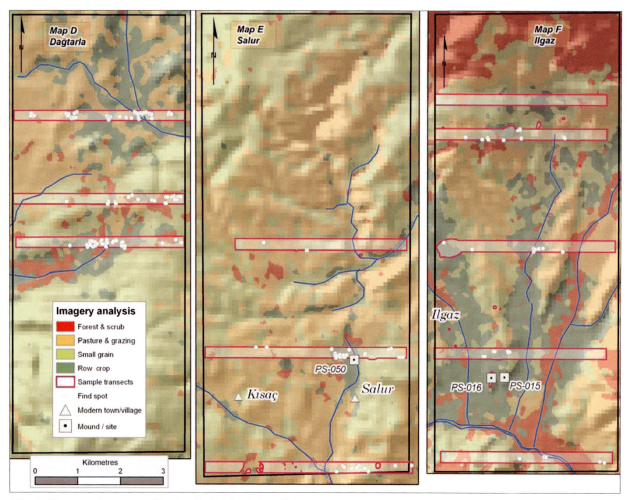

Fig. 2.23. Intensive survey blocks: Dağtarla, Salur, Ilgaz

Deep, dark soils cover most of the upland. Soil quality is very high, even supporting row crops above the level of irrigation supply. The floors of the flat-bottomed valleys have excellent soils, with access to irrigation water. The northward edge of the plateau supports extensive tracts of barley and wheat. The south slope is harsh and unfarmed. The survey block maps as 63% excellent farmland. No good building stones at all occur in this block, although basaltic rubble can be collected in the south and east parts of the unit, but no coherent lithologies are present. Commercial extraction of rocksalt is ongoing at the south end of the survey unit.

Water supply on the upland is poor, because streams and groundwater sink quickly into the porous marl. Settlement today is localised on the shoulder of the north slope of the plateau, where springs are concentrated. This region was probably less altered by human use since earlier times than most other intensive units. The flat upland was relatively immune to erosion. The valley walls that bound the plateau on the south and west have retreated significantly (as attested by the stream entrenchment undercutting the mound Çivi 05S01 at the edge of the block to the south), but the total amount of lost land is minor.

Bölükören (figs 2.22C, 2.30, 2.31)
The Bölükören block covers a complex topography developed on a complex geology. From the south end of the block the land rises 250m out of a gorge, onto a shoulder of flat fertile land. The edge of this shoulder is dominated by an isolated round hill of siliceous rock, and the shoulder extends 3km to a bare limestone ridge which is backed by a dissected mountainous region. Even today access to the region is difficult, following a narrow track out of the gorge to the flat upland which connects to several medium-sized towns on the high basalt landscape to the east.

The small plateau of Bölükören is favoured with very good soils derived from the limestone and basalt bedrocks. Most of the flat land is of high quality; the exceptions being saturated lowlands near the streams, and some gravelly fan deposits coming off the mountains. Higher lands around the plateau bear thin soils and offer very low productivity.

Contexts of Human Interaction: Geology, Geography, Geomorphology and Environment

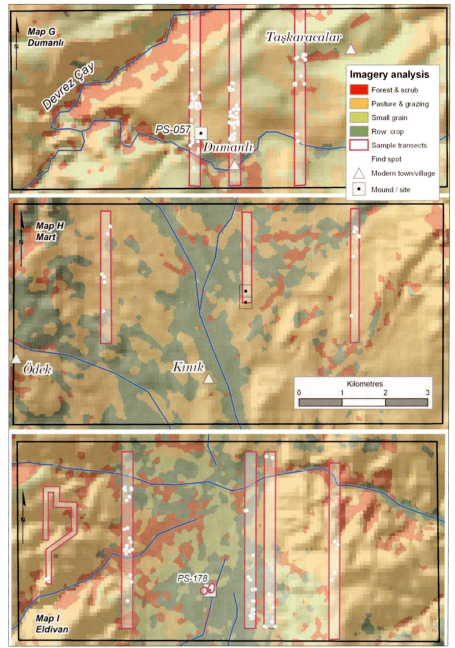

Fig. 2.24. Intensive survey blocks: Dumanlı, Mart, Eldivan

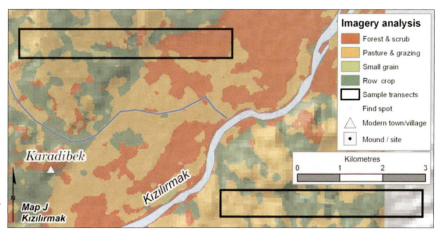

Fig. 2.25. Intensive survey block: Kızılırmak

Chapter Two

Fig. 2.26. General view of Çerkeş survey block

Fig. 2.27. General view of Çerkeş survey block

Contexts of Human Interaction: Geology, Geography, Geomorphology and Environment

Fig. 2.28. General view of Çivi survey block

Fig. 2.29. General view of Çivi survey block

Fig. 2.30. General view of Bölükören survey block

Fig. 2.31. General view of Bölükören survey block

The survey block maps as 16% excellent farmland and 35% small-grain agriculture. The abundant streams in the Bölükören area are somewhat unusual in that they flow north and west, away from the adjacent canyon. Surface water is widely available along the streams and below the uplands. Good village sites are located in well-watered spots between the fertile plains and the ringing uplands. This general type of location describes the placement of the large *höyük*, PS122 (İnceboğaz), in the landscape.

As rich as this block is, its previous state was much richer. Most of the uplands are made of limestone and basalt rocks that can be expected to have carried soil sufficient for good grazing and even grain production. These uplands have been thoroughly stripped of soil by rapid runoff from the bare upper slopes; deep soil and gravel now covers the lowlands and has degraded that landscape, as attested by the wetlands, the aggraded streams and the gravel fans.

Dağtarla (figs 2.23D, 2.32, 2.33)
The Dağtarla survey block lies in the main east-west valley crossing the Inner Paphlagonia region, on a low saddle between the broad valleys of the Devrez Çay to the east and the Çerkeş Çay to the west. This valley system forms a section of the historic Silk Road passing through this region (connecting to the Ilgaz block to the east) and provides excellent communications through the unit. Topography of the survey block features two small disconnected basins in the northern half, one draining to the Devrez Çay and the other to the Çerkeş Çay, and a significant upland in the south, Dumanlı Dağı. Beyond the western margin of the unit, a wide, fertile valley opens out for tens of kilometres.

The southern half of the block lies on basic volcanics, and the northern half is on sandstones and pyroclastics. The southern volcanics support reasonable soils, even on slopes, and the uplands are widely amenable to small-grain agriculture. The two basins in the north are floored with alluvium from the uplands, which provides rich soil. Presently the survey block maps as 17% excellent farmland and 54% small-grain agriculture. The ridges and divides between those basins are developed from the sparse sandstone bedrock, and have poor soils. Both basins are well watered from the uplands and provide numerous protected locations for settlement.

Since pre-agricultural times, human impact in this block has thinned the upland soils, aggraded the lowland soils, buried archaeological evidence in the valleys, decreased spring discharge and dry-season stream flow, and laid unproductive swaths of gravel across the plains of the larger streams.

Fig. 2.32. General view of Dağtarla survey block

Fig. 2.33. General view of Dağtarla survey block

Salur (figs 2.23E, 2.34, 2.35)
The Salur survey block stretches over a complex array of geological elements that have created a deceptively simple landscape. The unit is roughly an open trough, rising gradually from the flood-plain of a major branch of the Devrez Çay to the south, through a broad alluvial valley holding the village of Salur, to a series of dissected eastward-sloping pediments, to an irregular upland in the north. The valley is bounded on the east by a basaltic ridge and to the west by rhyolitic hills. The landscape is highly accessible from the broad valley to the south and the low hills to the east, although these areas are themselves rather isolated from the rest of Anatolia by the heavily dissected surrounding uplands. Soils of the wide valley bottom are rich and moderately well watered. Narrow valleys cut into the northern dissected pediment are richer still. Both are now in garden and row crops. The side-slopes of the wide valley and the dissected pediments support productive small-grain agriculture in their lower parts and rich grazing above. Presently the survey unit only maps as 3% excellent farmland, primarily limited by water supply, and 42% small-grain agriculture. Good pasture is 54% of the block; it extends over the basaltic hills to the east and onto the flatter parts of the western rhyolitic ridges. The northern mountains are only sparsely wooded. Basaltic uplands provide building stone of moderate quality and sizable obsidian deposits occur in the rhyolite not far from the multi-period mound of Salur, PS050 (see Chapter Three). Large streams flow through the block, but lie low on the landscape and offer little irrigation water. Numerous small streams emerge at the foot of the uplands. It is at a cluster of such springs that the village of Salur is located; the *höyük* at the north end of the broad valley is also near several of these springs.

The impact of humans on the environment of Salur is similar to that at the other sites. The soil depth in the uplands, especially the basalt ridge to the east, is significantly reduced. Rapid erosion is typical of these basalt soils, and the blocky, thin soils of the upland reflect that event. More and larger springs would have been present when soil on the uplands was deeper. The soils of the flat tops of the wide pediments are very well preserved; the dark surface horizon typical of mollisols is still visible indicating less than a few centimetres of erosion. The valley bottom has suffered significant alluviation over the centuries. The streams feeding into the valley have several metres of silty fill, the valley middle is boggy from the clays that have been washed in, and the flood-plain of the major stream in the south is covered by a recent, extensive gravel layer that prevents farming.

Ilgaz (figs 2.23F, 2.36, 2.37)

The Ilgaz survey block is a dramatic and diverse landscape. The survey unit spans the junction of two major stream valleys and extends up into the foothills of the Pontic range. The major east-west lineation that the unit crosses is a topographic expression of the NAFZ. The stream from the north, the Gök Çay, is highly energetic as it drops rapidly from the sparse uplands. The bulk of the survey unit consists of a 'staircase' of faulted silty alluvial fan deposits that descends from the north. Wide, shallow north-south valleys dissect the fan deposits. The north and the east edges of the unit include isolated modern settlements in narrow valleys cut into the steep uplands. East-west travel throughout the entire Paphlagonian region has been funnelled into the lowland of the Ilgaz unit, along the Devrez Çay, still a major route today as in antiquity. The Gök Çay valley to the north traces a logical route into the mountains, but the high energy of the stream makes road maintenance difficult, and transport climbs with difficulty, especially in winter, the steep 1,400m-high mountain flank. Access from the south, over the 500m rise, is challenging but passable in numerous places, both where the contemporary road switches back into Ilgaz and at the path of the Roman road, further to the west.

Very rich, well-watered bottomlands cover the southern end of the survey unit, extending onto the lower parts of the faulted fan. This land was recently in cotton; it is now in high-value market vegetables. The upper fan

Fig. 2.34. General view of Salur survey block

Fig. 2.35. General view of Salur survey block

Fig. 2.36. General view of Ilgaz survey block

Fig. 2.37. General view of Ilgaz survey block

surfaces are rich soils, but unwatered; they carry small-grain agriculture. Lying at the foot of extensive mountain regions, the Ilgaz block receives abundant water, but the streams are frequently uncontrollable. The Gök Çay, from the north, has a very 'flashy' regime, with high, damaging winter flows alternating with very low summer flows. The foothills section of the unit bears many good springs, but the steep and unstable slopes inhibit effective canal distribution systems. The survey unit maps as 24% excellent farmland and 28% small-grain agriculture.

A variety of good building stone is present in this region, including granite blocks, sandstone, highly carveable pyroclastic deposits to the south (which host rock-cut tombs or shrines – see site PS010, İnköy) and abundant river cobbles. Mineral deposits are likely in this tectonically active hard-rock landscape, but none were mapped in this survey. This is a very hazardous environment in which to live. Earthquakes have always been a fact of life in this region (see above). The steep, faulted, unconsolidated fan deposits to the north are highly prone to slope failure. A huge slide cut through the survey region within the last decade, dissecting a Byzantine site at its upper end and potentially burying settlements at its lower end (fig. 2.7). Evidence of damaging floods for the Gök Çay includes the massive boulder deposits on the flood-plain and the placing of modern settlements many metres above the elevation of that stream.

Modern settlement in the Ilgaz region is widespread along the wide stream valleys in the lowlands: Ilgaz has the highest modern population density of all the survey blocks. In the uplands the settlements are typically nestled in narrow valleys, constrained by the location of good springs and the small patches of flat lands. The steep landscape of the Ilgaz unit has evolved considerably since earliest settlement: erosion has thinned upland soils and removed entire hillsides, while vigorous stream action has covered areas around the major streams with boulder bars and fan deposits. However, the agriculturally important parts of the unit – small valleys and fan tops – are geomorphically stable, so the total change in arable land has not been high.

Dumanlı (figs 2.24G, 2.38, 2.39)
The Dumanlı survey block covers a dissected rolling upland of volcanic rocks. The centre of the unit is a high 'prow' of a plateau, bounded in the south by a sheltered small stream valley and in the north by the 250m-deep canyon of the Devrez Çay, the major through-cutting stream. The Dumanlı region is generally inaccessible because of its landscape of deep canyons and rocky slopes.

Dumanlı is the least agriculturally productive of the survey units. Much of the basaltic upland and valley sides support only grazing and the highest parts are planted in small grains. The alluvial southern valley is fertile and well watered, but less than 1km wide. The area is only

Fig. 2.38. General view of Dumanlı survey block

1% top-quality vegetation and 42% small-grain agriculture. Useable water is sparse in the Dumanlı unit. A large stream flows through the unit, but it is hundreds of metres below most of the landscape. The basaltic bedrock is quite porous, permitting surface water and groundwater to sink below the uplands, although minor springs dot the edges of the upland. Only in the narrow southern valley near the village of Dumanlı, and around the lake in the east, is ready water found at the surface for municipal or irrigation use. Modern settlement is concentrated in those two areas. Building stone is very abundant, as can be seen in the substantial Late Bronze Age wall structure on the west point of the triangular upland at site PS057, Dumanlı (see Chapter Four).

Dumanlı's rural landscape has been dramatically degraded by soil erosion over the years. Extensive areas of well-preserved abandoned field walls and cropping systems testify to relatively recent economic or environmental change. Piles of stones in the upland fields, up to 4m high and 10m across, probably represent many generations of stone picking, as new stones were revealed each year by erosion.

The piles invite excavation and palaeopedological analysis to understand better the erosional chronology. Earlier settlement may have been possible at the shoulders of the uplands, where small spring-fed gardens are now seen.

Mart (figs 2.24H, 2.40, 2.41)

The Mart block lies across a broad north-south valley cut into the high mountains of the southern part of the survey region. The valley is 2–3km wide, between ridges 400–1,000m above the valley floor. The main central valley branches into several smaller basins, separated by gravelly ridges. The Mart valley joins the Terme Çay to its south, and the Terme Çay valley carries a major modern highway route. A significant Roman road is mapped passing southwest-northeast through the Mart unit, to cross from the Terme Çay valley to the Eldivan Dağı uplands and on toward Eldivan and Çankırı (see Chapter Six).

Upland geology is marble and basic volcanics and the valleys are floored with sediment washed off the hills. Mart is similar to the Eldivan site in landscape, soils and situation, but the area of rich lands is somewhat larger. Land quality in the Mart block is strongly bimodal: only poor grazing land and rich row-crop land are present. Rich, well-watered lowlands and valley flood-plains are surrounded by sparse uplands developed on hard bedrock. Presently the survey unit maps as 29% excellent farmland and only 1% small-grain agriculture, but 64% grazing land. Much nearby land along the several streams is also productive, placing the Mart unit in a larger agricultural region. Numerous sites within the unit would be well watered and near rich land, and

Fig. 2.39. General view of Dumanlı survey block

Contexts of Human Interaction: Geology, Geography, Geomorphology and Environment

Fig. 2.40. General view of Mart survey block

Fig. 2.41. General view of Mart survey block

contemporary villages in and near the block are consistently situated above flood level on ridges near the larger streams.

Post-agricultural human impact on this area includes massive soil loss from hill slopes, significant aggradation of the alluvial lowlands, loss of dry-season water supply and accumulation of sterile gravel on flood-plains.

Eldivan (figs 2.24I, 2.42, 2.43)
The Eldivan survey block lies across an oval basin, 3km by 6km, in the first range of hills west of Çankırı. The basin floor is about 300m below the ringing uplands. Best access to the region is presently up the outlet stream toward the east. The Roman road between Ankara and Çankırı passed through the plain, running over the now unoccupied uplands north of the outlet stream. The stream valley may have been too unruly in which to maintain a road when the western uplands were more barren.

The Eldivan basin is floored with deep silt alluvium, brought into the valley from the surrounding uplands. The floor of the Eldivan valley is well watered from the several streams entering from the west and north. Highly productive row crop and fruit agriculture is found in the lower parts of the basin. The hills to the west rise abruptly, and bear little soil today. The bounding ridge to the east supports good grazing and small-grain agriculture. The survey unit maps as 17% excellent farmland and 14% small-grain agriculture. Availability of building stone is low in the productive parts of the landscape, but clay and mud for ceramics and brick are abundant. Present settlement is arrayed around the periphery of the basin, near mountain-side springs and away from the waterlogged bottomlands.

A reconstruction of earlier environmental conditions would highlight these important changes: more excellent soil would have been available in the lowlands as presently the middle of the valley is waterlogged and unfarmed, as a consequence of sedimentation of the upper part of the outlet stream. There are also extensive fan deposits of coarse gravel overlying good soils at the mounts of the canyons entering the valley. Soils would have been thicker and farming more productive in the uplands to the north and east of the valley, so that the area in small grains would have extended much higher. Spring flow would have been higher, supporting more irrigation on the valley slopes.

Kızılırmak (figs 2.25J, 2.44, 2.45)
The Kızılırmak survey block lies on a simple landscape in the extreme southeast of the Paphlagonia region. The unit stretches across the 2.5km width of the flood-plain

Fig. 2.42. General view of Eldivan survey block

Fig. 2.43. General view of Eldivan survey block

Fig. 2.44. General view of Kızılırmak survey block

Chapter Two

Fig. 2.45. General view of Kızılırmak survey block

of the Kızılırmak, the major river draining north-central Anatolia. The flood-plain covers about 40% of the area of the unit. Beyond the flood-plain, the bedrock is dominated by light silts and marls, which support low, heavily-dissected ridges rising up from the river. Access to the region is very good, along the river valley, but the site is distant from significant modern settlements.

Soils of the uplands were originally thin but productive silt loams. Bottoms of the lateral valleys would support thicker versions of the same soils, and the pre-agricultural valleys would have had similar thick, silty soils. The optimal settlement sites would have been on the spurs of the interfluves between the lateral streams, near springs and farmland but above the wet bottoms. The productivity of this area has been degraded by human agricultural activity over the millennia. The steeper hillsides eroded rapidly and the soils were thinned. Several metres of siltation have degraded the productivity of the river plain, largely by rendering it swampy. Timing of this in-filling is unknown, but evidence from other Anatolian watersheds suggests that it was progressive from the Early Bronze Age and continues to the present. This deposition would have obliterated any evidence of human occupation near the river. Thick brush is the typical flood-plain vegetation on Anatolian river plains without modern mechanised drainage and clearing; the survey unit is 31% forest and scrub, mostly along the Kızılırmak river. Nevertheless, a significant factor in the lack of agricultural exploitation of the main valley is the high salinity of the water and immediately adjacent land, caused by the river's course through a Miocene rock-salt plateau at this point. Lack of ancient sites in the region indicates that high salinity and poor soil quality are long-standing problems here. The adjacent valley floors, however, can support rich agriculture. Presently the survey unit maps as 25% excellent farmland and only 1% small-grain agriculture.

Palaeolimnological investigations in Paphlagonia
By Neil Roberts, Warren Eastwood and Julian Carolan
Introduction
The analysis of lake sediments, or palaeolimnology, can provide important insights into historical changes in environmental and climatic conditions, both locally and regionally. A key attribute of palaeolimnological study is that multiple proxy indicators can be analysed from the same sediment core. From a single lake core, for example, pollen can provide an indication of past changes in vegetation and land use, mineral magnetics can indicate changes in soil erosion and landscape stability, while sediment chemistry may be used to infer past climatic conditions.

As part of wider palaeolimnological investigations into Anatolia's environmental history (for example, Eastwood et al. 1998; Roberts et al. 2001), we undertook a survey of potential lake coring sites in Çankırı province in summer 1999. This section reports results from that survey and analysis of a 2,000 year-long lake sediment sequence. We follow this with some wider comparisons with other published palaeoenvironmental histories from adjacent areas of northern and central Anatolia.

Lake survey

In total, seven lakes were visited (fig. 2.46; table 2.9) during September 1999. Sites were probed for bottom sediments, and modern lake water and surface sediment samples collected, along with field measurements of pH and conductivity. Of these sites, the most promising for full coring was a series of four small lakes of solution origin located on the Miocene gypsum plateau immediately east of Çankırı town. All contain brackish-saline water as a result of gypsum dissolution. This same process has led to the rivers that receive drainage from the gypsum plateau being saline and non-potable; hence also the ancient name of Halys for the modern Kızılırmak. Oxygen-isotope enrichment between spring and lake waters at Siviş shows that the latter have additionally been affected by summer evaporation; that is, the naturally high salinity levels of the lake water have been raised further by climatic aridity. A 3m-long core was collected from one of these lakes (Çöl Göl) and the results of detailed laboratory analysis of this core follow below. Çöl Göl contains abundant aquatic macrophytes and algae, and its lower waters are anoxic. In addition a 1.4m core was collected from Dipsiz; a lake that is not in fact bottomless, although deep for its small size.

In addition, a number of small–medium size freshwater lakes, mainly of tectonic origin, lie along the NAFZ at the western edge of the Project Paphlagonia survey area in Bolu province. A number of these were sampled and cored in a summer 2000 season under a separate collaborative field programme with the MTA Institute. At Keçigöl, 20km east of Gerede, a 2.5m-long sediment Livingstone core was taken, while Yenicağa, a shallow freshwater lake west of Bolu, was also cored (this site had previously been studied by Beug [1967] and Bottema et al. [1993/1994]; see further details below).

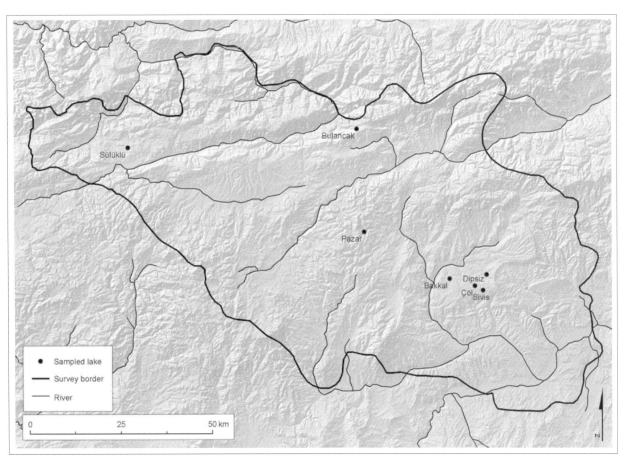

Fig. 2.46. Map of survey region showing location of visited lakes

Lake	Elevation (masl)	Maximum water depth (m)	pH	Conductivity mS/cm^{-1}	Notes
Çöl	1,028	5.8	7.7	4.55	3m core collected
Siviş	1,043	n.d.	8.4	6.86	
Siviş spring	1,060	n.a.	7.0	2.48	
Dipsiz	930	7.4	7.4	4.00	1.4m sediment core
Bakkal	860	n.d.	7.9	25.6	
Pazar	1,430	0.5	6.3	0.25	
Sülüklü	1,150	1.5	7.5	0.75	True to its name
Bulancak	1,840	n.d.	-	-	

Table 2.9. Lakes sampled in Çankırı province during 1999 field season and modern water chemistry

Field and laboratory methods

Lake coring at Çöl Göl was undertaken by Glew gravity surface sediment sampler (upper 0.5m) followed by Livingstone piston corer for underlying sediments, from an inflatable Avon boat with integrated coring platform at a water depth of 5.8m (fig. 2.47). Coring was stopped by a hard layer at ~3m sediment depth. Livingstone cores were extruded in the field into downpiping tubes cut lengthways, and wrapped in non-PVC cling film and heavy-duty plastic sleeving (fig. 2.48). Upon return to the laboratory in the UK, cores were kept in dark cold store at ~4°C. The sediments were described in the field and again in the laboratory.

The pollen preparations were carried out at the University of Birmingham using standard processing procedures (Faegri, Iversen 1989). This involved digestion in 10% HCl, followed by treatment by 10% NaOH. Clay-rich samples were subjected to 5% Na$_4$P$_2$O$_7$ and sieved at 5µm and 150µm mesh sieves. Minerogenic samples were treated with 60% HF acid before Erdtman's acetolysis. Exotic *Lycopodium* tablets of a known concentration were added in order to calculate pollen concentrations. Samples from 34 core depths were mounted in glycerine jelly and where possible a total of 300 pollen and charcoal grains were counted.

Sediment dry weight was measured as weight loss after 24 hours drying at 105°C and organic content by loss on ignition at 550°C for two hours at the University of Plymouth. In addition, the same samples were combusted at 900°C. Normally this would provide a measure of carbonate content, but in this case, other precipitates may also have been lost by combustion. Whole core mineral magnetic susceptibility was measured using a Bartington meter and loop sensor at 2cm intervals. In addition 19 samples were prepared for diatom analysis using H$_2$O$_2$ and HCl reagents, although most proved sterile, so were not counted systematically (see below).

Analytical geochemistry and particle size analyses were undertaken on 41 sample depths at Reading University. The latter were homogenised and disaggregated in sodium hexametaphosphate, but not otherwise chemically pre-treated. Particle size analysis was performed on a Coulter LS 230 laser granulometer, and relevant statistics calculated using LS 230 and PIDS software. For XRD and XRF analysis, samples were oven dried at 40°C for 72 hours and then ground until the

Fig. 2.47. Inflatable boat on Paphlagonian lake

Fig. 2.48. Extrusion of core into piping tubes

sample was a fine powder <20μm. XRD was performed with an automatic Siemens D5000 diffraction system, with the percentage of the various mineral phases calculated from bulk mineral diffractograms, using the intensity of the strongest peak for each mineral. Samples were prepared for XRF as pressed tablets ~2mm thick and analysis performed using a Phillips PW1480 X-ray fluorescence spectrometer. ICP-AES analysis involved a three-stage extraction. Solution A (carbonate bound fraction) was reacted with acetic acid, Solution B (iron bound fraction) involved the addition of moydroxalamine hydrochloride, Solution C (organic bound fraction) involved reaction with hydrogen peroxide. Additionally a limited number of samples (carbonate fraction) were tested for stable isotope analysis ($\delta^{18}O$ and $\delta^{13}C$), but results were inconsistent and are not reported here.

Finally, ^{14}C dates were obtained on three samples at the Beta-Analytic laboratory, using conventional (i.e. non-AMS) determinations. Calibrated age ranges are based on INTCAL.

The core from Çöl Göl (COL99)

Çöl Göl is located 12km east of Çankırı town on an extensive Miocene plateau which to the south is cut by the Kızılırmak river. It is one of a series of small ancient lakes of the region.

Chronology

Two samples were initially sent for ^{14}C dating, from depths of 93–96cm and 238–42cm (table 2.10). The latter, however, produced an unexpectedly young date of only 180 ± 40 BP, so a third sample from near the base of the core was dated, which gave an age of 1740 ± 60 BP. The 238–42cm sample (Beta-136284) had been measured on a reed stem. Aquatic plant remains are abundant in the lake and its sediments, so we assume that one such stem was pushed down by the core barrel to a lower depth and incorporated into the core. The date of 180 ± 40 BP is therefore ignored in calculating the core chronology. The two remaining ^{14}C dates, along with core top (assumed to date to the present-day) give a very

Sample depth cm	Material dated	Lab number	^{14}C age BP (uncal)	Calibrated age range (2 sigma)
93–96	Organic sediment	Beta-136283	620 ± 40	1290–1410 AD
238–242	Reed stem	Beta-136284	180 ± 40	1650–1950 AD
263–267	Organic sediment	Beta-141984	1740 ± 60	135–425 AD

Table 2.10. ^{14}C dates for COL99

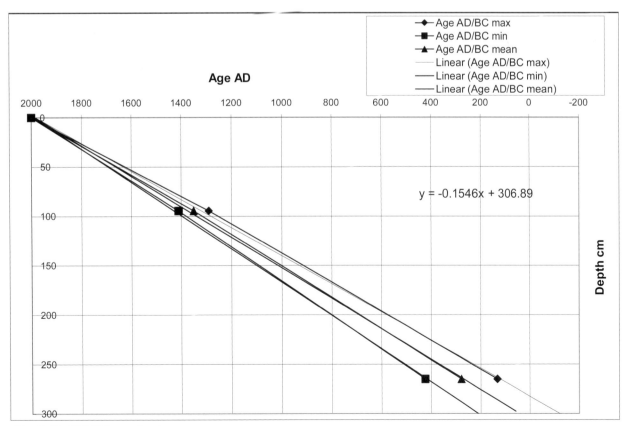

Fig. 2.49. Çöl Göl age depth curve

consistent, nearly linear age-depth relationship, with a mean value equation of x = (306.89-y)/0.1546 (fig. 2.49). This would give a basal age for the core in the mid-first century AD, although at 95% statistical confidence this could be as old as ~100 BC or as young as ~AD 200. In addition, the high water content in the upper 70cm of the core makes it unlikely that this age-depth relationship was truly linear all the way to the core top. Overall, these dates indicate that core COL99 covers approximately the last two millennia.

Lithology, sedimentology and geochemistry
The sediments of the COL99 core comprise sulphur-rich organic algal muds and chemical precipitates, and exhibit some marked down-core changes in lithology (fig. 2.50, table 2.11). The upper 70cm of the core has a water content between 41% and 67%, below which it stabilises at lower values, generally around 30–40%. The organic content of the core is >10%, except for the basal levels, and reaches values as high as 37%, probably reflecting both high algal productivity and the anoxic conditions at

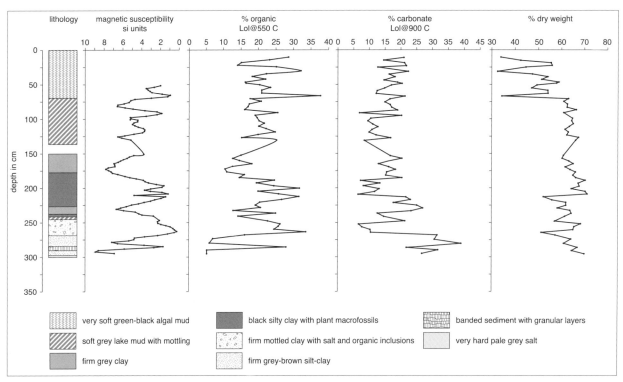

Fig. 2.50. Lithology, loss-on-ignition, magnetic susceptibility, and grain-size analyses for COL99

Depth cm	Description
0–10	No recovery
10–70	Green-black, gell-like algal mud with some plant macrofossil remains; very strong sulphide smell
70–136	Soft grey lake mud with mottling and white streaks (band of soft grey-green algal mud 93–96cm)
136–49	No recovery
149–76	Homogeneous, firm grey clay with occasional white specks
176–225	Black homogeneous organic silty clay; plant macrofossils visible
225–36	Firm grey clay with occasional plant macrofossils
236–40	Black organic silt-clay
240–44	Soft grey-brown mud with plant macrofossils (some woody)
244–67	Firm mottled clay with black and white inclusions
267–83	Firm homogeneous to weakly banded grey-brown silt-clay
283–89	Alternating bands of dark, white and buff sediments. Dry with some hard granular inclusions
297–298	Pale grey, hard 'salt' precipitate

Table 2.11. COL99 core description

the bottom of the lake. Magnetic susceptibility (MS) values are low throughout, which is unsurprising given the absence of ferrimagnetic rocks in the lake catchment. MS values show a striking negative correlation ($r^2 = -0.76$) with organic matter content of the core. This suggests that MS may have been influenced by autochthonous processes (such as bacterial magnetite production in a reducing environment) as much as by allochthonous ones. On that basis, it would seem unwise in this case to use MS as a direct record of catchment erosion history. This inference is further supported by the lack of correlation between MS and grain-size characteristics downcore. The increase in sand-sized particles in the lower half of the core is less likely to reflect allochthonous soil inwash than it is the formation of large-grained gypsum crystals (see below).

Of the full suite of major and minor element geochemical data, only selected results are presented here. In terms of abundance, silica, magnesium and calcium dominate the cat-ions, followed by iron and aluminium. This is reflected in the bulk mineralogy (fig. 2.51), which shows a dominance of silica and high-Mg calcite in the upper 85cm of the core, with gypsum dominant below this. Magnesite ($MgCO_3$) was found to be a major constituent of samples at 285.5cm and 298cm and, in addition, a substitution series was identified within the hexahydrite ($MgSO_4.6H_2O$) group. This mineral or assemblage of minerals occurred in most samples, and was a major constituent at 10cm and 68.5cm depths. The abundance of magnesite and hexahydrite could not be quantified using XRD and they are not included in the data shown in fig. 2.51. The silica comprises a mixture of detrital quartz and biogenic Si. Diatom preservation broadly correlates with bulk silica abundance, with diatom frustules preserved mainly above 95cm.

The diatom species present include some likely planktonic taxa (*Cyclotella, Nitszchia*) along with a variety of salt-tolerant benthic and periphtic taxa (*Amphora veneta, A. commutata, Campylodiscus, Anomoeneis sphaerophora, Mastogloia, Rhopalodia*). There are no obvious stratigraphic changes in diatom assemblages, and all the preserved samples indicate a prevalence of salt-water conditions in the lake.

Pollen analysis

Fig. 2.52 shows a percentage diagram of the main pollen taxa, zoned stratigraphically using CONISS (Cluster Analysis). In terms of abundance, the record is dominated by pine and grasses (Poaceae), including cereal-type grasses. Apart from pine, the only other common tree pollen type is oak (*Quercus*, probably deciduous). The occasional grain of *Picea* (spruce) and

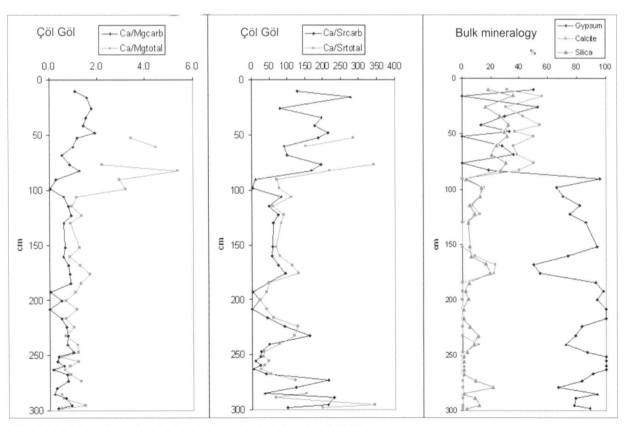

Fig. 2.51. Selected geochemical and mineralogical data for COL99

Chapter Two

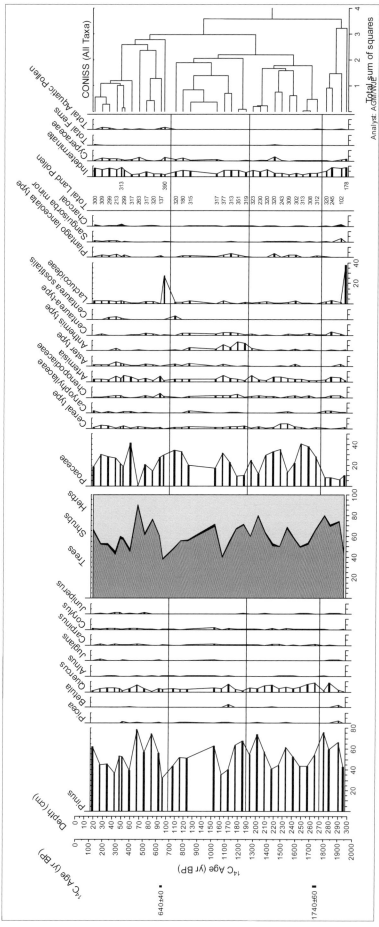

Fig. 2.52. Summary percentage pollen diagram for COL99

Betula (birch) almost certainly represent long-distance airborne transport from Pontic mountain forests. A wider range of herb-types is represented, including *Artemisia* and chenopods (steppe indicators), ribwort plantain (*P. lanceolata* – often considered an indicator of grazing land) and several herbs in the Asteraceae (daisy) family. Charcoal is sparse throughout the record, suggesting very limited burning activity of the immediate landscape, at least of woody biomass.

In pollen zone 1 (270–300cm), pine pollen percentages are high and grass pollen is relatively poorly represented. Zone 2 (190–270cm) sees an increase in grass pollen percent, including cereal-type, although both decline again in the upper part of the zone. Zone 3 (100–190cm) is marked by an increase in *Anthemis*-type pollen and a partial decline in oak pollen abundance. *Anthemis* is a genus of about 100 species of aromatic herbs in the aster family. In zone 4 (10–100cm) there is an initial increase in the relative abundance of pine pollen and, nearer to the present-day, a slight increase in cereal-type and *Plantago* pollen. There are two sharp peaks in Lactuceae pollen (also aster family) almost certainly produced by plants living close the lake.

Overall, the most significant feature of the pollen record is the lack of change downcore, which is in contrast to many other pollen diagrams from adjacent areas of Anatolia that span the same time period. Pine does not grow locally today, but is a pollen type well known for its wide airborne dispersal. In fact, pine is present at high relative abundance in most modern pollen samples from northern Anatolia, even when not present locally (Bottema et al. 1993/1994). The pine pollen at Çöl Göl therefore almost certainly originates as long-distance transport from pine woodlands at least tens if not hundreds of kilometres away to the north. Most of the remaining pollen types probably originate nearer to the lake. Excluding pine pollen, the diagram suggests that a relatively open landscape has prevailed on the gypsum plateau for the last two millennia.

Climate history
The COL99 core displays marked geochemical and lithological changes through time. These would have been caused primarily by changes in the lake hydrology and chemistry, although it is possible that some may also have been due to diagenetic (i.e. post-depositional) effects (Talbot, Kelts 1986). For example, the shift from calcite to gypsum dominance downcore broadly coincides with the stabilising of dry matter values in the core at around 70cm depth, and could potentially be linked to dewatering of the sediments linked to compaction. Some of the changes further downcore seem less easily explained in terms of a possible diagenetic origin. A second complicating factor is the unusual nature of Çöl Göl as a lake system, linked ultimately to the gypsiferous nature of the local bedrock. Gypsum dissolution has created a lake deep enough to become anoxic in its lower waters, leading to good preservation of organic matter in the sediments. At the same time, incoming waters are already charged in solutes, notably sulphates, even before they enter the lake. Normally, inflowing waters to a lake are chemically dilute (i.e. freshwater) with solutes only becoming concentrated within a lake through evaporation, in the absence of any surface or sub-surface outflows. The saline waters of Çöl Göl result from the combined effect of these two processes, i.e. evaporative concentration and solute-rich incoming waters. The changing nature of the COL99 lake sediments downcore is most likely to have resulted primarily from shifts over time in lake water balance that in turn would have been caused by climatic variations between drier and wetter conditions. Specific inferences about the significance of individual geochemical proxy data, however, are more problematic.

In most lake systems, calcium behaves conservatively as an element, and the ratio between it and other elements, such as magnesium and strontium, can sometimes be used to infer changes in lake salinity. This in turn might be considered a proxy for climatic aridity (i.e. higher lake salinity implying a negative water balance and a drier climate). On that basis, the changing Ca/Mg and Ca/Sr ratios in COL99 might lead one to infer lower lake salinity, and a wetter climate, in the upper 85–100cm of the core than in the underlying sediment layers (fig. 2.51). A similar argument might be used for the downcore switch from calcite to gypsum precipitation at the same depth, as the former is precipitated first in the Hardie-Eugster brine evolution model (Hardie et al. 1978; Teller, Last 1990).

On the other hand, Çöl Göl may be atypical with regard to its degree of saturation with respect to calcite and gypsum, and a different relationship could therefore apply. The geochemical change at around 90cm core depth, assuming that it is not diagenetic in origin (see above), is dated according to the available ^{14}C chronology to around AD 1400. From lake sediment records elsewhere in central Anatolia, this time – around the start of the European Little Ice Age – has been inferred to mark a significant shift to a drier, not to a wetter, climate. In particular, a highly-resolved, annually-laminated crater lake sequence from Nar Gölü in Cappadocia shows a clear switch in stable isotopes and carbonate mineralogy at this time (Jones et al. 2006). Plotting the Nar and Çöl records on a common timescale (fig. 2.53) shows a good overall correspondence between them, not only at this time, but also for earlier periods. This includes a shorter-lived phase of dry climate at Nar from AD 750 to 950, and relatively wet conditions from AD 550 to 750.

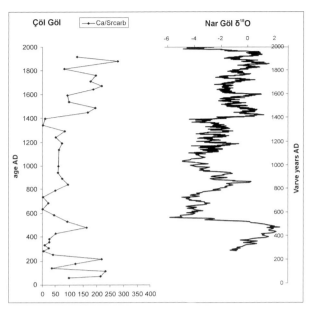

Fig. 2.53. Sr-Ca ratio for COL99 compared to $\delta^{18}O$ record for Nar Gölü (Jones et al. 2006) on common timescale

For the reasons outlined above, interpretation of the COL99 geochemical record in terms of specific changes in climate must remain tentative. None the less, it does suggest that strong century-scale climatic variations have occurred over the last two millennia. The correlation with the Nar record is striking, and it is certain that the two lakes would have experienced a common climate history.

Vegetation and land-use history
According to Bottema et al. (1993/1994), the 'natural' vegetation type for most of Çankırı province would be mixed broad-leaved and needle woodland resistant to cold. Deciduous oak would be the predominant tree type, with occasional small stands of black pine in mountainous areas with higher rain/snowfall (500–900mm p.a.). In lower-lying and more southerly parts of the region, where mean annual precipitation is below 400mm, this woodland would become increasingly open and steppic, characterised by *Artemisia* and chenopods. In contrast, the Pontic mountains to the north towards Kastamonu and west towards Bolu are much better watered and often densely forested, even today, with pine, fir, oak, hornbeam and beech.

There are no published pollen diagrams from Çankırı province, but there are some important pollen records from adjacent regions which we use here for comparison with Çöl Göl. Three of these, Abant and Yenicağa near Bolu and Ladik between Samsun and Amasya, extend back to the Late Glacial, at which time tree cover was greatly reduced and steppe vegetation much more extensive (Bottema et al. 1993/1994). Modern vegetation of the region has also been extensively studied (Akman et al. 1983). Woodland expanded during the early Holocene, but only achieved its maximum extent in the sixth millennium BC. In terms of comparison with the pollen sequence from Çöl Göl, the most relevant diagrams are those from Ladik, Kaz (southeast of Amasya), Demiryurt near Sivas (Bottema et al. 1993/1994), Nar Gölü in Cappadocia (England 2006) and lakes in the İznik region of northwest Turkey (Bottema et al. 2001). A characteristic feature of these sites is that they all record a cultural phase similar in nature to the Beyşehir Occupation phase of southwestern Anatolia (Eastwood et al. 1998). Although the dating of this cultural period is not always very precise in pollen diagrams from northern Anatolia, it began during the later second millennium BC after the volcanic eruption of Santorini (Bottema et al. 2001: 340) and ended during the mid-first millennium AD around the time of the Arab invasions of the Byzantine empire. It is marked by the presence of tree crops, such as walnut and olive, and cereal cultivation. After this phase ended, these cultural indicators disappear and there is a large and often sustained increase in pine pollen.

The Çöl Göl pollen record is notable for the absence of this Beyşehir Occupation-type phase. According to the ^{14}C dating, at the time of the end of this widespread cultural phase elsewhere (sixth to eighth centuries AD) there was a decline in cereal-type pollen at Çöl Göl and an increase in pine pollen percentage. Other cultural indicators, however, such as walnut (*Juglans*) do not show a continuous presence. Unless the ^{14}C chronology is in serious error, it can be concluded that the gypsum plateau around Çöl Göl experienced a different land-use history from most other areas of north-central Anatolia. In fact, this is not such a surprising conclusion. The gypsum plateau must always have been an adverse setting for agriculture on account of the saline soils and shortage of freshwater. Even prior to significant human impact, it would have represented a difficult environment for tree growth. The Çöl Göl pollen diagram indicates that the gypsum plateau has been a relatively open landscape for at least 2,000 years, with a limited amount of agro-pastoral activity and little woodland cover. By contrast, in more favourable parts of Paphlagonia, land-use history probably followed a similar course to that recorded in the pollen diagrams from Kaz and Ladik, with a cultural landscape created during the Iron Age and sustained through Hellenistic, Roman and early Byzantine times. For most of the last 13 centuries, pollen evidence of human activity is much less evident and is associated with pastoralism rather than with tree crop or cereal cultivation.

Conclusions

Çöl Göl is one of a series of small saline lakes formed by dissolution on the Miocene gypsum plateau east of the town of Çankırı. The lake's lower waters are anoxic, which has led to the preservation of organic-rich sediments. A 3m-long core spanning the last two millennia shows marked changes in sediment stratigraphy and geochemistry that are likely to have been caused by climatic fluctuations. The unusual nature of the lake's hydro-chemistry, however, makes it difficult to attribute these changes to wetter or drier periods with any precision. In contrast to the sediment geochemistry and also to other pollen records from the region, the vegetation around Çöl Göl shows little evidence of change through time, implying that it was insensitive to both climatic variations and to human-induced landscape transformations. The gypsum plateau appears to have been a marginal environment for human populations since at least Roman times, just as it is today, at least in terms of settlement, if not in terms of agricultural and pastoral exploitation.

Chapter conclusion

By Roger Matthews

In this chapter we have examined a range of physical and ecological contexts within and upon which the successive episodes of human settlement took place, as discussed in succeeding chapters. We have stressed the significance of the differential distribution of raw materials, of arable land, of water resources, of building materials and of other physical aspects of this highly diverse region in structuring a dialectic between people and place that forms the key theme running through the survey project. The importance of soil and good soil quality in enabling agricultural productivity cannot be overstressed – without it there would have been little incentive to farm the land – but, as we discuss in subsequent chapters, of equal significance is the political climate, which in so far as it offered an environment of calm and stability could alone permit the safe spread of human society, generally in small communities, across the land of Inner Paphlagonia. The impact of erosion on the soil quality and quantity of the region is undeniable but more intensive programmes of investigation, involving coordination with ongoing excavation of settlement sites, is needed before significant progress can be made in associating episodes of soil erosion with the history of human settlement in the area.

Chapter Three

Silent Centuries:
Paphlagonia from the Palaeolithic to the Early Bronze Age, 200,000–2000 BC

Roger Matthews

Introduction

The prehistoric human occupation of north-central Anatolia is a subject clouded in uncertainty and obscurity. While archaeological surveys in the region occasionally encounter fragments from its prehistoric past, there have been extremely few projects, even fewer involving excavation, specifically addressing the region's prehistory. Archaeological encounters with the region's pre-Hittite societies have until recently been accidents of discovery made without forethought or adequate provision of the meticulous techniques needed in the recovery and recording of often scanty prehistoric remains (Schoop 2005a). The early prehistory, in particular, remains almost totally unexplored. A glance through the site distribution maps provided in the TAY (*Türkiye Arkeolojik Yerleşmeleri*) series of volumes serves to make this point very sharply. For the long Palaeolithic period only a handful of sites occur in north-central Anatolia on the TAY map (Harmankaya, Tanındı 1996: ek 3), while for the Neolithic period there is but one candidate and that is a highly debatable occurrence of lithic material, with no Neolithic pottery (Harmankaya et al. 1997: ek 3; Marro 2000: 951). For the subsequent Chalcolithic and, especially, Early Bronze Ages the picture is slightly fuller, as we shall see.

Before we consider the various phases of the Palaeolithic period it is worth mentioning the importance of this region for a much earlier field of enquiry, that of the Miocene era, dating to around 15 million years ago. Exposed Miocene beds in north-central Turkey, including some in Çankırı province at Candır and Paşalar, have yielded fossil evidence of an otherwise unknown species of hominoid as well as a host of associated fossilised faunal remains (Alpagut et al. 1990).

The Palaeolithic phases, 200,000–12,000 BP

In a recent survey of the Palaeolithic period of Turkey the observation is made that 'The range of things one would like to know about the Turkish Paleolithic contrasts sharply with what is actually known about it' (Kuhn 2002: 198), a statement that applies with special aptness to north Anatolia. In all of Turkey, fewer than 25 out of at least 200 known Palaeolithic sites have been excavated, and only a small proportion of those have been adequately published (Kuhn 2002: 199). Despite the undoubted importance of Turkey within the story of human evolution, and in particular as regards the communication and movement of early hominin forms, including *Homo sapiens*, between Asia and Europe (and vice versa), there is still almost everything to learn about the specifics of the role played by Anatolia in these highly significant developments. Almost no fossil remains of archaic Anatolian hominins have been recovered from any part of Turkey. Our own survey in Paphlagonia has not added immensely to the sum of human knowledge on these topics, but some relevant discoveries were made, as considered here (fig. 3.1).

For the Lower Palaeolithic period very few sites are known from the Anatolian plateau, in contrast to areas further southeast, for example, where finds are more abundant (Garrard 1998). Relatively frequent occurrences of Miocene finds from the plateau, including those from Paphlagonia mentioned above, may indicate a generally high degree of erosion of Pleistocene contexts within which early Palaeolithic sites may have been located. In Project Paphlagonia we located no definite sites of Lower Palaeolithic date and only a few dubious contenders for Lower Palaeolithic implements, all heavily abraded and eroded (figs 3.2–3.3).

Chapter Three

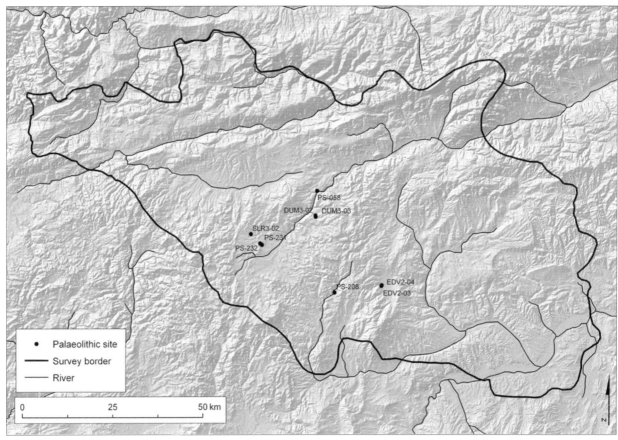

Fig. 3.1. Palaeolithic sites located in Project Paphlagonia

Fig. 3.2. Possible Lower Palaeolithic implement from PS058

Fig. 3.3. Possible Lower Palaeolithic implements from Dumanlı 03S03

The picture for the Middle Palaeolithic, ca. 200,000–40,000 BP, is slightly fuller. During this period hominins of Neandertal type evolved in Europe and gradually made their way into Western Asia, where they have been encountered in excavations at sites such as Shanidar in north Iraq, Dederiyeh in north Syria and cave sites in the Levant (Matthews 2000e). To reach these regions from Europe, Neandertals almost certainly passed through Anatolia. Finds of Middle Palaeolithic stone tools are indeed relatively common in Turkey as elsewhere in Western Asia, although extremely few of these known sites have been excavated. The most important excavations in Turkey have been at the cave site of Karain near Antalya, the only site in Turkey to have yielded archaic hominin remains, in the form of a handful of fragments reported to be 'Neandertaloid' in morphology (Kuhn 2002: 203). Lithics of Middle Palaeolithic date from Turkey appear quite mixed in their forms and technologies, combining elements of assemblages from both the Balkans and the Zagros mountains (Kuhn 2002: 207), and perhaps underlining the transit role of Turkey between these two regions.

Apart from occasional stray finds of Middle Palaeolithic stone implements, significant assemblages of Middle Palaeolithic material in Project Paphlagonia were encountered at four sites, three in the course of intensive survey and one in extensive survey. The largest spread takes the form of two adjacent lithic sites, Eldivan 02S03 and Eldivan 02S04, both on raised slopes overlooking the shores of what must once have been a Pleistocene lake and is today the fertile Eldivan plain (fig. 3.4). Covering in total more than 2ha, these two sites comprise fairly dense scatters of lithic material in the form of tools, flakes, chips and cores, all of a light-grey flint alien to the immediately local geology but similar to deposits in the Orta region 40km to the northwest (figs 3.5–3.6). Numerous pieces show evidence of the Levallois technique of tool manufacture, characteristic of the Middle Palaeolithic period, and are broadly comparable to material from one of the very few excavated Middle Palaeolithic sites of the region at Etiyokuşu just north of Ankara (Kansu 1940). In view of their location, we interpret the Eldivan lithic scatters as the remains of camps situated at prime localities where hominins, almost certainly Neandertals, took advantage of good availability, doubtless seasonally determined, of animals and plants to be hunted and gathered in and around a Pleistocene lake. Other Middle Palaeolithic sites found in the survey include Levallois type artefacts from Salur 03S02 and from PS208 in the vicinity of a spring in the Şabanözü area.

As with many other regions of Turkey and Western Asia, there is a striking absence of sites of Upper Palaeolithic date, ca. 40,000–12,000 BP, in north-central Anatolia, and none at all were encountered in the course of fieldwork in Paphlagonia. As Kuhn has noted (2002: 204) during this period in Europe caves higher than 500m above sea level were not occupied at all, and so at 1,000m and more the entire Anatolian plateau may have been totally unattractive to human presence in these centuries, due to climatic severity at the peak of the Late Glacial Maximum, as is indicated for other parts of the

Fig. 3.5. Middle Palaeolithic implements from sites Eldivan 02S03 and Eldivan 02S04

Fig. 3.6. Middle Palaeolithic implements from sites Eldivan 02S03 and Eldivan 02S04

Fig. 3.4. Sites Eldivan 02S03 and Eldivan 02S04, on foreground slopes

Anatolian plateau (Vanhaverbeke, Waelkens 1998) and adjacent regions such as Armenia (Dolukhanov 2007). In lower regions of Turkey, where the climatic impact will have been less powerful, Upper Palaeolithic sites have been found in the course of survey, for example in the southeast (Garrard 1998). In all, we still have almost everything to learn about all aspects of the Palaeolithic past of Anatolia, in all its regions and we may agree with Kuhn that: 'The potential of Turkey's Pleistocene archeological and paleontological records will not be fully realized for years to come' (Kuhn 2002: 208).

The Neolithic period, 10,000–6000 BC

Since Seton Lloyd made his now famous statement that 'the greater part of modern Turkey, and especially the region more correctly described as Anatolia, shows no sign whatever of habitation during the Neolithic period' (Lloyd 1956: 53), ongoing surveys and excavations have established a significant Neolithic presence in many parts of Anatolia, with sites such as Can Hasan, Aşıklı, Çatalhöyük and others discovered, excavated and well established on the archaeological scene. North of the Konya plain, however, there is still no convincing evidence for a definite Neolithic presence in Anatolia, as the TAY map illustrates (Harmankaya et al. 1997: ek 3). As discussed in Chapter One, a major aim within Project Paphlagonia was to explore the issue of a Neolithic presence or absence in north-central Anatolia. Through five seasons of fieldwork, extensive and intensive, we failed to identify any definite traces of Neolithic occupation within the survey region. It has to be stated, however, that there are special difficulties in attempting to identify a possible Neolithic presence in north-central Anatolia where the traditions of painted pottery are extremely weak. As Lichter (2005: 7) has recently underlined, in the absence of a painted pottery tradition in northwest Anatolia it may be impossible to distinguish a Late Neolithic presence from an Early Chalcolithic one. This rider holds true for the Paphlagonia region, where we have several fragmentary ceramic assemblages from surface collection, such as that from Salur Höyük (PS050), which elsewhere might be assigned, however tentatively, to the Neolithic period. Pending more definitive evidence, however, we prefer to err on the side of caution for the time being.

This apparent, or real, absence of Neolithic sites matches the results of other surveys across the entirety of north Anatolia (Işın 1998; Marro 2000; Dönmez 2006a; Düring 2008), but is especially significant in that even with the deployment of techniques of intensive survey in Project Paphlagonia no convincing Neolithic sites were located. In an articulate review Marro (2000: 951–53) has considered the possible explanations for the apparent absence of Neolithic sites in north Anatolia: either the region was not occupied in the Neolithic, or it was occupied but Neolithic material traces have not been correctly identified, or existing Neolithic sites have been covered by more recent alluvial deposits. Marro's interpretation is that the natural abundance of edible animal and vegetal resources of the region must have attracted a human presence in the Neolithic period, even if that presence may have been characterised by a lifestyle principally of hunting and gathering as opposed to permanent sedentism and plant/animal cultivation. Summers (2002) reaches similar conclusions in his study of this problem.

It is important to keep in mind that even when we consider central Anatolia, where Neolithic sites have been explored over the past half century, the density of Neolithic occupation is relatively sparse. Survey on the Konya plain, for example, has detected extremely few sites contemporary with the great focal node of Çatalhöyük (Baird 2001: 16; 2002: 147). Furthermore, the arrival of a Neolithic economy in central Anatolia at around 8000 BC is a late phenomenon compared to developments further east in the Fertile Crescent. There is no suggestion yet from decades of survey and excavation across the Anatolian plateau that any part of it was densely occupied by large numbers of sizeable sedentary communities in the Neolithic. We should not then expect to find a considerable and dense Neolithic occupation along the northern fringes of the Anatolian plateau.

In a stimulating recent study Schoop (2005b) has delineated a cultural *koiné* of central Anatolia in the Neolithic as characterised by small numbers of quite large, dense settlements – Can Hasan, Aşıklı, Çatalhöyük – whose inhabitants engaged in sheep/goat herding and extensive hunting of wild cattle, equids and other animals. Schoop contrasts this *modus vivendi* with that attested to the west in the Lake District and adjacent regions of western Anatolia, emphasising the even later incipience of a Neolithic economy in this region at around 6400 BC and a heavier reliance on domesticated animals as opposed to hunting of wild herds (Schoop 2005b: 48–50). Schoop's interpretation is that for some 1,500 years the Neolithic mode of life was constrained within the central plain of Anatolia by the geography, cultural as well as physical, of the region and its surroundings, where it thrived in a steppe environment rich in, above all, herds of large wild animals highly suited to hunting. Once beyond the central Anatolian plain, in the mid-seventh millennium BC, a distinctive Neolithic way of life developed out of the interaction between existing and new modes of food production and social intercourse, evolving into a form of existence that rapidly spread across western Anatolia, into Mediterranean Europe and beyond (Schoop 2005b: 53). In this spread, northern Anatolia seems to have been essentially by-passed. As Roberts (1982: 243) has phrased it: 'the initial wave of Neolithic colonisation appears to have skirted northern Anatolia and instead proceeded westwards'.

The negative Neolithic results from Project Paphlagonia add increased weight to the argument that any postulated Neolithic settlement of north Anatolia must have been extremely sparse at most. We need much further work, particularly in the form of intensive survey, before we can assert with confidence that north Anatolia was entirely devoid of human presence in the Neolithic. But as the years pass and more and more survey work is conducted in this broad swathe of territory and still no Neolithic sites are encountered, the balance of interpretation swings further towards that of an almost total absence of human occupation, especially as such an absence can be viewed as a continuity from the Upper Palaeolithic and Epipalaeolithic periods, also unattested in the north Anatolian region. As we have seen, for the Upper Palaeolithic such an absence may be understood as resulting from the severity of the climate at such altitudes in the Late Pleistocene. Dense and rapid forest development in the region through the Early Holocene (Roberts 1982: 235), coupled perhaps with continuing severely cold winters, along with issues of socio-cultural and economic preferences, may have meant that human communities of Neolithic Anatolia chose not to engage in depth with north Anatolia at this time. By the very close of the Neolithic, at some time around 6000 BC, scraps of evidence such as Sakaeli obsidian found at Ilıpınar (see below) suggest that the region's long isolation was coming to an end.

The Chalcolithic period, 6000–3000 BC

In considering the 3,000-year span of the Chalcolithic period in the context of north-central Anatolia there are several factors to take into account (see Schoop 2005c for detailed discussion of this topic). Firstly, it is worth reiterating that there have been extremely few projects, survey or excavation, which have set out to explore sites and phases of this period in this region or indeed in adjacent regions, as again a glance at the appropriate TAY map (Harmankaya et al. 1998: ek 3) swiftly demonstrates. We therefore lack secure, independently dated sequences of cultural material to assist in situating scraps of sherds from surface reconnaissance. For our purposes relevant excavated sites include İkiztepe, Dündartepe, Büyük Güllücek, Alişar, Boğazköy-Büyükkaya and Yarıkkaya, all broadly to the east and southeast of our survey region, along with Demircihüyük and Orman Fidanlığı to the southwest. Results from broad-ranging surveys in adjacent regions such as Kastamonu, Samsun, Çorum, Ankara and beyond are also of some relevance.

Secondly, north Anatolia hosts a highly conservative tradition in its ceramic trajectories, characterised by a reluctance to indulge in the decoration of ceramic vessels, often in contrast to other parts of Anatolia and neighbouring regions, and an adherence to stable ceramic forms, fabrics and manufacturing techniques over long time periods. These characteristics apply well beyond the Early Chalcolithic period in Paphlagonia. The ramifications are that we generally lack from our survey the sorts of highly distinctive decorated sherds – painted, incised, impressed, modelled – that are so often the key elements in relating assemblages of material across time and space. Without these key elements it can be hazardous to postulate relationships, spatial and chronological, between assemblages on the basis of often simple and long-lasting fabrics and forms.

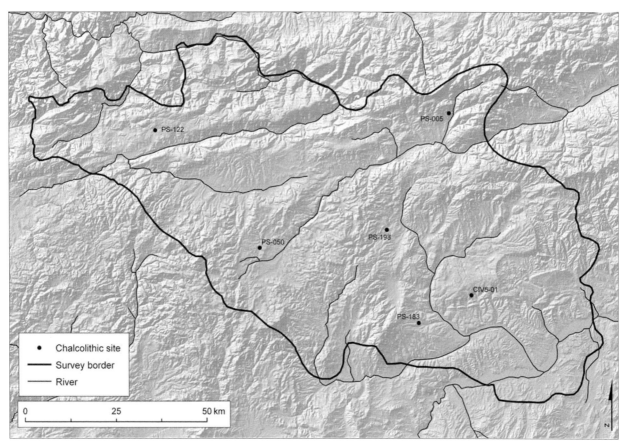

Fig. 3.7. Chalcolithic sites located in Project Paphlagonia

Thirdly, despite the paucity of projects that have addressed the Chalcolithic period of north Anatolia and the difficulties inherent in approaching associated ceramic assemblages, there nevertheless does appear to be a genuinely low level of human settlement in this region throughout the entire Chalcolithic. From our survey a total of only six sites can with some confidence be dated to the Chalcolithic (fig. 3.7), certainly an increase over the nil levels of the Neolithic period but hardly evidence for a massive ingress of peoples at any time prior to 3000 BC. We may assume that through these centuries small groups of farmers, herders, traders and adventurers were steadily spreading and negotiating their way through the often difficult terrain of the region, adapting to local circumstances and bringing with them ideas and traditions from outside the region as well as starting to shape a local trajectory of socio-cultural development. As we shall see, these peoples are likely to have been attracted into the hills, high plains and river valleys of Paphlagonia by some of the natural and mineral resources available there.

Fourthly, with the above factors in mind, we do not propose here to provide an exhaustive account, let alone a reworking, of the intricacies of Chalcolithic chronology as it applies to north-central Anatolia and adjacent regions (and the same applies for the Early Bronze Age), as our evidence is too slim to make a significant contribution and others have already taken this subject as far as it can go without further targeted excavation (Thissen 1993; Steadman 1995; Schoop 2005a; 2005c). What we essay here is to establish the level and spread of Chalcolithic occupation in Inner Paphlagonia, to consider economic, social and cultural factors shaping that level and spread, and to situate the results within the broader field of Anatolia and beyond in this period.

As discussed by Thissen (1993: 207), paucity of material means it is difficult to sub-divide the Chalcolithic of this region into valid phases but the period as a whole spans some 3,000 years from about 6000 BC, conventionally divided into three phases across Anatolia: Early, Middle and Late.

Early Chalcolithic

A rare hint of activity at the transition from the Late Neolithic to the Early Chalcolithic in the region of Inner Paphlagonia is provided by the presence in phases X–IX at the site of Ilıpınar in northwest Anatolia of obsidian probably from a source by the village of Sakaeli in the Orta region of Çankırı province (Bigazzi et al. 1995: 148). The obsidian in the Sakaeli region occurs in the form of strata of volcanic ash containing nodules of obsidian and perlite (Keller, Seifried 1990: 61), some large enough to be knapped into tools (fig. 3.8). Nearby hills, north of Orta town, comprise significant deposits of flint and chert beds and cobbles, also likely to be attractive to prehistoric, and historic, occupants of the region and beyond. The location of site PS050, Salur Höyük, close to both the obsidian and flint/chert deposits is unlikely to be coincidental (fig. 3.9). Although a small site at just under 1ha, Salur's surface is littered with potsherds ranging from the Chalcolithic through the Early Bronze Age, second millennium and Iron Age. It is tempting to consider Salur as serving as a focus of contact between external communities, as at Ilıpınar, and the earliest settlers of post-Pleistocene north-central Anatolia in the Late Neolithic–Early Chalcolithic period, although it is not possible to assign any of the sherds found at the site definitively to the Late Neolithic as attested in phase X at Ilıpınar. In truth, the fragmentary nature of the surface sherds, from Salur as elsewhere, makes it difficult to compare them in detail with the often subtle and sinuous shapes of the Late Neolithic and Early Chalcolithic material from sites such as Ilıpınar (Thissen 1995; 2001) or Demircihüyük on the Eskişehir plain, where the Neolithic wares A–C (Seeher 1987: Taf. 1–7) find no completely convincing parallels in our Paphlagonia material.

Fig. 3.8. Obsidian strata in layers of volcanic ash near PS050 Salur Höyük

Fig. 3.9. PS050 Salur Höyük

Salur is, however, one of the few surveyed sites to have yielded painted ceramics of Early Chalcolithic type, with red-brown paint in zigzag motif on a beige slip (fig. 3.10 top right), as well known from sites far to the south such as Hacılar as well as, in smaller quantities, sites of central-western Anatolia such as Demircihüyük, where it is designated as ware D (Seeher 1987: 76–77, Taf. 8, 9). A few sherds of this type occur at four sites in total from the Paphlagonia survey: Salur (PS050), PS122, PS183 (see fig. 4.31 right centre) and Çivi 05S01.

Schoop's recent analysis (2005a; 2005c) of the Early Chalcolithic material from Boğazköy-Büyükkaya highlights several characteristics of the material, some shared with the Demircihüyük assemblages of similar date, including a predominance of brown and grey surface colours, a lack of organic temper and a common use as temper of crushed limestone and mica schist, even occasionally asbestos, giving a fine sheen to the burnished surfaces of vessels. Shapes are simple, including bowls, splaying and carinated, with rare lugs and no handles. Decoration is restricted to the so-called stab-and-drag technique perhaps designed for a paste infill, also found at Alişar (Von der Osten 1937: fig. 65) and in the west at Orman Fidanlığı (Efe 2001: 44–45).

Amongst the Paphlagonia material there are only a couple of sites that have yielded sherds probably comparable to the Boğazköy-Büyükkaya material presented by Schoop (2005a; see also Parzinger 1993; and for proximate assemblages at Yarıkkaya and Yazılıkaya, see Hauptmann 1969; 1975) as well as to contemporary material from other sites. Site PS005 has some plain sherds with micaceous mineral temper in forms similar to those of Boğazköy-Büyükkaya as well as a sherd (fig. 3.11 bottom left) with parallel fluting comparable to material from phases I–IV at Orman Fidanlığı, thus of Early Chalcolithic date. Site PS198 has closed carinated bowl forms in micaceous grit tempered fabric. No sherds with stab-and-drag decoration have been identified in the survey material.

In sum, in the Paphlagonia material there are slight and rare hints at the participation of the region within the world beyond during the sixth millennium BC. As Efe (2001: 55) has stressed, the ceramic evidence in the Early Chalcolithic suggests a degree of contact and interaction over a geographical range reaching from inside the Kızılırmak bend westwards to the Eskişehir region and showing at least an awareness of contemporary communities someway to the south, at Hacılar and elsewhere. The participation of the central Black Sea region in these interactions, however, is all but negligible (Dönmez 2006a: 92).

Fig. 3.10. Early Chalcolithic painted sherd from PS050 Salur Höyük (top right)

Fig. 3.11. Chalcolithic and Early Bronze Age sherds from PS005

Middle–Late Chalcolithic

By the Middle and Late phases of the Chalcolithic period the ceramic evidence for interaction amongst the regions of Anatolia and beyond is notably strengthened, although the Paphlagonia material itself continues to be scant and difficult to situate. Thissen (1993) has revisited the Late Chalcolithic material from sites of the Turkish Black Sea coastal region, principally İkiztepe and Dündartepe, showing that contacts between this area and communities of western Anatolia, the Balkans and the Aegean are clearly established by the fifth millennium BC, with evidence during the Middle–Late Chalcolithic, in the form of horned handles and white-painted decoration, for the participation of sites such as İkiztepe and Büyük Güllücek in these wide-ranging, if perhaps not highly-intensive, interactions. Immediately to the north of Çankırı province, survey in Kastamonu has recovered limited evidence relating to all phases of the Chalcolithic period, in particular showing affinities with Middle Chalcolithic material from the sites of Kes Kaya and Orman Fidanlığı on the Eskişehir plain, thus linking the Kastamonu region into the broad Thracian-Anatolian complex that incorporates eastern Macedonia, Thrace and the Marmara basin (Efe 1989–1990; Marro 2000: 950). The high-collared carinated vessels and large flat strap handles that characterise these connections are not readily identified in our Paphlagonia material, but again Salur, site PS050, has some candidates.

Similarly, there are but rare occurrences in the Paphlagonia evidence for ceramic connections with sites such as Demircihüyük, where wares F–G characterise the Late Chalcolithic occupation there (Seeher 1987: 77–78). White-painted ware, ware H, generally taking the form of open bowls with parallel white stripes on the interior of the rim (Seeher 1987: Taf. 28, 29), has its own special problems as it may occur in several periods, ranging from Middle–Late Chalcolithic, as at Büyük Güllücek (Koşay, Akok 1957: Taf. XI–XIII) and Orman Fidanlığı (Efe 2001: fig. 17, 269–79), and into the Early Bronze Age (Thissen 1993: 222–25; see Seeher 1987: 67–71 for discussion of white-painted wares of Anatolia and beyond). From Paphlagonia site PS122 we have a single rim sherd from an open bowl with three faint white stripes on a red burnished surface (fig. 3.35:1). The strong red hue favours a dating of this sherd to the Early Bronze Age (see below). From the same site comes a single instance of a Late Chalcolithic horned handle, a widely-occurring type across Anatolia and beyond. No examples of Late Chalcolithic fruit-stands were encountered in the Paphlagonia survey.

The elaborately incised and impressed vessels and sherds of Büyük Güllücek (Koşay, Akok 1957), Alişar (Von der Osten 1937) and Gelveri-Güzelyurt (Esin 1993) find no parallels at all in the surface material from Project Paphlagonia, underlining the impression of asceticism in the ceramic traditions of the region. In addition to the Kastamonu survey mentioned above, other surveys in north-central Anatolia have recovered generally scant traces of Chalcolithic occupation, most commonly from the Late phase, as at Sinop, Samsun and Amasya (Işın 1998; Dönmez 1999) and Çorum (Branting 1996; Yıldırım, Sipahi 2004). Surveys around all sides of the Salt Lake in central Anatolia have indicated a significant increase in settlement in the Chalcolithic period as a whole (Omura 2002: 61; 2005: 61; see also Yakar 1994: 41) and have emphasised the role of the Kızılırmak river as a boundary between Chalcolithic sites of Alişar type to the north and sites of Konya plain type to the south. Evidence from Todd's central Anatolian survey, with its relative dearth of Konya plain style Chalcolithic evidence (Todd 1998: 24), suggests an eastern boundary for these wares. The importance of rivers as boundaries between cultural entities, however defined, resonates through many periods of the Paphlagonian past, as we shall see.

In conclusion, the Chalcolithic evidence from Inner Paphlagonia is scant indeed even if we may have erred on the side of caution in identifying comparanda for our material. The slight evidence so far suggests that Inner Paphlagonia played a minimal role in trans-regional interactions of the Chalcolithic period. For the early phase there are hints of connections to the west and southwest, while some evidence intimates the tentative participation of the region within a cultural interaction sphere as delineated by earlier scholars to include much of west and central Anatolia as well as Thrace and the Balkans (Thissen 1993; Steadman 1995; Özdoğan 1996).

Much of the inter-regional contact amongst these broad zones must have been conducted by sea, particularly the Black Sea (Thissen 1993: 207), and will doubtless have featured a concern with access to, and distribution of, differentially occurring raw materials. It is also in this period, around 5000 BC, that the gradual transformation of the Black Sea from an inland, semi freshwater lake into a semi marine environment appears to have been completed and the region reached its Holocene climatic optimum around 5500 BC (Yanko-Hombach 2007; *contra* Ryan, Pitman 1998), factors which may have played a role in the intensification of interaction during the Chalcolithic.

In this light, Inner Paphlagonia becomes significant on two counts: firstly as a potential source of raw materials and secondly as a transit zone between inland resource areas and the Black Sea. The location of the few identified Chalcolithic sites, all of them *höyüks*, in Inner Paphlagonia appears very neatly to fit such an interpretation. Site Çivi 05S01, Sariçi Höyük, sits directly beside massive deposits of rock-salt (fig. 3.12), for which there is evidence of mining from the Early Bronze Age up to, and including, the present-day. There can be little doubt that Chalcolithic communities also took advantage of the abundance here of this essential mineral, perhaps as a key component of the intake of their herded animals as well

Fig. 3.12. Site Çivi 05S01, Sariçi Höyük

as an item to be traded near and far. The location of Salur Höyük, site PS050, has already been commented upon as significant in its proximity to deposits of nodular obsidian and flint/chert, again suitable for exploitation throughout the Chalcolithic period. The other Chalcolithic sites of Paphlagonia sit astride major natural routes of communication, site PS005 being on the only north-south route across the Ilgaz mountains (fig. 3.13), connecting Çankırı to Kastamonu and the Black Sea beyond, a route that appears to survive through all subsequent periods up to the present-day. Sites PS122, PS183 and PS198 are situated also at natural passes and routes through the often difficult landscape. We may therefore surmise that the principal stimulus to engagement of human communities with Inner Paphlagonia in the Chalcolithic was their desire to obtain natural resources of specialised types and to transport them across the region up to the Black Sea coast. There is so far little evidence for a major incursion of Chalcolithic settlers practising extensive and intensive methods of farming and animal husbandry, although there can be no doubt that further Chalcolithic sites remain to be discovered in this region.

Fig. 3.13. Site PS005, atop flat summit

The Early Bronze Age, 3000–2000 BC
The third millennium BC sees a significant increase in the human settlement density and extent across Inner Paphlagonia as with all other regions of Anatolia, with a total of 26 sites in the survey area yielding ceramic remains of the Early Bronze Age (hereafter EBA) (fig. 3.14). This evidence generally takes the form of handmade, burnished sherds from jars, cups, bowls and other vessels well known from excavated sites in the vicinity and beyond. For our purposes the most significant excavated sites in the region include the EBA cemetery at Balıbağı just east of Çankırı town (Süel 1989), settlement and burial excavations at İkiztepe on the Black Sea coast (Alkım et al. 1988), as well as ongoing explorations at the site of Kınık-Kastamonu (Çınaroğlu, Genç 2004; 2005) and a host of more distant excavated sites across north Anatolia and well beyond (for syntheses, see Yakar 1985; Harmankaya, Erdoğu 2002).

Survey and excavation across all regions of Anatolia indicate a sharp rise in settlement intensity with the onset and unfolding of the Early Bronze Age, a dramatic shift in the human settlement of the area that has to be viewed as an integral part of an immense and highly complex social phenomenon: the rise of urban, sometimes literate, society in southwest Asia. While commencing in the late fourth millennium BC in southern Mesopotamia, by the middle of the third millennium BC, at the latest, these sweeping developments had impacted, however indirectly, as remote a region as Inner Paphlagonia. The rise and spread of complex political communities in third-millennium Anatolia cannot be viewed in isolation from earlier and contemporary developments in the world beyond (Efe 2003). In an insightful recent study Çevik (2007) has deconstructed the concept of 'urbanisation' in the Anatolian context, in its place seeing a tripartite social development, with distinct zones of Anatolia following their own socio-political trajectories through the Early Bronze Age. Thus in southeast Anatolia true urbanisation occurs, while central and western Anatolia undergo a more diffuse process of 'centralisation'. Much of the rest of Anatolia, however, including we argue here its north-central region, remains distinctly 'rural', characterised by dispersed patterns of occupation, small size of sites and little or no clear settlement hierarchy.

A major aspect of Anatolia's role within this overarching process was its rich potential as a source of raw materials desired by burgeoning élites in urban societies both at home and abroad. Metals in particular played a key role in these interactions and Inner Paphlagonia's part in the overall process was significantly structured by that factor. At the same time as the Early Bronze Age revolution was impacting the region, however indirectly, it is important to stress that a uniquely local socio-cultural trajectory continued to evolve, rooted in already centuries of development of local communities with specialist knowledge of their physical and cultural circumstances and maintaining their own material culture traditions.

In the vicinity of Inner Paphlagonia, surveys have yielded results that strongly underline the increased intensity of settlement in the third millennium BC. To the north, in Kastamonu (Marro 2000), Sinop (Işın 1998) and Samsun (Dönmez 1999) large numbers of EBA sites appear where previously scant occupation had existed, and such a pattern is repeated across the region, in

Chapter Three

Ankara and Konya (Omura 2002; Baird 2001), in Amasya, Tokat (Özsait 1994; Özsait, Koçak 1996) and Çorum (Yıldırım, Sipahi 2004), across all of northern Anatolia (Burney 1956) and at all points beyond (Parzinger 1993).

Thissen (1993: 219) has stressed the apparent break with tradition inherent in many aspects of EBA pottery as compared to its Late Chalcolithic predecessors in north-central Anatolia, with new shapes, fabrics and decoration appearing at the start of the third millennium BC. Attempts to associate such material culture shifts with origins and movements of ethno-linguist groups, including Proto Indo-Europeans (Bilgi 2001), raise interesting but perhaps ultimately unanswerable questions. More substantively, Sherratt (1986: 441) has associated the appearance of new ceramic assemblages at the start of the EBA with a shift in farming, cooking and eating practices, and an increased emphasis on the production and consumption of dairy products and wine. Within the context of Inner Paphlagonia the break in ceramic tradition at the start of the EBA is less clearly visible and a major element of long-term continuity remains the dour reluctance of local potters to indulge in flippant adornment of their drab vessels. Once more, with a few much-appreciated exceptions, this ceramic asceticism denies us the benefit of distinctive decorated sherds from the surfaces of sites with which to make ready comparison with material from other sites in the vicinity and beyond.

For our purposes, sites of EBA date within the Paphlagonia survey are identified as such on the basis of the occurrence of types of sherds known to be of EBA date from excavated sites. Most of our EBA sites are only loosely datable within the EBA on the basis of these types and, as mentioned for the Chalcolithic, there is no attempt here to construct a detailed chronology for the EBA of north-central Anatolia on the basis of such thin evidence. Of the 26 identified Paphlagonia EBA sites, most yielded solely material of generic EBA type from which little more than an EBA presence at the site can be deduced. The occasional find of specific types such as horizontal-handled red-cross bowls (figs 3.15 centre; 3.16 bottom left, 3.35:6, 7), as at sites PS174 and PS187, establishes a chronological link with their widespread occurrence across central and western Anatolia in the very late EBA, as at Beycesultan (Lloyd, Mellaart 1962: 257, map X). A handful of our sites, however, produced rather more significant surface assemblages of EBA material and the following discussion centres on these sites in turn.

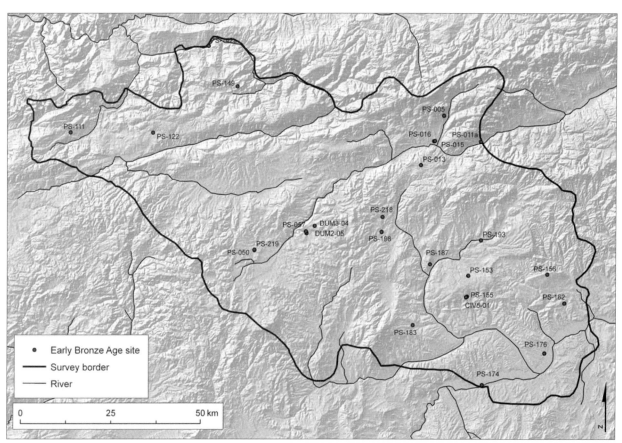

Fig. 3.14. Early Bronze Age sites located in Project Paphlagonia

Fig. 3.15. Selected sherds from site PS187

Fig. 3.16. Selected sherds from site PS174

Western connections: Yazıboy (PS111)
The site of Yazıboy is located in the far west of the Project Paphlagonia survey region, to the west of Eskipazar town (fig. 3.14) and lies atop a flat promontory, adjacent to travertine cliffs, which sits 30m above a small tributary stream of the Eskipazar Çay (fig. 3.17). The site, as defined by the distribution of surface pottery, covers only 0.12ha in area, and has access to high-quality agricultural land in the immediate vicinity. The surface of the promontory is littered with sherds of handmade, usually highly burnished, pottery. The forms include (figs 3.18–3.25, 3.34:2–18) large numbers of rims from jars and bowls with an applied strip or cordon on the exterior surface decorated with finger-indents. These sherds are often burnished on the interior only. On the exterior some of them, not all, lack burnishing and are lightly rusticated below the cordon, a very distinctive trait. Other decoration includes examples of rows of punctates and incised linear designs. One sherd has a hand in relief on its exterior surface. A range of well-formed knobs and handles is attested. Surface colour of sherds ranges from black through beige, with a high frequency of light red. Temper is almost always only mineral.

Parallels for the Yazıboy assemblage of surface sherds come most convincingly from the west, and in particular from sites in Turkish and Bulgarian Thrace, Greek east Macedonia and Romania. An Anatolian situation of this sherd collection is suggested only by a few occurrences of so-called Yenişehir ware of the Iznik region, with black interior, black upper exterior and paler lower exterior (French 1967: 59), while other areas of northwest Anatolia (French 1969) generally provide few convincing comparanda for the Yazıboy material, especially the forms with applied/indented cordon decoration. Parallels for the applied hand on a vessel exterior do, however, include very similar examples from Demircihüyük (Efe 1988: Taf. 23:5–6; Bittel, Otto 1939: Taf. 13:4).

To the west the parallels are much more thorough-going. The technique of applied/indented cordon has been identified as a long-lasting feature of the ceramics of Turkish Thrace, surviving from the later EBA into the Iron Age (Özdoğan 1982: 45), well attested at, for example, the site of Hasköy Höyüğü in Edirne province not far from the Aegean coast (Başaran 1999: Lev. 3:6–7). The Yazıboy material sits comfortably within the milieu of the Thracian later EBA as identified by Özdoğan at sites such as Salhane near Kırklareli (Özdoğan 1982: Lev. XVII:4), which themselves look further west towards the Balkans in this period. Excavations at the site of Kanlıgeçit by Kırklareli (Özdoğan 1998; 2001; Özdoğan et al. 1999) have revealed a remarkable occupational sequence of later EBA date, commencing with a modest rural village with typical Bulgarian-Ezero material. This layout is dramatically transformed in late EBA III into a fortified stone enclosure encircling three megarons in what appears to be a sacred temenos reminiscent of the famous Troy II city plan, with an extensive lower town. The excavator's

Fig. 3.17. PS111, Yazıboy, view: the site sits atop the small flat promontory in the mid-left of the image, directly above foreground trees

Chapter Three

Fig. 3.18. Sherds from PS111, Yazıboy

Fig. 3.22. Sherds from PS111, Yazıboy

Fig. 3.19. Sherds from PS111, Yazıboy

Fig. 3.23. Sherds from PS111, Yazıboy

Fig. 3.20. Sherds from PS111, Yazıboy

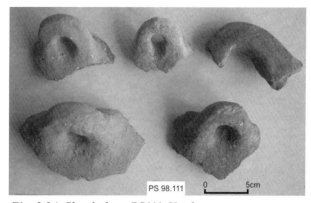
Fig. 3.24. Sherds from PS111, Yazıboy

Fig. 3.21. Sherds from PS111, Yazıboy

Fig. 3.25. Sherds from PS111, Yazıboy

interpretation is that the fortified enclosure is constructed and occupied, from ca. 2400 to 2100 BC, by colonists from Anatolia, utilising their own pottery styles, with an interest in securing control over significant deposits of copper in the nearby Istranca mountains (Özdoğan 2001: 62). The colony is destroyed by fire at the end of the EBA and not subsequently occupied.

Within Greek east Macedonia the two sites of Sitagroi and Dikili Tash on the Drama plain also provide excellent parallels for the Yazıboy material, not least because of the multiplicity of associations. Thus, from phase Vb at Sitagroi (Sherratt 1986: figs 13.20–13.27, pls XCIX–CI), of EBA III date, comes a raft of close similarities, including fabric, form and decoration such as applied/indented cordons, rows of impressed dots, and assorted lugs and handles, all in mineral-tempered handmade wares. Here the cordons are interpreted as possible devices for securing covers over the mouths of pots or decorative representations of cords originally serving such a purpose, and are associated with the broad world of Europe in the Bronze Age (Sherratt 1986: 439). At Dikili Tash, too, the strata of the latest EBA at the site (level 3b = EBA II), although dated slightly earlier than Sitagroi Vb, contain many parallels to the Yazıboy material, especially in the form of vessels with applied/indented cordons (Séfériadès 1996: fig. 14).

The Bulgarian connections of the Yazıboy pottery are clearly established via the sites just examined. Thus in Ezero I phase, later EBA, at the site of Ezero in central Bulgaria vessels with finger-impressed cordons and other forms match well with Sitagroi Vb (Sherratt 1986: 446). Other Ezero forms featured in the Yazıboy material include crescentic finger-impressed cordons, notched vertical handles, a range of applied knobs, punctate decoration and a human hand in relief on a vessel exterior (Georgiev et al. 1979: pl. 155), all told some of the best parallels for the Yazıboy assemblage. Many of these traits are also matched by Bronze Age ceramics from the nearby site of Karanovo (Hiller, Nikolov 1997: Taf. 143–64). Further north still, in central Romania, the late EBA site of Zoltan yields good parallels for the Yazıboy sherds, including applied/indented cordons, often with a rusticated lower exterior surface below the cordon, a marked characteristic of some of the Yazıboy sherds, as well as similar handles and impressed/incised decorative techniques (Cavruc 1997).

These assorted ceramic comparanda for the Yazıboy surface material congregate chronologically around the horizons 11–12 discerned by Parzinger (1993) across the Balkans and Anatolia as spanning the latter part of the EBA. They vividly demonstrate the participation of the small community resident at Yazıboy during the later EBA in a geographically immense series of complex socio-cultural processes attendant upon the rise of complex society in the area at large. The regions of northwest Anatolia, the north and east Aegean, the Bulgarian plains east of Sofia and areas beyond all participated in this complex, shifting dialogue of culture (Nikolova 1999; Menkova 2000). A major driving force for the development of such wide-ranging relationships across time and space must undoubtedly have been the desire of certain elements of sophisticated communities to acquire, and/or to control access to, relatively limited supplies of metal and metal ores, principally those of copper but also of gold and silver. The presence of copper ores and gold in the mountains of Bulgaria (Leshtakov 1996: 266) and of copper and lead in north-central Anatolia (Özgüç 1978: 98–99; Yakar 1985) is certainly significant here. Recent discoveries of large amounts of finished gold objects from late EBA contexts at Dabene in addition to well-known finds of gold-work from the EBA tombs at Alaca (Thissen 1993: 221) strongly reinforce the importance of this metal in structuring social relations throughout the EBA. Equally important in shaping the trajectories of these long-distance relationships was the physical topography of the landscape. The east-west trending ranges and valleys of the Pontic zone encouraged throughout time a tendency for communications to succeed in these directions, especially when married with a maritime inclination, while north-south interactions at times were adversely affected by those same factors. Thus it was possible for communities of Inner Paphlagonia, as instanced at Yazıboy, to engage in direct relations with distant cousins to the west while at some levels bypassing their closer neighbours to the south.

In search of protection: Dumanlı 03S04
A notable element of several of the EBA sites in Inner Paphlagonia is evidence that they were protected by surrounding walls of dry stone. Of the 26 sites with EBA pottery on their surfaces, seven show traces of surrounding stone fortification (Çivi 05S01, Dumanlı 03S04, PS016, PS050, PS057, PS122, PS218). Many of the remaining sites are situated on ridges or promontories where a defensive concern might be to the fore. It has to be conceded that several of the fortified sites have occupation also into the Middle–Late Bronze Age and without excavation it is not possible to date the construction of their surrounding walls firmly to the EBA nor to separate what may be EBA phases from later phases. Nevertheless, there are good parallels for fortified EBA sites outside Inner Paphlagonia and there is reason to accept that we have them too in this region. In most of our seven cases, the evidence takes the form of scattered traces of collapsed surrounding walls, occasionally with encircling ditches, as at Çivi 05S01.

Only at one site, Dumanlı 03S04, is there convincing evidence for an exclusively EBA occupation in association with a fortified enclosure. This site sits on a small summit at the end of a low ridge not far from the Devrez Çay (fig. 3.26), and comprises a collapsed rubble enclosure wall defining a sub-quadrangular plan ca. 40m across with remains of internal structures and perhaps external ones as well. A scattering of handmade EBA sherds was recovered from within the enclosure.

Fig. 3.26. Dumanlı 03S04, atop summit in mid-distance

An excellent parallel for Dumanlı 03S04 can be found at the excavated EBA II site of Karaoğlan Mevkii near Afyon (Topbaş et al. 1998), where an 80m wide enclosure of dry stone contains a rather haphazard arrangement of stone structures, very similar in layout to Dumanlı 03S04. At Karaoğlan Mevkii the surrounding wall includes external buttresses and a gate with ramp and bastions, all features that occur on several of the Paphlagonia sites but which, as mentioned above, it is difficult to attribute exclusively to the EBA when there are sound reasons for dating many of them, at least in final form, to later in the Bronze Age (see Chapter Four). EBA fortifications are also well-known at Demircihüyük (Seeher 1987; see also De Vincenzi 2008), where early in the EBA a coherent plan of radially-arranged structures is enclosed within a compound wall, and at Elmalı-Karataş north of Antalya (Warner 1994). Closer to Çankırı province, survey in the Çorum region (Yıldırım, Sipahi 2004: 310) has revealed a common occurrence of small fortified mounds of EBA date, while at Tavium, also in Çorum province, there are indications of a major fortified EBA site (Gerber 2005: 87). In Kastamonu province, directly north of Çankırı, ongoing excavations at the site of Kınık-Kastamonu (Çınaroğlu, Genç 2004; 2005) are exposing an intriguing settlement of late EBA date with rare and extensive evidence for on-site metallurgy, including kilns, slag and working tools, at a location not far from the Küre deposits of copper ores. An associated massive wall appears to date slightly later than the workshop activity.

This evidence for the fortification of small mounded sites in the EBA has an important bearing on our understanding of the nature of EBA settlement in the region. It is clear that the Chalcolithic settlement of north-central Anatolia was never highly intensive and that it is during the EBA that the first significant ingress of human populations into the region was taking place. As already indicated, a major stimulus to that ingress, and to the development of locally situated communities, was the presence in the region of special materials and commodities valued by incoming and external societies, perhaps above all the presence of metals, a factor adduced in the case of the Kanlıgeçit fortified colony of the late EBA (Özdoğan 2001), as mentioned above. A need to defend settlements by encircling them with often quite grand stone structures may have arisen due to fierce competition over access to such raw materials, but perhaps also over another commodity in relatively short supply in the region: arable land. As discussed in Chapter Two, Paphlagonia does not host extensive tracts of fertile plains. To the contrary, much of the region is impossible to farm in conventional arable ways. Incoming farming communities, then, may have encountered some difficulty in claiming and securing rights to arable territory adjacent to their settlements, and the fortification of their small villages may be understood as a manifestation of a society that, while sharing many traits of material culture, was undergoing severe internal conflict throughout the third millennium BC. The use of land for burial of the dead is another means by which EBA societies may have sought to enhance their claims to tracts of territory and we may now consider another site in Inner Paphlagonia that sheds some light on this issue.

Death and burial: Salur North (PS219)
Salur North is located in the sub-province of Orta in Çankırı province, 45km west of Çankırı town. The site takes the form today of a scatter of material in an arable field, covering an area of 40m by 25m. Just to the south of the cemetery site lies the mound of Salur Höyük, itself a major feature of the prehistoric and early historic landscape of the region, as mentioned above (fig. 3.27). We assume that the EBA occupants of Salur Höyük buried their dead in the nearby cemetery of Salur North (Matthews 2004a). The cemetery itself was located as we field-walked the environs of the *höyük*. Modern ploughing of the field is annually destroying the integrity of the site, and so we made regular visits to this field in order to recover and record freshly revealed material.

Finds include numerous sherds from sizable pithos vessels, fragments of human bone and three metal objects, all suggesting use of the site as a cemetery of single-period date.

Looking firstly at the recovered pottery, it is striking that almost all the sherds come from substantial storage vessels, and it can be assumed that the dead were buried inside these vessels, a practice well known from other EBA cemeteries, including Balıbağı not far to the east in Çankırı province (Süel 1989). It is furthermore notable that almost all the attested pithos rims show slight differences in their manner of finish and decoration, with features such as appliqué strips, incised notches and other simple elements (figs 3.28–3.31, 3.36:1–11, 3.37:4–8, 3.38:2–9). These characteristics enable us to estimate a minimum number of recovered vessels and thus of individual human burials, assuming one individual to each pithos. On the basis of the rim varieties, we can say that at least 40 individual pithoi/burials were situated at this cemetery site, set into pits in the ground as at Balıbağı and elsewhere. The characteristic of distinguishing pithos rims with subtle decoration does not appear to occur at other EBA pithos cemeteries and burials of the region, such as Demircihüyük-Sarıket (Seeher 2000a), İkiztepe (Alkım et al. 1988), Alişar (Von der Osten 1937), Kaklık Mevkii (Topbaş et al. 1998) and Küçükhöyük (Gürkan, Seeher 1991), amongst others. The density of burials over quite a restricted area at Salur North suggests that each grave may have been marked in the EBA by an above-ground feature of some sort, perhaps of wood, in order to avoid overlapping of graves. Apart from the pithos sherds, fragments of finer vessels indicate that grave goods included small pots, though not in large numbers.

The finding of three metal items further strengthens the identification of this site as a cemetery. These objects comprise two pieces of copper alloy and one of gold, all

Fig. 3.28. Selected sherds from PS219, Salur North

Fig. 3.29. Selected sherds from PS219, Salur North

Fig. 3.30. Selected sherds from PS219, Salur North

Fig. 3.27. PS219, Salur North, in foreground with PS050, Salur Höyük, beyond

Fig. 3.31. Selected sherds from PS219, Salur North

surviving in good condition (figs 3.32, 3.39:1–3). The copper alloy pin has a round-sectioned shank, broken at one end, with a hexagonal head and a neck decorated by two raised cordons. The razor is made of a thin sheet of copper alloy, at one end drawn and bent to form a loop-handle, with the tip of the blade carefully bent back on itself. It is likely that this deliberate bending of the razor signifies a symbolic act of closure of the razor at the time of its deposition with the dead individual. Deliberate folding or bending of metal items deposited in cemeteries is known from other contemporary sites, as at Balıbağı (Süel 1989: figs 16–17), Alişar (Von der Osten 1937: figs 142, 153, 159, 160), Maşat Höyük (Emre 1979: figs 61–63, pl. XIV), as well as at Mahmatlar and Horoztepe (Özgüç, Akok 1958), all in north-central Anatolia. The gold pendant from Salur North is cut from a sheet of hammered gold stock less than 0.5mm thick. At the top a projecting strip was folded over in order to form a suspension tube. Cutting of the pendant was not neatly executed, the edges indicating where the cutting tool slipped during manufacture. A finer tool was used to inscribe lines running down the centre of the cross of the pendant, whose lower part is missing, perhaps again deliberately broken. The three metal objects were found in close proximity to each other and may have been deposited in the same grave. One example of a rough bead of soft white stone and a broken grind-stone, perhaps originally used to cover the mouth of a pithos as attested at many other EBA pithos cemeteries, were also found at Salur North.

The EBA cemetery site at Salur North can best be appreciated through comparison with similar cemetery sites of north and central Anatolia. At the cemetery of Balıbağı, within Çankırı province and only 60km east of Salur, rescue excavations uncovered numerous burials of EBA date, many in pithos vessels and others in stone-lined cist graves (Süel 1989). Grave goods include pottery vessels and many metal items of copper alloy, principally pins, all dated by the excavator to the later third millennium BC on the basis of comparisons with material from Alaca Höyük (but see Thissen 1993: 221 for a dating of Alaca to earlier in the third millennium BC). Our own survey of the Balıbağı EBA cemetery (PS155) indicates its extent over some 4ha and suggests limited continued use into the second millennium BC (see Chapter Four). Other EBA pithos burials, with associated metal grave goods, are known from the sites of Oymaağaç, Göller and Kalınkaya, all in north-central Anatolia (Özgüç 1978), while excavations at Maşat Höyük uncovered further EBA burials inside pithoi, again with associated metal objects such as pins and ear-rings (Emre 1979). As at Balıbağı, the EBA cemeteries of Demircihüyük-Sarıket (Seeher

Fig. 3.32. Metal objects from PS219, Salur North

2000a), Küçükhöyük (Gürkan, Seeher 1991) and Kaklık Mevkii (Topbaş et al. 1998) contain inhumations in both pithos vessels and stone-lined cist graves, with grave goods of pots, metal items and beads. EBA burials at Alişar show the same pattern of inhumation within pithoi and stone-lined pits along with grave goods of vessels, beads and metal objects, especially pins of which many are deliberately bent (Von der Osten 1937). At İkiztepe on the Black Sea coast west of Samsun, burials of very late EBA date include at least one in a pithos and many simple inhumations, with a range of ceramic and metal grave goods (Alkım et al. 1988: 203). Way to the southwest, in the Turkish Lake District, EBA pithos burials with grave goods of pottery and metal have been excavated at Harmanören (Özsait 2000a) and to the northwest at Ilıpınar (Roodenberg 2003).

Conclusions: a world taking shape

In conclusion, by the end of the long prehistoric past of Paphlagonia the EBA evidence from north-central Anatolia notably augments our rather poor understanding of the cultural position of the region within the world at large throughout the third millennium BC. Three related elements stand out in the EBA: metals, fortifications and burials. As we have seen, the evidence for these aspects of life and death in the EBA of north-central Anatolia is rich and can comfortably be situated within a narrative that sees the first extensive human occupation of this region from about 3000 BC, perhaps initially attracted by the presence of scarce raw materials and resources, including salt, obsidian, flint, metals and arable land. All identified EBA sites in the region are small and most take the form of *höyüks*. A concern to establish and maintain claims over land and landscapes, physical and cultural, is manifest in the very substance of the settlement mounds themselves (Bailey 1999), in the construction of fortifications around sites or parts of sites and in the practice of burying the dead in dedicated plots of land adjacent to settlements.

The engagement of these increasingly sophisticated and often competing polities with the world beyond is amply demonstrated by commonalities in pottery fabrics, forms and styles, while at the same time there is a clear local trajectory of material culture that, for example, eschews the use of decoration on ceramic vessels and that adheres firmly to long-standing traditions in technology and manufacture. Wider world contacts, as has been discussed above, are at least partially predicated on desire for access to and use of metals and metal ores, increasingly important as the prehistoric era came to a close. The role of Inner Paphlagonia in these broad processes is most sharply illuminated by sites such as Salur North, Dumanlı 03S04 and Yazıboy, as we have seen, as well as by continuing excavations at Kınık-Kastamonu where metal-processing appears to lie at the core of the settlement's existence. The network of interactions and communications established in the centuries of the Early Bronze Age set the scene for early second millennium developments in the region and beyond, as considered in the following chapter.

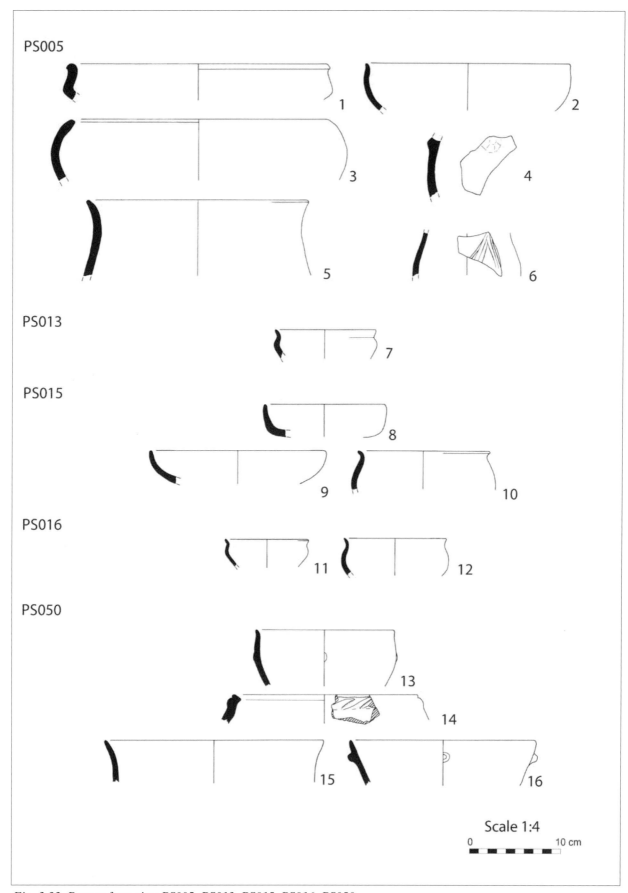

Fig. 3.33. Pottery from sites PS005, PS013, PS015, PS016, PS050

Fig. No.	Site No.	Hand	Wheel	Inclusions	Colour	Finish
1	PS005		X	dense min, mica	7.5 YR 6/4	ext and int brn
2	PS005	X		m min, veg	int 2.5 YR 4/6 ext 10 YR 5/4 core grey	ext and int highly brn
3	PS005	X		dense min	5 YR 4/4, core grey	ext and int brn
4	PS005	X		m min	int 7.5 YR 6.4 ext and core grey	ext and int brn knob ext
5	PS005	X		dense min	5 YR 4/4	ext and int brn
6	PS005		X	f min	surfaces and core 7.5 YR 6/6	ext incised decoration
7	PS013	X		sparse f min, veg	5 YR 7/6	ext and int red 2.5 YR 5.6 brn slip
8	PS015		X	m min, veg	5 YR 6/4	
9	PS015		X	v f min	2.5 YR 5/6	ext and int brn
10	PS015		X	dense min	int 10 YR 6/3 core grey	ext brn
11	PS016	X		min, veg	5 YR 5/1	ext and int brn 2.5 YR N3
12	PS016	X?		m min	7.5 YR 5/2	ext and int brn
13	PS050	X		sparse f min	int 7.5 YR 3/2 ext 5 YR 4/6 to 10 R 5/6	brn
14	PS050	X?		dense m min	5 YR 6/6 core pale brown	rim red brn paint 10 R 5/8 int brn; incised decoration ext below rim
15	PS050	X		sparse f min	ext and int 2.5 YR 5/6	ext and upper int brn int N 2.5/0
16	PS050	X		sparse f min	ext 5 YR 5/6	int and upper ext brn N2.5/0

Fig. 3.33 (catalogue). Pottery from sites PS005, PS013, PS015, PS016, PS050. Abbreviations used in the pottery and object figure catalogues: h = high; m =medium; l = low; min = mineral; veg = vegetal; inc = inclusions; v = very; f = fine; c = coarse; ext = exterior; int = interior; brn = burnished; smoo = smoothed

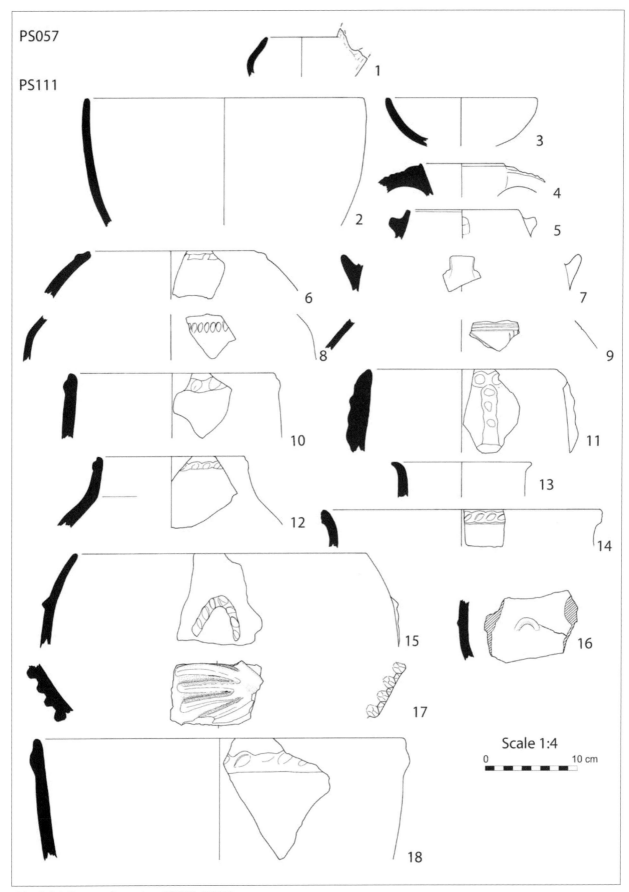

Fig. 3.34. Pottery from sites PS057, PS111

Fig. No.	Site No.	Hand	Wheel	Inclusions	Colour	Finish
1	PS057	X		f-m min, some c	7.5 YR 6/4 to 6/6 core grey	brn
2	PS111	X		m min, veg	2.5 YR 5/4 core grey	ext and int brn
3	PS111	X		m min	7.5 YR 6/4	ext and int brn
4	PS111	X		m min, sparse veg	2.5 YR 5/4 core grey	ext and int brn decorated ridge on top of handle
5	PS111	X		m min	7.5 YR 6/2 core grey	int brn
6	PS111			m min, sparse veg	2.5 YR 5/4 core grey	int brn ext below rim applied band with indents
7	PS111			m min	grey/black core beige	ext and int brn ext lug handle
8	PS111	X		dense min	7.5 YR 4/2	ext and int brn row of indents on shoulder
9	PS111	X		m min	10 YR 6/3 int 2.5 YR 5/4	ext and int brn ext incised decoration
10	PS111	X		dense min	7.5 YR 6/4 and 7/4 core grey	int brn (5 YR 6/3 to 5/3) ext below rim applied and indented decoration
11	PS111	X		dense min	ext 5 YR 6/4 core 5 YR 5/2	int brn 2.5 YR 5/4 and 4/2 ext coarsely applied decorative bands
12	PS111	X		m min, veg	ext 2.5 YR 4/6 int 5 YR 5/4 core grey	ext and int brn ext below rim applied band with indents
13	PS111	X		m min	2.5 R 5/6 core grey	ext and int brn
14	PS111	X		dense min	5 YR 5/6	ext and int brn ridge with decoration below ext rim
15	PS111	X		m min	int 5 YR 5/2 ext 2.5 YR 4/6 core grey	ext applied ridge with dents
16	PS111			f-m min	ext brn 7.5 YR 6/4 int 7.5 YR 6/2 core yellow brown	ext brn horseshoe-lug
17	PS111	X		dense f-c min	int 2.5 YR 6/2 ext 2.5 YR 4/6 core grey	ext red slip? brn ext moulded hand
18	PS111	X		dense min, grog	5 YR 6/4	int brn ext below rim applied ridge with coarse dents

Fig. 3.34 (catalogue). Pottery from sites PS057, PS111

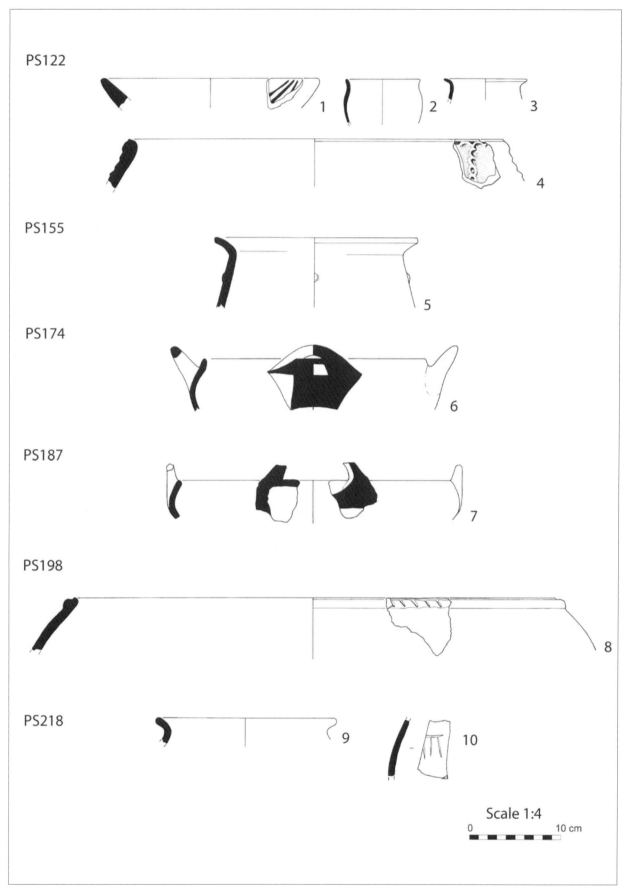

Fig. 3.35. Pottery from sites PS122, PS155, PS174, PS187, PS198, PS218

Silent Centuries: Paphlagonia from the Palaeolithic to the Early Bronze Age, 200,000–2000 BC

Fig. No.	Site No.	Hand	Wheel	Inclusions	Colour	Finish
1	PS122	X?		m min	10 R 5/6 to 10 R 6/6	ext scraped decoration
2	PS122	X		f inc	5 YR 6/6	ext brn 2.5 YR 5/8
3	PS122			f-m	10 YR 5/8	ext and int brn
4	PS122	X		m inc, some c	core 7.5 YR 6/3	ext brn paint 10 R 5/6 ext rim plastic decoration
5	PS155	X		dense f min	10 YR 5/8	ext and upper int brn slip 2.5 YR 5/6
6	PS174		X	m min, mica	7.5 YR 5/6	ext and int partial brn slip 2.5 YR 5/6
7	PS187	X		v dense min	7.5 YR 7/6	ext and int partial brn paint/slip 7.5 YR 6/6
8	PS198	X		min, mica	10 YR 5/2 core 2.5 Y N4 ext 5 YR 6/6 to 10 R 5/6	applied impressed ridge
9	PS218					
10	PS218		X?			ext incised sign

Fig. 3.35 (catalogue). Pottery from sites PS122, PS155, PS174, PS187, PS198, PS218

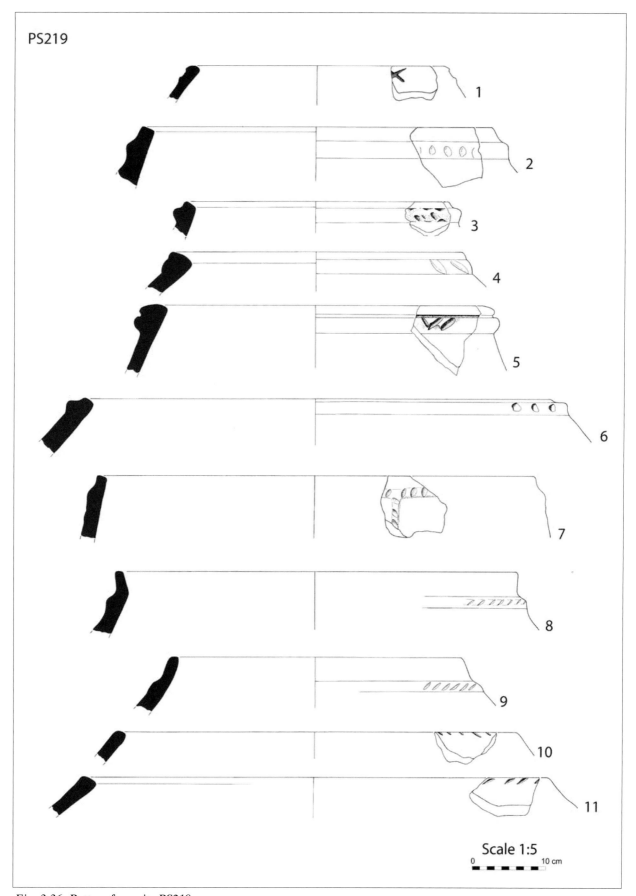

Fig. 3.36. Pottery from site PS219

Fig. No.	Site No.	Hand	Wheel	Inclusions	Colour	Finish
1	PS219	X		dense c min	5 YR 6/4 core and lower body 7.5 YR 6	ext incised cross
2	PS219	X		dense min, veg	10 YR 7/3 core grey	ext and int brn ext ridge with indents
3	PS219	X		c inc	5 YR 7/4	ext impressed design
4	PS219	X		dense min	10 R 4/6 core grey	ext and int brn ext indents on ridge
5	PS219	X		c min	int 7.5 YR 7/2 core 2.5 YR N5/grey	ext paint 10 YR 7/2 ext below rim irregular impressed design
6	PS219		X	c min	5 YR 7/4 core grey	brn, ext ridge impressed decoration
7	PS219	X		dense min, veg		ext and int brn
8	PS219	X		dense min, mica	10 YR 7/3	ext and int brn
9	PS219	X		dense min	10 R 4/6 core 10 YR 7/3	ext and int brn ext ridge with indents
10	PS219		X	f-c min, mica	5 YR 7/4 core grey	ext rim incised decoration
11	PS219	X			5 YR 7/3 core 7.5 YR 5/grey	ext rim impressed decoration

Fig. 3.36 (catalogue). Pottery from site PS219

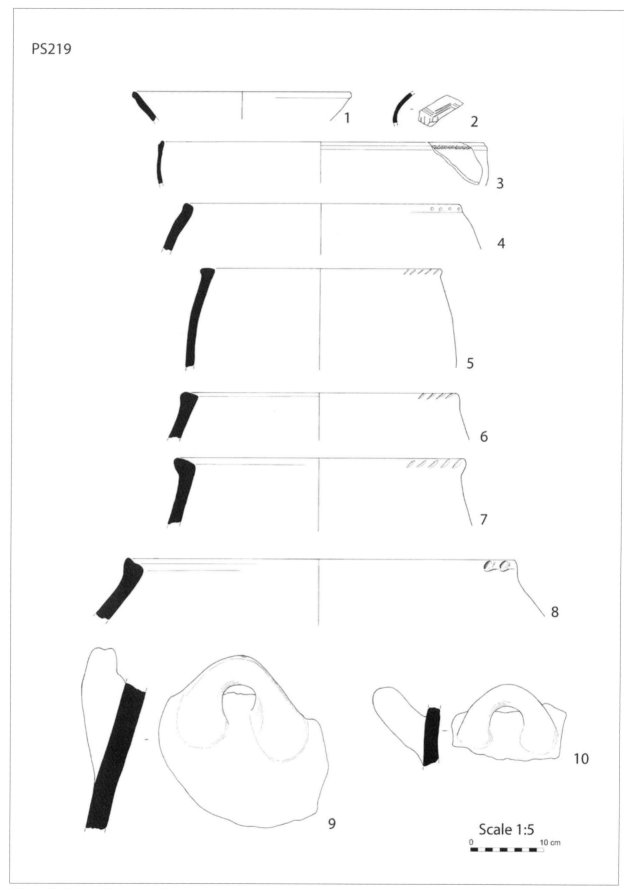

Fig. 3.37. Pottery from site PS219

Fig. No.	Site No.	Hand	Wheel	Inclusions	Colour	Finish
1	PS219	X		dense min	10 R 5/6 core grey	ext and int brn
2	PS219	X		m min, low veg, mica	5 YR 6/3	ext lightly incised design ext and int brn
3	PS219	X		c min	5 YR 6/3 core 7.5 YR 5/grey	ext lightly brn ext rim punched decoration
4	PS219	X		dense min, veg	2.5 YR 6/6	ext rim red inlaid circles
5	PS219	X		dense min	ext 7.5 YR 7/4 core grey	ext and int rim red brn paint 10 R 5/6 ext rim incisions
6	PS219	X		dense min, veg	10 R 4/6 core grey	brn, ext indents on ridge
7	PS219	X		dense min, veg	2.5 R 6/4	ext and int brn ext indents on ridge
8	PS219		X	c min	5 YR 7/3 core grey	ext ridge impressed decoration
9	PS219	X		dense min, veg	5 YR 6/6	ext slightly brn dent on top of handle
10	PS219	X		dense min, veg		ext and int brn

Fig. 3.37 (catalogue). Pottery from site PS219

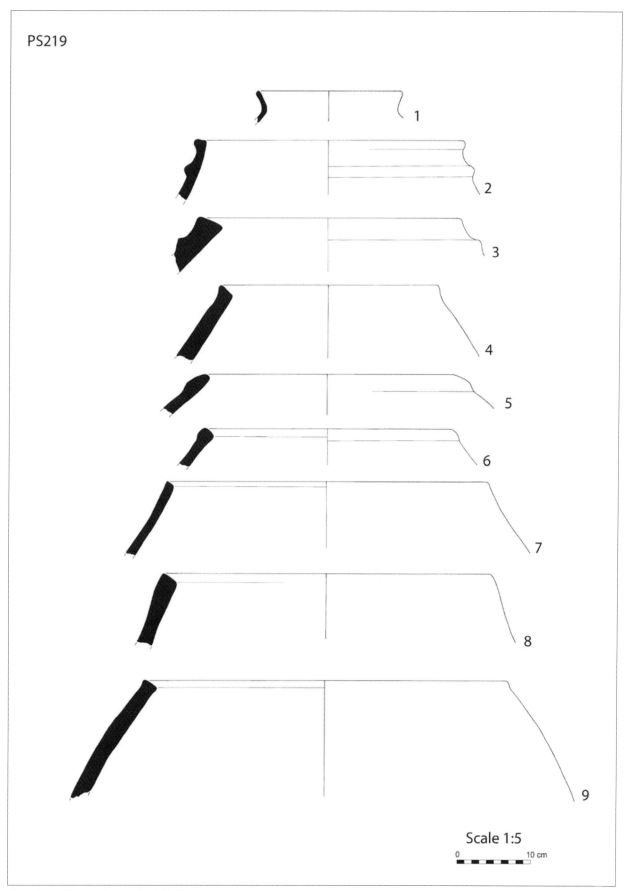

Fig. 3.38. Pottery from site PS219

Fig. No.	Site No.	Hand	Wheel	Inclusions	Colour	Finish
1	PS219	X		m min, sparse veg, mica	10 YR 5/6	ext and int brn
2	PS219	X		veg	ext 7.5 YR N5/grey int 7.5 YR 8/4	
3	PS219			c min	int 5 YR 7/4 core 7.5 YR 6/grey	ext and rim painted 10 R 6/6
4	PS219	X		dense min	10 YR 7/3	
5	PS219	X		dense min	5 YR 6/4	
6	PS219	X		f-m inc	core 7.5 YR 6/grey	paint 7.5 YR 7/4
7	PS219	X		m min, veg	surfaces 10 YR 7/3 core grey	
8	PS219			dense min, mica	10 YR 7/3	ext and int brn
9	PS219	X		dense min, veg	5 YR 5/4	ext and int brn

Fig. 3.38 (catalogue). Pottery from site PS219

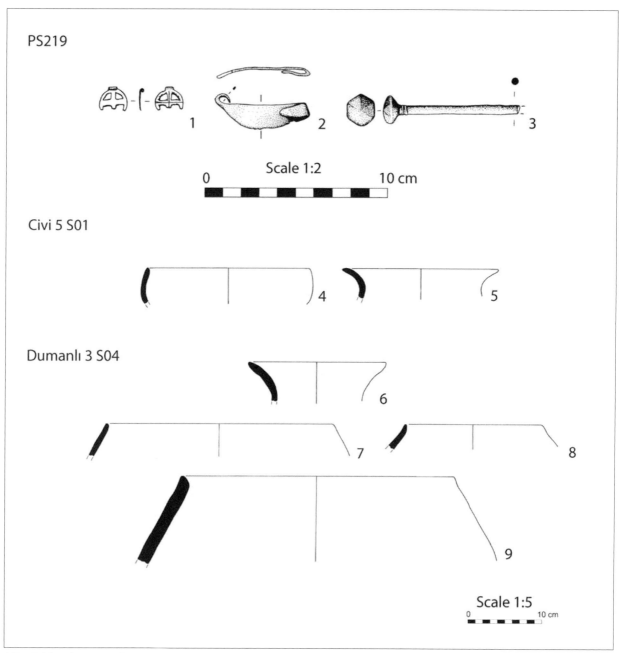

Fig. 3.39. Objects and pottery from sites PS219, Çivi 05S01, Dumanlı 03S04

Fig. No.	Site No.	Hand	Wheel	Inclusions	Colour	Finish
1	PS219			gold		
2	PS219			cu-alloy		
3	PS219			cu-alloy		
4	Çivi 05S01	X			5 YR 7/4-7/6 and 6/6	brn
5	Çivi 05S01	X			surfaces 5 YR 6/4 and 5/4	ext brn
6	Dum 03S04	X		m min, veg	10 R 4/3	ext brn
7	Dum 03S04	X		m min, veg	ext 2.5 YR 6/4 int 10 R 4/3	int brn
8	Dum 03S04	X		m min	surfaces 2.5 YR 6/6 core grey	
9	Dum 03S04			m min, veg	ext 10 R 4/3 int 5 YR 4/2 core grey	ext and int brn

Fig. 3.39 (catalogue). Objects and pottery from sites PS219, Çivi 05S01, Dumanlı 03S04

Chapter Four

A Landscape of Conflict and Control: Paphlagonia during the Second Millennium BC

Claudia Glatz, Roger Matthews and Andreas Schachner

Introduction

The second millennium BC constitutes one of the most striking and significant time-frames within the Paphlagonian past. Notably, for the first time we have contemporary textual sources, almost exclusively originating from outside Paphlagonia itself, which enable the development of scenarios that attempt to accommodate both the textual and the archaeological evidence. For much of the second millennium BC the dominant socio-political event of Anatolia as a whole is the rise, fluorescence and fall of the Hittite state, and Inner Paphlagonia played a highly important role within these developments, as we shall see, not least because of its proximity to the Hittites' capital city, Hattusa. While the relative richness of the historical context can be beguiling, it is vital that the archaeological realities of second-millennium BC north-central Anatolia are kept firmly in mind, in particular as regards the problem of assigning pots and potsherds to specific phases of that millennium, as we discuss below.

In the previous chapter we saw how the communities of Inner Paphlagonia in the Early Bronze Age participated in a broad range of interactions with their contemporaries near and far, with evidence for exchanges of technologies and material culture attributes in directions to the west, into southeast Europe and the Balkans, as well as to the south and east into the heart of Anatolia and beyond. We also saw how the location of many Early Bronze Age sites in Inner Paphlagonia may plausibly be connected to the occurrence of natural minerals and commodities, including metals, flint, obsidian, rock-salt and timber. With the onset of the Middle Bronze Age (hereafter MBA) the sources for early Anatolia for the first time take the (barely) usable form of written documents, principally as cuneiform texts associated with the so-called Old Assyrian trade. Here is not the place to review the evidence and interpretations for this important episode (Veenhof 1995), but in view of the undoubted inclusion of north Anatolia within the world system, *senso latu*, of this economic and political network, it is necessary to consider how our survey region related to this broader structure of interaction. Such a review may also provide a useful backdrop against which to situate the political and settlement developments of subsequent centuries of the Late Bronze Age (hereafter LBA).

Pottery and chronology in the second millennium BC

It is important to emphasise the considerable difficulties in establishing chronological precision as regards almost all the MBA–LBA evidence, not only from Project Paphlagonia but also from all material collected in surveys in north-central Anatolia and indeed even from sites excavated in the region, including Boğazköy-Hattusa itself. The question of the dating of second-millennium BC and Hittite pottery has received fresh study in recent years and there is a new willingness to accept that there are major problems in the dating of these ceramics, along with an increased suspicion of previously accepted wisdom on the intricacies of chronology reliant on ceramic sequences. A new scepticism toward the glib association of scant historical records to excavated 'events', such as destruction levels, is rooted in a healthy sense of doubt and a determination to define and establish 'an *archaeological* chronology of Hittite culture' (Schoop 2003a: 168, italics in original; see also Seeher 2001).

One element is the marked conservatism of MBA–LBA potters, manufacturing similar vessel forms from similar fabrics over long time periods; a problem increasingly being faced in current work at Boğazköy-Hattusa (Schoop 2003a; 2003b; 2006; forthcoming). Many LBA forms show great continuity with preceding MBA types. At the other end of the LBA, there is the suggestion that ceramics of 'Hittite' type continued to be made and used even after the fall of the empire, as indicated by evidence from the Upper City and Büyükkaya at Boğazköy-Hattusa (Schoop 2003a: 172). The ceramic chronology of the LBA in north-central Anatolia is by no means fine enough to allow correlation of sites and associated pottery with kings' reigns, for example, or often even with entire episodes of the Hittite past. To some extent, then, our attention is shifted away from the niceties of chronological connection and more to broad-scale concerns such as the structuring principles of the MBA world, the interaction of local (Kaska?) with Hittite traditions, large-scale issues of continuity from third-millennium communities of the region and the potential association of the recovered material with postulated strategies of control and interaction.

Prior to Project Paphlagonia, the region had been subject to little systematic archaeological exploration (see Chapter One). The lack of excavations and the consequent absence of local MBA and LBA stratigraphic and ceramic sequences are the most immediate impediments to the evaluation of materials from archaeological field survey in north Anatolia, as mentioned in other chapters throughout this volume. Typological and chronological assessment of the Paphlagonia ceramic evidence, therefore, has to rely on comparisons with archaeologically better-understood parts of Turkey.

The Paphlagonia surface material does not include painted pottery diagnostic of the transitional EBA–MBA phase in central Anatolia such as Alişar III or Intermediate Ware (for example, Orthmann 1963b), which hampers the identification of settlements from this crucial period. A certain degree of stability in the Bronze Age settlement system may be inferred, however, from the continuity in occupation of many *höyük* settlements from the Chalcolithic to the EBA and into the second millennium BC (see Chapter Eight). Interaction between Paphlagonia and the central Anatolian plateau is indicated, by the pottery, as starting during the later parts of the MBA and fully during the LBA.

The later MBA and LBA ceramic evidence from the Paphlagonia survey shows definitive links with the pottery tradition characteristic of Hittite centres such as the imperial capital at Boğazköy-Hattusa. Local styles or variations on common types, however, are difficult or impossible to identify and to integrate chronologically (see also Kuzucuoğlu et al. 1997: 292). Recent work (Müller-Karpe 1988; Parzinger, Sanz 1992; Schoop 2003a; 2003b; 2006; forthcoming) on the pottery of Boğazköy-Hattusa, the type-site of LBA north-central Anatolian material culture, has brought to broader attention the problematic nature of the north-central Anatolian MBA–LBA ceramic sequence, challenging previously accepted practices of dating archaeological material on and beyond the central plateau.

Formal conservatism and continuity have long been observed as the characteristics of the north-central Anatolian LBA ceramic tradition (for example, Fischer 1963). With few exceptions, the Boğazköy-Hattusa assemblage remains virtually unchanged in formal terms over several centuries. Thus, the historical periods that are used to divide the second millennium BC into the Old Assyrian Merchant Colony period (MBA), the Old and Middle Hittite kingdoms (MBA–LBA I) and the Hittite empire period (LBA II) are not neatly matched by the ceramic record, as has been strongly reaffirmed in a recent article by Schoop (2003a: 168): 'It is important here to understand one general property of Hittite pottery, namely, its fundamental typological continuity from the beginning of the *karum* period onwards to the very end of the Hittite empire' (see table 4.1).

While comparatively clear ceramic changes characterise the transition from the EBA to the MBA (see Orthmann 1963a), the pottery tradition of the Old Hittite kingdom develops apparently seamlessly from the previous *karum* Ib phase in spite of the fundamental socio-political reconfigurations indicated by the texts; although a number of new shapes are introduced into the repertoire in the Old Hittite phase. Neve (1984: 89), for instance, remarked that, without corroborative contextual information, the ceramic inventory of a securely stratified Old Hittite house in the lower city at Boğazköy-Hattusa could easily have been assigned to the preceding phase. Similar observations were made with regard to the Hittite centre of Kuşaklı-Sarissa (Mielke 1998: 123–29). By the same token, many vessel forms that appear for the first time in the Old Hittite phase, or earlier, continue to be produced until the end of the LBA (Fischer 1963; Neve 1984; Müller-Karpe 1988; Parzinger, Sanz 1992; Schoop 2003a; 2003b; forthcoming) and even for a short period after the final destruction of Boğazköy-Hattusa (Genz 2003: 181). The continuous as well as slow ceramic development impedes the identification of 'type fossils' for dating purposes (Schoop 2003a: 168).

The scarcity of chronologically sensitive vessel types or forms in the pottery assemblages of north-central Anatolia during the MBA–LBA carries significant implications for both survey and excavation projects, which rely on north-central Anatolian-style pottery from Boğazköy-Hattusa not only for stylistic comparisons but also for the dating of local materials. In the light of these relatively well-known observations, but in their newly and more strongly formulated form, the standard typological approach to dating newly discovered archaeological materials based on comparisons to Fischer's (1963) monograph *Die Hethitische Keramik von Boğazköy* is no longer valid (Schoop 2003a: 167). Alter-

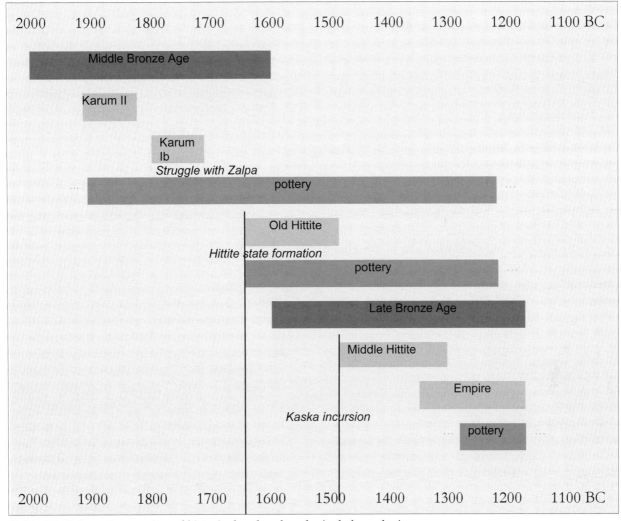

Table 4.1. Schematic overview of historical and archaeological chronologies

native approaches to the problem of north-central Anatolian ceramic chronology have to be quantitative. The first quantitative studies of pottery from the Upper City (Müller-Karpe 1988; Parzinger, Sanz 1992) and Büyükkaya (Schoop 2003a; 2006) were able to identify parameters that are chronologically more sensitive than formal, typological attributes.

Variation within the Boğazköy-Hattusa assemblages appears to be proportional (Müller-Karpe 1988; Parzinger, Sanz 1992; Schoop 2003a: 168). Different types of vessels or formal variants have numerically differential representations in the assemblages of different phases, as identified through other means of dating. General trends in ceramic development have been observed (see Müller-Karpe 1988: 161–62; Parzinger, Sanz 1992; Schoop 2003a: 172–73; forthcoming for details) but it has to be kept in mind that only the pottery from levels dating to the 13th century BC and later have been analysed so far. Thus, the pottery of the later imperial phase at Boğazköy-Hattusa is characterised by a general trend of decreasing attention to surface treatment, and reduction of the overall repertoire as well as formal simplification and standardisation. In terms of formal development, a proportional change of sub-types within functional categories as well as a general trend towards more pronounced rim strengthenings may be observed.

A realistic evaluation of north-central Anatolian pottery from surface collection has to accept that dating is only possible in very broad terms. The loose, and to some extent necessarily arbitrary, chronological categories proposed here divide the second millennium BC into early, middle and late phases. The early phase comprises broadly the Old Assyrian Colony period (mainly MBA). The middle phase is characterised by ceramic types assignable within the Old Hittite to earlier imperial sequence (MBA II–LBA I and some LBA II) while the late phase comprises the final stages of the Hittite empire (LBA II). For the sake of convenience, MBA denotes the *karum* period while the LBA is used to describe the entire 'Hittite' sequence, even though technically the beginning of the Old Hittite period still falls within the last decades of the MBA.

A compound methodology has to be adopted. Taking into account a basic bias in publication preference in favour of fine as well as complete vessels for the larger part of Anatolian archaeology's history, the proportion of red to brown slipped and burnished/polished vessels is higher in the earlier parts of the second millennium BC than during the Hittite empire period (Schoop forthcoming: 2). While this type of surface treatment may be taken, at least, as a general indicator for either an Old Assyrian Colony or Old Hittite date, red to brown slipped vessels continue, albeit in smaller numbers, right until the end of the Hittite empire period, where the majority of the repertoire is of the so-called 'drab ware' variety, an unslipped, buff-coloured ware. White slipped wares are found in only small numbers during the early part of the sequence but they increase as time progresses (Schoop forthcoming: 3) and may in association with other criteria be seen as indicating an LBA date.

Early phase
A small number of vessel types appears to be sufficiently chronologically restricted to the early phase of the second millennium, which, combined with surface treatment, allows a general differentiation from later materials.

> Triangular, horizontal handles, often covered in high-quality red slips and belonging to bowls with an inverted upper body, are a feature of the *karum* period. There are pieces from later contexts (Fischer 1963: 67, Taf. 104–08), although they seem to disappear from the repertoire soon after the beginning of the Old Hittite period (Schoop forthcoming: 4).
> Spouts, covered in slip as well as plain variants, are also found in the Paphlagonia material. In the central Anatolian sequence spouted vessels such as the so-called *Niedere Tüllenkannen* ('teapots') are found in MBA levels at, for instance, Hattusa (for example, Orthmann 1963a: Taf. 1, 33, Taf. 20, 173, 175–78, Taf. 22, 211; 1984: Abb. 3, 52, Abb. 12, 115, Abb. 15, 144–48) but also in the Old Hittite period (for example, Neve 1984: Abb. 5, 25–26). For the purpose of the Paphlagonia material they are used to indicate an MBA–Old Hittite presence.
> Large jars with V-shaped rims and a carination on the shoulder are another feature of the late EBA/MBA in western Anatolia (for example, Kull 1988: Taf. 10, 4, 6, 8, Taf. 17, 10–11) and on the central plateau (for example, Orthmann 1963b: Taf: 23, 213–18, Taf. 32, 308–10).

Middle phase
As mentioned above, the north-central Anatolian ceramic tradition of the second half of the second millennium BC, our middle phase, is characterised by increasing standardisation and formal simplification as well as by decreasing efforts in surface treatment on medium coarse clays. A predominance of simple, unslipped vessels may thus be treated as an indication of a likely LBA date of the assemblage together with the occurrence of specific vessel forms that are characteristic of the second half of the second millennium BC at Hattusa and elsewhere, even if forerunners are present in earlier contexts. Chronologically sensitive shapes present in the Paphlagonia survey material include the following.

> Bowls with internally angled and pointed rims (*Schwapprandschalen*) (type S5 in Müller-Karpe 1988, or type I 3 in Parzinger, Sanz 1992), which appear in quantities at the beginning of the Old Hittite period, are hallmarks of the Middle Hittite phase but also make up a substantial part of the repertoire of the early imperial phase in the Upper City of Hattusa (Müller-Karpe 1988; Parzinger, Sanz 1992; Mielke 1998; Müller-Karpe 1998; Schoop forthcoming). Bowls of this type, however, are only found in rather limited numbers in the last phase of the Hittite empire in the Upper City (Müller-Karpe 1988; Parzinger, Sanz 1992). In this study they are used to indicate a broad Old Hittite–early empire sequence.
> Some of the bowls in the Paphlagonia material are partially red slipped on the upper part of the vessel. The technique of partial slips appears in the *karum* period and continues into the Old Hittite period, while both the shapes typically associated with partial slips and the technique itself decline during the middle phase of north-central Anatolian ceramic development (Schoop 2003b: 15; forthcoming: 13–14).
> A particular aspect of the tradition of partial slips is the restriction of the slipped area to the inverted rim of bowls of the S5 or I 3 variety. They are typical of the middle part of the sequence (Schoop 2003b: 15; forthcoming).
> Large bowls with thick walls and strengthened rims of the type S1 (Müller-Karpe 1988) are related to the S5/I 3 variety mentioned above but are larger in size. They too are typical for the early part of the LBA and are particularly pronounced during the Middle Hittite phase (for example, Müller-Karpe 1998).
> Plates (large, shallow vessels with stepped rim profiles) are a characteristic component of the LBA north-central Anatolian pottery assemblage. They appear in the repertoire after the *karum* period

(Schoop forthcoming: 5). Towards the final phase plates with strongly stepped rim profiles appear to diminish proportionally towards the end of the LBA sequence and undergo a development towards smaller, less pronounced forms and a change in clay composition (Müller-Karpe 1988: 162; Parzinger, Sanz 1992: 61, Abb. 35; Schoop 2003a: 173; forthcoming: 5). Like the bowls with internally angled rims, strongly accentuated plates are here treated as indicators of an Old Hittite–early empire date.

> A few instances of fragments of small, hemispherical bowls with tapered rims and very thin walls of the so-called 'egg-shell' ware also appear in the Paphlagonia material. They are a fineware, which appears to have been used during the imperial phase (Schoop forthcoming: 3), with some possible earlier examples in Old Hittite contexts (for example, Neve 1984: 87, Abb. 11, 80–84).

> A number of jars found in the Paphlagonia material are also diagnostic of at least the LBA sequence. These are mostly restricted to the type T12 (Müller-Karpe 1988) of relatively large vessels with constricted neck, flaring upper body and everted rim. The shape is prominent in the earlier part of the LBA sequence (for example, Schoop 2003b: 18; Müller-Karpe 1998) but is also found in the last imperial phase at Hattusa (Müller-Karpe 1988).

> Few instances occur of possible T1 type (Müller-Karpe 1988), which is more characteristic of the later phase of the empire period (Schoop 2003b: 18).

Late phase

Formal types characteristic of, but not exclusive to, this later imperial phase that are also represented in small numbers in the Paphlagonia survey material are as follows.

> Flat, shallow bowls with only slightly thickened rims of the type S2 or S3 (Müller-Karpe 1988) or I 1.1 (Parzinger, Sanz 1992).

> Bowls with everted and/or thickened (interior and exterior) rims of the type S4 (Müller-Karpe 1988) or I 4 and I 5 (Parzinger, Sanz 1992).

The archaeological and historical contexts

There is evidence for the existence of a powerful Anatolian kingdom during the middle MBA at Zalpa in the Black Sea region (Bryce 1998: 25), whose location seems confirmed as the modern site of İkiztepe (Alkım 1973; Forlanini 1977: 199–200) at the mouth of the Kızılırmak river. The importance of this evidence lies in the picture it generates of the integration of the indigenous polities of the north-central region within the broad cultural and economic sphere of central-south Anatolia and the wider world beyond, particularly that of the Old Assyrian trade network. It is clear that Zalpa and adjacent regions of north Anatolia partook fully of the commercial world so vividly attested in the cuneiform texts from Kültepe-Kaneš and elsewhere, with evidence for movement of people and seafood, perhaps shrimps, from Zalpa to Ališar, for example (Dercksen 2001: 60). A continuation of this sense of productive interaction between north and central Anatolia can be detected in the early phases of the Hittite kingdom, when the northern regions were under the control and influence of Hattusa. Early Hittite texts, such as the Anitta inscription, record intensive trade with the Black Sea region without mention of hostile tribes (von Schuler 1965: 10). One suggestion (Bryce 1998: 74) is that the location of Hattusa as the Hittite capital, at the northern marches of the kingdom, was determined by the need for Hattusili I (1650–1620 BC) to campaign regularly in the north against the cities of Sanahuitta and Zalpa, which may have begun to resent burgeoning Hittite influence by that time.

Archaeological survey in the provinces of Kastamonu, Sinop and Samsun supports the notion of relative stability and peaceful north-south interaction in the MBA, with evidence for a significant spread of settlement followed by what appears to be a dramatic fall-off in settlement at the start of the LBA or a little later (Kastamonu: Marro et al. 1996; 1998; Kuzucuoğlu et al. 1997; Sinop: Işın 1998; Samsun: Yakar, Dinçol 1974; Dönmez 1999). Excavations in Sinop province at Boyabat-Kovuklukaya, as well as numerous metal finds from the nearby Hıdırlı cemetery, indicate a thriving society, with sophisticated metallurgical capabilities, participating fully in trade and interaction across MBA Anatolia (Dönmez 2006b). In the case of Samsun, both on the coast and inland, a degree of MBA evidence is followed by approximately a millennium without any convincing settlement evidence (Işın 1998: 110). Well to the south, survey around Gordion also indicates a major expansion of settlement in the MBA, but in this region the extent and intensity of settlement are sustained into the LBA (Kealhofer 2005: 146, table 11.2).

A high degree of uniformity in ceramic forms across much of central and northern Anatolia in the MBA is further evidence of a strong sense of regional integration at this time, more so than at the height of Hittite power some centuries later. Thus, MBA ceramics from İkiztepe (?Zalpa) are virtually identical to those from contemporary levels at Kültepe-Kaneš (Müller-Karpe 2001: 440–41), which, in the later *karum* phase, strongly resemble ceramics at Acemhöyük, Alaca, Ališar and Hattusa (Emre 1966: 141). A factor underlying this high level of ceramic comparability across Anatolia in the

MBA may be the fact that potters throughout the region were taking their inspiration from forms and decorative techniques displayed on increasing quantities of contemporary metal vessels (Emre 1966: 142).

The correlation of Hittite historical and genealogical elements as well as archaeological evidence with the absolute chronologies of the east Mediterranean and Middle East has proven difficult for a number of reasons (table 4.1). Suffice it here to point out that even though the issue of high, middle or low is still unresolved in the Anatolian case (for example, Müller-Karpe 2003), several recent treatments of the subject favour various combinations centred on the middle chronology (*contra* Kühne 1987; Wilhelm, Boese 1987; Gorny 1989; also chronology charts in Kunst 2002). Bryce (1998: 414), for instance, proposes a middle to low chronology. Beckman (2000) has evaluated, on philological grounds, the recently posited ultra-low chronology against the rather flimsy Hittite chronological evidence and found that the best fit, not totally convincing, comes from the middle chronology while not ruling out the high chronology. A more archaeologically centred reassessment of the dating of İnandıktepe and comparison to Kuşaklı-Sarissa suggests a fit with the middle or a shortened middle chronology (Mielke 2006). The chronological scheme outlined in table 4.1 thus broadly follows the middle chronology.

When considering the LBA landscape of Inner Paphlagonia the most significant factor is the region's role as a physical context for the most persistent and chronic problem faced throughout the history of the Hittite state: how to deal with the peoples known as Kaska, who dwelt in the upland zones bordering Hatti to the north and northeast, and who constituted a ceaseless source of trouble and conflict for the Hittite king and his people. This chapter is not the place for an exhaustive review of the Hittite-Kaska relationship in the light of the available textual evidence (von Schuler 1965; Glatz, Matthews 2005), nor for a detailed consideration of the implications of our fieldwork for an understanding of the historical geography of the region (see Matthews, Glatz forthcoming). Rather, we aim here to focus on the results of the survey itself within the general context of our archaeological understanding of this issue.

Texts from the Hittite state, principally from Hattusa, indicate a range of modes of interaction between the Hittites and the Kaska from ca. 1500–1200 BC, involving at least the following elements (see Glatz, Matthews 2005 for further detail; see also the insightful discussions by Singer 2007; Zimansky 2007):

> Frequent Kaska raiding and burning of Hittite settlements, crops and temples;
> Virtually annual campaigning by the Hittite king into the mountains of the Pontic zone;
> Destruction of Kaska settlements by Hittite troops;
> Fortification or refortification of settlements by the Hittites and Kaska;
> Hittite concern to garrison and protect settlements through a system of routes, look-out posts and watch-towers;
> Occasional agreement of treaties between the Hittites and at least elements of the Kaska;
> Fluidity of people and settlements across the Hittite-Kaska divide.

These various elements fit well within an interpretive framework of frontier studies, best encapsulated in Lightfoot and Martinez's (1995: 471) phrase 'zones of cross-cutting social networks' (see also Lattimore 1962: 472–74; Zimansky 2007). A principal concern in this chapter is to explore how the textually-attested strategies and tactics might be manifest in the archaeological record within the Project Paphlagonia survey region.

The possible significance of cult and ritual practice as a structuring factor in the Hittite-Kaska dialectic should not be underestimated. Certainly the cultic centre of Nerik, home of the Storm-God of Nerik, was located somewhere within the Kaska zone, perhaps not far to the east of our survey region around Vezirköprü (Macqueen 1980; Czichon, Klinger 2005), and throughout the LBA formed a major issue of contention between the two enemies. An indicator of the cultic significance of the region may be the distribution of the so-called cultic vases, so far found at Hattusa, Hüseyindede, İnandık and Bitik (see map in Sipahi 2000: 64). The distribution of these find-spots along what was to become the Hittites' northern frontier zone is striking.

The archaeology of the Hittite-Kaska frontier zone and of the Kaska homelands is an undeveloped area of research. Among the few excavations in north-central Anatolia of relevance here are those at İnandık, Balıbağı, Kınık and Hüseyindede, as well as recently started investigations at Oymaağaç near Vezirköprü (Czichon et al. 2006). Recent and ongoing surveys in the modern provinces of Çankırı, Karabük, Kastamonu, Sinop, Samsun, Çorum, Amasya and Sivas have also contributed significant information. There can be no doubt that a systematic programme of targeted survey and excavation both in the Hittite-Kaska frontier zone and in the heartland of Kaska settlement would greatly augment our evidence and understanding of this critical episode in the history of LBA Anatolia, as well as more broadly shedding light on a textually well-documented interaction between an imperial power and a people at the margins of empire.

Within the Project Paphlagonia survey area, the site of İnandık and its nearby settlement at Termehöyük were excavated in the 1960s by Tahsin Özgüç (1988). The main LBA occupation layer, level IV, was dated by the excavator to the early Old Hittite period on the basis of a land-grant document found associated with this level (Balkan 1973), while the main architectural feature of level IV was identified as a Hittite temple (Özgüç 1988). According to Özgüç (1988: 110), there was no evidence of later, imperial, material culture at either site. Mielke (2006) has recently put forward a convincing challenge to both the conventional chronological assessment of İnandık as well as to the identification of the structures of level IV as a Hittite temple. For the assessment of the Paphlagonia survey, a redating of the only excavated LBA settlement in the survey region has wide-ranging implications. A closer look at surface collection material from İnandık, if not lending conclusive support, by no means contradicts Mielke's (2006) approach.

The chronological argument is based on historical and philological considerations, which questions the reasoning behind Balkan's (1973) attribution of the tablet to the early Old Hittite phase (for slight variations see, for example, Easton 1981; Carruba 1993). The numerous land-grant documents brought to light in the excavations of the Upper City of Hattusa have been shown to date to the Middle Hittite period, while those with anonymous Labarna seals may be assigned to the reign of Telipinu or, perhaps a little earlier, to Huzziya I in the case of the İnandık tablet (Wilhelm 2005, cited in Mielke 2006; see also Klinger 1995: 76–78). In addition, the land-grant document from İnandık can be associated with documents from the early occupation phase at Kuşaklı-Sarissa, with which İnandık demonstrably shares strong ceramic similarities (Mielke 2006). The foundation of Kuşaklı-Sarissa, however, can be relatively securely dated on the basis of dendrochronology to the last quarter of the 16th century BC (middle chronology). An additional, external ceramic *terminus post quem* for the destruction of level IV is available through a spindle bottle associated with the Red Lustrous Wheelmade tradition (Mielke 2006; originally published as a 'light grey slipped' spindle bottle: Özgüç 1988: 79, pl. 27.1) from İnandık that favours a redating towards the end rather than the beginning of the Old Hittite phase. Of importance for the chronology of other Hittite sites is the reasoning behind the original dating of the İnandık relief vase to the Old Hittite period purely on the basis of the, now shown to be clearly problematic, date assigned to the land-grant tablet (see Mielke 2006).

Level IV at İnandık and the contemporary settlement at Termehöyük, the details of which are not published, were apparently destroyed by fire, and at the former site there is evidence for a small-scale, short-lived reoccupation, level III, following the abandonment of the earlier, more substantial structures. Re-use and modifications to the architecture are attested in the area of the central courtyard and the southern rooms in addition to other structural remains (Özgüç 1988: 69, 74). According to the chronological framework proposed by Mielke (2006), the İnandık level IV destruction had to happen sometime after the last quarter of the 16th century BC. Direct textual evidence for the Kaska invasion also dates from the Middle Hittite period onwards, even if later texts appear to place the beginning of the conflict into a more distant past (see below; Klinger 2002). With the proposed redating of İnandık IV and, consequently also level III, the site's archaeological evidence may also be brought into closer alignment with the region's historical development. While level III receives little attention in the excavation report, it may be of some interest in seeking to reconstruct Hittite-Kaska interaction in the Paphlagonia region. Hittite textual material indicates a fluidity with which settlements and regions passed from Hittite to Kaska control and vice versa. The violent conflagration of the structures of level IV at İnandık as well as the flimsy reoccupation, perhaps not long after the conflagration, may be evidence of such a changeover in occupation. Archaeological support for the above arguments of redating also come from our own surface collections at İnandık, which yielded a number of sherds that find their best fit in the middle of the Hittite ceramic sequence alongside some later, conventionally imperial, forms (figs 4.29–4.30, 4.43:10–22).

Ongoing excavations at the site of Hüseyindede, 45km northwest of Hattusa, have yielded architectural evidence, identified as a cult location, and material culture in the form of relief vases and other pottery dated by the excavators to the Old Hittite period (Yıldırım 2000; Sipahi 2003). One of the relief vases has scenes in four panels similar to those on the İnandık vase, while the other has a single decorated panel with scenes of dancers, musicians and a bull with acrobats (Sipahi 2001). The site is dated by the excavators to the later part of the 17th century BC on the basis of similarity to the İnandık vessel and other ceramic similarities to Old Hittite levels at Hattusa and Alaca Hoyuk (Sipahi 2001: 117). Considerations relating to the difficulty of associating ceramic shapes with any of the historical periods in the Hittite sequence (see above), as well as concerns about the dating of İnandık as outlined by Mielke (2006), consequently also put into question the dates proposed for the Hüseyindede material through direct correlation with İnandık.

Perhaps the most intriguing discoveries relating to Hittite-Kaska relations have been unearthed at Kınık in Kastamonu province (Emre, Çinaroğlu 1993), where a spectacular assemblage of silver vessels was recovered during construction work. The likeliest interpretation of how this collection of clearly Hittite material arrived in Kastamonu, well to the north of the Hittite core region, is that it had been seized by the Kaska from a Hittite temple or temples and taken to the north. A subsequent threat to Kaska security, such as one of the many attested Hittite military incursions into the hills, may have led the Kaska holders of the material to deposit it in the ground as a hoard with the intention, unrealised as it happened, of returning in safer times to reclaim it. The results of recent excavations reveal an intriguing mix of craft activity at the site, with evidence for EBA metal-working, including crucibles and slag, and pottery production, as well as storage (see Chapter Three). Level 2 at the site includes a massive stretch of walling at least 51m long and 2.5m wide, which may date to the early second millennium BC (Çınaroğlu, Genç 2005).

Archaeological survey in north-central Anatolia, generally of the extensive type, has been thriving in recent years and it is fortunate that the results from Project Paphlagonia can be situated within a broad geographical context, at least for some periods and in some respects. In general, Old Hittite sites have been claimed in considerable numbers across north-central Anatolia, especially in regions to the north of Hattusa, with a significant reduction of settlement in the imperial phase. In view of the overlap of the ceramic phases across historical episodes, however, such clear-cut chronological definitions should be understood with caution. Thus, the claim that survey in Çorum province has found numerous Old Hittite sites but, surprisingly, no imperial Hittite sites between Hattusa and the Kızılırmak to the northwest (Sipahi, Yıldırım 2001: 105; Yıldırım, Sipahi 2004: 310) may be overstating the potential of the archaeological record as currently understood.

To the north of the Project Paphlagonia survey region, survey in Kastamonu province, deeper into Kaska territory, appears to have recovered only a few sites with Hittite ceramics, generally in commanding positions and with a better representation of early second-millennium material than imperial Hittite, agreeing with the general pattern of settlement shift in the north, which may be associated with a gradual southwards expansion of the western Kaska groups through the second millennium BC. Further north still, in Sinop province, a total lack of Hittite material and a dramatic decline in settlement density over the course of the Bronze Age is attested, with 41 sites of the EBA, eight of the MBA and none at all of the LBA (Işın 1998). The complete absence of even Early Hittite sites in this region, in contrast to a significant MBA presence, indicates that a major settlement shift had happened in the far north of central Anatolia before it happened in regions to the south, supporting the idea of a north-south drift of settlement disjunction over several centuries from perhaps 1650 BC onwards. Features of this disjunction may have included an abandonment of traditional mounded sites, an increased use of wooden structures (archaeologically all but invisible), a decreased use of pottery and an increased element of transhumant mobility.

Moving eastwards, into the central Kaska zone, the picture from Samsun province agrees with that just described for Sinop, with a dramatic decrease in and abandonment of settlement from the MBA into the LBA (Yakar 1980: 84; Dönmez 2002: 275). While the site of İkiztepe on the Bafra plain shows a strong cultural integration with central Anatolia in the MBA, such connections are severed through the LBA (Dönmez 2002: 247) and settlement on the Bafra plain generally appears to collapse (Yakar, Dinçol 1974: 91). Surveys in the Samsun region indicate a very low or non-existent level of occupation in the LBA (Yakar, Dinçol 1974: 93; Dönmez 2002 denies any LBA presence in the Samsun region). Excavations at sites such as Dündartepe, Kavak, Höyük Tepe and Sivritepe also indicate LBA material at an extremely low (Yakar, Dinçol 1974: 87) or totally absent level (Dönmez 2002: 274–75).

Further east still, Hittite settlements have been found to the south of what may have been a frontier line along the Kelkit river, but not to the north of the Kelkit nor to the east of the lower Yeşilırmak (Yakar 1980: 77–81). The most important excavated Hittite site to the southwest of, and therefore within, this natural line of defence is Maşat Höyük (Hittite Tapigga), with a floruit in texts and architecture of around 1400 BC and a subsequent decline (Özgüç 1978; Alp 1991). LBA sites are more common in Amasya province than in areas to the north and east, with settlements spanning both Early Hittite and the imperial phase (Dönmez 2002: 275). Large, long-occupied sites such as Vezirköprü Oymaağaç Höyük, Merzifon Onhoroz Tepe and Alacapınar Tepe, all in Amasya province, may have functioned as frontier sites throughout much of the entire Hittite period (Dönmez 2002: 276).

In Sivas province, the region between Maşat-Tapigga and Kuşaklı-Sarissa, LBA settlement appears to have centred around four large sites, each between 18–26ha in area and located in broad fertile plains, with smaller sites at key strategic locations such as passes (Ökse 2000; 2001: 502–04, Abb. 1), a settlement nucleation and location likely to indicate an increased concern with security in this Hittite border zone. In Tokat province, less proximate to the frontier, Early Hittite materials have been found at 15 sites and imperial Hittite at 11 sites. Within Tokat province a total of 19 sites dating to the second millennium has been found, with an emphasis on Early Hittite materials (Özsait, Özsait 2001).

If we look briefly to the south of Hattusa, towards the modern provinces of Konya and Aksaray, we see a mixed picture, with a spread of Old Hittite settlements and an overall decrease of sites with Hittite imperial pottery, with some new establishments in the late phase (Omura 2000: 47). To the west, the region of Gordion hosts a scattering of small LBA villages with elements of classic Hittite imperial pottery assemblages (Henrickson 1995), sustaining through the LBA a high intensity of settlement that commences in the MBA (Kealhofer 2005). The shift of Hittite settlement is clear: a drift of site abandonment from north to south at some time around the early–middle LBA. It is highly likely that a major cause of this drift was the hostile and unsettled environment of the north-central frontier zone, an atmosphere that failed to impact upon the pattern of settlement in safer, calmer regions to the south and west, such as Gordion and Konya. The timing of the settlement shift seems to sit well with an interpretation of the textual record to the effect that late Hittite texts, such as Hattusili III's treaty with the frontier town of Tiliura, which place the earliest Kaska incursions as early as Hattusili I, are in fact late retrojections of highly questionable historicity, with the earliest secure attestations of the Kaska more likely to be of 15th century BC date, certainly by the time of the prayer of Arnuwanda (1420–1400 BC) and Asmunikkal (von Schuler 1965: 29). While our confidence in Hittite ceramic chronology remains low, for reasons explained above, we may nevertheless speculate that the north–south settlement shift took place at around the same time.

The archaeology of the second millennium BC in Inner Paphlagonia

A total of 29 sites located in Project Paphlagonia yielded sherds that can be dated to some phase of the second millennium BC (fig. 4.1; table 4.2). Once more it is worth stressing that these sites constitute but a sample of the totality of MBA–LBA sites of the region, although a highly significant one, we hope. Gaps in the distribution pattern are certain to be filled in by ongoing (Yıldırım, Sipahi 2004) and future work in the region. As fig. 4.1 clearly demonstrates, MBA–LBA sites are distributed principally across the southeastern half of the survey region, with the Devrez Çay markedly bisecting the site distribution. To the northwest of the Devrez there are extremely few MBA–LBA sites, while to the southeast significant numbers occur. At a glance, then, the role of the Devrez Çay as a border or boundary in this period is

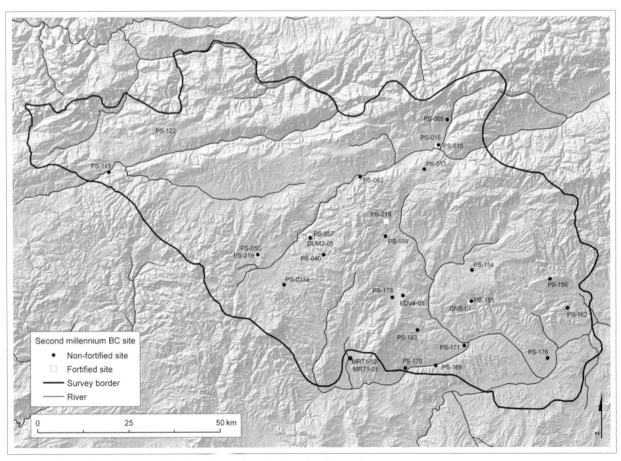

Fig. 4.1. Second-millennium BC sites located in Project Paphlagonia

Chapter Four

Site	MBA to LBA	MBA (gen.)	MBA II to OH	LBA (gen.)	OH to Early Empire	Later Empire	Size (ha)	Site type	Classification
PS005				X	X		0.16	cemetery	G
PS013	X		X	X	X	X	0.79	*höyük*	M
PS015	X	X		X	X		0.61	*höyük*	M
PS016	X	X	X	X	X	X (?)	1.4	fortified lowland	D
PS033a	X	X		X	X		0.03	sherd scatter	Q
PS040				X	X		19.63*	sherd scatter	A
PS050	X		X	X	X	X	0.97	*höyük* (fortified)	M
PS052				X	X		0.08	*höyük*	M
PS057		X		X	X		3.3	fortified lowland	D
PS113			X	X			0.16	sherd scatter	C
PS122		X		X	X	X	1.5	fortified lowland	D
PS154		X					1.18	*höyük*	M
PS155		X (?)		X	X		4	cemetery	G
PS156				X	X	X (?)	0.79	*höyük*	M
PS162		X		X	X		0.8	*höyük*	M
PS169				X	X	X	1	*höyük*	M
PS170	X			X	X	X	1	*höyük*	M
PS171				X	X	X	1	*höyük*	M
PS176			X	X	X	X (?)	0.5	*höyük*	M
PS178		X		X	X		0.79	*höyük*	M
PS183		X		X	X	X	6.3	*höyük*	M
PS198				X		X	1.77	*höyük*	M
PS218	X	X		X	X		1.5	fortified lowland	D
PS219				X	X		0.1	slip from PS050	G
Çivi 05S01		X		X	X		0.5	*höyük* (fortified)	M
Dumanlı 02S05			X	X			2.25	flat settlement	B
Eldivan 04S01				X	X		0.01	look-out post	S
Mart 01S01	X	X	X	X	X	X	1.02	*höyük*	M
Mart 01S02				X			16.38*	slip from Mart 01S01	A

*Table 4.2. Sites of second-millennium BC date and their attributes. Sites marked * have occupation principally of Roman–Byzantine date and are not included in the spatial and settlement analyses for the second millennium BC*

apparent, fitting neatly with an idea originally posited by von Schuler (1965: 62) in his definition of the territory of the so-called Western Kaska group as extending northwards from the north bank of the Devrez Çay.

The types of MBA–LBA sites are indicated in table 4.2. Two of these sites (PS219, Mart 01S02) are clearly small scatters of sherds from immediately adjacent second-millennium sites, and they do not therefore feature in the subsequent discussion and analyses as true second-millennium sites. Two sites (PS005, PS155) comprise second-millennium sherds associated with what are primarily EBA cemeteries, which may thus represent continued use of those cemeteries into the second millennium. Three cases (PS033a, PS040,

PS113) are scant occurrences of little more than single sherds that we hesitate to define as discrete second-millennium sites. A single site (Eldivan 04S01) appears to be a look-out post situated high on a ridge strategically overlooking the plains on either side. Deducting all these sites we are left with a total of 21 substantive settlement sites of MBA–LBA date. Of these, 16 take the form of *höyüks* (two of which have evidence of fortification), four are fortified lowland sites (that is, not hilltop refuges and not *höyüks*, but sites situated on natural lowland eminences with traces of fortification) and one is a substantial flat settlement.

The *höyük* sites are generally modest in size, ranging from a tiny 0.08ha, in the case of the severely truncated mound at PS052, to the massive size, by Paphlagonian standards, of Maltepe (PS183); at 6.30ha by far the largest *höyük* encountered in the entire survey programme. All the other MBA–LBA *höyüks* fall in the range 0.5–1.77ha, with many of them around the 1ha mark. The significance of Maltepe cannot be ignored (fig. 4.2). This large multi-period mound dominates the entire southern reaches of the survey region and its location immediately to the north of the fertile valley of the Terme Çay is no coincidence, for this valley forms a major east-west route behind Hittite lines, connecting directly to the Kızılırmak in the southeast of our survey region, and thence to Hattusa. Maltepe can be viewed as the most important staging post for Hittite military activity in this part of the Hittite-Kaska frontier and must certainly feature by name in Hittite accounts of their campaigns in this region.

It is striking that almost all the sites with evidence of fortifications (PS016, PS050, PS057, PS122, PS218, Çivi 05S01) either cluster close to the banks of the Devrez or, in the case of PS122, are situated well beyond the river in what, for the Hittites, we take to be frequently enemy territory. As mentioned in the previous chapter, it is impossible definitively to associate surface sherds with evidence of fortifications, but in the cases listed above there seems little doubt that such an association can be made, particularly where the site is single period. The distribution of these fortified sites reinforces the case for the Devrez as a major frontier marker.

It is worth focusing here on some specific sites in order to give an idea of their characteristics. Especially notable are the fortified lowland sites (PS016, PS057, PS122, PS218), each of which is greater in area than the mean (1.26ha) for all 16 *höyüks*. Indeed if we exclude the exceptionally large site of Maltepe and the truncated PS052, the mean *höyük* area is only 0.91ha, while the fortified lowland sites have a mean area of 1.93ha. These sites dominate their surroundings and like many of the *höyüks* are clearly located with a strategic purpose in mind, that is to control key routes of communication. Immediately adjacent to the older site of Salman East (PS015), Salman West (PS016) sits today close to the modern intersection of the north-south Çankırı-Kastamonu road with the east-west Istanbul-Samsun road, directly to the north of the Devrez Çay (fig. 4.3). There are traces of a Roman/Byzantine road heading north into the Ilgaz mountains at this point (French

Fig. 4.3. PS016, Salman West, and PS015, Salman East, looking north from İnköy

Fig. 4.2. PS183, Maltepe

1988a: 9) and there is no reason to doubt that the major MBA–LBA route to Kastamonu and the Black Sea headed this way too, constrained by the exiguous contours of the region. Salman West will thus have functioned as a major base-camp and halting-place for the Hittite king and his troops before they made the ascent into the mountains and the forested homeland of the enemy (fig. 4.4). Around the site's summit there are traces of *in situ* stone masonry and clear access ramps scarped into its sides (figs 4.5–4.6). Sherds from the surface of the site cover all phases of second-millennium occupation (figs 4.23–4.26, 4.40).

Further west along the Devrez, on its south bank, the extensive site of Dumanlı (PS057) also appears to control a line of access where a tributary flows to join the Devrez to the north. The site is fronted by an 85m-long stretch of revetment walling, standing in places over 5m high, built of massive stones in staggered sections each some 12m long (figs 4.7–4.11), with echoes of Troy VI in its means and scale of construction. The revetment wall cuts off a long neck of land over which there is a light scatter of pottery of exclusively earlier second-millennium phase (figs 4.27–4.28, 4.42:1–8). Construction of this site must have been a major undertaking and it has to be viewed as one element in a system of landscape control and defence. Not far to the east of Dumanlı, the site of Kanlıgöl (PS218) also controls a major communication route in the form of what today is a minor road from modern Korgun to Kurşunlu. Before the construction of the modern Çankırı-Ilgaz road this route was the sole means of access from Çankırı to Kurşunlu, and such is likely to have been the case in the second millennium BC as there are traces of ancient tracks in this region, doubtless also Roman/Byzantine, paralleling the route of the early 20th-century railway (fig. 4.12). Kanlıgöl itself is a highly impressive site, sitting squat on a prominence that provides excellent visibility for great distances in all directions. There are good traces of circumvallation, a superb access ramp to the main gate and collapsed stone structures on the interior (figs 4.13–4.16). The site is occupied over several periods, from the EBA to Phrygian period, and association of the walls with any single period is risky, but the absence of later imperial Hittite material and its proximity to Dumanlı suggest that its main use as a defensive site was as part of that same system of defence and control attested by many of these sites in the first half of the second millennium BC. Far to the north of the Devrez the imposing site of İnceboğaz (PS122) sits astride a natural pass, dominating the strategic landscape (fig. 4.17), and yielding pottery of a range of periods including all phases of the second millennium BC (figs 4.32, 4.42:10–22).

Fig. 4.4. Ilgaz mountains behind PS016, Salman West

Fig. 4.5. Ramps of PS016, Salman West

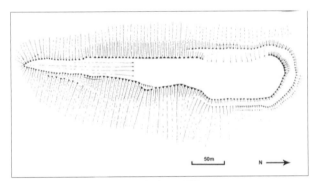

Fig. 4.6. Plan of PS016, Salman West

Clear and defensible routes of communication between the sites of this coherent system would have been fundamentally important. One element is that of tracks and, as we have seen, there is some evidence to associate specific tracks and routes with the distribution and location of second-millennium sites. Another element, commonly attested in Hittite textual sources (Goetze 1960), is that of look-out posts. Clearly such sites would have been located at points in the landscape with excellent all-round visibility and where rapid communication, probably in the form of bonfires on stone platforms, could be transmitted to nearby settlements or garrisons in order to warn of movements of potentially hostile groups. We were fortunate indeed in one of our transects to encounter what appears to be exactly such a site at Eldivan 04S01, comprising a collapsed circle of stones, 9m in diameter with an adjacent stone bank 6m long and 3m wide (figs 4.18–4.19). A few scraps of pottery suggest an early LBA date. Views from this point are extensive in all directions, with the MBA–LBA mound of Eldivan Höyük (PS178) clearly visible way below on the plain to the west and PS171 in sight far off to the southeast. The site of Eldivan 04S01, and perhaps the nearby stone banks of Eldivan 04S02, can only have functioned as look-outs, no doubt manned by a detachment of troops from the garrison below accompanied by a few storage and cooking vessels for their immediate needs, whose sherds we encountered in survey.

Conclusions: a contested landscape

In sum, the picture generated by the second-millennium evidence from Paphlagonia is one of conflict and control (Matthews 2004b), with the probable exception of the MBA evidence (although, as discussed above, it is not possible convincingly to separate the MBA evidence from the MBA/LBA evidence).

Fig. 4.7. PS057, Dumanlı. The main wall runs across the centre of the image in the middle distance

Fig. 4.8. PS057, Dumanlı, main wall

Fig. 4.9. PS057, Dumanlı, detail of main wall showing stepped alignment

Fig. 4.10. PS057, Dumanlı, access ramp at south end of main wall

Chapter Four

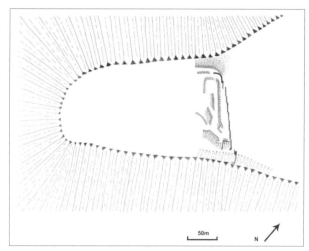

Fig. 4.11. Plan of PS057, Dumanlı

Fig. 4.12. Ancient tracks in the region of PS218, Kanlıgöl

Fig. 4.13. PS218, Kanlıgöl, located on the flat promontory on the horizon

Fig. 4.14. PS218, Kanlıgöl, with figures ascending the access ramp

Fig. 4.15. PS218, Kanlıgöl, collapsed stone circumvallation

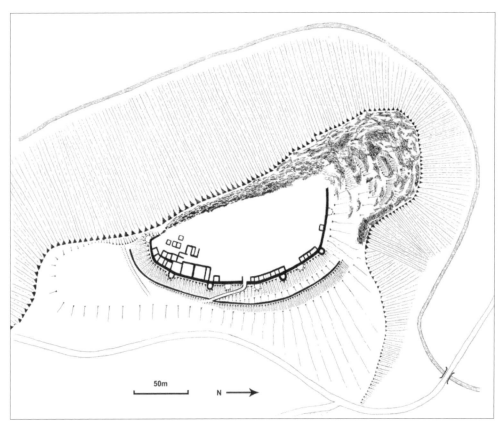

Fig. 4.16. Plan of PS218, Kanlıgöl

Fig. 4.17. PS122, İnceboğaz. To the left an Iron Age tumulus sits atop the Bronze Age access ramp

A Landscape of Conflict and Control: Paphlagonia during the Second Millennium BC

Fig. 4.18. Look-out site Eldivan 04S01

Fig. 4.19. Looking east across the Eldivan plain. In the centre Eldivan Höyük (PS178) stands out amongst the vegetation, with the look-out site, Eldivan 04S01, located on the centre of the high ridge beyond

A total of 11 settlements sites yielded materials that can be assigned with some confidence to the MBA. Settlement in Inner Paphlagonia concentrated on the larger mounds already occupied in the preceding periods, but there is also a recognisable shift to new settlement locations during the MBA. The exploitation of raw materials and strategic positioning with respect to inter-regional communication routes were clearly important in this phase. An intensification of interaction between Inner Paphlagonia and the regions to the south and east, an important catalyst for which must have been the Old Assyrian trading network, is evident in the central-Anatolian characteristics of the local pottery. This trait is shared by other MBA settlements on the Black Sea and in its hinterland (Müller-Karpe 2001). Sometime during the 16th and 15th centuries BC, however, these regions underwent a major transformation, manifested in the apparent cessation of permanent settlement and the absence of recognisable LBA pottery from the Black Sea region. In contrast, regions further to the south such as Inner Paphlagonia, inland Samsun and Amasya experienced settlement continuity into the LBA.

The LBA countryside of Inner Paphlagonia is not populated with scattered hamlets and villages maximising agricultural potential of the valleys and plains: the landscape was not safe enough for that. Nor is there much of a settlement hierarchy in terms of site size and significance, with only Maltepe standing out for its large size. Arguably all the second-millennium sites located in Project Paphlagonia can be tied into a Hittite system of control, each site capable of supporting, through farming and herding in the site's immediate environs, its own small population who may, as at Maşat, have included a permanent military garrison. Each site has good visibility, a freshwater source with some arable land and is situated on routes that enable rapid communication and interaction with neighbours and ultimately with the Hittite heartland around Hattusa to the southeast. We are confident that the coherent system of communication and control represented by the archaeological evidence recounted above can be understood as the Hittite response to the recurrent Kaska threat along the Hittite's northwest frontier, as vividly attested in numerous texts of the time.

We may also surmise that many of these sites must have swung between Hittite and Kaska control over the several centuries of their interaction, and that Hittites and Kaska will have co-existed for episodes at particular sites, as masters and slaves for example (Houwink ten Cate 1967: 53; Glatz, Matthews 2005). We should therefore be cautious in using terms such as 'Hittite' in relation to assemblages of pottery from specific sites. There is the possibility that potters from the Hittite heartland continued producing 'Hittite' pottery while under Kaska suzerainty, as may have happened immediately after the fall of Hattusa itself at the very end of the LBA (see Chapter Five; Genz 2004a: 48), as well as of Kaska potters imitating 'Hittite' types and styles. What we have not been able to detect at any of these sites or elsewhere in the survey region is a distinctive material culture, in the form of pottery, which can unequivocally be equated with a Kaska presence. It is likely that only excavation of a Kaska site deep in Kaska territory will assist in this regard, and we may look to ongoing work at Kınık-Kastamonu to provide some clear answers in due course. In any case, the indubitable textual evidence for a Kaska presence in north-central Anatolia from the 15th century BC onwards, coupled with the archaeological evidence for lack of sites in the same region from even earlier in the LBA, strongly suggests that the material culture of the Kaska has not left us a loud and clear archaeological signal. The texts tell us the Kaska are there but the archaeology indicates abandonment over much of the region. It is clearly the case that Kaska sites are difficult or impossible to find, and that they may be characterised by small-scale settlement, lack of dressed-stone architecture, minimal use of pottery and a tendency for frequent site relocation, all factors that militate against their discovery and identification in archaeological survey.

A major factor in structuring the Hittite-Kaska dialectic was the landscape itself. The rolling plains and gentle contours of the central plateau, the Hittite heartland, succumb in the north to the severe mountains and gorges of the Pontic zone, where the Kaska had their home. Inner Paphlagonia precisely straddles the transitional area between these two ecozones, forming a natural arena for the acting out of the Hittite-Kaska drama over several centuries. Of key significance were the rivers of Inner Paphlagonia. For the Hittites the Kızılırmak/Marassantiya may have seemed attractive as a natural frontier zone, perhaps especially where it cuts through the barren rock-salt plateau to the southeast of Çankırı town, but it is too close to Hattusa to act as a last line of defence for the capital city and its associated settlements. Hittite military policy against the Kaska comprised a ceaseless attempt to push the frontier zone as far to the north and northwest as possible, frequently taking the fight into the mountains themselves, though with limited success. A more substantive solution to the problem was for the Hittites to establish a frontier zone on the next major river valley north from the Kızılırmak/Marassantiya, that is the Devrez Çay, which, in its steep-gorged sections, forms an extremely effective obstacle to communication. As we have seen, the distribution of MBA–LBA sites is clearly bisected by the Devrez, with very few sites to its northwest and several instances of major fortified sites along or near its banks, strongly suggesting Hittite use of the Devrez as a natural frontier against the Kaska (fig. 4.20).

Fig. 4.20. The Devrez Çay near Sakaeli, Orta

It remains to consider briefly the historical geography of this region, in view of the input from the archaeological evidence. This is not the place for an exhaustive treatment of relevant toponyms attested in Hittite texts dealing with the Kaska problem (for which, see Matthews, Glatz forthcoming), but it is worth considering one key feature: the localisation of the Dahara river. Studies by Goetze (1960) and Güterbock (1961) made significant strides in establishing an outline of Hittite historical geography in the north-central region, building on a breakthrough by Forrer (1932) in associating the Classical regions of Blaënë and Domanitis, described by Strabo as lying around Mount Olgassys/Ilgaz, with the Hittite lands of Pala and Tumana. Problems in localising the campaigns of Mursili II (1339–1306 BC) in the vicinity of the Dahara river continued to arise from the suggested association of the Dahara river with the Gök Irmak (Houwink ten Cate 1966; 1967), which put much of the Hittite-Kaska action far to the north. Forlanini's (1977) suggestion that the Hittite Dahara river should equal the modern Devrez Çay brilliantly solved this problem, with the net effect of bringing much of the military action closer to the Hittite heartland and situating it along the banks of the Devrez itself. The archaeological evidence reported on in this chapter neatly complements the now widely accepted interpretation of the Hittite campaign texts, convincingly supporting Forlanini's Dahara/Devrez equation and stressing the fundamental role of that river within Hittite defence policy against the Kaska. As we have seen, no other explored region of north-central Anatolia, such as Kastamonu or Sinop to the north, shows such a pattern of LBA fortified settlement. As the evidence exists, then, only the region of Çankırı province stands out as a candidate for the physical arena within which relations between the Hittites and the northwest Kaska groups were played out, for only here are found candidates for the fortified towns and settlements, and the militarised border zone, which feature in the relevant Hittite texts.

Fig. 4.21. Pottery from site PS015, Salman East

Fig. 4.22. Pottery from site PS015, Salman East

Chapter Four

Fig. 4.23. Pottery from site PS016, Salman West

Fig. 4.27. Pottery from site PS057, Dumanlı

Fig. 4.24. Pottery from site PS016, Salman West

Fig. 4.28. Pottery from site PS057, Dumanlı

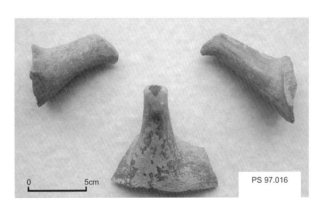

Fig. 4.25. Pottery from site PS016, Salman West

Fig. 4.29. Pottery from site PS170, İnandık

Fig. 4.26. Pottery from site PS016, Salman West

Fig. 4.30. Pottery from site PS170, İnandık

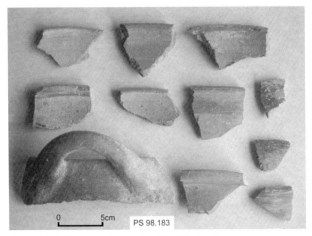
Fig. 4.31. Pottery from site PS183, Maltepe

Fig. 4.35. Pottery from site Mart 01S01

Fig. 4.32. Pottery from site PS122, İnceboğaz

Fig. 4.36. Pottery from site Mart 01S01

Fig. 4.33. Pottery from site Mart 01S01

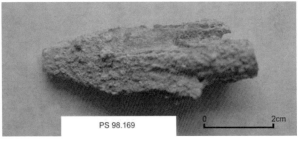
Fig. 4.37. Copper alloy projectile point from site PS169, Kara Mustafa Höyük

Fig. 4.34. Pottery from site Mart 01S01

Fig. 4.38. Copper alloy projectile point from site Çivi 05S01

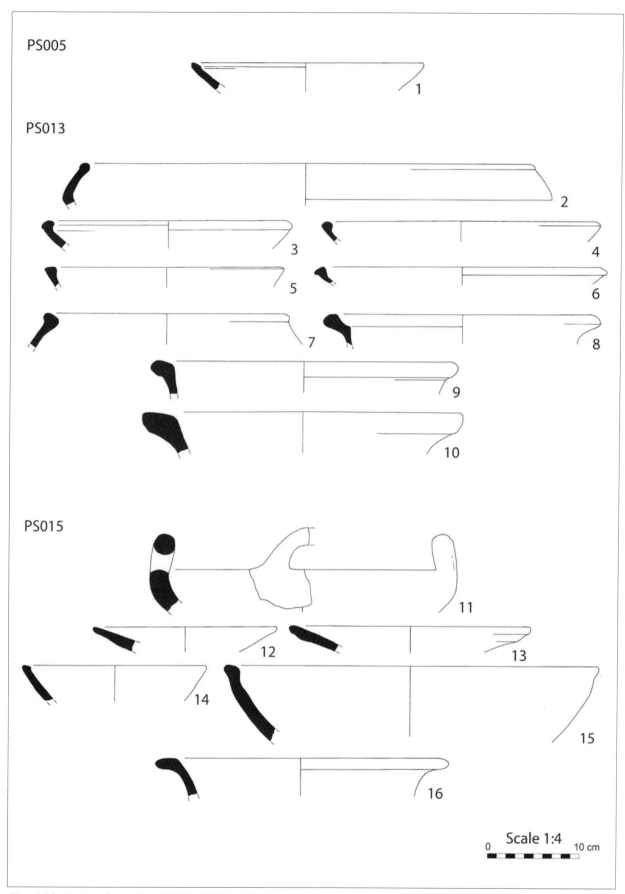

Fig. 4.39. Pottery from sites PS005, PS013, PS015

Fig. No.	Site No.	Hand	Wheel	Inclusions	Colour	Finish
1	PS005		X	m min and mica	10 YR 6/2	int and ext brn
2	PS013		X	f-m min and veg	7.5 YR 7/4	red brn slip 5 YR 5/5 to 2.5 YR 5/6 ext and upper int
3	PS013		X	min, mica and veg	7.5 YR 7/4	int and ext brn 7.5 YR 5/4
4	PS013		X		2.5 YR 6/6 ext 5 YR 7/6 to 7.5 YR 7/4	red slip 2.5 YR 5/6 int and top ext
5	PS013		X	m min, sparse veg	5 YR 6/6	traces of brn ext
6	PS013		X	m min, sparse veg	5 YR 6/6	traces of brn ext
7	PS013		X	c min, m veg	7.5 YR 6/4 to 5/2	
8	PS013		X	m and c min and veg	7.5 YR 7/4	ext and int brn upper rim 7.5 YR 6/6
9	PS013		X	min, sparse veg	2.5 YR 6/6 to 5 YR 6/6	
10	PS013		X	sparse veg and f min with mica	surfaces 2.5 YR 6/1 ext and int 2.5 YR 6/6 core 5 GY 6/6	
11	PS015		X	min (white)	7.5 YR 5/4	int brn
12	PS015		X	m min	2.5 YR 5/4	
13	PS015		X	m min	5 YR 6/4	
14	PS015		X	m min	5 YR 5/6	ext and int brn
15	PS015		X	m min	7.5 YR 4/2	ext and int brn
16	PS015		X	f min	7.5 YR 5/6	ext brn

Fig. 4.39 (catalogue). Pottery from sites PS005, PS013, PS015. Abbreviations used in the pottery and object figure catalogues: h = high; m = medium; l = low; min = mineral; veg = vegetal; inc = inclusions; v = very; f = fine; c = coarse; ext = exterior; int = interior; brn = burnished; smoo = smoothed

Chapter Four

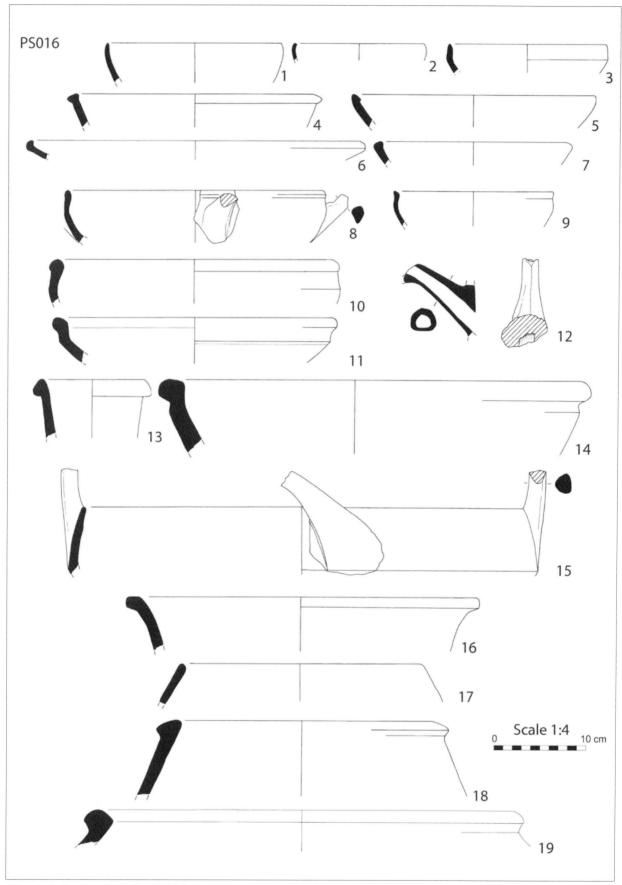

Fig. 4.40. Pottery from site PS016

A Landscape of Conflict and Control: Paphlagonia during the Second Millennium BC

Fig. No.	Site No.	Hand	Wheel	Inclusions	Colour	Finish
1	PS016		X	m min	7.5 YR 5/4	ext and int brn
2	PS016		X	m min	5 YR 6/6	
3	PS016		X	f min	7.5 YR 6/6	ext and int brn
4	PS016	X?	X	m min	2.5 YR 5.4	top brn
5	PS016		X	m min	2.5 YR 6/6	ext and int brn
6	PS016		X	m min	7.5 YR 4/4	ext and int brn
7	PS016		X	m min	5 YR 6/4	
8	PS016		X	min	5 YR 6/4 to 5 YR 7/6	ext and int brn 2.5 YR 5/6
9	PS016		X	sparse min, veg	5 YR 6/4	ext and int brn 7.5 YR 6/4 to 5 YR 5/6
10	PS016		X	m min	4 YR 6/4	
11	PS016		X	m min	5 YR 6/4	rim and ext paint 2.5 YR 6/4
12	PS016			sparse min	7.5 YN 6 7.5 YR 7/4	vertical brn slip 5 YR 5/6 to 7.5 YR 6/4 on ext
13	PS016		X	m min	7.5 YR 6/4	brn ext
14	PS016		X	m min	5 YR 6/4	
15	PS016			min, veg (?)	5 YR 7/6	ext and int brn 2.5 YR 5/6
16	PS016		X	sparse min	2.5 YR 6/6	ext and top brn
17	PS016		X	min	5 YR 6/4 ext 10 R 4/3 to 10 R 6/4 to 2.5 YR 6/4	
18	PS016		X	m min	5 YR 6/4	
19	PS016		X	m min	5 YR 6/4	

Fig. 4.40 (catalogue). Pottery from site PS016

Chapter Four

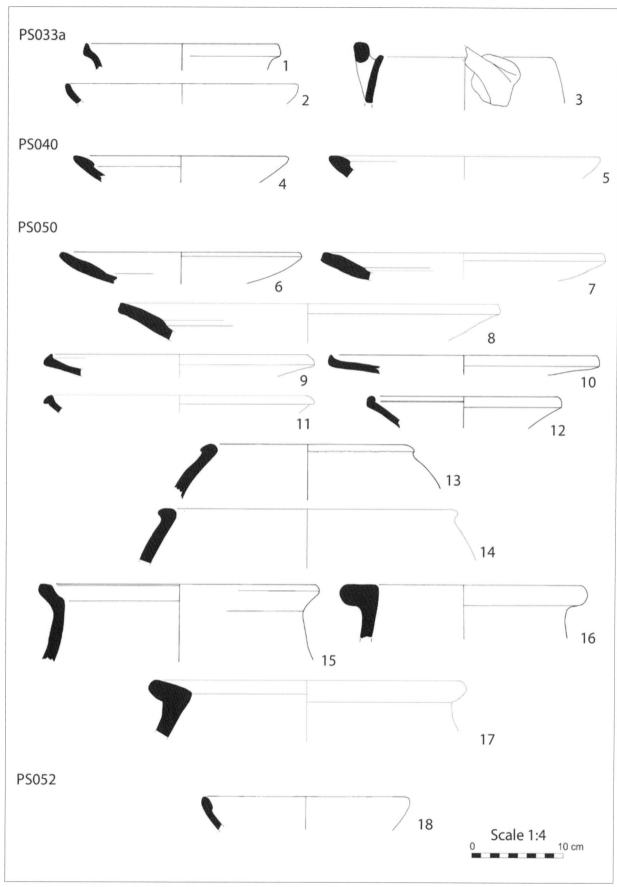

Fig. 4.41. Pottery from sites PS033a, PS040, PS050, PS052

134

Fig. No.	Site No.	Hand	Wheel	Inclusions	Colour	Finish
1	PS033a		X	dense min	7.5 YR 6/4	
2	PS033a		X?	m min	7.5 YR 6/6	ext brn
3	PS033a		X?	m min	5 YR 5/6	ext and int brn
4	PS040		X	m min	7.5 YR 6/4	
5	PS040		X	m min	7.5 YR 5/4	ext and int top brn
6	PS050	X		dense min	7.5 YR 5/4	int brn 10 R 5/6
7	PS050	X		dense min	5 YR 6/6	ext and int brn
8	PS050		X	min	ext 2.5 YR 6/6 to 7.5 YR 6/2 int 6 YR 5/6	streaky ext
9	PS050		X	dense f min	5 YR 6/3	
10	PS050		X	dense f min	5 YR 6/6	ext and int white slip 10 YR 8/2
11	PS050		X	m min		
12	PS050		X	dense min	5 YR 6/6	
13	PS050		X	f-c min	7.5 YR 7/2 surface brown core grey	
14	PS050		X	c min	7.5 YR N5 ext 5 YR 6/6 int 5 YR 6/3	
15	PS050		X	dense min	5 YR 6/6	ext and int brn
16	PS050		X	sparse min	ext 5 YR 8/1 int 7.5 YR 5/grey	
17	PS050		X	dense min	ext 2.5 YR 6/6 to 7.5 YR 6/2 int 6 YR 5/6	streaky ext
18	PS052		X	m min	7.5 YR 6/4	brn ext

Fig. 4.41 (catalogue). Pottery from sites PS033a, PS040, PS050, PS052

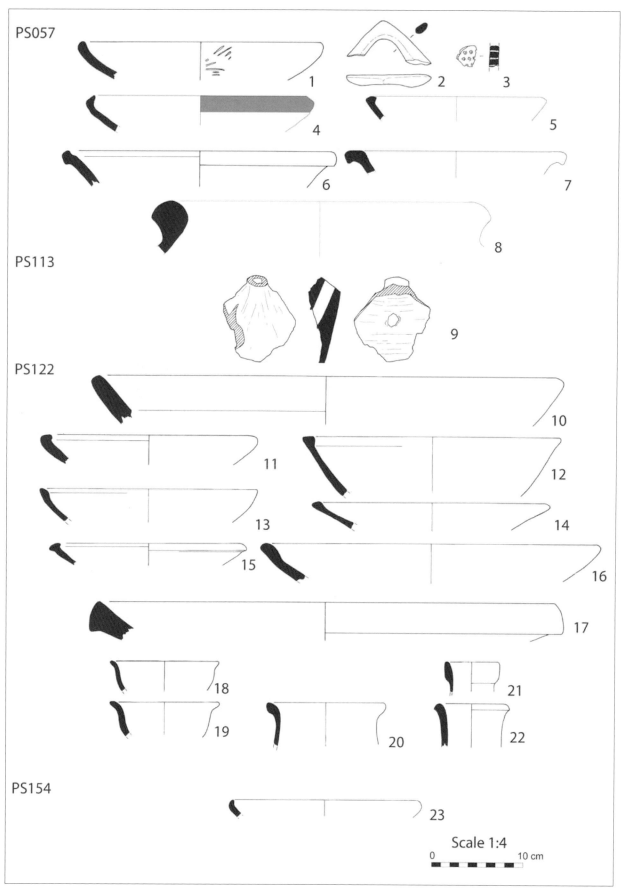

Fig. 4.42. Pottery from sites PS057, PS113, PS122, PS154

Fig. No.	Site No.	Hand	Wheel	Inclusions	Colour	Finish
1	PS057		X	m min	7/5 YR 5/2	
2	PS057			f	7/5 YR 6/4	slip 10 R 5/6
3	PS057			no visible inc	2.5 YR 5/2	
4	PS057		X	f min	10 YR 7/4	int and upper ext brn slip 7.5 YR 6/4
5	PS057		X	f min	7.5 YR 7/4	brn ext and int
6	PS057		X	f-m min	7.5 YR 7/4-6/4	slight brn, traces of red paint on lower body
7	PS057		X	m min	5 YR 6/3 5 YR 5/1	
8	PS057		X	h min	7.5 YR 6/4 7.5 YR N5	
9	PS113		X	f min	int 5 YR 6/6	ext brn 2.5 YR 4/6-3/6
10	PS122			f-c min	core red-brown	slightly brn 5.5 YR 5/3
11	PS122		X	sparse f min	7.5 YR 6/4	int rim slip 7.5 YR 6/6 ext and int brn
12	PS122		X	f-m min	5 YR 7/3	
13	PS122		X	dense f-m min	2.5 YR 4/6	
14	PS122		X	min inc	ext 5 YR 7/6 int 7.5 YR 6/6	ext and int rim brn 2.5 YR 6/7
15	PS122		X	dense f min	10 YR 7/4	top brn paint/slip 5 YR 5/6
16	PS122		X	m min	5 YR 7/4	
17	PS122		X	m min	2.5 YR 5/4	ext and int brn
18	PS122		X	min	5 YR 6/5	
19	PS122		X	min	10 R 6/6	
20	PS122		X	f min	5 YR 7/4	
21	PS122		X	f dense min	5 YR 7/6	
22	PS122		X	f min	10 YR 8/4	ext brn ext and int slip 2.5 YR 6/6
23	PS154		X	m min	5 YR 6/6	

Fig. 4.42 (catalogue). Pottery from sites PS057, PS113, PS122, PS154

Chapter Four

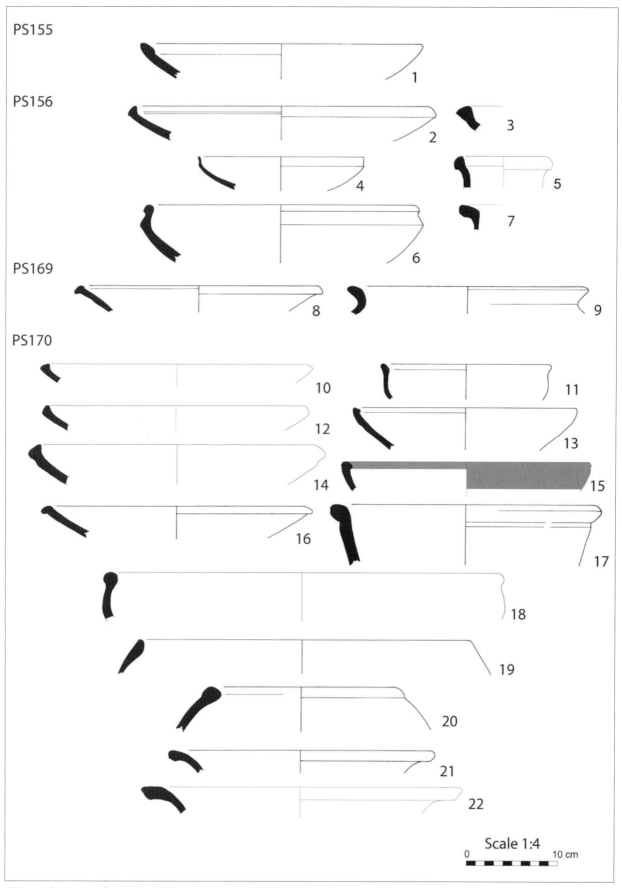

Fig. 4.43. Pottery from sites PS155, PS156, PS169, PS170

A Landscape of Conflict and Control: Paphlagonia during the Second Millennium BC

Fig. No.	Site No.	Hand	Wheel	Inclusions	Colour	Finish
1	PS155		X	dense min	7.5 YR 7/6	ext rim and int brn
2	PS156		X		7.5 YR 7/4	upper ext reddish-brown 5 YR 5/3 stripe; ext slightly smoo/brn
3	PS156		X	min	reddish-yellow	
4	PS156		X	sparse grit, veg	5 YR 7/5	ext and int brn
5	PS156		X	min	5 YR 6/6	ext brn 10 YR 7/4
6	PS156		X	sparse grit, vesicles, chaff	5 YR 6/6	ext brn 2.5 YR 5/6 int 10 YR 8/3
7	PS156		X	min	2.5 YR 8/2	
8	PS169		X	min	7.5 YR 7/6	
9	PS169		X	min	7.5 YR 5/4	ext and int brn 10 R 5/6
10	PS170		X	m min	2.5 YR 5/6	
11	PS170		X	min, f veg (?)	10 YR 8/3	int rim 5 YR 5/3-6/4 ext 10 YR 8/2-8/3 int 5 YR 5/3
12	PS170		X	dense min	fabric 7.5 YR 7/4 surfaces 10 YR 8/4	
13	PS170		X	dense c min	5 YR 7/4	
14	PS170		X	dense min, veg (?)	fabric 10 YR 8/3 surfaces 19 YR 8/2-8/3	int brn/smoo
15	PS170		X	min	fabric 2.5 YR 5/6 to 5 YR 6/6 int 7.5 YR 8/4 to 10 YR 8/4	int rim and ext upper body painted red 2.5 YR 5/6 ext and int brn
16	PS170		X	dense min	core 2.5 YR 5/4 surfaces 7.5 YR 6/4	
17	PS170		X	dense min	2.5 YR 5.4 ext 2.5 Y 8/2	ext below rim punctuation
18	PS170		X	dense min	surfaces 10 YR 8/3 fabric 7.5 YR 7/4	
19	PS170		X	min	5 YR 6/6	ext brn
20	PS170		X	dense min	5 YR 5/4	
21	PS170		X	dense c min	7.5 YR 7/6	ext strip of white on rim 2.5 Y 8/2 ext 7.5 YR 6/4-3/2 int brn 7 YR 4/2
22	PS170		X	m min	core grey surfaces 2.5 YR 5/8	int brn to rim edge

Fig. 4.43 (catalogue). Pottery from sites PS155, PS156, PS169, PS170

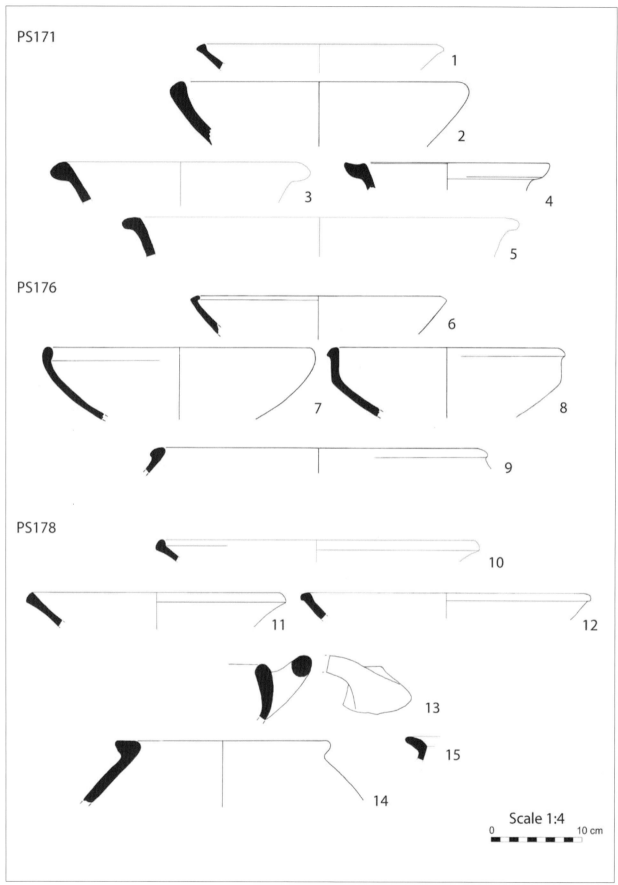

Fig. 4.44. Pottery from sites PS171, PS176, PS178

Fig. No.	Site No.	Hand	Wheel	Inclusions	Colour	Finish
1	PS171		X	dense min	7.5 YR 7/6	
2	PS171		X	dense min	2.5 YR 6/2	
3	PS171		X	dense min	10 YR 7/4 core grey	
4	PS171		X	dense min	10 YR 7/4	
5	PS171		X	dense min	2.5 YR 5/6	
6	PS176		X	c min	10 YR 7/4	
7	PS176		X	min	5 YR 6/4 ext 10 YR 8/3	
8	PS176		X	dense min	7.5 YR 7.4 core 2.5 YR 5/2	brn
9	PS176		X	min	2.5 YR 8/4	
10	PS178		X	fine clay	5 YR 6/6	
11	PS178		X	min	5 YR 6/3	
12	PS178			m min	2.5 YR 6/4	
13	PS178		X	m min		
14	PS178		X	m min	7.5 YR 6/6	ext and rim top brn
15	PS178			fine clay	5 YR 7/3	

Fig. 4.44 (catalogue). Pottery from sites PS171, PS176, PS178

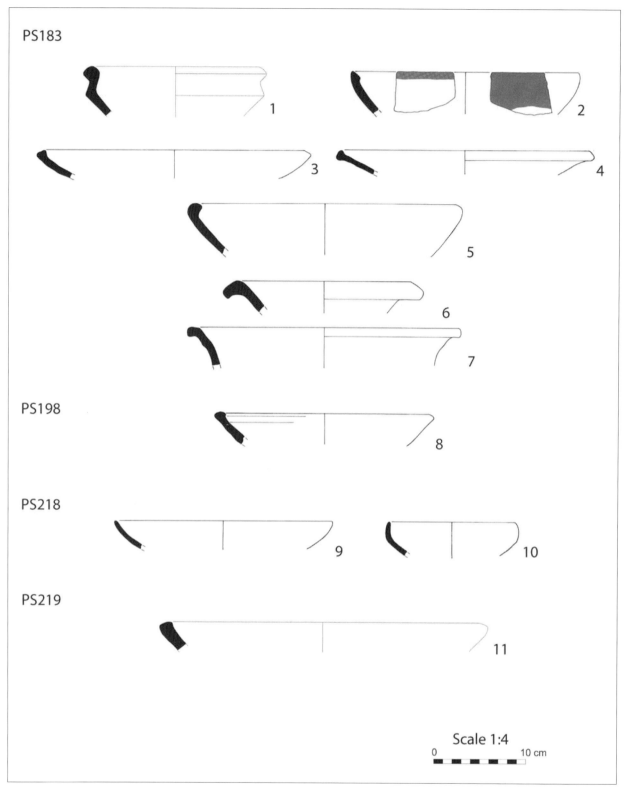

Fig. 4.45. Pottery from sites PS183, PS198, PS218, PS219

A Landscape of Conflict and Control: Paphlagonia during the Second Millennium BC

Fig. No.	Site No.	Hand	Wheel	Inclusions	Colour	Finish
1	PS183		X	dense min	7.5 YR 6/6	
2	PS183		X	dense min	2.5 YR 7/4	int rim and ext upper body paint 5 YR 5/6
3	PS183		X	dense min	7.5 YR 6/6	ext and int brn
4	PS183		X	dense min	7.5 YR 7/4	
5	PS183		X	dense min	5 YR 5/8	ext brn
6	PS183		X	dense min	10 YR 6/6	ext and int brn
7	PS183		X	dense min	2.5 YR 7/4	int slip/paint 2.5 YR 5/4
8	PS198		X	sparse min	5 YR 6/3	ext and int dark reddish-grey to reddish-brown brn 5 YR 4/2-5/3
9	PS218		X	sparse min	5 YR 6/4	ext and int brn
10	PS218		X	m min	5 YR 6/4	ext and int brn
11	PS219		X	m min	5 YR 5/4	

Fig. 4.45 (catalogue). Pottery from sites PS183, PS198, PS218, PS219

Chapter Four

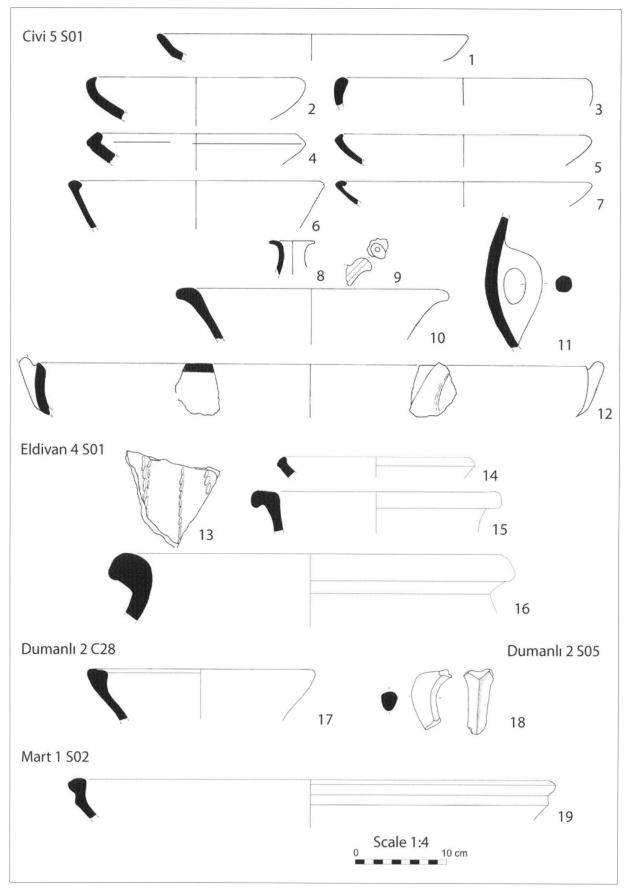

Fig. 4.46. Pottery from sites Çivi 05S01, Eldivan 04S01, Dumanlı 02C28, Dumanlı 02S05, Mart 01S02

A Landscape of Conflict and Control: Paphlagonia during the Second Millennium BC

Fig. No.	Site No.	Hand	Wheel	Inclusions	Colour	Finish
1	Çivi 05S01		X?		ext 10 YR 7/4-5/6 int 10 YR 7/4-6/6	
2	Çivi 05S01		X	m min	10 YR 7/3	
3	Çivi 05S01		X	dense f min	10 YR 8/3	
4	Çivi 05S01		X	dense f inc	10 YR 7/3	ext grey-white slip
5	Çivi 05S01		X	dense min	ext 5 YR 7/4 int 2.5 YR 6/6	
6	Çivi 05S01		X	dense f inc	10 YR 6/4	
7	Çivi 05S01		X		10 YR 6/2-7/6	brn
8	Çivi 05S01		X	min, veg	5 YR 5/4	
9	Çivi 05S01		X	m min	10 YR 8/3-7/4	
10	Çivi 05S01			f min	2.5 YR 5/8	int green-white slip ext line of slip
11	Çivi 05S01		X		2.5 YR 6/6	
12	Çivi 05S01	X?		min	2.5 YR 7/4	ext brn 2.5 YR 6/4 and 6/6
13	Eldivan 04S01	X?		c min	2.5 YR 6/4	ext cord impressions
14	Eldivan 04S01		X		2.5 YR 6/6	
15	Eldivan 04S01		X		7.5 YR 6/6	
16	Eldivan 04S01		X		5 YR 6/3	rim brn
17	Dum 02C28		X		5 YR 5/2	rim 5 YR 5/2
18	Dum 02S05				5 YR 4/1 surfaces 5 YR 6/4	traces of red slip 10 R 5/6
19	Mart 01S02		X		5 YR 6/4	ext brn

Fig. 4.46 (catalogue). Pottery from sites Çivi 05S01, Eldivan 04S01, Dumanlı 02C28, Dumanlı 02S05, Mart 01S02

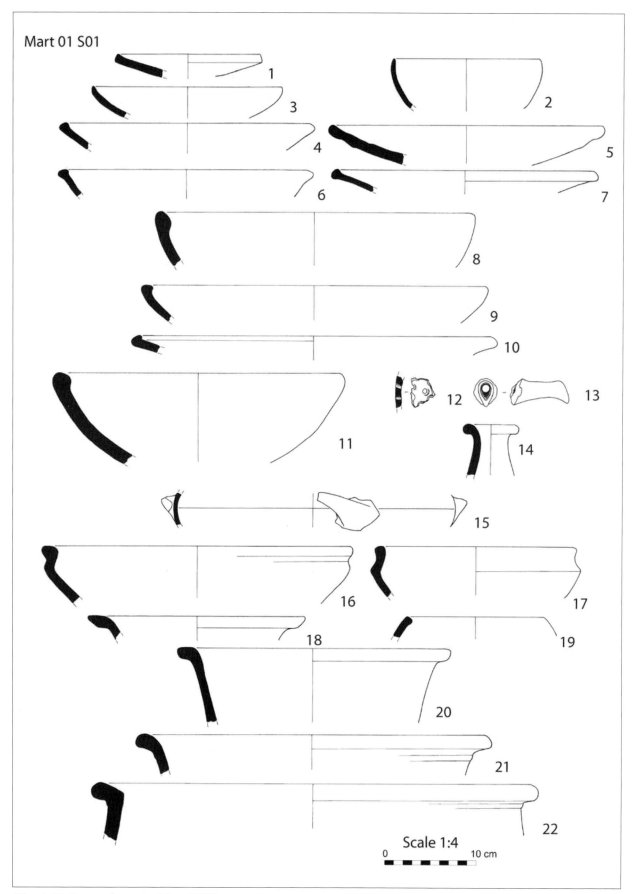

Fig. 4.47. Pottery from site Mart 01S01

Fig. No.	Site No.	Hand	Wheel	Inclusions	Colour	Finish
1	Mart 01S01		X	m min and veg	7.5 YR 7/4	ext and int brn
2	Mart 01S01		X	dense m min	5 YR 7/3	
3	Mart 01S01		X	f min	5 YR 7/6	
4	Mart 01S01		X	dense f min	7.5 YR 8/2	cream slip originally?
5	Mart 01S01		X	m min	2.5 YR 5/4	
6	Mart 01S01		X	min	2.5 YR 6/6	ext and int brn
7	Mart 01S01		X		10 YR 8/2	
8	Mart 01S01		X	f min	5 YR 7/6	
9	Mart 01S01		X		5 YR 5/4	
10	Mart 01S01		X	h min	5 YR 6/4	brn originally?
11	Mart 01S01		X	c-m min	5 YR 7/6	
12	Mart 01S01			m min	10 YR 5/1	
13	Mart 01S01		X	fine ware	2.5 YR 5/6	ext brn
14	Mart 01S01		X	low min, veg?	10 YR 7/4	ext and int brn
15	Mart 01S01		X	low min	2.5 YR 5/4	
16	Mart 01S01		X	f min	5 YR 6/4	
17	Mart 01S01		X	m min	2.5 YR 6/4	ext and int brn
18	Mart 01S01		X	h min	7.5 YR 7/4	
19	Mart 01S01		X	f min	2.5 YR 5/4	ext and rim brn
20	Mart 01S01		X	m min	5 YR 6/4	brn originally?
21	Mart 01S01		X	f min	5 YR 7/6	
22	Mart 01S01		X	f min	int 10 YR 8/2 ext 5 YR 8/3	

Fig. 4.47 (catalogue). Pottery from site Mart 01S01

Chapter Five

A Dark Age, Grey Ware and Elusive Empires: Paphlagonia through the Iron Age, 1200–330 BC

Roger Matthews

Introduction

In approaching the surviving traces of the Iron Age in Inner Paphlagonia we are faced initially with the by now familiar challenge of detecting associations and connections between often scant and fragmentary surface remains and assemblages of material from excavated sites of the region. The ongoing reluctance of Paphlagonian potters to adorn their vessels with incision, paint or other decorative elaboration once more renders it difficult to tie our drab surface assemblages into the more ebullient materials recovered from Iron Age levels at excavated sites and beyond. An encouraging aspect is that there are three well-excavated and well-published sites, with major Iron Age levels, located not too far from our survey region: Boğazköy, Gordion and Kaman-Kalehöyük. In order to approach the evidence for this period our first step is to define a chronological framework, a relatively straightforward matter given the schemes that have been established on the basis of the excavated Iron Age levels at the sites mentioned above. The Gordion sequence provides a good basis for such a framework, particularly in view of the recent redating of the Early Phrygian destruction level to 830–800 BC (Voigt 2002; 2005; DeVries et al. 2005). The Gordion/Yassıhöyük scheme divides the Iron Age, and the subsequent phases of the first millennium BC, as outlined in table 5.1.

On the basis of the Boğazköy sequence, Genz (2004a: 34; see also Genz 2004b) has consolidated these divisions in defining an Early Iron Age as 1200–950 BC and a Middle Iron Age as 950–550 BC. We can add the Late Iron Age as covering 550–330 BC, corresponding to the period of Achaemenid political domination of Anatolia. Use of the terms Early, Middle and Late Iron Age is here preferred over the Gordion terminology so as to avoid ethnic or socio-cultural associations of terms such as 'Phrygian', which may or may not apply in regions outside, or indeed inside, Gordion (Durbin 1971: 103; Summers 1994: 241; Genz 2000a: 111; 2004a: 49). In this chapter we are concerned with the time-span covered by the Early, Middle and Late Iron Age phases of the first millennium BC, which are here treated in turn. The Hellenistic and Roman phases will feature in Chapter Six.

Period	Approximate dates	Yassıhöyük Stratigraphic Sequence (YHSS)
Roman	1st century BC–3rd century AD	YHSS 2
Late Hellenistic (Galatian)	3rd century BC–189 BC	YHSS 3A
Early Hellenistic	330 BC–3rd century BC	YHSS 3B
Late Phrygian (Achaemenid)	540–330 BC	YHSS 4
Middle Phrygian	800–540 BC	YHSS 5
Early Phrygian Destruction	800 BC	
Early Phrygian	900–800 BC	YHSS 6A
Initial Early Phrygian	950–900 BC	YHSS 6B
Early Iron Age	1200–950 BC	YHSS 7A–B

Table 5.1. Iron Age chronology, based on Gordion/Yassıhöyük sequence

Chapter Five

In all, a total of 19 sites within the survey region (other than tumuli and rock-cut sites, see below) yielded surface material indicative of an Iron Age presence (fig. 5.1; table 5.2). Most of these sites have only a small handful of sherds definitively dating to the Iron Age but several of them produced more substantial collections of Iron Age material, especially of Early and Middle Iron Age date. Several sites are datable to the Iron Age, but not to a specific phase within it.

The Early Iron Age, 1200–950 BC

Following the collapse of the Hittite state at some time around 1200–1180 BC (see Chapter Four), much of Anatolia entered an era that for us remains largely obscure and has therefore been labelled a Dark Age. The term is useful in indicating an absence of written documents where once they existed, but the trend in recent years has been to minimise its use in an attempt to avoid value-laden implications concerning social collapse and population depletion rather than a possibly temporary state of archaeological ignorance (Matthews 2008). Nevertheless, there is no denying that after the collapse of the Hittite state the socio-political scene in Anatolia is quite dramatically changed, and that the evidence for written texts ceases for a lengthy period. As concerns north-central Anatolia, locally situated evidence for writing stops for almost the entire first millennium BC, as there are no Phrygian or Achaemenid inscriptions at all from this region (Prayon, Wittke 1994: Karte 15). This shift does not seem quite so dramatic when we remind ourselves that even during the height of the Hittite state the only known texts north and northwest of Hattusa are the scraps of cuneiform evidence from İnandık, Alaca and those recently encountered at Oymaağaç near Vezirköprü (Czichon et al. 2006). Inner Paphlagonia, at the edge of empires, was never a highly literate zone.

On the basis of the Büyükkaya evidence from Boğazköy, Genz (2004a; 2005; see also Genz 2000b; Seeher 2000b for Büyükkaya sequence) has discerned three phases of an Early Iron Age presence in this part of the site, radiocarbon dated to ca. 1200–950 BC. These phases are characterised by a hybrid pottery assemblage that includes a significant proportion of wheelmade forms, in the Hittite tradition (31% in the earliest phase), alongside a resurgence of handmade vessels. In later phases of the Early Iron Age the wheelmade wares seem to have disappeared and vessels are almost exclusively

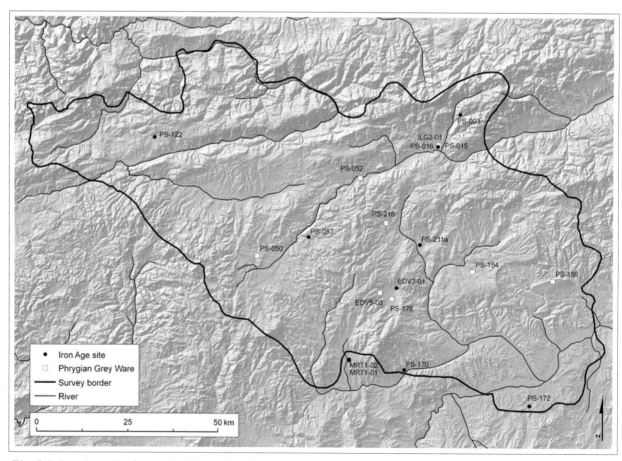

Fig. 5.1. Iron Age sites located in Project Paphlagonia

Site number	Site name	Village	İlçe	Type of site	Site area (ha)	Size category	Classification category	Genz 2004a ceramic type
PS003	Kurmalar	Kurmalar	Ilgaz	settlement	19.63	7	A, I	B7
PS015	Salman Höyük East	Ilgaz	Ilgaz	höyük	0.61	4	M	B6, B7, B14 (x 5), D1, D4, F4, H3
PS016	Salman Höyük West	Ilgaz	Ilgaz	fortified lowland	1.40	5	D	B3, B7, D1, F4
PS050	Salur Höyük	Salur	Orta	höyük	0.96	4	M	B2, B8, G1.1 (x 4)
PS052	Kızılca Tepesi	Kızılca	Kurşunlu	höyük	0.08	2	M	B1, B11, C3, D4, F4 (x 3), G1.1
PS057	Kale Mevkii	Dumanlı	Kurşunlu	fortified lowland	3.30	5	D	G1.1 (x 2)
PS122	İnceboğaz Tepe	İnceboğaz	Eskipazar	fortified lowland	1.50	5	D	B6, D5
PS154	Çivi Höyük	Çivi	Merkez	höyük	1.18	5	M	B14, C3, G1.1
PS156	Çapar Höyük	Ünür	Merkez	höyük	0.79	4	M	
PS170	İnandık Tepe		Merkez	höyük	1.00	4	M	B5, B9
PS172	Saraycık Höyük		Kızılırmak	höyük	0.20	3	M	G1.1
PS178	Höyük Tepesi	Eldivan	Eldivan	höyük	0.79	4	M	B6, B14
PS211a	Deliklikaya		Merkez	settlement	0.25	3	C	G1.1
PS218	Kanlı Göl Mevkii	Mandırlı	Korgun	fortified lowland	1.50	5	D	B8, B14, G1.1
Ilgaz 02S01		Candere	Ilgaz	settlement	3.00	5	B	
Eldivan 03S01			Eldivan	settlement	3.00	5	B	B14, F5
Eldivan 05S03			Eldivan	settlement	0.16	3	C	
Mart 01S01			Mart	höyük	1.02	5	M	B6, B7, B9, F4
Mart 01S02			Mart	settlement	16.38	7	A	B7, G1,1

Table 5.2. Iron Age sites and their attributes

hand-formed. It thus appears that 'Hittite' or 'Hittite-style' potters survived for perhaps a generation after the political end of the Hittite state and continued to produce their wares in a drastically changed world. Genz points out that the Early Iron Age 'Hittite' wares can be distinguished from forms of truly Late Hittite imperial date by their surface finish – burnished rather than simply wet-smoothed (Genz 2004a: 48).

As to the handmade wares of the Early Iron Age at Büyükkaya, these appear in a range of simple forms with usually burnished but undecorated surfaces. Genz (2004a: 49) has rightly pointed to the lack of external parallels for these wares and forms, and has instead situated them within a local trajectory that sees either a reversion to the Early and Middle Bronze Age ceramic traditions of Anatolia or the hitherto unrecognised continuation of the handmade tradition throughout the Bronze Age and into the Early Iron Age. His suggestion that Early–Middle Bronze Age traditions of pottery production and use may have survived through the Late

Bronze Age by being sustained in such areas as the Kaska-dominated Pontic mountains (Genz 2004a: 49; 2005: 82; see also Glatz, Matthews 2005) is intriguing but ultimately answerable solely through excavation of sites of the relevant period in the region of Paphlagonia.

As far as the survey material from Paphlagonia is concerned, there are occurrences of Early Iron Age material at a total of seven sites, as characterised by sherds referable to the types identified by Genz (2004a) from Early Iron Age levels at Büyükkaya (table 5.3).

Thus none of these putative Early Iron Age sites includes material seen by Genz as belonging to the early phase of the Early Iron Age. The Paphlagonia sites of the middle phase of the Early Iron Age are widely distributed across the survey region, and it is notable that all but one of them (Eldivan 03S01) are situated atop sites that had already been occupied in the Bronze Age, an attribute noted by Genz (2003: 179) as applying to excavated Early Iron Age sites across central Anatolia. At İnandık (PS170) there is clear evidence, in the form of two sherds (fig. 5.16:6–7), for red-painted finer buff ware that features in the middle–late phases of the Early Iron Age at Büyükkaya (Genz 2003: 181), while less certain occurrences are found at sites PS111 and PS156. At site PS211 a grooved sherd from a carinated bowl matches well with an example from YHSS 7A (Early Iron Age) at Gordion (Henrickson 1994: fig. 10.6e; Voigt, Henrickson 2000: fig. 5.1), but otherwise the parallels with Early Iron Age material from Gordion are scarce. The pottery from Early Iron Age level IId at Kaman-Kalehöyük (Matsumura 2000: 120) appears mixed in character and is not easy to situate within either the Büyükkaya sequence (Genz 2003: 181) or our Paphlagonia material.

The Early Iron Age evidence from Paphlagonia is rather sparse but suggestive of some level of settlement continuity from the preceding Bronze Age, even if there may have been a hiatus in settlement lasting a century or so at the very start of the Iron Age and following the collapse of the Hittite state, doubtless contemporary with the detected hiatus in the Late Bronze–Early Iron Age transition at Gordion (Henrickson 1994; Muscarella 1995: 94; Genz 2003: 185; but see Voigt 1994: 276). This apparent hiatus in settlement in Inner Paphlagonia is arguably matched by what has been identified as an absence of evidence for Early Iron Age material from surveys and excavations across the central Black Sea region of north Anatolia (Dönmez 2003: 214; 2005: 68), although in fact Early Iron Age red-painted wares are found in surveys of the Amasya-Çorum-Samsun region. Certainly within our survey region and adjacent territory there is little surface evidence to support a contention that here is where Kaska or Kaska-related groups maintained a distinctive ceramic tradition that was to come to prominence in the immediately post-Hittite levels at Boğazköy. Either way, the evidence is extremely scant relating to an Early Iron Age presence in Inner Paphlagonia. As Genz (2003: 179) has pointed out, Early Iron Age levels at excavated sites in central Anatolia have yielded evidence suggestive of village or hamlet-level occupation with no trace of monumental architecture or of fortification. The highly limited ceramic material from the region adds a small piece to the puzzle of ceramic regionalisation that typifies central Anatolia in the aftermath of the collapse of the Hittite state (Genz 2003: 185), but the paucity of the evidence does not allow us to associate the region with a putative pattern of major immigration of Phrygian peoples from Thrace and the west at this time (Voigt, Henrickson 2000: 46; Voigt 2002: 192).

The Middle Iron Age, 950–550 BC

Middle Iron Age forms at Boğazköy once more assist in identifying sites of this date in Paphlagonia, in particular the levels known as Büyükkaya-Stufe and Büyükkale IIa–b (Genz 2004a: 48; Bossert 2000). At Boğazköy these levels are characterised by the continuation of

Site number	Name	Genz 2004a type	Genz 2004a dating
PS003	Kurmalar	B7	Middle Early Iron Age
PS015	Salman East	B7	Middle Early Iron Age
PS050	Salur	B2	Middle Early Iron Age
PS122	İnceboğaz	D5	Middle Early Iron Age
PS170	İnandık	B9	Middle Early Iron Age
PS170	İnandık	Red-painted x 2	Middle–Late Early Iron Age
Eldivan 03S01		F5	Middle Early Iron Age
Mart 01S01	Mart	B7	Middle Early Iron Age
Mart 01S01	Mart	B9	Middle Early Iron Age

Table 5.3. Sites with material of Early Iron Age date

many forms, fabrics and decorative techniques from Early Iron Age levels alongside new forms such as whole-mouth jars with interior rim-ledge, trefoil-mouthed jugs and craters (Genz 2004a: 48), as also attested at Early Phrygian Gordion (Henrickson 1994: 111). New fabrics include, above all, the so-called grey wares often associated with a Phrygian presence. Radiocarbon dates at Boğazköy put the Büyükkaya-Stufe into the ninth century BC, while the Büyükkale IIa-b levels appear to date to the eighth century BC and have material comparable to that from Maşat III-II, Kültepe Iron Age and Kaman-Kalehöyük IIc-a (Genz 2004a: table 6). The painted wares that characterise Middle-Late Iron Age assemblages from excavated sites and surveyed regions to the south and southeast of Inner Paphlagonia, as at Gordion (Sams 1994), Pazarlı (Koşay 1941) and many other sites across to Tokat and Sivas (Durbin 1971), are conspicuous by their absence from our survey region. Earlier surveys across north Anatolia by Burney (1956) and Dengate (Durbin 1971), as well as more recent work in Kastamonu (Marro et al. 1998), also recovered almost no painted Iron Age wares.

The appearance of so-called Phrygian grey ware provides a useful point of identification for mid-later Iron Age material in the Paphlagonia surface collections, while bearing in mind that at Gordion grey wares are dominant, in a limited range of forms, from YHSS5 through YHSS3, that is from Middle Phrygian to Hellenistic (Sams 1994; Voigt et al. 1997: 14). In all, grey ware occurs at nine sites within the survey region (fig. 5.1): PS015, PS050, PS052, PS154, PS156 (fig. 5.2), PS178 (figs 5.3, 5.17), PS218 (also with trefoil rim sherd), Ilgaz 02S01 and Eldivan 05S03. As with the Early Iron Age sites, these locations are broadly distributed across the survey territory. Forms in Phrygian grey ware in Paphlagonia are dominated by crater rims with distinctive interior ledges, as is the case with similar material from Todd's central Anatolia survey (Summers 1994). The fabric is fine, with minute mineral inclusions and a burnished soapy texture to the surface often with a 'silvery sheen' (Summers 1994: 241), obtained by the application of a solution of fine-grained mica prior to firing (Matsunaga, Nakai 2000).

The distribution of Phrygian grey ware in central Anatolia has been taken as evidence for an extension of the Phrygian state to the east of the Kızılırmak river (Summers 1994: 244), supported by scattered occurrences in parts of Tokat and Sivas provinces (Durbin 1971; Ökse 1999), although survey work in central Anatolia has indicated a role for the Kızılırmak as a boundary between two Middle Iron Age cultural spheres (Omura 2000: 47). This point resonates rather nicely with Herodotus' statement that the Halys (= Kızılırmak)

Fig. 5.2. Pottery from PS156

Fig. 5.3. Phrygian grey ware sherds from PS178

formed the boundary between Cappadocia and Paphlagonia (*Histories* I.7). We need in any case to be cautious in associating a ceramic fabric, Phrygian grey ware, with a political entity, the Phrygian state (Summers 1994: 244). A major tributary of the Kızılırmak, the Delice river, also appears to serve as a boundary between a zone with Phrygian grey ware, towards the Kızılırmak, and a zone without Phrygian grey ware, to the north (Omura 2002: 61). Furthermore, a significant fall-off of occurrences of grey ware to the south of the Kızılırmak in Aksaray province has suggested that the origins of this ware may be sought in west-central Anatolian ceramic traditions (Matsumura 2001: 101; Omura 2001: 48). The major concentrations of Phrygian grey ware are indeed in west-central Anatolia (Sams 1994: 177), with rarer occurrences further east, as at Kültepe, and the fabric endures through the Middle and Late Iron Ages and perhaps into the Hellenistic period (Matsumura 2000: 121). At Kaman-Kalehöyük it is commonest in levels IIb and IIa, dated to the Middle-Late Iron Age, where it forms more than 20% of recovered sherds, and is there explicitly associated with an increased cultural impact of Phrygia (Matsumura 2001: 108).

Chapter Five

In the case of Çankırı province we surmise that the scattering of sites with Phrygian grey ware approximates, however indirectly, the northern limits of the Phrygian state through the last few centuries of its existence, thus matching the shifting extent of political control of the Hittite state of a few centuries earlier. In this connection it is striking how many of the Inner Paphlagonia sites with Phrygian grey ware, six out of eight (PS015, PS050, PS052, PS154, PS178, PS218), are situated atop sites with Late Bronze Age occupation, presumably thus sharing a mindset of defence and control as clearly manifest in the Late Bronze Age landscape of Çankırı province (see Chapter Four). Survey in Çorum province, east from Çankırı, indicates increasing occurrences of both Phrygian grey ware and painted Iron Age wares as one heads south on the central Anatolian plateau (Yıldırım, Sipahi 2004: 310), while survey in the environs of Gordion, capital of Phrygia, demonstrates a maximum expansion of settlement in the Middle Phrygian period (Kealhofer 2005). Directly to the north of Çankırı, survey in Kastamonu province has detected a few sites with Phrygian grey ware, notably distributed along the valley of the Araç Çay immediately north of the Ilgaz range (Marro et al. 1996: 284; Kuzucuoğlu et al. 1997: 288; see also Dönmez 2006b: 17) with one large outlier at Gavurevleri on the Gökırmak near Daday (Marro et al. 1998: 322). In Sinop province only a handful of sites with 'Late Phrygian' pottery was located in survey, none apparently with grey ware (Işın 1998: 98, table 1). Indeed, the Sinop region, like Samsun, appears to lack trace of human occupation for the entire period between the 18th and eighth centuries BC (Işın 1998: 110; see also Chapter Four this volume). It thus seems reasonable to postulate the north Çankırı and south Kastamonu region as a frontier zone between a Phrygian state in the south and its neighbour(s) to the north, whoever those neighbours may have been.

In our survey, an especially notable concentration of Phrygian grey ware and other Iron Age types occurs at site PS052, Kızılca Tepe, located on a bluff dizzyingly high above the Devrez river (figs 5.4–5.5). This site has been severely truncated by ancient and recent quarrying of rich deposits of the pink andesite stone that underlies the bluff and its surrounding land. There are traces of quarrying activity, using the wooden wedge method, for some distance around the site and a substantial tumulus (PS052a) 300m to the north. Evidence for use of pink andesite in the construction of burial chambers within tumuli, as at the illicitly excavated site PS061 (fig. 5.6), indicates a possible destination for at least some of the stone blocks quarried from this site.

Fig. 5.4. PS052, Kızılca Tepe

Fig. 5.5. Pottery from PS052, Kızılca Tepe

The Late Iron Age, 550–330 BC

As we enter the Late Iron Age we are able, for the first time since the late 13th century BC, to employ contemporary written documents, though originating from outside the study region, to complement the relatively laconic archaeological information (for a summary of ancient Greek and Latin sources concerning Paphlagonia and the Black Sea, see Işık 2001). Paphlagonia and Paphlagonians enter the historical record at the very dawn of history in the Greek world, described by Homer as led by 'Pylaemenes of the shaggy breast' from the land of the wild mules (*Iliad* 2.851–55). Herodotus (*Histories* I.27) cites Paphlagonia, along with several adjacent territories, as subject to Croesus of Lydia, ca. 560–540s BC, and a Paphlagonian contingent, led by one Dotus son of Megasidrus, features as an element in Xerxes' army of 480 BC (*Histories* VII.72). Herodotus enumerates Paphlagonia as one of the peoples on the southern shore of the Black Sea jointly paying 360 talents to king Darius in 522 BC (*Histories* III.90). How securely we can take Herodotus' account of the structure of the Achaemenid Persian empire in the light of contemporary textual and archaeological evidence from within that empire is of course highly questionable (Kimball Armayor 1978).

What is beyond doubt is the difficulty in detecting archaeological evidence for an Achaemenid impact on many levels of society and culture across Asia Minor following its political absorption into that empire (Erciyas 2006a: 56; for Persian influence on coins from Sinope in Outer Paphlagonia, see Keleş 2006). An innovative suggestion by Root is that the apparent dearth of Achaemenid impact on the material and social culture of the western empire is the result of a deliberate policy of the Achaemenid rulers that for political and administrative reasons 'sought to play down the conspicuous presence of Persian power in the provinces on a variety of social/cultural levels' (Root 1991: 3). By this standard, the Achaemenid rulers' success in imple-

Fig. 5.6. Stone-lined burial chamber at tumulus PS061

menting a strategy of low-impact governance is appropriately measured through its minimal archaeological signature. In any respect, it remains an elusive empire, and the inhabitants of Paphlagonia at this time, as so often, teeter on the brink of history, epitomised by shadowy individuals such as king Otys (also known as Gyes by the Oxyrhynchus Historian) who hosts a visit from the Spartan king Agesilaus in 395/394 BC and provides him with 1,000 cavalry and 2,000 peltasts (IV.1.1–4). The end of Paphlagonia as an Achaemenid subject territory is marked by the visit of a deputation to Ancyra/Ankara in Galatia in order to submit to Alexander the Great directly following Alexander's swift and sharp resolution of the Gordion knot problem (Arrian II.4). The lack of mention of a specific Paphlagonian ruler's name in this exchange suggests that, as in the Late Bronze Age a thousand years earlier, no single king was in charge of the Paphlagonians but they were rather acting as a loose federation of tribal groups.

In terms of pottery, continuity of ceramic forms and fabrics from the Middle Iron Age into the Late Iron Age is well attested at Gordion (Henrickson 1993; 1994: 113), which makes it often difficult or impossible for us to distinguish sites as specifically Middle or Late Iron Age. Rare occurrences of Achaemenid-style carinated bowls, however, do allow us to assign a Late Iron Age date in such cases as sites PS015 (fig. 5.14:3) and PS172 (fig. 5.16:9–10), as attested at Gordion YHSS 4 (Henrickson 1994: fig. 10.9b), clearly ceramic skeuomorphs of metal forms known from, for example, Achaemenid levels at Hasanlu (Dyson 1999: 102, fig. 1). Indeed the Gordion evidence suggests a significant Achaemenid impact most notably on the élite finewares, with otherwise marked continuity in the utilitarian and cooking ceramic traditions (Henrickson 1993: 147; 1994: 113–14; Voigt et al. 1997: 16; Voigt, Young 1999: 192). Looking northwards, the Late Iron Age painted pottery of İkiztepe near the Black Sea coast (Bilgi 1999) finds no clear parallels in the Paphlagonia survey material. Apart from pottery, finds of terracotta tiles at many sites in Inner Paphlagonia are hard to date but some may belong to the Late Iron Age, although there are no good parallels for the 'spouted-eaves-tile' type attested in Achaemenid levels at Gordion (Glendinning 1996) nor for the rather fancy roof tiles of the Middle–Late Phrygian period at the same site (Glendinning 2005). In this connection, use of terracotta roof tiles, often decorated, in sites inland from the southern Black Sea coast is likely to indicate significant influence on local élites from early Greek communities settled along that coast from the seventh century BC onwards (Summerer 2007; see also Mitchell forthcoming). A

Fig. 5.7. Architectural tile from PS015, Salman East

single fragment of what may be an element of architectural decoration (figs 5.7, 5.14:17), possibly depicting the rear quarters and part of a curled tail of a lion (or flower volute?), with traces of black paint, was recovered from PS015 (Salman East), reinforcing this site's identity as a settlement of some significance in this period.

Burial sites of the Iron Age

The introduction of new burial practices into Anatolia in the Iron Age, doubtless associated with shifting socio-cultural connections and at times involving movements of peoples, generates for our purposes two types of funerary monument that require consideration in the context of this chapter: tumuli and rock-cut tombs (table 5.4).

Tumuli

In all, 52 tumuli were identified and catalogued during the five seasons of Project Paphlagonia (fig. 5.8). In some cases there was room for doubt over whether a specific mound constituted a tumulus, a *höyük* or occasionally a natural hillock, but in the majority of instances the definition as tumulus was clear: a discrete artificial mound built to mark and contain one or more human burials. Tumuli occur all over the Paphlagonian landscape and we essayed to record every tumulus that came into our view, but there are certainly many more of them than those recorded in our survey. By comparison, in three seasons of the Kastamonu survey, of 143 total sites 33 were tumuli (Marro et al. 1996: 279; Kuzucuoğlu et al. 1997: 275; Marro et al. 1998: 317), a percentage (23%) not far from the proportion of tumuli to recorded sites (52 out of 337 = 15%) located in Project Paphlagonia. As rather distinctive topographic features in the landscape, known often to contain spectacular grave goods, they have long attracted the attention of illicit diggers, sometimes employing mechanical equipment to reach the burial chamber within the mound (fig. 5.9).

Site number	Site name	Village (or nearest)	İlçe	Type of site	Site area (ha)	Size category	Classification category
PS011	Çeltikbaşı	Çeltikbaşı	Ilgaz	tumulus	0.13	3	H
PS014	Olukbaşı	Ilısılık	Ilgaz	tumulus	0.02	2	H
PS017	Danişment	Danişment	Ilgaz	tumulus	0.01	2	H
PS020	Basil Avci	Ilgaz	Ilgaz	tumulus	0.07	2	H
PS021	Ilgaz tumuli	Ilgaz	Ilgaz	tumulus	0.28	4	H
PS022	Ilgaz lions	Ilgaz	Ilgaz	stones, not *in situ*	0.00	1	T
PS024	Kayı	Kayı	Ilgaz	rock-cut tomb	0.01	2	F
PS027	Osman Gölü		Ilgaz	tumulus	0.21	3	H
PS047	Gâvur Evleri	Kayıören	Orta	tumulus	0.02	2	H
PS052a	Kızılca Tepesi	Kızılca	Kurşunlu	tumulus	0.02	2	H
PS061	Alakır Mevkii	Yeşilöz	Kurşunlu	tumulus	0.03	2	H
PS073	Bozoğlu tumulus	Bozoğlu	Çerkeş	tumulus	0.01	2	H
PS076	Ağaca tumulus	Ağaca	Çerkeş	tumulus	0.02	2	H
PS082	Dere Yaylası		Çerkeş	rock-cut site	0.01	2	F
PS083	Karamustafa		Çerkeş	rock-cut tomb	0.02	2	F
PS106	Çeştepe Mahallesi	Eskipazar	Eskipazar	tumulus	0.07	2	H
PS107	İstasyon Mahallesi	Eskipazar	Eskipazar	tumulus	0.07	2	H
PS123	İnceboğaz Tepe		Eskipazar	tumulus	0.03	2	H
PS128	Sadeyaka		Eskipazar	tumulus	0.26	4	H
PS129	Saraycık	Saraycık	Eskipazar	tumulus	0.28	4	H
PS132	Bölükören Mevkii	Bölükören	Eskipazar	tumulus	0.03	2	H
PS142	Karakoyunlu	Karakoyunlu	Ovacık	rock-cut tomb	0.02	2	F
PS145	Kuz Mevkii	Yüreören	Ovacık	tumulus	0.02	2	H
PS145a	Kuz Mevkii	Yüreören	Ovacık	tumulus	0.02	2	H
PS146	Kuz Mevkii	Yüreören	Ovacık	tumulus	0.07	2	H
PS164	İç Yenice		Merkez	tumulus	0.03	2	H
PS164a	İç Yenice		Merkez	tumulus	0.03	2	H
PS175	Eski Mezar Mevkii	Alagöz	Kızılırmak	tumulus	0.02	2	H
PS187	Güvey Tepesi	Çankırı	Merkez	tumulus?, cemetery?	1.50	5	H
PS192	İkizören		Yapraklı	tumulus	0.02	2	H
PS200	Dikenli		Korgun	tumulus	0.03	2	H
PS211	Deliklikaya		Merkez	rock-cut tomb	0.01	2	F
PS213	Bağkapısı	Belenli	Bayramören	tumulus	0.02	2	H
PS215	Dere Mağarası	Dere Mahallesi	Bayramören	natural cave/ rock shelter	0.01	2	F
PS220	Çatalkaya Tumulus	Salur	Orta	tumulus	0.02	2	H
PS223	Siviş Göl	Çivi	Merkez	tumulus	0.02	2	H
PS225	Bulancer Göl	Yeşil Dumlurpınar	Kurşunlu	tumulus	0.02	2	H
PS228	Eskipazar	Eskipazar	Eskipazar	rock-cut steps	0.36	4	F
PS234	Dedeköy Tumulus	Dedeköy	Çivi	tumulus	0.02	2	H
PS236	Şabanözü Tumulus	Şabanözü	Eldivan	tumulus	0.02	2	H

Table 5.4. Tumuli and rock-cut sites

Chapter Five

Site number	Site name	Village (or nearest)	İlçe	Type of site	Site area (ha)	Size category	Classification category
PS237	İnceboğaz Mevkii	İnceboğaz	Eskipazar	tumulus	0.02	2	H
PS241	Tokmakoğlu		Eskipazar	tumulus	0.02	2	H
PS242	Kadıköy		Çerkeş	tumulus	0.07	2	H
Çivi 03S01				tumulus	0.02	2	H
Çivi 03S02				tumulus	0.05	2	H
Çivi 03S03				tumulus	0.01	2	H
Çivi 03S04				tumulus	0.01	2	H
Çivi 03S05				tumulus	0.01	2	H
Çivi 04S03				tumulus	0.02	2	H
Ilgaz 01S04				tumulus	0.01	2	H
Ilgaz 05S02				tumulus	0.05	2	H
Eldivan 05S01				tumulus	0.02	2	H
Dumanlı 02S01				tumulus	0.02	2	H
Dumanlı 02S02				tumulus	0.02	2	H
Dumanlı 02S03				rock-cut tombs	0.50	4	F
Dumanlı 03S01				tumulus	0.02	2	H
Salur 02S05				tumulus	0.02	2	H
Dağtarla 01S01				tumulus	0.01	2	H
Dağtarla 01S02				tumulus	0.06	2	H
Dağtarla 01S03				tumulus	0.02	2	H
Dağtarla 03S01				tumulus	0.01	2	H

Table 5.4 (continued). Tumuli and rock-cut sites

A Dark Age, Grey Ware and Elusive Empires: Paphlagonia through the Iron Age, 1200–330 BC

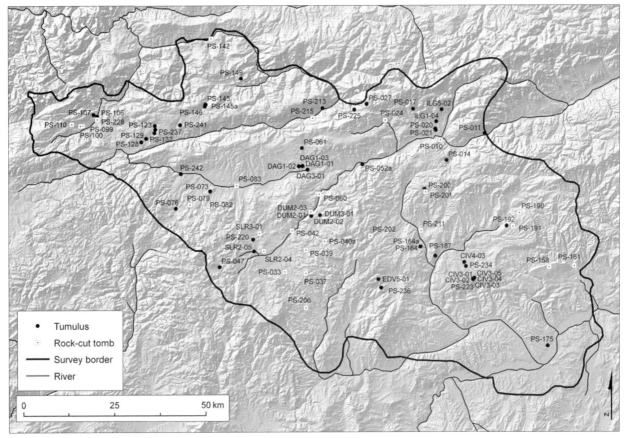

Fig. 5.8. Burial tumuli and rock-cut tombs located in Project Paphlagonia

Fig. 5.9. Illicitly excavated tumulus PS129

In Anatolia tumuli are used as a means of human burial for several centuries through the first millennium BC and a little beyond, originating in burial practices of Thrace and southeast Europe. Legally excavated examples in Anatolia span at the latest the eighth century BC at Kaynarca near Niğde (Summers 1994: 245) and at Ankara (Strobel 2002: 9), with many cases also known from the Hellenistic period (Bilgi 1999; Strobel 2002: 20), as at İnandık (Özgüç 1988: xxx), and into Roman times as indicated by a group of over 100 tumuli around the Roman site of Sarnıç-Küçükkuyu in central Anatolia (Omura 2003: 54, figs 3–4). Clear evidence for continued use of tumuli into the Roman period is attested by inscribed funerary stelae intended to be erected on or beside tumuli as grave markers (Marek 2003: 137; see also Chapter Six this volume). Chambers of dressed stone, often exquisitely shaped and fitted, characterise the interiors of many tumuli across Anatolia (Koşay 1941: pl. 45), a feature also of Iron Age tumuli in Thrace (Kitov 1999). As mentioned above, evidence for such stone-work is clear in several of the illicitly excavated tumuli in Paphlagonia, as at PS061 (fig. 5.6).

Tumuli in Project Paphlagonia are located either on natural ridges and spurs, where a desire for maximum visibility was clearly paramount (fig. 5.10), or less frequently on and around lowland plains usually as single tumuli (fig. 5.11). This latter group comprises generally much larger tumuli than those found on high ridges, which more frequently occur as groups of aligned tumuli. There are no obvious connections between the geographical distribution of tumuli and that of Iron Age settlement sites.

Rock-cut tombs and sites

It has been proposed that tombs cut into vertical rock faces, encountered sporadically in the often vertiginous Paphlagonian landscape, have their ancestry in Achaemenid burial practices in Iran (L'vov-Basirov 2001), while the co-existing practice of burial under tumuli indicates an adoption of existing Anatolian burial tradition into the scope of Achaemenid funerary custom. More specifically Gropp (2001: 40) suggests that the rock-cut tomb at Kalekapı near Süleymanköy/Koryleion, in Kastamonu province, which von Gall (1966: 14; 1967) posits as that of a local Paphlagonian king of fifth to fourth century BC date, could more likely be that of the Persian satrap Orontobates. Generally, von Gall (1966: 122) dates the Paphlagonian rock-cut tombs to

Fig. 5.10. Tumulus PS017 on high spur

A Dark Age, Grey Ware and Elusive Empires: Paphlagonia through the Iron Age, 1200–330 BC

Fig. 5.11. Lowland tumulus PS021

comparability in political terms to its Hittite predecessor is increasingly being proposed (Postgate 2007: 149). Significant continuities in occupation of Paphlagonian sites from the Late Bronze Age into the Middle Iron Age, with or without an Early Iron Age component, further strengthen such a proposal.

The Late Iron Age evidence from our survey is perhaps the most difficult of all to characterise and interpret, tempted as we are to adduce the available written sources, though from outside the region, as a framework for comprehension of the region's socio-political development through this period. What cannot be denied is the broad range of influences, from all points of the compass, on the communities of Inner Paphlagonia during the last centuries of the Iron Age, epitomised not only in their ceramic repertoires but most vividly in their varied and distinctive burial practices.

within a period stretching from the early fifth century BC to the third century AD. In our survey six single rock-cut tombs, probably all of Late Iron Age date, were recorded (PS024, PS083, PS142, PS201, PS202 [see Marek 2003: Abb. 53], PS211 [fig. 5.12]), plus one agglomeration of at least a dozen tombs along the banks of the Devrez as it cuts through a steep gorge (fig. 5.8). These latter were first identified by Leonhard in his travels of 1899–1903 (Leonhard 1915). The most significant rock-cut tomb in Inner Paphlagonia is that of Karakoyunlu (PS142), a spectacular monument already published in full by Leonhard (1915: 269–77) and von Gall (1966: 73–82), and dated to the second half of the fourth century BC (Marek 2003: 32) (fig. 5.13). Other groups of rock-cut tombs lacking chronologically specific features are impossible to date with certainty and many are likely to be of Hellenistic/Roman/Byzantine construction and use.

Fig. 5.12. Rock-cut tomb PS211, Deliklikaya

Conclusions: imperial impacts?

In conclusion, we can state that the Iron Age evidence from Project Paphlagonia is patchy and not easy to interpret. Available stratified ceramic sequences from not too distant sites such as Boğazköy, Gordion and Kaman-Kalehöyük at least enable us to situate the Paphlagonia Iron Age sites within a relatively secure chronological framework, even if the socio-political contexts remain largely aloof. Following the collapse of the Hittite state at the end of the Late Bronze Age, Inner Paphlagonia partakes of a regional episode of obscurity arguably characterised by a hiatus in settlement, followed by sporadic evidence for a resurgence of settlement spread and density that may accompany the rise to ascendancy of a powerful, Phrygian state whose

Fig. 5.13. Rock-cut tomb PS142, Karakoyunlu

Chapter Five

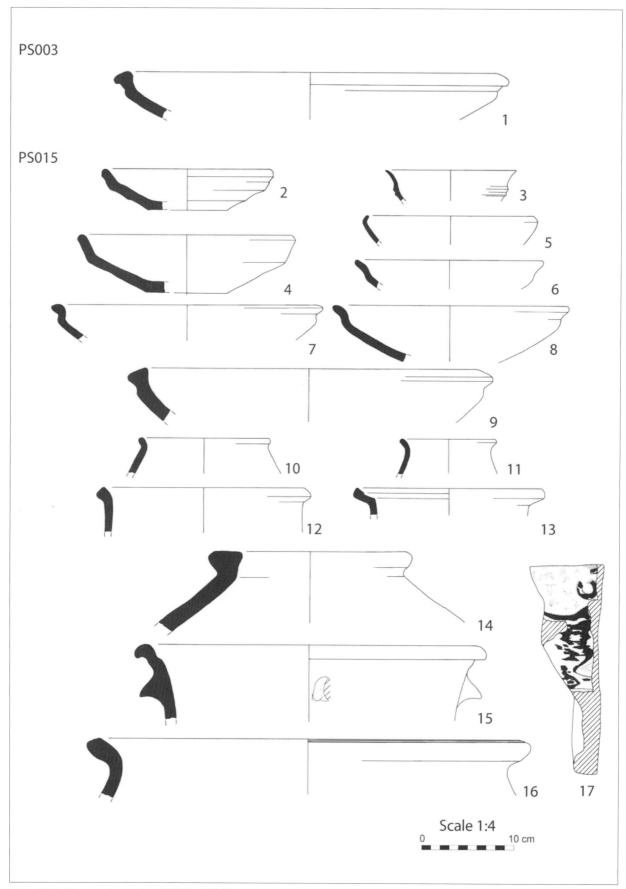

Fig. 5.14. Pottery from sites PS003, PS015

Fig. No.	Site No.	Hand	Wheel	Inclusions	Colour	Finish
1	PS003			mf min	7.5 YR 5/2 surface 7.5 YR 6/4	brn int and ext
2	PS015		X	m dense min	fabric 10 YR 5/2	ext traces of brn
3	PS015		X	f min	2.5 YR 5/6	ext and int brn; ridges
4	PS015		X	m min	5 YR 5/3	
5	PS015		X	m min	2.5 Y 5/2	ext and int brn
6	PS015		X	dense min	10 YR 6/3	ext and int brn
7	PS015		X	f min	5 YR 5/6	ext and int brn
8	PS015		X	f sparse min	2.5 YR 5/6	ext and int brn
9	PS015		X	dense min	7.5 YR 5/2	
10	PS015		X	dense min	10 YR 6/3	ext brn
11	PS015		X	shell	7.5 YR 4/0 core dark grey	ext and int brn
12	PS015		X	m min	5 YR 6/4	
13	PS015		X	dense min	dark grey N4/0	ext and int brn
14	PS015		X	m min	10 YR 6/4	ext brn
15	PS015		X	m min	7.5 YR 4/2	ext and int brn
16	PS015		X	f min	5 YR 6/4	ext and int brn
17	PS015				2.5 YR 5/6	white paint 10 YR 8/2 dark grey paint 7.5 YR N/4

Fig. 5.14 (catalogue). Pottery from sites PS003, PS015. Abbreviations used in the pottery and object figure catalogues: h = high; m =medium; l = low; min = mineral; veg = vegetal; inc = inclusions; v = very; f = fine; c = coarse; ext = exterior; int = interior; brn = burnished; smoo = smoothed

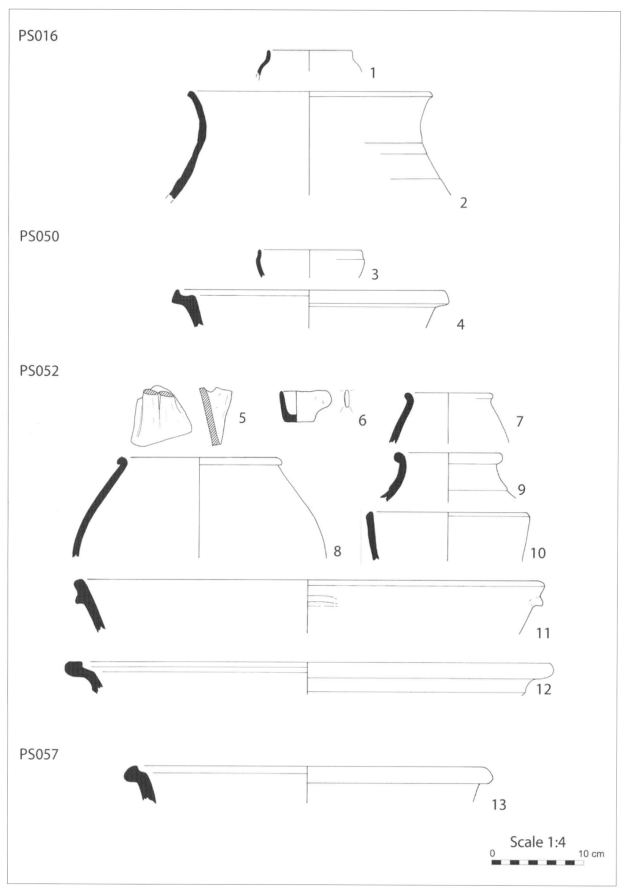

Fig. 5.15. Pottery from sites PS016, PS050, PS052, PS057

A Dark Age, Grey Ware and Elusive Empires: Paphlagonia through the Iron Age, 1200–330 BC

Fig. No.	Site No.	Hand	Wheel	Inclusions	Colour	Finish
1	PS016		X	sparse min, veg	2.5 YR 6/6	ext and int rim brn 2.5 YR 5/6
2	PS016		X	min, veg	5 YR 6/4	ext upper rim traces of red brn 2.5 YR 4/4
3	PS050	X		sparse min	5 YR 7/4 core grey	ext and int brn int 2.5 YR 6/6
4	PS050		X	f min	2.5 YR 5/6	top rim and ext brn int slipped 7.5 YR 7/6 ext 7.5 YR 6/8
5	PS052		X	sparse f min	10 YR 5/1	ext brn
6	PS052		X	m min	7.5 YR 6/4	ext upper body and int slightly brn
7	PS052		X	dense min	5 YR 6/4	ext upper body and int slightly brn
8	PS052		X	dense min	7.5 YR 6/4	ext upper body and int slightly brn
9	PS052		X	dense min	7.5 YR 5/2	upper body ext and int slightly brn
10	PS052	X		m min	7.5 YR 5/2	brn
11	PS052	X		dense min	10 YR 6/2	lug handle
12	PS052		X	sparse f min	10 YR 5/1	ext and int brn
13	PS057		X	f-m min	pink	lower body traces of red paint 7.5 YR 7/4-7/6

Fig. 5.15 (catalogue). Pottery from sites PS016, PS050, PS052, PS057

Chapter Five

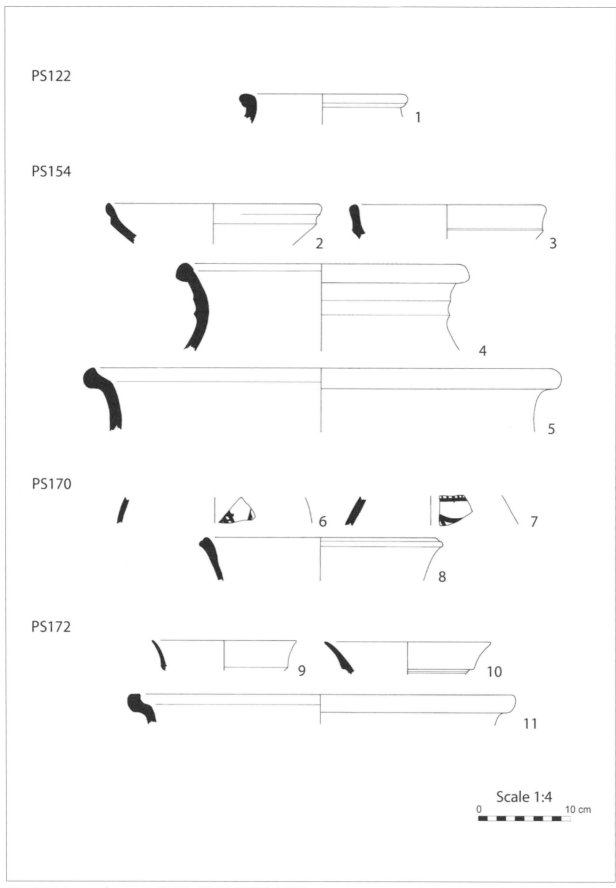

Fig. 5.16. Pottery from sites PS122, PS154, PS170, PS172

Fig. No.	Site No.	Hand	Wheel	Inclusions	Colour	Finish
1	PS122		X	sparse f min	5 YR 7/6	ext lightly smoo int finishing marks
2	PS154		X	f-m min	10 YR 4/1	ext brn
3	PS154		X	dense f min	2.5 Y 4/0	ext and rim top brn
4	PS154		X	dense min	10 YR 5/1	
5	PS154		X	f-m min	10 YR 4/1	ext brn
6	PS170		X	m min	5 YR 6/4	ext slip 10 YR 7/6 paint 5 YR 5/6
7	PS170		X	m min	5 YR 6/4	ext slip 10 YR 7/6 paint 5 YR 5/6
8	PS170		X	c min	7.5 YR 7/4 surfaces 10 YR 8/4 to 2.5 Y 8/2	
9	PS172		X	no visible inc	core 5 YR 6/6	ext and int slip 10 R 5/4
10	PS172		X	no visible inc	core 5 YR 6/4	ext and int slip 10 R 5/6
11	PS172		X	sparse min, veg	5 YR 6/6	ext and int brn

Fig. 5.16 (catalogue). Pottery from sites PS122, PS154, PS170, PS172

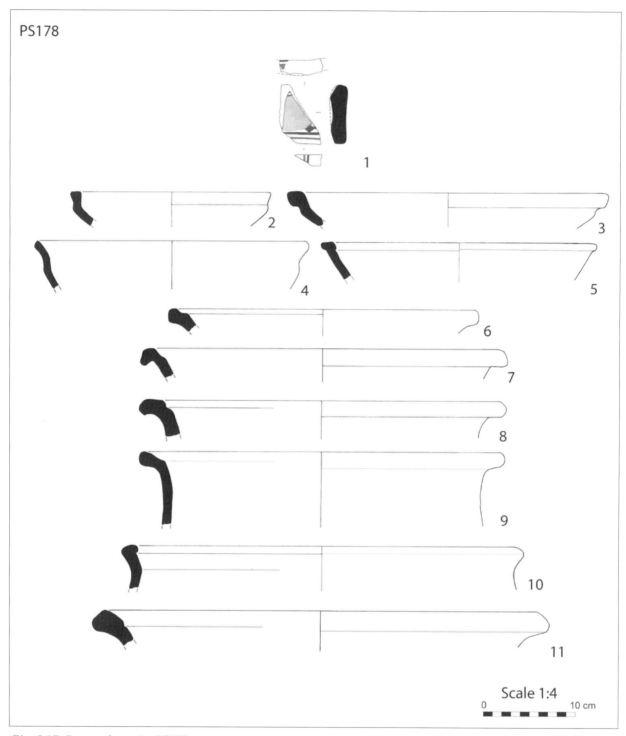

Fig. 5.17. Pottery from site PS178

Fig. No.	Site No.	Hand	Wheel	Inclusions	Colour	Finish
1	PS178			no visible inc		painted decoration 5 YR 7/5, 5 YR 5/6, 5 YR 4/1
2	PS178		X?	m min	10 YR 6/2	ext top and int brn
3	PS178		X	sparse min	10 YR 5/2	ext brn
4	PS178		X	sparse min	10 YR 5/2	ext brn
5	PS178		X	m min	10 YR 5/1	
6	PS178		X	sparse min, veg	2.5 YR 6/4	ext and int brn
7	PS178		X	sparse min	10 YR 5/2	ext brn
8	PS178		X	sparse min	10 YR 5/2	ext brn
9	PS178		X	sparse min, veg	10 YR 5/1	ext and int brn
10	PS178		X	f min	5 YR 7/1	brn
11	PS178		X	sparse min	10 YR 5/2	ext brn

Fig. 5.17 (catalogue). Pottery from site PS178

Chapter Five

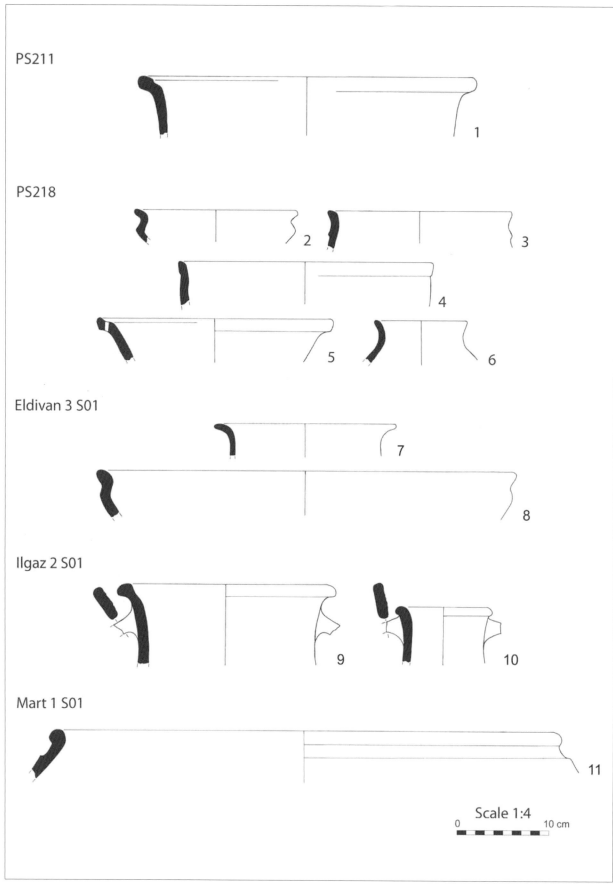

Fig. 5.18. Pottery from sites PS211, PS218, Eldivan 03S01, Ilgaz 02S01, Mart 01S01

Fig. No.	Site No.	Hand	Wheel	Inclusions	Colour	Finish
1	PS211		X	min, sparse veg	5 YR 4/2 ext 5 YR 5/3	ext and int brn (?)
2	PS218			m min	Phrygian grey ware	ext brn
3	PS218			m min	Phrygian grey ware	ext brn
4	PS218	X		m min		
5	PS218					
6	PS218			m min	Phrygian grey ware	ext brn
7	Eldivan 03S01			s-m min	5 YR 7/3	
8	Eldivan 03S01			s-m min	5 YR 6/6	
9	Ilgaz 02S01			dense min, mica	10 YR 6/1	
10	Ilgaz 02S01			m min	2.5 YR 6/6	
11	Mart 01S01			m-c min	5 YR 7/6	

Fig. 5.18 (catalogue). Pottery from sites PS211, PS218, Eldivan 03S01, Ilgaz 02S01, Mart 01S01

Chapter Six

Landscapes with Figures:
Paphlagonia through the Hellenistic, Roman and Byzantine Periods, 330 BC–AD 1453

Roger Matthews, Michael Metcalfe and Daniela Cottica

Introduction

Alexander's march and the progress of the Hellenistic age across Anatolia do not appear to have had a significant material impact upon the inhabitants of Inner Paphlagonia, just as the preceding centuries of Achaemenid rule are hard to discern in material culture attributes, as we have seen in the previous chapter. From the historical and archaeological sources, however, it is possible to pick out distinctive elements that appear to characterise an Inner Paphlagonian trajectory through the period in question, as we consider below. It is not the intention here to provide an exhaustive discussion of every historical event or source relating to the past of Inner Paphlagonia over such a long and eventful time period, but rather to employ the sources to construct a meaningful framework of social and political context within which the significance of the detected settlement patterns and other evidence may most suitably be appreciated.

The rather lengthy period in question can most validly be considered in three sequential stages, in each case taking the form of a historical sketch followed by a discussion of the relevant archaeological evidence from the survey. We treat each section by firstly providing a chronological framework rooted in the now relatively rich and diverse historical sources, before reviewing the archaeological evidence from the region for settlement and land use, concluding with a consideration of the epigraphic evidence recorded within the remit of Project Paphlagonia.

Problems of identification and interpretation

As with other periods of the Paphlagonian past there are special issues in dealing with the available ceramic evidence from all phases reviewed in this chapter. Above all, the absence of excavated well-stratified assemblages from the region renders difficult almost all identifications. Only the most egregious finewares and forms can with some confidence be assigned to specific episodes within the Hellenistic, Roman and Byzantine periods, and even here the comparanda are from distant locations, generally far to the west and southwest in the Aegean world. A host of coarsewares cannot be assigned to any particular period. Other specific ceramic issues include: the relative lack of clearly Hellenistic material, with some evidence for continuity of form and finish from the preceding Iron Age into the Hellenistic era, as also attested on the Konya plain and in the Amasya region (Dönmez 2005: 69); the common occurrence of late Roman and early Byzantine red-slipped wares; the occasional presence of medieval and post-medieval forms and fabrics (also poorly understood) and; a lack of knowledge of local traditions in pottery manufacture in terms of wares, forms and decoration. As with the prehistoric and early historic periods discussed in earlier chapters, there is every possibility of morphological and fabric continuity over centuries within the periods studied here. Only excavation of appropriate sites in the region of Paphlagonia will begin to ameliorate the impact of these and other factors. Overall, the best attested episode of occupation is early Roman, while the Byzantine period is most richly attested by coarsewares that are usually awkward to date precisely. Frequent occurrences of baked clay tiles are even more difficult to assign to specific periods.

At the broader level, our attempt here to situate the specifics of the Paphlagonia results for the Hellenistic, Roman and Byzantine periods within a wider geographic remit is fraught with difficulties, the major one being the relative lack of interest displayed by most survey directors in these periods. Many survey projects pay no respect at all to this almost 2,000-year long era, or fail to distinguish sufficiently between the various episodes of which it is constituted, or do not establish an appropriate site categorisation that might enable detection and exploration of size hierarchies and other demographic concerns (these issues as they relate to the Hellenistic period have been neatly critiqued by Erciyas 2006a: 4–5, 55–56). Nevertheless, keeping these problems firmly in mind, we may take some tentative steps along the synthetic road, encouraged not least by the stimulating work of Alcock (1994; 2001) in essaying broad syntheses of settlement patterns, demography and society across the entire Hellenistic world.

A Hellenistic highland kingdom, 330–6 BC

> The interior, on the other hand, like Pontus, was wholly Asianic in character. Its mountain-folk, largely small farmers, lived in the primitive village-organizations characteristic of a country which was unaffected by Hellenism. The only city of which we know was Gangra, not, geographically speaking, in Paphlagonia at all, but in the fruitful valley of a river which flows southward from the watershed separating the district from Galatia.
>
> (Magie 1950: 188)

Recent studies of the Pontic region and the royal house of Pontus have stressed two features in particular (Bosworth, Wheatley 1998; Mitchell 2002; forthcoming; Erciyas 2006a; 2006b): the distinctive character of the societies of the region through the Hellenistic age (and beyond) and the deliberate association of the Pontic élite, in the form of the Mithridatid dynasty, with a claimed Achaemenid Persian past. The key event for our purposes is the rise to power in the last years of the fourth century BC of Mithridates Ctistes, the 'Founder', who at the death of his uncle, also Mithridates, a ruler in the region of Mysia to the west of Paphlagonia, founded a new fortified base at a place called by Strabo (12.3.41) Kimiata in the region of Kinistene, lying beneath the mountain Olgassys (=modern Ilgaz range). According to Strabo, this site was used by Mithridates Ctistes as a base for operations in the Pontic region, and it was from here that Mithridates moved against Amaseia (=modern Amasya, Strabo's home town) where in turn a substantial stronghold was established (Magie 1950: 189; Mitchell 2002: 55). The subsequent twists and turns in the fortunes of the Mithridatic kings and their immediate successors over a period of some three centuries need not detain us here (see McGing 1986; Erciyas 2006a; 2006b): suffice to state that in the conflict between them and the rising power of Rome it is not hard to see a rerun of the Hittite-Kaska struggle of a millennium earlier, with a predominantly lowland power attempting to control and subdue a recalcitrant highland kingdom. The difference with the Rome-Mithridatid case, however, is that, unlike the Hittites, the Romans did succeed in subduing the highland zone and in incorporating the region fully into their empire by the end of the first century BC, with significant impacts on settlement and land use, as we shall see.

A key consideration for the Hellenistic period is the possible location of the site called Kimiata by Strabo, a fortified stronghold established by Mithridates Ctistes at the end of the fourth century BC and localised by Strabo as below the mountainous country of the Olgassys (Marek 1993: 123–24). Inscriptions found at and near the village of Deresamail close to Eskipazar indicate that Strabo's toponyms should be emended to Kimista of the region Kimistene (Bosworth, Wheatley 1998: 164; Mitchell 2002: 53). One inscription (PPI.13), on a statue base dedicated to the Roman emperor Caracalla, AD 211–217, mentions the people and elders of Kimistene (Kaygusuz 1983a: 112, no. 1; *SEG* 1983: 1097). This statue base now lies on its side (figs 6.82–6.83) towards the summit of Asar Tepe (PS096), a towering peak that dominates the local landscape and enjoys commanding views of the valley far below (fig. 6.1). In the same field lies a fragment with an inscription dedicated to Diocletian, AD 284–305 (Kaygusuz 1983a: 113, no. 2; *SEG* 1983: 1098).

Asar Tepe is briefly discussed, although not visited, by Leonhard (1915: 146) under the name of 'das Kale bei Samail'. Earlier still, at the end of the 19th century, the site was visited by Mendel who first recorded the dedication to Zeus Kimistenos discussed below (Mendel 1901: 24, no. 161). Mendel relates how he conducted excavations here without unearthing new inscriptions but encountering many architectural fragments – columns, square column bases, entablature, sarcophagus pieces – as well as a large stone plaque with a depiction of a bearded horseman. The site is reported by Kaygusuz (1983a: 112; 1984) as being a major settlement with associated inscriptions, but he holds back from identifying the location with Strabo's Kimiata, partly due to the Kimiata/Kimista confusion, but also because his candidate for Kimiata is a site, 100km to the east, at Kurmalar near Ilgaz town, an identification followed by Foss (2000: map 86 D3) in his recent map of Paphlagonia in the Greek and Roman periods. As Kaygusuz notes (1983b: 60), Kurmalar (our site PS003) does indeed have pottery ranging in date from the seventh century BC to the third century AD and sits on a level high terrace overlooking the valley of a tributary of the Devrez (fig. 6.2; see also Marek 2003: Abb. 153), but the site is not defensively situated and inscriptions from the nearby village do not mention Kimiata or Kimiatene. Earlier

Fig. 6.1. View from summit of Asar Tepe, PS096, facing northwest, with extensive platform in the foreground and traces of illicit digging

Fig. 6.2. Site PS003, Kurmalar

attempts to date one inscription from Kurmalar (PPI.1; *SEG* 1983: 1113) to the Hellenistic period are not convincing. Doubtless the proximity of the site to the looming peaks of Ilgaz/Olgassys encouraged Kaygusuz to see here the location of Strabo's Kimiata, broadly agreeing with an earlier attempt at the localisation of Kimiata by Leonhard in the vicinity of modern Ilgaz town (named as Kotshhisar on Kiepert's map in Leonhard 1915).

The hilltop site of Asar Tepe (our site PS096) by Deresamail is the strongest candidate in the entire Çankırı/Karabük region for Strabo's Kimiata. It lies at the junction of two major routes, one east-west across northern Anatolia, another south-north to Safranbolu and the Black Sea beyond. Reached by a stiff climb from Deresamail village, Asar Tepe comprises many elements, loosely spread over a total area of some 50ha, including inscriptions, rock-carvings (one horse and rider), rock-cut tombs and steps, and a light scatter of pottery and tile. A significant feature is a deliberately levelled terrace of ground, ca. 40m by 40m in dimensions, which has received much attention from illicit diggers (fig. 6.1). Here there are clear traces of finely constructed dressed stone walls around the edges and in the interior of the terrace, as well as superbly carved architectural elements that have been unearthed and smashed by treasure hunters, including representations of an eagle and an elephant, sadly no longer recognisable as such (figs 6.3–6.5).

Fig. 6.4. Architectural element illicitly excavated at Asar Tepe, PS096. Parts of an eagle in relief can be discerned at the right

Fig. 6.5. Architectural element, said originally to have had a depiction of an elephant, at Asar Tepe, PS096

Fig. 6.3. Architectural element illicitly excavated at Asar Tepe, PS096

At the eastern corner of the terrace there is a rock outcrop that serves as a natural gateway to the pinnacle of Asar Tepe and here an inscription (PPI.14) has been cut into the rock face within a dove-tail cartouche (*tabula ansata*) (fig. 6.84). The inscription is a Roman imperial dedication to Zeus Kimistenos (Mendel 1901: 24, no. 161; Robert 1980: 222; Kaygusuz 1983a: 113, no. 3; *SEG* 1983: 1099), and is also in danger of destruction by modern hacking at the adjacent rock. There can be little doubt that Asar Tepe hosted a temple or shrine dedicated to this local divinity. Another inscription from Pompeiopolis, 150km to the northeast across the Ilgaz range, mentions a certain Synphorus, a citizen of Hadrianopolis, as setting up an altar to Zeus Kimistenos, clearly a local deity (Wilson 1960: 159–60). Hadrianopolis is located immediately west of the modern town of Eskipazar (see below) and only 12km from Asar Tepe. We may assume that these Roman-period associations of Zeus Kimistenos with the vicinity of Asar Tepe and Hadrianopolis were rooted in existing patterns of cult and religion of Hellenistic and doubtless earlier date. Indeed, recent work by Laflı in and around Asar Tepe has recovered sherds of Phrygian grey ware, suggesting a long history to occupation at this site (Laflı, Zäh 2008).

Strabo (12.3.39) mentions such shrines as densely distributed across the Olgassys mountain (Robert 1980: 214). Two inscriptions from Kurmalar near Ilgaz relate to a temple of Hera of Kandara, mentioning stoas, a banqueting hall and kitchens (PPI.1A–B; Kaygusuz 1983b: 59–60; Mitchell 1993b: 23; Marek 2003: 107, Abb. 153–55; SEG 1983: 1113–14) (figs 6.61–6.62). Other parallels for such shrines in the Pontic region in the Hellenistic period can be found at locations such as another Asar Tepe, this one on a ridge high above the Black Sea coast near Sinop, where finds of pottery, bull figurines and Mithridatic coins confirm its Hellenistic date (Işın 1998: 109, site 44). Other sites of this date located through survey in the Sinop region, such as Çukurhankale (Işın 1998: 105, site 31), are also likely to have served as strategically located fortified bases during the decades of conflict between the Pontic kings and Rome.

Lying as it does at the western outliers of the Olgassys range, it is highly probable that Asar Tepe is indeed the location of Kimiata/Kimista in Kinistene/Kimistene and thus served as the base for the Pontic operations of Mithridates Ctistes as he founded and expanded his highland kingdom in the years around 300 BC. As with countless other sites in this and other parts of Turkey, Asar Tepe is in sore need of an integrated programme of recording, survey, excavation, preservation and, above all, protection.

The migration from Europe into Anatolia in the 270s BC of significant numbers of Celtic Galatians and their settlement in the region broadly centred on modern Ankara (Mitchell 1993a: 19) appear not greatly to have impacted on the archaeology of the adjacent region of Inner Paphlagonia. The distinctive fine painted pottery known as Galatian ware (Strobel 2002: 28) is not found in our survey region, but appears to be largely localised within the area of Galatian settlement. The temptation to associate hilltop fortified sites across north-central Anatolia with a Galatian presence needs to be resisted, while strongest and most justified in the areas of the Galatian settlement itself, such as Ankara province (Darbyshire et al. 2000). As we discuss below, fortified hilltop sites in our survey region are difficult to date, given the scarcity of pottery in and around the sites, but where there is good dating evidence it almost always suggests a date, of occupation if not also construction, in the later centuries of the Byzantine age (see below).

Due to the special problems of ceramic dating outlined above, we have no great confidence in the authenticity of the distribution map of detected Hellenistic (plus Hellenistic–Roman) sites in Paphlagonia (fig. 6.6), even accepting it as a highly refined sample study. Nevertheless, the apparent rarity of sites of this period in our survey does fit with a broader pattern that may be detected both locally and globally in the Hellenistic world. In the Kastamonu survey several sites, including cist-grave cemeteries, are claimed as being of Hellenistic date but it is not clear on exactly what basis in terms of ceramic types (Kuzucuoğlu et al. 1997: 288). Erciyas's bold study (2006a: 53–62) of settlement distribution and continuity across north-central Anatolia, directly east of Paphlagonia, highlights a dramatic decline, by about 50%, in settlement from the Late Iron Age into the Hellenistic period, a pattern she associates with a possible trend to urbanisation and settlement agglomeration in certain regions. These local trends agree well with apparent global shifts in settlement style and distribution underlined in Alcock's studies of the Hellenistic world, where she points to an abandonment of rural settlement and associated increased urbanisation as key characteristics of the Hellenistic and perhaps early Roman periods (1994: 188; 2001: 332). Other regions of Anatolia, however, appear to host a steady rise in both numbers of settlements and aggregate site area from the Iron Age into the Hellenistic era (Baird 2004: 232).

Undoubtedly a major factor in determining settlement preferences in Paphlagonia through the Hellenistic centuries was the unremitting warfare and disquiet visited upon the region in the course of the Mithridatic wars. Expanding on our earlier parallel with the Hittite-Kaska situation of the Late Bronze Age, it is improbable that farmers and villagers felt confident enough to live in isolated farmsteads and hamlets without complete security in the countryside. Once more at empire's edge, the region was too vigorously contested for that, and remote hilltop sites such as Asar Tepe, PS096, are more likely to be quite typical of the place and period. It is also notable that of the few securely identified Hellenistic sites in our survey, a few take the form of settlement on *höyüks*. This represents the last flourishing of this *modus vivendi*, for from the Roman period onwards *höyüks* are more or less totally abandoned in favour of living on flat expanses of land either adjacent to existing *höyüks* or in completely new locations, a phenomenon that appears common to all of Turkey.

Tumuli, terraces, lions
Burial of the dead in lined or constructed chambers under mounds of earth in the form of tumuli appears in Anatolia earlier in the first millennium BC (see Chapter Five) and, as with use of rock-cut tombs, continues as a common practice into the periods considered in this chapter. In the Hellenistic and early Roman periods there is good evidence for the construction of a flat terrace adjacent to

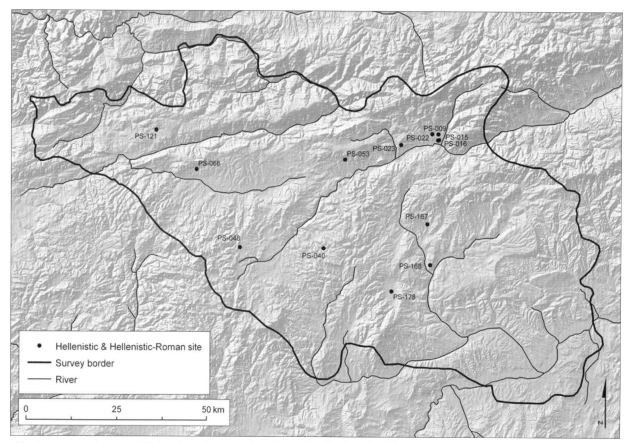

Fig. 6.6. Hellenistic and Hellenistic–Roman sites located in Project Paphlagonia

tumuli as a location for sculpture and doubtless the practice of a cult of the dead (Strobel 2002: 19). Illegal excavations at the Danacı tumulus near Tavium recovered at least one, probably two, stone lions and lion fragments were found during legal excavations at the great Karalar tumulus of the younger Deiotarus, just north of Ankara (Strobel 2002: 19). A few of our tumuli have clear evidence for an associated earthen platform to one side, (fig. 6.7), which may well have been adorned with cultic structures and lion sculptures. Stone lions found during our survey generally lack secure provenance but are likely to originate from such tumuli and associated terraces, of Hellenistic or early Roman date. Two stone lions currently on display in front of the *kaymakamlık* at Ilgaz (figs 6.8–6.9) are doubtless the same as those alleged to have been excavated from Salman East in the early 20th century (Belke 1996: 224). In the adjacent province of Kastamonu finds of stone lions have also been dated to the Hellenistic period (Marro et al. 1998: 326), while more broadly, the large-scale depiction of lions in stone in north-central Anatolia may date back to the Persian period (Durugönül 1994: 152). There are also indications from later, Roman, inscriptions that funerary stelae were occasionally erected on top of tumuli to mark and name the inhabitant of the grave within (Marek 2003: 137, Abb. 205).

In the Roman empire, 6/5 BC–AD 285

Thus ... northern Asia Minor developed from a rude barbarian tract of unexploited mountainous country, devoid of civilization, to become part of a complex urbanized empire, whose relics (though sparse) are still to be seen by the diligent enquirer.

(Wilson 1960: 544)

By the time of its absorption into the expanding Roman empire at the end of the first century BC, Inner Paphlagonia, like much of Asia Minor, had seen several centuries of recurrent warfare. It is hardly surprising that in this environment, as in the Late Bronze Age a millennium earlier, the intensity of human settlement remained patchy and hesitant: 'If inland Pontus had made little progress beyond that stage of development where the populace lived in villages and the princes in rocky fortresses, inland Paphlagonia had made none at all' (Wilson 1960: 481). Following Pompey's defeat of Mithridates and the latter's death in 63 BC, the lands of Paphlagonia were divided between Attalus and Pylaemenes (Mitchell 1993a: 33). Pompey's efforts to integrate the region into the Roman world included the founding of five cities along the line of the northern

Fig. 6.7. Tumulus with adjacent earthen platform, PS128

Fig. 6.8. Stone lion at the kaymakamlık *of Ilgaz, PS022*

Fig. 6.9. Stone lion at the kaymakamlık *of Ilgaz, PS022*

steady increase in the density and intensity of settlement and ever-expanding agricultural exploitation of the resources of the land. These developments were no doubt encouraged by the incorporation of Inner Paphlagonia into the province of Galatia in 6/5 BC (Mitchell 1993b: 152), although the Kaisareia Hadrianopolis region appears to have been annexed to Bithynia already in 63 BC (Mitchell 1993a: 92–93). We can examine this broad process through historical and archaeological study of the major urban centres of the region, few as they are, followed by a consideration of the settlement patterns discernible through our survey work.

Cities, towns and roads of Inner Paphlagonia

Inner Paphlagonia, like much of its surrounding territory, has never been a heavily urbanised area. Long and painful episodes of conflict, involving chronic raiding and occasionally severe military activity, have not encouraged the aggregation of large proportions of the population in cities or even large villages. When threats have come, as often they have, the default response has been to run for the hills and hide. For the proper administration and efficient taxation of the region, however, as required by an imperial power with designs on the area, the presence of an urban network was essential. Only so could be provided the facilities and accoutrements of bureaucracy and control, along with the amenities – baths, temples, imported goods, metalled roads – demanded by a landed gentry serving as an imperial administrative élite. As elsewhere in their empire, Roman annexation of Paphlagonia thus naturally led to the imposition of a system of control rooted in a network of towns and cities connected by secure and reliable roads. But this system was always fragile and would survive only as long as the imperial impetus that generated it:

> The urbanization of Bithynia, Paphlagonia, and Pontus retained to the end the artificial character which it had had at the beginning. The inhabitants of these regions did not take naturally to city life. The few cities that there were were either Greek colonies or artificial creations of the central government, and these cities ruled enormous territories where the primitive village life of the natives continued to flourish unaffected by them. Pompey had partitioned up the kingdoms into city territories for administrative convenience, and his system was maintained and extended by later rulers for the same motive. It had no effect on the civilization of the district, which remained essentially of a rural type.
>
> (Jones 1971: 172)

route through north-central Asia Minor (Marek 2003: Karte II), including Pompeiopolis itself (=modern Taşköprü) in the Amnias valley (=Gök Irmak). At this stage the Devrez valley with its own major east-west route through the region remained in the hands of local Paphlagonian princes (Magie 1950: 372). From then onwards, for a period of several centuries, we see a

We here examine the few attested cities and towns that formed part of that transient episode of control and administration when Inner Paphlagonia was integrated into an imperial system for the first time in its history. The cities that developed were perforce unique and fragile creations, nicely encapsulated in Yegül's phrases as 'a synthesis of ultimate and immediate sources, cosmopolitan practices, local needs and Anatolian traditions' (2000: 148).

Gangra, later Germanikopolis

Situated on the sweet waters of the Tatlı Çay, the modern town of Çankırı controls the approaches from the Anatolian plateau to the south to the Pontic ranges and the Black Sea itself to the north. It is not surprising that this city has a long and distinguished ancient history that includes millennia as a regional capital, as it remains to this day. Its modern name, Çankırı, is a direct descendant of its Iron Age name of Gangra, meaning 'goat' (Wilson 1960: 168), a name that may refer to the difficulty in ascent of the citadel that still towers over the town (fig. 6.10). The inhabitants of Gangra regarded their city and its nearby mountain, Olgassys, as 'the hearth of the gods' (Mitchell 1993b: 23). The visible ancient remains of Çankırı relate almost entirely to its role within the Byantine empire (see below) and it is unfortunate that we know much less about its history and especially its archaeology in earlier times (see also Belke 1996: 196–99).

In 179 BC a local prince, Morzius, was confirmed by the Romans as king of Paphlagonia, and a treasure taken by Pharnaces of Pontus from the treasury on the citadel at Gangra was returned (Polybius XXV.ii.9). Gangra remained the seat of local dynasties until the death of Deiotarus Philadelphus and the subsequent annexation of Inner Paphlagonia into the Roman province of Galatia in 6/5 BC (Mitchell 1993b: 152). Thereafter Gangra continued as regional capital, as indicated by the fact that the oath of allegiance sworn by the Paphlagonians in 4/3 BC was taken there (Magie 1950: 465; Jones 1971: 167; Mitchell 1993a: 92). A Roman town developed on the slopes below the citadel, taking the name of Germanikopolis at the time of Tiberius or Claudius, and coins of Caracalla struck at Gangra indicate that Gangra and Germanikopolis were one and the same place (Wilson 1960: 168; Jones 1971: 168; Mitchell 1993a: 93; Marek 2003: Abb. 93–94). These coins, which are issued in 'une orgie de monnayage' in the years AD 208–214 (Robert 1980: 219), boast of the city's status as 'most ancient of Paphlagonia' and portray the tall towers and structures of the citadel (Marek 2003: 64, 161). Coin depictions of a river bearing the name Xanthos have been interpreted as referring to the Tatlı Çay (Robert 1980: 209), which enters Çankırı from the north and provides the waters that give the immediate environs of the city its fertile aspect (fig. 6.11). Directly south of the city the

Fig. 6.10. Site PS168, Çankırı citadel, in distance with goat in foreground

Landscapes with Figures: Paphlagonia through the Hellenistic, Roman and Byzantine Periods, 330 BC–AD 1453

Fig. 6.11. The Tatlı Çay as it enters Çankırı town

Fig. 6.12. The Acı Çay to the south of Çankırı town

Fig. 6.13. Construction work on ancient site of Çankırı in 1997

river flows through a great rock-salt plateau which turns the waters bitter, giving the modern name Acı Çay; a salty stream capable of supporting none but the most salt-tolerant plants (fig. 6.12), which flows on to join the Kızılırmak. The Byzantine name for the Acı Çay appears to have been Halmyros (Belke 1996: 206; Foss 2000: 1219, map 86; but note that on Foss's Paphlagonia map the location of the Xanthos/Tatlı Çay needs to be placed to the north of Çankırı not to the south).

181

Archaeologically we know nothing about what must have been an extensive Roman and Byzantine town that grew up on the lower slopes of the citadel. Its remains are buried still under the modern town but occasional construction work encounters scraps of evidence in the form of columns, tiles and sherds (fig. 6.13). The remains visible today on the citadel date exclusively to the Byzantine and early Turkish era and are discussed below.

Kaisareia Hadrianopolis
A visit by Mendel in the late 19th century to the region of Eskipazar, then called Viranşehir or 'ruined city' and today in Karabük province, established through inscriptions the localisation of Kaisareia Hadrianopolis in this region (Mendel 1901; Marek 1993: 117). The foundation of the city under the name Kaisareia of the Proseilemmenitae is probably attributable to Augustus at the time of the annexation of Inner Paphlagonia to Galatia in 6/5 BC (Wilson 1960: 156; Jones 1971: 168). As Wilson (1960: 156) points out: 'Cities in Paphlagonia have always been relatively rare, and at this date were scarce indeed; the creation of a new city was perhaps an administrative necessity'. The inclusion of Kaisareia Hadrianopolis within Galatian Paphlagonia by at latest the time of Hadrian is indicated by an inscription mentioning C. Iulius Scapula, a governor of Galatia, AD 136–138, who is also attested in inscriptions from Ankyra (Marek 1993: 118; Mitchell 1993a: 93; 1993b: 53). The city was later refounded by Hadrian (or according to Mitchell 1993a: 93 not founded at all until then). Under the major reorganisation of Diocletian in the late third century AD Hadrianopolis was taken from Paphlagonia and added to the new province of Honorias in eastern Bithynia, and it is listed as a town by Hierocles and Justinian in the sixth century AD (Jones 1971: 537). It continues to be attested well into Byzantine times, for example in the march of the rebel Saborius from Melitene (Malatya) to Hadrianopolis in AD 668 (Treadgold 1997: 320) with other less certain attestations perhaps as late as the 11th century AD (Belke 1996: 156).

Kaisareia Hadrianopolis is likely to have been the administrative centre of a wide area in the early empire, and may have been assisted in this regard by a dozen or so hyparchies based on existing tribal foci, which in turn developed into towns themselves in at least some cases. This compound system of administration, melding local and Roman elements of control, may have been 'an adaptation of the old tribal organization with the addition of just sufficient cities not to lose sight of the normal Asiatic provincial system' Wilson suggests (1960: 158, 509; see also Marek 1993; Mitchell 1993a: 91–92).

The site of Kaisareia Hadrianopolis lies in the hills just west of Eskipazar. The modern villages of Hacımatlar and Budaklar appear to be the main focus of the city and there are carved and inscribed stones in several surrounding villages. A small hill forms the centre of the city, and there is a nearby necropolis with chambers cut into the rock. There are also traces of what may have been a church. But the surviving standing remains of the city are minimal indeed, doubtless, for one reason, due to its proximity to the North Anatolian Fault Zone. In 1901 Mendel (1901: 8) had already mused that the city's utter destruction may have been due to earthquake damage.

Sites PS098–PS105 include remains of the city of Kaisareia Hadrianopolis. At PS098 (figs 6.14–6.15) illicit excavations have uncovered a mosaic floor and elaborate architectural elements, probably from a church, while PS099 (fig. 6.16) comprises a series of graves cut into the rock. Further to the west the modern road from Eskipazar to Mengen passes through a natural gap in a limestone spur, PS100 (fig. 6.17), which shows traces of modification in the form of dressed stone facing and features cut into the summit, which may have been a fortified entrance into the city. Sites PS101–PS104 consist of non-*in situ* finds of architectural elements, including columns, statue bases and crucifixes, scattered in surrounding villages (fig. 6.18), and at PS105 (fig. 6.19) there are intact remains of a brick dome or vault, perhaps the remains of an underground cistern. Recently started intensive survey and excavations at Kaisareia Hadrianopolis by Dr Ergün Laflı of Dokuz Eylül University, Izmir, are steadily increasing our understanding of the topography and history of this important Paphlagonian city (Laflı 2007; Laflı, Zäh 2008; see also Marek 2003: Abb. 89, 91, 107–09, 184, 191–92, 209–13, 232 for excellent images of remains from the site and territory of Kaisareia Hadrianopolis; and fig. 6.20).

By north Anatolian standards the territory of Kaisareia Hadrianopolis is rich in inscriptions, and it is worth considering them in some detail at this point, at the same time broadening the discussion beyond the immediate topic of Kaisareia Hadrianopolis itself (fig. 6.21). It is worth noting, in contrast, that the territory of Gangra/Germanikopolis, the only other urban area located within Çankırı province, appears somewhat lacking in inscriptional evidence. This discrepancy is in part the result of the disparity in effort that has been expended on these two sites by epigraphically-minded travellers of the 18th–20th centuries, but even though future work may go some way towards redressing this balance, it is doubtful that it will ever completely balance the scales. As things stand, the western stretches of Çankırı province, which correspond to a major part of the

Landscapes with Figures: Paphlagonia through the Hellenistic, Roman and Byzantine Periods, 330 BC–AD 1453

Fig. 6.14. Kaisareia Hadrianopolis, PS098, mosaic floor in illicit excavations

Fig. 6.15. Kaisareia Hadrianopolis, PS098, architectural element

Fig. 6.16. Kaisareia Hadrianopolis, PS099, group of rock-cut graves

Fig. 6.17. Kaisareia Hadrianopolis, PS100, stone-clad entrance to the city

Fig. 6.18. Kaisareia Hadrianopolis, PS101, broken column

Chapter Six

Fig. 6.19. Kaisareia Hadrianopolis, PS105, brick dome or vault, largely underground

Fig. 6.20. Kaisareia Hadrianopolis, PS109, architectural element now in Eskipazar belediye *garden*

territory of Kaisareia Hadrianopolis, provide a good deal of information about the social customs of its inhabitants during the Roman imperial period, while the eastern stretches, which correspond to the territory of Gangra/Germanikopolis, provide very little. Any discussion of the social content of the inscriptions of Çankırı province is therefore essentially an account of the epigraphic habits of a single city, the urban centre of which is no longer located within Çankırı province. In fact, even the old borders of Çankırı province, which were those followed throughout Project Paphlagonia, did not encompass the entirety of the territory of Kaisareia Hadrianopolis, and any discussion of the epigraphy of this city would thus be restricted to a part of an interesting whole if these modern provincial borders were strictly adhered to. It is for this reason that they have not been, and in what follows, evidence from the inscriptions of Kaisareia Hadrianopolis that were found in the closely adjoining districts of neighbouring provinces has been included without being specified as such.

The most important parameter in this discussion is periodisation, and here we are dealing principally with the first four centuries AD, with some later instances (see catalogue for dating of inscriptions). The Roman imperial period inscriptions show that marble and limestone were abundantly used, and that the quality of the carving and the material chosen could be very high (for example, PPI.13) or very low indeed (for example, PPI.4, 6). At a basic level, this indicates that the requisite skill level, and aesthetic taste, was present in Inner Paphlagonia, and that even people of comparatively limited means (or taste) wished to express their values through the epigraphic medium.

The shapes that these stones were carved into is important, although it must be remembered that not all were carved into free-standing monuments, as at least two were carved into the living rock itself (PPI.12, 14), presumably because on both occasions there was a suitable rock face available in close proximity to monuments for the deities that were being honoured in these inscriptions. The shapes assumed by these free-standing stones are necessarily dependent upon their intended function, and in the case of the funerary inscriptions this is principally that of a round funerary *bomos* (=altar: Coulton 2005: 131) that had a moulded top and bottom, sometimes with raised bands between the moulding and the main field that was to be used for the inscription. The top of these columns was smoothed flat, and they may have been used as display platforms for busts of the dead or offerings. They would have been placed over the tomb (as specified in some inscriptions) or close to it. In addition to the inscription that they carry, several were also adorned with inscribed leaves or ears of corn, or symbols that reflect the life and work of the deceased. A few examples of triangular-shaped gables have also been found (for example, PPI.18, 23), in which sculptural motifs (sometimes of people, sometimes of flowers, etc) were placed in niches above the inscriptions, as well as some semi-circular stones that functioned in the same manner (for example, PPI.4, 6), and at least one grave stele (PPI.11).

These stones were only one part of the funerary customs that were observed, and the inscriptions they bear sometimes provide more information about how these were articulated, although the words used to describe the receptacle of the body (for example, τύμβος, τάφος and ἡρίον) perhaps demonstrate a greater variety than the actuality of the conditions of the grave. Although it is the grave marker that is often said to have been set up, rather than the grave itself, graveside actions of the families of the deceased are sometimes described, as in PPI.22, where the wife and mother of the deceased are said to have embraced the

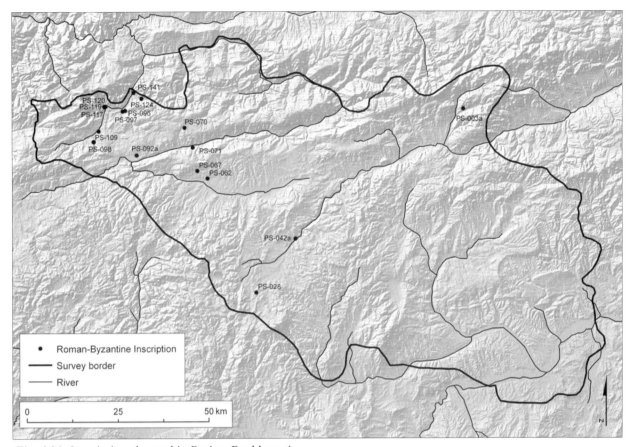

Fig. 6.21. Inscriptions located in Project Paphlagonia

tomb while numerous other relatives wept and grieved. Parents bury their children, children bury their parents, spouses bury spouses and friends bury friends. Sometimes groups of people club together to pay for the stone, and sometimes the epitaphs are brief and simple statements ('Apphus and Markianos for Tourigos, their dearest father, in memory': PPI.21) while others are complicated, and sometimes very accomplished, verse epitaphs that display a considerable linguistic skill on the part of the poet (for example, PPI.18, 19). This display of literacy cannot, unfortunately, be used as direct evidence for the literacy of the population at large, as the poetry need not have been composed by the dedicator of the inscription, but was more likely the result of a commission, as the stone itself would have been. It does, however, attest a level of appreciation for this literary form and its appropriate use on the part of the person who commissioned the work. The profession that the deceased had been engaged in is seldom stated, but a soldier, farmers, a trader and merchant, and a doctor are all attested (Marek 1993: Kaisareia 79; PPI.9 = *SEG* 1982: 1261). The mode of death is also infrequently declared, although Marek 1993: Kaisareia 27 (killed by a poisoned drink?) and PPI.19 (slain by barbarians) are interesting exceptions.

Another type of inscription that is regularly attested in this region is that of the inscribed statue base set up by communities to honour certain individuals, which are often square blocks of stone with moulded tops designed to hold a stone or metal statue. The examples that have so far been discovered, together with sundry other honorific inscriptions that did not directly accompany statues, show that a large number of Roman emperors were honoured in this way, together with a governor of Galatia of the time of Hadrian (Marek 1993: Kaisareia 2), which incidentally shows that Kaisareia Hadrianopolis was a part of the province of Galatia at this time.

The final category of inscription present in this region is the religious, which includes dedications of entire temples (PPI.12), or parts thereof (PPI.1), or fulfilment of personal vows (Marek 1993: Kaisareia 20). Several deities are mentioned in these (for example, Demeter and Kore, Artemis, Zeus, the mother of the Gods and the Supreme God), with many different epithets (for example, Zeus Kimistene, Zeus Karzene, Zeus Epikarpios), and they were set up by both individuals and entire subcommunities of Kaisareia Hadrianopolis (on which see below). The formal structures of the temples were supplemented by cult statues (for example, PPI.12) and inscribed altars (Marek 1993: Kaisareia 21–22, 24), which were the focus of the rites carried out in these sacred areas, irrespective of whether they were equipped with a formal temple or not. The diffusion of these inscriptions throughout the territory shows that the worship of these deities was not confined to the urban area – far from it in fact – and that various individuals and communities were prepared to spend significant sums of money on these structures and items, and to record the fact epigraphically (an action which in itself was not cheap).

The sub-communities that are attested within the region of Kaisareia Hadrianopolis are all recorded in the form of ethnics, from which the proper name of the community must be derived. This fact has caused some problems when scholars have made reference to them, and it is not unusual to come across references to the community, as, for example, that of Kimistene, when it should be something like Kimista. These ethnics are sometimes attested in situations where the people in question have made a decision (for example, PPI.13, where the people of Kimista honour Caracalla with an inscription and statue), or they are sometimes deducible from the use of locality-based epithets of deities (for example, Zeus Karzene; Marek 1993: Kaisareia 16). Several such communities are attested, most of which would have consisted of a central village and its surrounding area, which may have included outlying hamlets, although at least one (Kimista) may have been of greater importance than this, as it consisted of at least one fortified settlement replete with sacred areas and perhaps another entire village (Endeiron), which may have been located ca. 2km distant from it (PPI.12, with commentary). These ethnics are witness to a level of organisation within the region that operated below that of the cities, which must have existed before Kaisareia Hadrianopolis was created and which was presumably the building block from which this city was eventually fashioned. Such villages and rural areas continued to function as political entities in certain situations. Thus it was the people of Kimista who set up the aforementioned statue of Caracalla and carved an inscription into its base stating this fact, not the people of Kaisareia Hadrianopolis as a whole, and it is probable that the urban centre that was developed over time at Eskipazar never completely displaced them as the central organising and controlling influence in the lives of the people who lived within these villages.

Çerkeş/Kızıllar (Antoninopolis?)

One of the hyparchy towns associated with Kaisareia Hadrianopolis is likely to be located near Çerkeş. According to the Peutinger Table this may have been Antoniopolis or perhaps Antoninopolis (Wilson 1960: 159), but we need to treat this source with extreme caution: it does not, for example, feature Kaisareia Hadrianopolis, the major town of the region. Furthermore, we have to wonder why Antoninus Pius, the successor to Hadrian, would attempt to diminish the significance of Hadrian's (re)foundation at Kaisareia Hadrianopolis by establishing another major settlement in its eastern marches at the alleged site of Antoninopolis. Mordtmann (1925: 244) claims to have seen at and around Çerkeş traces of an amphitheatre, columns, frieze pieces and inscriptions, while Ainsworth (1842: 38) recorded the ruins of two posting stations or guardhouses just west of the town. Amphitheatres, however, are extremely rare in Asia Minor and we should be sceptical about Mordtmann's sighting of one at a location such as Çerkeş.

Nevertheless, surviving traces do reveal the existence of a long-lasting ancient town barely 4km to the northwest of Çerkeş. The village of Kızıllar has yielded stelae, stone lions, altars (Wilson 1960: 159). In the centre of Çerkeş today, PS062, in a municipal garden there sits a funerary stele in primitive style (PPI.4; figs 6.66–6.67; see also Marek 2003: Abb. 204), as well as other scattered traces of its pre-Turkish past (Belke 1996: 172, Abb. 11–13), but the bulk of the ancient remains are scattered thinly through the fields around the villages of Bedil, PS063 (fig. 6.22), and, especially, Kızıllar, PS064–PS067 (fig. 6.23). Sherds and tile, from Hellenistic to late Byzantine in date, are found over an area of almost 30ha, and at one point there appears to be a dug-over cemetery. Ploughing occasionally brings to the surface stone slabs of some note, including one inscribed gravestone, PS067/PPI.6 (figs 6.71–6.72). The location of this long-lived settlement, like modern Kızıllar, directly on a major fault of the North Anatolian Fault Zone and attractive to settlement because of the eruption of water sources to the earth's surface at this point, means that the town must have experienced major destructive earthquakes during the several centuries of its existence.

Fig. 6.22. Antoninopolis, PS063, remains at Bedil village

Fig. 6.23. Antoninopolis, PS064, located across the fields to the west of the modern village of Kızıllar

Roman roads

Of major significance to the incorporation of the region into the Roman state was a system of roads (French 2003: 51–54; Mitchell 2003: 23–24). As Mitchell (1993a: 127) has put it 'After the decline of the Roman system, parts of which were certainly in use in the early seventh century AD, Anatolia had to wait until the end of the nineteenth century before it acquired new roads on a remotely comparable scale'. As we have discussed in previous chapters, there certainly existed a network of tracks and routes in earlier periods of the Paphlagonian past. In particular, Hittite attempts to control this highly-contested frontier region only make sense if involving a good system of communication and movement of often substantial numbers of humans, carts and animals over considerable distances. For the Romans, once the region had been brought under control, the requirements were principally for efficient and smooth communications and transport of people and commodities between towns and cities of the ever-expanding empire (for a detailed and exhaustive study of the Roman roads of the entire region of north-central Asia Minor, see Wilson 1960: 311–414; see also Magie 1950: 1083–86, building on the earlier work of, *inter alios*, Ramsay 1890; for the Byzantine road system of the region, in most respects maintaining the Roman network, see Belke 1996: 117–35; see also French 1980). In general, milestone evidence from Galatia and Pontus indicates three main episodes of road building in this region: AD 80–82, AD 97–100 and AD 119–122 (Mitchell 1993a: 124; French 2003: 53). It may thus be that other roads in our region were completed or repaired at this time, even if the milestone evidence itself is largely lacking from Inner Paphlagonia. We should nevertheless be aware that episodes of intensive road building may well have taken place without leaving significant epigraphic traces.

Of most importance for our survey region is the great east-west route originating from Istanbul, running through Çerkeş in the west, eastwards partly along the Devrez valley through Ilgaz, Tosya, to Amasya and beyond; still a highly important route today (fig. 6.24). A more northerly east-west route, running along the Gök Irmak valley in Kastamonu province and including the territory of Pompeiopolis, at times served as the most important means of access from the west into north and east Asia Minor, all the way to the great legionary fortress at Satala (Mitchell 1993a: 127). Although not attested by Roman milestones, the more southerly Devrez route features in the Peutinger Table and Wilson's study of this difficult document suggests a localisation of Antoninopolis at Çerkeş (not wholly accepted here: see above), of Anadynata at Kurşunlu (Belke 1996: 171–72) and of an unknown station at or near modern Ilgaz town. For this last possibility, the best candidate is the multi-period site of Salman East, located at an intersection of modern routes, east-west and north-south, and where Wilson (1960: 353) also postulates the existence in Roman times of a major crossroad (see also the useful map in Marek 2003: Karte V, suggesting a major intersection of routes north of Gangra at the location of modern Ilgaz, as does Belke 1996: 118). This point is also close to the location of Kandara-Cendere (Belke 1996: 224), our site PS009. Further to the west, traces of this road have been detected around Kurşunlu and Çerkeş (French 1988a: 9).

The major north-south route of the region ran from Ankyra (=Ankara) north to Gangra and on to Kastamonu and the Black Sea beyond. A series of 28 milestones from north Galatia, including several along the road from Ankyra to Gangra/Germanikopolis, all mentioning the name of A. Larcius Macedo, governor of Galatia AD 122, suggests an intensive burst of road building to complete the Roman programme of road construction in central Anatolia (Mitchell 1993a: 122, fig. 22). The Ankyra-Gangra road can be traced today at several points (Belke 1996: 135), in particular where it crosses the high ground to the west of Eldivan Dağı (sites Eldivan 02S02, 05S02 comprise robbed-out stretches of this road, set in a course 3.5m in width; figs 6.25–6.26), unlike the modern road which keeps to the east of this mountain, before traversing the Eldivan plain and heading northeast to Gangra. A milestone associated with this route, found at Yukarı Yanarlar southwest of Gangra, is also related to the road-building programme of the Galatian governor, A. Larcius Macedo in AD 119–122 (French 1988a: 9), while a possible milestone from Mart to the southwest of Eldivan Dağı probably dates about a century later, to the reign of Severus Alexander in AD 222–235 (French 1988b: no. 318) and attests the same route (von Flottwell 1895: Blatt 3). A further milestone inscription, if

Fig. 6.24. Main east-west route in region of Ilgaz, looking north, mounds of Salman East and Salman West visible in centre

Fig. 6.25. Robbed-out stretch of Roman road on west side of Eldivan Dağı, Eldivan 02S02, 05S02

correctly restored, shows that Gangra/Germanikopolis was a city of Galatia under Hadrian, but a city of Pontus by the time of Diocletian (French 1991: 81–83). A short section of road visible near the village of Kisecik (Leonhard 1915: 121; Wilson 1960: 357; French 1989: 275; Belke 1996: 135) belongs to this route (fig. 6.27). North of Ilgaz the road has been traced ascending a shoulder of the Ilgaz range (French 1988a: 9), much as the modern road to Kastamonu does. This road is unlikely to have been passable in winter months.

Fig. 6.26. Robbed-out stretch of Roman road on west side of Eldivan Dağı, Eldivan 02S02, 05S02

The main route from Gangra to Anadynata/Kurşunlu did not, as today, head north to Ilgaz and then west along the Devrez valley (although that was also an option in Roman–Byzantine times) but instead ascended the harsh terrain west of modern Korgun to arrive more directly at Anadynata (Foss 2000: 1223). Traces of this road and even earlier tracks, probably of Late Bronze Age date (see Chapter Four), are clearly visible through this desolate stretch of country today (fig. 6. 28).

The Roman settlement pattern of Inner Paphlagonia
The distribution in Inner Paphlagonia of sites of Roman date (including those only identifiable as either Roman or Byzantine) (fig. 6.29) differs dramatically from all earlier patterns, and indeed compares well only with much later settlement systems as in the Ottoman period and that of AD 1950. Two major features may be stressed. Firstly, there is a spread of settlement over almost the entire survey region, with the northwest section for the first time in its already long history hosting significant numbers of human settlements. Such a spread is attributable to the establishment of an atmosphere of peace and security that enabled safe exploitation of often small and isolated parcels of arable land, vivid demonstration of the impact of the *pax Romana*. Secondly, for the first time there is a clear hierarchy of settlement with sites ranging from tiny hamlets and farmsteads, through villages to quite sizable towns. In keeping with local Paphlagonian tradition, however, even the largest sites are modest and the majority of settlements cluster at the smaller end of the scale, doubtless a factor of the scattered and patchwork distribution of pockets of arable land as well as the difficulty of movement over many parts of the region. The chronology of the spread of Roman settlement into and within the survey region remains a topic for future study dependent on a richer understanding of ceramic development through this period, and there is scope too for a ceramic-based appreciation of how the communities of Inner Paphlagonia related to their contemporaries on the Black Sea coast to the north.

In apparent contrast to the Hellenistic pattern, the development of agglomerated settlement in Inner Paphlagonia in the Roman period did not occur at the expense of rural occupation, which flourished like never before, indicating a steady increase in population in an environment of safety. Exactly this pattern has been detected in other survey projects throughout Anatolia and beyond, and quite clearly is a fundamental characteristic of the Roman period across vast regions. Thus Erciyas (2006a: 61; 2006b: 228) points to a general increase of rural settlement in concert with the development of urban centres through the Roman period across north-central Anatolia, while in regions to the west, including Phrygia

Fig. 6.27. Stretch of Roman road near Kisecik, south of Ilgaz

Fig. 6.28. Traces of roads and tracks west of Korgun

(Kealhofer 2005: 148) and Lydia (Pleket 2003: 89), to the south on the Konya plain (Baird 2004: 232), around Sagalassos (Vanhaverbeke et al. 2004: 255) and in Cilicia (Blanton 2000: 60) the simultaneous thriving of urban and rural settlement in the Roman period can have been supported only by demographic growth and economic prosperity. What is distinctive about the Inner Paphlagonian settlement trajectory for this period within the context of Asia Minor at large is the apparently minimal part played by urban communities as key elements, a characteristic feature of the region in the long-term perspective.

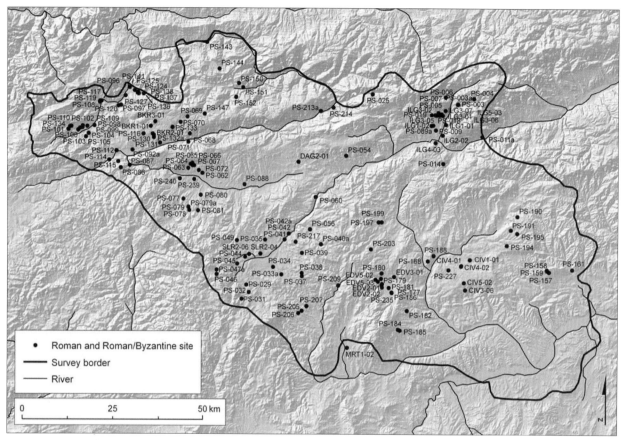

Fig. 6.29. Roman and Roman–Byzantine sites located in Project Paphlagonia

Late Roman–Byzantine retrenchment, recovery, retreat, AD 285–1453

> The interlude of classical urbanism was finally over, and Paphlagonia returned to a pattern of dynastic strongholds similar to that prevailing before Pompey's defeat of Mithridates in the first century BC.
>
> (Crow 1996: 35)

This volume is not the place for a grand overview of the history of the Byzantine state through more than a thousand years of its often turbulent life (for which see Treadgold 1997), nor even for a history restricted to those parts of the state now in our survey region (Belke 1996: 57–102 provides an excellent historical overview of Paphlagonia through the Byzantine and early Turkish periods). As in previous sections of this chapter our aim here is to highlight those aspects and elements of the historical framework that may have some bearing on the nature, distribution and hierarchy of settlement across the landscape through this period.

The most significant feature of that history is the uncertainty, often heightening to terror, attendant upon increasingly forceful and effective incursions into this part of Byzantine territory by outsiders, firstly Arabs and subsequently Turks, over a period of some 500 years. Inner Paphlagonia once more stood at the edge of an empire and once more hosted a drawn-out and debilitating episode of conflict (Vryonis 1971) that could only have had a powerful impact upon the ways in which the landscape was settled. Following the dramatic rise of Islam, Arab armies under Maslamah and other commanders drove deep into Anatolia in the eighth century AD, reaching as far north as Gangra in AD 712 and 727 (Brandes 1989: 65, 69; Belke 1996: 196; Treadgold 1997: 343, 353). Failure to take the citadel of Gangra led to its being called Hısnu'l Hadid (Iron Fortress) by Al-Ya'kubi (II: 292, 300). It is doubtless starting from this time that we can date the widespread use of fortified sites in our region (see below) as elements of a settlement pattern under severe threat from outside. By the late 11th century Turkish troops and settlers had pushed through Paphlagonia to the Bosporus. A further focus of instability attended the rebellions and counter-insurgency operations at the time of emperor John II Comnenus in AD 1130–1135, when the region of Gangra and Kastamon swung between rebel and imperial hands on several occasions (Vryonis 1971: 119; Treadgold 1997: 631–32). By the mid-12th century all of Inner

Paphlagonia had been lost to Byzantium and had come under the sway of the Danishmendid emirates, from which time we can date the development of a truly Turkish pattern of settlement that survives to this day. What impact did these developments have on the settlement of human communities in the region? To address this question we here examine three strands of evidence: cities, rural settlement and fortified refuge sites.

Cities

We are reasonably well informed on the earlier Byzantine political geography of Paphlagonia through the Synecdemus of Hierocles and the novels (28, 29, 31) of Justinian, which show that there had been very little change since the second century AD, with survival of the Roman towns of Inner Paphlagonia into the sixth century AD and the addition of some new ones (Jones 1971: 171). Through the fifth and sixth centuries AD, however, major changes were underway in the structure of social life in Asia Minor, involving a fundamental shift in the civic life of cities (Mitchell 1993b: 120–21), changes that continued to affect urban life across the entire region into the seventh and eighth centuries and beyond (Brandes 1989). Thus, while continuing as centres of trade and specialist manufacture, Anatolian cities lost their role as foci of civic and public activity, with the result that the urban élite turned to their landed estates as sources of power, hiring their own gangs of armed bodyguards to protect and impose their interests against those less able to look after themselves. A mid-sixth-century AD inscription from Hadrianopolis (Mitchell 1993b: 121; *SEG* 1985: 1360) comprises an imperial edict, promulgated through the local bishop, with the aim of curbing the power of mobs of mounted club-bearers employed by local landowners, thus demonstrating at once both a breakdown of civic order and a centralised attempt, doomed to failure, to conscript the church into the exercise of imperial policing and control. This inscription indicates that the city was a part of the province of Honorias at the time.

Accompanying these changes and integrated with them was a process that has been described as a 'transfer from *polis* to *kastron*' (Crow 1996: 23), whereby the Classical city was steadily replaced by the medieval castle through the later Byzantine period. Indeed the widespread occurrence of fortified sites, of many shapes and sizes, including refuges, appears to co-occur with the decline of the city in many areas of Asia Minor at this time, and by the 11th century at the latest, much earlier in some regions, the urban experiment in Inner Paphlagonia had totally collapsed, the region returning to its default setting of 'a pattern of dynastic strongholds' (Crow 1996: 35).

With the rise to prominence of Christianity in the later Roman and early Byzantine decades Gangra played an increasingly significant role, hosting at some time around AD 343 the famous Council of Gangra, attended by 13 bishops and with the specific aim of countering the new and contagious fad of ascetic monasticism as advocated by Eustathius, who was roundly castigated in a letter sent by the bishops to their colleagues in Armenia, power-base of Eustathius (Mitchell 1993b: 112; Belke 1996: 197). Despite these censures and entreaties, from this time onwards, and surviving for many centuries, monasticism thrived in the rural environment of Paphlagonia as elsewhere in Anatolia (Mitchell 1993b: 69, 115). In any case, Gangra retained its status as a metropolis into the 11th century (Crow 1996: 20), finally ceasing to exist in this capacity only in the 14th–15th centuries (Vryonis 1971: 302; Belke 1996: 112).

As mentioned in Chapter One, Gangra became a focus for religious exile through much of the Byzantine period. In AD 452 the emperor Marcian banished Dioskoros of Ephesos to Gangra where he died in AD 454, while a few years later Leo I exiled the heretic known as Timothy the Cat to Gangra, where, Theophanes Confessor tells us, 'the Cat began to hold rival assemblies and cause disturbances, on learning of which the emperor re-exiled him to Cherson' (Mango, Scott 1997: 172). In AD 518, his first year as emperor, Justin I exiled Philoxenos, bishop of Hierapolis, firstly to Philippupolis and then again to Gangra (Mango, Scott 1997: 250).

The importance of Gangra as the major, often sole, urban focus of Inner Paphlagonia continued throughout the Byzantine era (Belke 1996: 197–99) and indeed without significant hiatus up to modern times. In this respect is it unique amongst the towns and cities of the region. In the light of the *polis* to *kastron* shift discussed above, the significance of Gangra is the relative ease with which the one could be transformed into the other by the simple expedient of moving up the hill and fortifying its summit. Other towns of the region, such as Hadrianopolis and Çerkeş/Kızıllar, lacked natural citadels as effective and imposing as that of Gangra and thus failed to make the *polis* to *kastron* shift.

In terms of visible remains on Çankırı citadel (PS168) today, there is not much to see, most of the walls having been removed by local builders or destroyed by earthquakes and severe erosion (fig. 6.30). There are remains of two substantial towers, one with two clear phases (figs 6.31–6.32), as well as one enormous cistern (fig. 6.33), at least 50m deep, and two smaller ones. Much of the fortification building is likely to date to the 12th century AD when Gangra was most directly involved in assault and counter-attack by Byzantine and Turkish forces. Scattered pottery on the citadel dates

Chapter Six

Fig. 6.30. Çankırı citadel, PS168 general view

Fig. 6.32. Çankırı citadel, PS168 multi-phase tower

Fig. 6.31. Çankırı citadel, PS168 multi-phase tower

from the Hellenistic through Roman–Byzantine and into the Turkish periods (figs 6.34, 6.104:10–15). It is interesting to note that Çankırı citadel hosted a crowded quarter of dwellings until AD 1847 when an outbreak of cholera obliged its inhabitants to move down the hill. The citadel was in ruins when visited by von Flottwell in 1893 (Ayhan 1998: 105).

Fig. 6.33. Çankırı citadel, PS168 cistern in interior

Fig. 6.34. Pottery from PS168, Çankırı citadel

Rural settlement

As discussed above, there are insurmountable problems in disentangling some of the Byzantine from the Roman evidence in Inner Paphlagonia, but nevertheless there does appear to be a fall in settlement spread and hierarchy occurring at some stage during the Byzantine era (fig. 6.35). Episodes of rural abandonment undoubtedly occurred during periods of conflict and high instability, in particular through the centuries of the steady collapse of Byzantine control over north-central Anatolia, when villagers are likely to have moved into large towns for protection whenever possible. The shortage of suitable large towns in Inner Paphlagonia – only Gangra of any note and that itself not immune to assault – may have meant that significant tracts of the entire region were devoid of human settlement for long stretches at a time, as stated in accounts by Crusaders passing through Kastamonu and Gangra to Amasya in AD 1101 as well as in slightly later Danishmendid sources (Vryonis 1971: 162, 168–69). Mitchell (1993a: 239) has suggested that despite indications of urban decline by the late third century AD, there is evidence to support the idea of rural resilience in Anatolia throughout this period, for example in the form of funerary inscriptions, and this picture doubtless holds true for the centuries up to AD 700 or so. Thereafter, for the fragile regions of north Anatolia the trend appears to be one of steady rural collapse as attested, however tenuously, in survey evidence from Samsun and Tokat (Erciyas 2006a: 59) as well as Gordion (Kealhofer 2005: 148), while marginal regions far to the south, such as Cilicia, also suffered dramatic declines in population and rural settlement through the Byzantine period (Blanton 2000: 60). On the Konya plain a steady trend of demographic increase shudders to a halt around AD 700, also probably in association with the Arab raids that were well underway by then (Baird 2004: 245), while rural settlement in the territory of Sagalassos suffers a similar fate at about the same time (Vanhaverbeke et al. 2004: 272).

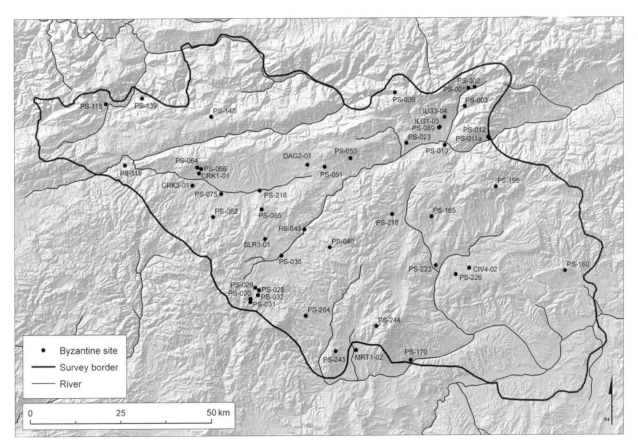

Fig. 6.35. Byzantine sites located in Project Paphlagonia

Chapter Six

Elements of surviving Byzantine rural settlement in Paphlagonia include churches and monasteries, attested by architectural pieces such as fonts with incised crosses, often no longer *in situ*, as well as sometimes elaborate rock-cut chapels and chambers as best known at İnköy, PS010 (figs 6.36–6.37) and newly discovered at Salur 03S01 (figs 6.38–6.39). Such sites are likely to have hosted small monastic communities and their associated cemeteries (Belke 1996: 219, see 103–13 for discussion of the role of the church in Paphlagonia). Byzantine inscriptions attest the spread of Christianity in the countryside, including baptismal fonts, an inscribed passage from the bible and prayers made to an archangel or to God (PPI.2, 3, 8; Marek 1993: Kaisareia 55). But, aside from demonstrating that this area was following the same broad trajectory as the rest of central and northern Anatolia in the Byzantine period, they allow us to discern little specific about the rural life of the people of this area at this time.

Site PS196, Zırçalı Mevkii, with its moulded Christian tiles, high-quality glass and rare fine painted pottery (figs 6.40–6.43, 6.105), is clearly a remote yet important monastery or church site, suffering badly now from illicit digging. Pig-keeping was certainly practised, the region being famous in high Byzantine society for its pork, which was exported to Constantinople (Belke 1996: 144; Magdalino 1998: 142). Several illegally excavated cemeteries of Byzantine date are attested by use of the distinctive tiles with triple parallel impressed lines running diagonally across the tile's surface (figs 6.44–6.45).

Fig. 6.36. Monastery/chapel site at İnköy, PS010

Fig. 6.38. Monastery/chapel site at Salur 03S01

Fig. 6.37. Monastery/chapel site at İnköy, PS010

Fig. 6.39. Monastery/chapel site at Salur 03S01

Landscapes with Figures: Paphlagonia through the Hellenistic, Roman and Byzantine Periods, 330 BC–AD 1453

Fig. 6.40. Site PS196, Zırçalı Mevkii, with illicit excavation in foreground

Fig. 6.43. Pottery from site PS196, Zırçalı Mevkii

Fig. 6.41. Site PS196, Zırçalı Mevkii, moulded tile with cross motif

Fig. 6.44. Tile with triple impressed lines, PS115

Fig. 6.42. Site PS196, Zırçalı Mevkii, moulded tile fragments

Fig. 6.45. Tile with triple impressed lines, PS064

Fortified refuges

At least a dozen fortified hilltop sites were discovered or newly recorded during our survey. There are certainly many more of them to be encountered by archaeologists in the future, as we did not attempt to visit every likely looking hilltop during our traverses of the landscape. By definition, all these sites are on top of hills and many of them are also rather remote, so that the time needed to reach and record them is always considerable. With many other calls on the limited time at hand, then, it was not often a priority to spend an entire morning or even day verifying reports of refuge sites on top of distant hills. As ever, what is presented and discussed here must be viewed as a sample.

Chapter Six

The location of the fortified hilltop sites (fig. 6.46) varies from rather low-lying eminences, as at Kurşunlu, PS051 (Crow 1996: 25), to extremely remote and precarious summits, as at Gavur Kale, PS043. By virtue of their position, all of them have good all-round visibility and most are situated a considerable vertical distance from the nearest water source and arable land. We may assume that in case of urgent need arrangement must have been made for an ongoing maintenance of essential supplies – water, grain, etc. – within the refuge walls. Sherds of ribbed storage jars are indeed found at several of the sites.

We are now convinced that almost all the fortified hilltop sites encountered in Project Paphlagonia date first and foremost to the centuries from AD 700, with the first incursion of Arab forces, to around AD 1200 with the final absorption of the region into the Turkish world. We do not believe that any of them can convincingly be demonstrated as belonging to the Hellenistic or Galatian periods (as tentatively suggested in Darbyshire et al. 2000: fig. 3, 91; *contra* see Strobel 2002: 35–37). As the sites are for refuge use only, and indeed in some cases may never have been used as refuges at all, there is always a restricted amount of pottery to be found within them, which makes dating difficult. Where pottery does survive, however, it almost always fits the AD 700–1200 bracket. The vernacular peculiarities of the architecture of these structures, where discernible, also do not generally allow a precise chronological resolution. These sites are almost exclusively dry-stone built, with minimal or no use of mortar, using readily available field stone and very capably constructed.

A dating of the fortified sites to the period AD 700–1200 is supported by two other strands of evidence. Firstly, such a dating sits well within a now broad network of roughly contemporary sites detected over much of central Anatolia, including the adjacent province of Ankara, which has been characterised as a chain of 'reporting posts' for use only in times of acute danger (Strobel 2002: 35–37; Vardar, Vardar 2001). Strobel's argument (2002: 35–37) that the hilltop sites close to Ankara relate to the eighth century AD Arab incursions, while those further north, in Inner Paphlagonia, relate to the Byzantine defence of Paphlagonia and Honorias against the Turks in the 11th and 12th centuries AD is too fine a distinction to make in view of the fact that Inner Paphlagonia was equally affected by both series of events. Secondly, a significant historical source for the use of

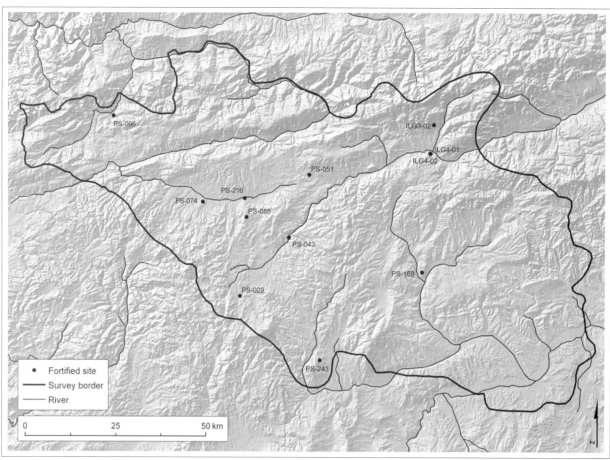

Fig. 6.46. Fortified hilltop sites located in Project Paphlagonia

Fig. 6.47. Fortified hilltop site, PS029, Gökçeören

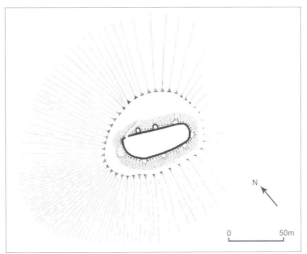

Fig. 6.48. Fortified hilltop site, PS029, Gökçeören, plan

Fig. 6.49. Fortified hilltop site, PS043, Gavur

fortified hilltop sites in the episode of stress and conflict that attended the final Byzantine collapse in Paphlagonia is the Danishmendname, which describes rural populations of the Pontic region as fleeing to the mountains and walled refuges or *kaleler* (Vryonis 1971: 169).

Plans and views of several of our fortified hilltop sites are shown in figs 6.47–6.54. Classic small refuge sites include the *kaleler* at Gökçeören (PS029), Gavur (PS043), Bozoğlu (PS074) and Yalakçukurören (PS085), each with narrow entrance and semi-circular bastions at regular intervals. These sites are not large, ranging from 40m to 100m on the long axis, and cannot have accommodated large numbers of people and/or animals for any length of time. Sherds of pottery from all four of the illustrated sites date exclusively to the Byzantine period (figs 6.55–6.56, 6.102:4–6, 6.103:7–10). Larger fortified sites, as at Kurşunlu (PS051) (figs 6.57–6.60) and Kanlıgöl (PS218) (see Chapter Four, figs 4.13–4.16), may have been intended for longer-term occupation and include clear traces of collapsed interior rooms and structures.

Chapter Six

Fig. 6.50. Fortified hilltop site, PS043, Gavur

Fig. 6.53. Fortified hilltop site, PS085, Yalakçukurören

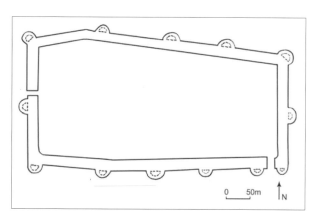

Fig. 6.51. Fortified hilltop site, PS043, Gavur, plan

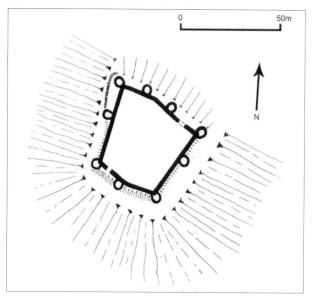

Fig. 6.54. Fortified hilltop site, PS085, Yalakçukurören, plan

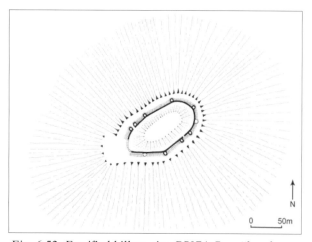

Fig. 6.52. Fortified hilltop site, PS074, Bozoğlu, plan

Fig. 6.55. Pottery from site PS074, Bozoğlu

Fig. 6.56. Pottery from site PS043, Gavur

Fig. 6.57. Fortified hilltop site, PS051, Kurşunlu

Fig. 6.58. Fortified hilltop site, PS051, Kurşunlu

Fig. 6.59. Fortified hilltop site, PS051, Kurşunlu

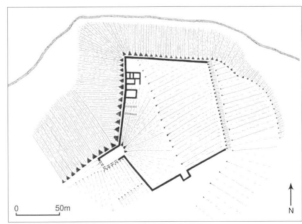
Fig. 6.60. Fortified hilltop site, PS051, Kurşunlu, plan

Epigraphic evidence from Project Paphlagonia

Nature of the sample

The inscriptions presented here were discovered and recorded through the duration of the project by a number of participants who photographed, transcribed and sometimes took squeezes of the stones (fig. 6.21). In 2001, the author (Metcalfe) joined the project for a number of weeks in order to record and document the inscriptions with a view to preparing them for publication. Of the 24 inscriptions on stone that were discovered, nine were previously unpublished (PPI.2–4, 6–8, 16, 23–24) and new readings (often minor, such as the moving of brackets or confirmation of the hypotheses of others) were made of a further five (PPI.5, 9–10, 13, 20). The only stones that were not revisited by the author were PPI.23, which was lost between 1998 and 2001, and PPI.14.

Çankırı province, although squarely placed on a major east-west route and in close proximity to Ankara, has not often been visited by epigraphically-minded travellers. Those who have made the effort have focused largely on the westernmost part of the province, in the area of modern Eskipazar, corresponding in the Roman and Byzantine period to the urban site of Kaisareia Hadrianopolis and a number of its dependent villages. The east of the province, which roughly corresponds to the area controlled by Gangra/Germanikopolis, has received much less attention and it was hoped that this project might uncover more epigraphic material relating to this region. Of the newly discovered inscriptions, however, only two (PPI.2–3) may have originated in sites connected with Gangra/Germanikopolis, and even these are in the border zone between that city and Kaisareia Hadrianopolis, and may therefore have been within the orbit of the latter rather than the former. All of the remaining newly discovered inscriptions (PPI.4, 6–8, 16, 23–24), together with all but one (PPI.1) of the previously published inscriptions, can be placed within the territory of Kaisareia Hadrianopolis. This distribution might suggest that Gangra/Germanikopolis was a place that made little use of inscriptions, but although it does not seem to have been as epigraphically active as its neighbours, the degree of difference is exaggerated by the nature of this brief catalogue, which is not a corpus of all inscriptions ever found within the borders of Çankırı province. It is, rather, a publication of only those inscriptions that were (re)discovered during the course of Project Paphlagonia. The previously published inscriptions from Çankırı province that do not appear here are not necessarily lost or destroyed, and several are stored in Çankırı Museum. In fact, the six previously published inscriptions from the Gangra/Germanikopolis area that were not rediscovered (Legrand 1897: nos 20–21; Kaygusuz 1982: no. 2 = *SEG* 1982: 1261; 1983b = *SEG* 1983: 1113; French 1988b: 318; 1991: 81–83), together with five unpublished inscriptions currently in Çankırı Museum (as of 2001) and perhaps a further one from Gangra/Germanikopolis itself (Marek 1993: 130), suggest that a sustained survey of its eastern stretches might turn up more inscriptions related to this site.

The new inscriptions published here broadly conform to those already discovered in this area, in that they are mainly funerary inscriptions of the imperial period (PPI.4, 6–7, 23–24) or brief Christian inscriptions of the late imperial or early Byzantine period (PPI.2–3, 8, 16). They add a few new names to those already attested in the region, but do not change the broad picture of the history and society of Paphlagonia that has been outlined by Marek (1993; 2003).

The inscriptions are presented in the order in which they were discovered in the course of Project Paphlagonia, and they are edited according to the basic principles of the RECAM (Regional Epigraphic Catalogues of Asia Minor) publications of the British Institute at Ankara. The commentary has been restricted to basic details, partly for reasons of space. The only field that needs detailed explanation is the 'date'. Where no date is expressly given as part of the inscription, one has been assigned on the basis of the letter forms. As there is as yet no sufficiently-sized control group from this area (and good photographs of those that are published are scarce) against which these otherwise undated inscriptions can be compared and dated with precision, this has necessarily resulted in the somewhat unwieldy groups 'imperial' (first to fourth century AD) and 'Byzantine' (essentially fifth to eighth century AD). Kaygusuz and Marek (the epigraphists who have most recently studied this area) have concurred in accepting 6/5 BC as the beginning of the era date of Kaisareia Hadrianopolis, as has Leschhorn 1993, and this has been followed here.

Catalogue of inscriptions

PPI = Project Paphlagonia Inscription
SEG = *Supplementum epigraphicum graecum* (1923–1971, 1979–)
MAMA = *Monumenta Asiae Minoris Antiqua* (1928–)

<u>PPI.1. Dedication to Hera</u> (site PS003a; figs 6.61–6.62)
Location: In the yard of the school house in Kurmalar.
Publication: Kaygusuz 1983b: 60, no. 2; 1983c: 64–65, 66, no. 2; *SEG* 1983: 1114.
Description: Badly broken four-sided marble base or altar with moulding at the upper edge. Two faces are inscribed, with inscription B (fig. 6.62) on the face to the left of inscription A (fig. 6.61). The stone has suffered damage since Kaygusuz found it: letters no longer visible are underlined.

Fig. 6.61. PPI.1, site PS003a, inscription

Fig. 6.62. PPI.1, site PS003a, inscription

Dimensions (maximum preserved): Height 0.4m; width 0.52m; thickness 0.52m; letters 0.03–0.04m.
Text inscription A:
  [Θεᾷ Μ]εγάλῃ Ἥρᾳ
  [τὰ] θυρώματα τοῦ
  ναοῦ τὰ χάλκ[εα]
  καὶ τὸ π[ρόθυρον]
  - - - - - - - - - -

Translation: For the great [goddess] Hera, [the] bronze doorway of the temple and the s[pace before the door]...
Text inscription B:
  - - - - - - - - - -
  [. . . .]ιΔΕΙΤΗ[.]
  [. .]ΛΗΣ τῆς
  τοῦ ναοῦ κα-
  ταχεῖσθαι Ο[.]
  [. .]ΝΟΙ μετ[ὰ]
  - - - - - - - - - -

1–5 [Θεᾶι Μεγάληι] | [Ἥρα]ι δεῖ τῆ[ς] | [πύ]λης τῆς | τοῦ ναοῦ και|ταχεῖσθαι Kaygusuz.

Translation: ....]the[....]of the temple[...]to pour over[....
Date: Imperial. Kaygusuz dated (A) to the second half of the second century AD and (B) to the first half of the third century AD, but although the inscriptions do seem to be the work of separate hands, too little remains to be certain of their relative dating.
Comment: These inscriptions describe the construction or, more likely, renovation of a temple to Hera, together with an associated libation ritual. The identity of the individual or group responsible for these actions has been lost along with the lower lines of each inscription, but the use of bronze for the door fixtures means that it will have been a costly operation that would only have been undertaken on a building of especial importance for the parties involved. Kaygusuz found a second inscribed stone in the same village (*SEG* 1983: 1113), not rediscovered in Project Paphlagonia, which contained an earlier dedication to 'the Great Gods' (dated third/second century BC by Kaygusuz, but see *SEG* lemma for a dissenting opinion) of stoas (complete with kitchens) and an associated building. These inscriptions (which were not found *in situ*) probably relate to the same sanctuary, which is presumably that mentioned by Stephanus s.v. Κάνδαρα (Κάνδαρα, χωρίον Παφλαγονίας ὡς ἀπὸ σχοίνων τριῶν Γάγγρων, καὶ Θάριβα κώμη. οἱ οἰκήτορες Κανδαρηνοί και Ἥρας Κανδαρηνῆς ἱερόν). The precise location of this sanctuary has not yet been ascertained, but it cannot be far from the current location of the inscribed stones (see Marek 2003: 107, Abb. 153–55 for discussion of this sanctuary, and a spectacular picture of Kurmalar and its surrounding area).

PPI.2. Font (site PS028; fig. 6.63)
Location: In the front room of a house at the western end of Gökçeören.
Publication: None.
Description: Rectangular marble font. Inscription carved into the upper part of one short side, in the upper two quadrants of a cross. Two further crosses are carved into the long side to the left of the inscribed face, together with a badly-executed leaf adornment. The remaining sides are undecorated. A drainage hole beneath the cross on the inscribed face has been concreted over by the present owner, who has also repaired some damage to the rim, in order to make cheese inside.
Dimensions: Height 0.49m; width 0.67m; length 1.075m; letters 0.05–0.08m.
Text:
  †Φωνὴ Κ(υρίο)υ ἐπὶ
  τῶν ὑδάτ-
  ω<ν>
Ligatures: Line 2 ΔΑ.

Fig. 6.63. PPI.2, site PS028, inscription

Translation: The voice of the Lord is upon the waters.
Date: Byzantine.
Comment: The font is inscribed with a quotation from (Septuagint) Psalm 28.3 (=Masoretic Psalm 29.3) that was frequently used in inscriptions (see, for example, Becker Bertau 1986: 173.3; Corsten 1991–1993: 212.1) and was particularly fitting for use on a font. The letters are roughly cut and awkwardly placed, and show such variety in shape (contrast the lunate *omegas* in lines 1 and 2 with the angular one in line 3) that it is impossible to be more precise as to the date of the inscription. The physical difficulty of fitting the final word into the available space is presumably the cause of the missing *nu*, and it is in fact difficult to see how the stone-cutter could have balanced word division and space in a way that would have resulted in a neater presentation.

PPI.3. Prayer to an archangel (site PS042a; figs 6.64–6.65)
Location: In the front yard of a house in Sakaeli.
Publication: None. Squeeze in collection of the British Institute at Ankara.
Description: Column capital decorated with crosses and scroll-work, with three-line inscription on one face, which has suffered damage to the right and top edges.
Dimensions: Height 0.485m; width 0.505m; thickness 0.475m; diameter of column 0.3m; letters 0.045–0.05m.
Text:

    ✝'Αρχάγ[γελε – ca. 4–6 –]
    φύλατε τὸν δοῦλ[ον -]
    ΘΙΝ [– ca. 2–3 –]

Ligature: Line 2 OY.
Translation: Archangel [...] guard [your] serv[ant .]thin[...
Date: Byzantine.
Comment: If, as seems likely, the column capital was originally symmetrical, the lacuna at the end of the first line could accomodate any of the archangel's names in abbreviated form (it is highly doubtful that 'archangel' would have been abbreviated after the initial *gamma*), but only Michael's name is short enough if it was inscribed in full, although the letters would have been crowded. The lacuna at the end of the second line would have contained ca. 2–3 letters, which indicates abbreviation in the required restoration. In full, this space would be expected to contain the termination of the noun, the personal pronoun and the initial letter(s) of the name of the 'servant'. Either the noun was abbreviated, the personal pronoun understood or abbreviated and the available space given over entirely to the beginning of the name, or the noun was finished and the pronoun understood, leaving space for only a single letter at most for the beginning of the name, which would have continued on the other (now lost) side of the central cross. Potential names are greatly restricted by the extant letters and lengths of the lacunae, but Ἀθινίος (*MAMA* 3: 241a line 1) is possible.

Fig. 6.64. PPI.3, site PS042a, inscription

Fig. 6.65. PPI.3, site PS042a, inscription

PPI.4. Worn gravestone (site PS062; figs 6.66–6.67)
Location: In the garden of the *belediye* in Çerkeş (moved there from the schoolyard before 1997).
Publication: None (although photo in Marek 2003: 136, Abb. 204). Squeeze in collection of the British Institute at Ankara.
Description: A poorly carved semi-circular limestone grave marker. One line of text is carved into a narrow border that arches over the central relief and separates it from the unworked outer edge. Another five lines are inscribed below the relief. The relief depicts a family group consisting of one central figure with upraised hands and outstretched palms, flanked on either side by two smaller figures. There is a column underneath the right elbow of the central figure, and a disk (the sun?) above it in the space between the upraised hand and head. The poor quality of the carving (matched by the low quality of the stone) has been exacerbated by severe erosion to the face and damage to the lower edge that has resulted in the loss of a substantial part of the lower-left part of the main inscription.
Dimensions: Height 1.4m; width 1.81m (relief = 0.76m by 1.39m); thickness 0.41m at top, 0.28m at bottom; letters 0.04m above relief and 0.03–0.025m below relief.
Text:
 ΑΥΓΟΥΣ[.]ΑΠΡΟΤ[- 0.15 -]ΟΗΠΙΧ[- 0.06 -]ΟΝΑ[- 0.155 -]
    ΝΑ[- 0.52 -]Ι̣Σ[- 0.11 -]Ε[- 0.17 -]
 Relief
 [.]ΥΝ̣[- 0.13 -]Δ̣[- 0.07 -]Ε[- 0.82 -]Τ̣[- 0.14 -]Α[- -]
 [- 0.20 -]Ν[- 0.05 -]Λ̣ΙΥΤ[- 0.24 -]Π̣[- 0.04 -]ΝΤ̣[- -]
 [- 0.35 -]ΟΥΓ[- 0.04 -]ΗΤ̣[- -]
 [- - - - -]
 [- 0.90 -]ΕΠΙΧΑΙ[- -]
Date: Late Imperial/early Byzantine.
Comment: The stone was examined in a variety of light conditions both before and after cleaning, and a squeeze and photographs taken for later study, but only the first word of this originally lengthy text can still be read: it is almost certainly the personal name Αὐγοῦστα (for the use of which outside imperial contexts, see, for example, *MAMA* 4: 174 line 1).

PPI.5. Gravestone for Prokle (site PS062; figs 6.68–6.70)
Location: In the garden of the *belediye* in Çerkeş (moved from the *lokanta* in the centre of the village in 2001).
Publication: Marek 1993: Kaisareia 89; Merkelbach, Stauber 2001: 10/02/93. Squeeze in collection of the British Institute at Ankara.
Description: Round marble funerary column with moulded top, broken at bottom.

Fig. 6.66. PPI.4, site PS062, inscription

Fig. 6.67. PPI.4, site PS062, inscription

Dimensions: Height 0.58m; diameter 0.53m; letters 0.04m.
Text:
 Λαίνεον τόδε σῆμα
 Πρόκλῃ Θεωδότος ἀδελφῇ, /
 [καὶ] πόσις Ἀλέξανδρος Ε[-]
 [- - - - - - - - - -]
1 [.]αινεον Marek [λ]αίνεον Merkelbach, Stauber. 2 [Π]ρόκλῃ Marek. 3 πόσις Ἀλέξανδρος Marek.
Translation: Theodotos (erected) this stone grave marker for his sister Prokle, [and] husband Alexander [...
Date: Imperial.
Comment: With the stone disinterred from its original position it was possible to read slightly more of the third line than Marek, and also to make out traces of two letters (the apex of a lunate letter and a horizontal bar) of a fourth line directly below the second and third letters of πόσις. The first two lines form a hexameter (although Θεωδότος should be Θεοδώτος) but the three successive short vowels in the third line seem to rule out a continuation of the metre.

Fig. 6.68. PPI.5, site PS062, inscription, left section

Fig. 6.69. PPI.5, site PS062, inscription, middle section

Fig. 6.70. PPI.5, site PS062, inscription, right section

PPI.6. Gravestone for Markianos (site PS067; figs 6.71–6.72)

Location: In a field (Çayır Mevkii) due south of Kızıllar Kale. Uncovered by farmers in 1997; in 2001 it was still resting against the back wall of the hole in which it had lain.

Publication: None. Squeeze in collection of the British Institute at Ankara.

Description: A roughly-cut and heavily-worn semi-circular block of poor-quality pockmarked limestone. A semi-circular sunken relief occupies the uppermost section, in which a disk containing a symbol (a flower?) has been carved in a slightly off-centre position. Beneath this relief is a carelessly-carved three-line inscription: the lines dip as they progress, and the letters are lightly scratched into the surface and frequently vertically misaligned.

Dimensions: Height 1.1m; width 1.5m (relief = 0.565m by 1.21m); thickness 0.3m; letters 0.025–0.035m.

Text:

 Β. Αυρ. Α[- 2–3 -]ΑΚΟΥΛΙΛΛΟΥ σῆμα τ[όδ᾽]
 ἐξετέλεσσεν
 Μαρκιανῷ Ἀλεξάνδρου, ὃς φίλος ἦν ἅπασιν
 καὶ ἄ[γαλ]μα τόδ᾽ ἔθηκεν τύμβου ἀνδρὸς ἑῆ(ος)

Translation: B. Aur(elia) [...] finished this grave marker for Markianos, son of Alexander, who was a friend to all, and placed this s[tat]ue on the tomb of her husband.

Date: After 212 AD.

Comment: The initial *beta* is clear, if considerably smaller than the average for the letters in this first line, but may be a lapicidal error for *kappa* (Klaudia?), as the stone-cutter has clearly made a mess of the patronymic/ethnic of the dedicator of the inscription – perhaps a poor attempt at Aquillius? The third line could theoretically be restored as κατὰ [σῆ]μα τόδ᾽ ἔθηκεν κτλ., but there is no trace whatsoever of the horizontal bar of the would-be *tau*, and the faint letter traces in the

Fig. 6.71. PPI.6, site PS067, inscription

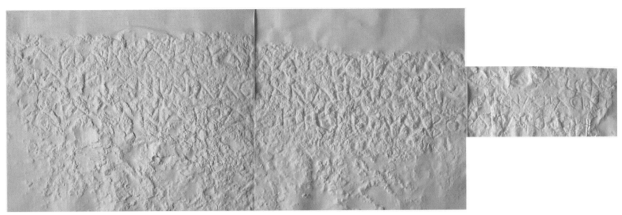

Fig. 6.72. PPI.6, site PS067, squeeze of inscription

lacuna seem to support the reading given in the text (although the letters would be crowded more closely together than in the rest of the inscription). The abbreviation at the end of the line was kindly suggested to me by Christian Marek. The inscription uses poetic language, and parts of it do scan, but it does not seem to be consistently metrical.

PPI.7. Gravestone for Diogenes (site PS070; fig. 6.73)
Location: In the entrance hall of the mosque in Beymelik.
Publication: None. Squeeze in collection of the British Institute at Ankara.
Description: Round marble funerary column with moulded top and five-line inscription. When first recorded in 1997 it was buried in the ground outside the mosque up to a point just below the fifth line. When revisited in 2001 it was broken into two pieces that were stored beneath a coffin and tea-tables in the entrance hall of the mosque. The largest piece consists of the top of the stone, including the entire inscription; the smaller (triangular-shaped) piece has broken off beneath the lower left-hand edge of the final line of the inscription. The right-hand side of the inscription has become heavily worn as a result of being dragged across rough ground by a tractor. The stone-cutter struggled to carve the letters around a curved surface, with the result that each line rises markedly as it progresses around the stone and some letters (for example, the first *omega* in line 1) are much wider than they should be.
Dimensions: Height 0.63m; diameter 0.38m; letters 0.03–0.04m.
Text:
  Πολλῶν σω-
  τὴρ κληθεὶς ἐν[θά-]
  δε κεῖμ' [Ἀμι]σ<ι>ηνός
  τὸ γένος οὔνο[μα]
5 Διογένης· χαίρετε

Translation: Known as the saviour of many, here lies a man of [Ami]sos by birth, named Diogenes. Farewell.
Date: Imperial.
Comment: I am much indebted to Santo Privitera and Christian Marek for help with this inscription. As the lacuna in line 3 does not seem to have space for three letters, the stone-cutter may have mistakenly placed the *iota* after the *sigma*, rather than before. The stone at the end of line 4 continues unbroken and smooth after a lacuna of a couple of letters at most, thereby excluding lengthier restorations such as οὔνο[μ' ἔχω], although the rest of the inscription does seem to have been intended to be metrical.

Fig. 6.73. PPI.7, site PS070, inscription

Chapter Six

PPI.8. Font (site PS070; fig. 6.74)
Location: Beymelik. Half buried upside-down in a patch of grass opposite a *çeşme* with an Arabic-script inscription.
Publication: None. Squeeze in collection of the British Institute at Ankara.
Description: Rectangular basalt font with a single cross carved in relief on one short side, and two similar crosses on the long side to its left. A badly-worn one-line Greek inscription was carved into a raised border between the crosses and the top of the font on both of these sides.
Dimensions: Height 0.535m; width 0.58m; length 0.725m; letters ca. 0.05m.
Date: Byzantine.
Comment: Presumably a single inscription beginning on the long side and moving around to the short. The faint letter traces do not allow any text to be reconstructed. Squeeze illegible.

Fig. 6.75. PPI.9, site PS071, inscription

Fig. 6.74. PPI.8, site PS070, inscription

Fig. 6.76. PPI.9, site PS071, inscription

PPI.9. Gravestone for Kyrittas (site PS071; figs 6.75–6.76)
Location: On the main road at the entrance to Akbaş Köyü, when starting on the mountain path from Kızıllar.
Publication: Marek 1993: Kaisareia 86; *SEG* 1993: 914. Squeeze in collection of the British Institute at Ankara.
Description: Round marble funerary column with nine-line inscription between a leaf and an ear of corn.
Dimensions: Height 1.815m; diameter 0.56m; letters 0.03–0.05m in lines 1–8, 0.04m in line 9.
Text:

    (leaf)
    Στήλην τήνδ' ἔστη-
    σαν ἐπ' εὐγήρῳ πατρὶ
    Κυρίττᾳ παῖδες
    Κύριλλος, Κυρίνας, οἱ φί-
5 λτατοι αὐτῷ, γεωργῷ, ἀγα-
   θῷ φίλῳ, ἐνπόρῳ ἱματιώνῃ,
   εἰς τέλος ἡδυβίου μνή-
   μης χάριν εὐσεβίης τε.
   ἔτους γκσ'
     (ear of corn)

1 τήνδε ἔστη- Marek. 7 ἡδυβίῳ Marek.
Translation: His children Kyrillos and Kyrinas, who were dearest to him, set up this stele over their long-lived father Kyrittas, farmer, good friend, trader and clothes merchant, at the end of a sweet life, in memory and reverence. Year 223.
Date: AD 218.
Comment: Marek noted in his brief commentary that ἱματιώνης is a hapax similar in sense to the more widely attested ἱματιαπράτης and ἱματιοπώλης.

PPI.10. Gravestone for Archelaos (site PS092a; figs 6.77–6.78)
Location: By the front porch of a house in Hamamlı.
Publication: Marek 1993: Kaisareia 91; *SEG* 1993: 916. Squeeze in collection of the British Institute at Ankara.
Description: Round marble funerary column with moulded top and seven-line inscription. Broken at bottom, hollowed out at top. The stone seems to have suffered more damage to the bottom since Marek recorded it, and only indistinguishable marks of the final four printed letters of the seventh line can now be seen.
Dimensions: Height 0.505m; diameter 0.56m; letters 0.025m.
Text:
 Ἀρχέλαος Ἀρχεδήμου ἡ-
 δὲ Κυρίλλης ἔνθα θανὼν κεῖται
 ὑπὲρ τύνβου γονέων φέρτατος
 ἠ{ω}ϊθέων· Μάνδανα ἀνέθηκ[ε συμ-]
5 βίῳ ἰδίῳ vac. Σευηρεῖνος
 οἱ υἱοὶ ΕΠΕΩΕΛΗΘΗΣ
      ἔτους τ[..]ʹ
1 Ἀρχέ[δη]μος Marek. 4 Μάνδανα Marek, Μάνδανα (nominative) Brixhe (1995: no. 583).
Translation: The best of the young men, Archelaos son of Archedemos and Kyrilla here lies dead above the grave of his parents. Mandana set this up for her husband. The sons Severinos [and...]. Year 3[..]
Date: The *tau* read by Marek in the final line dates the stone to the 300s of the local era, which equals AD 295–395.
Comment: The name of the deceased was read by Marek as Ἀρχέ[δη]μος, but there is space for only two letters between the extant *epsilon* and *omicron*, and the *mu* that Marek read before the *omicron* does not exist. There are clear traces of two diagonal letters within the lacuna, neither of which has a vertical bar at the base, and Marek presumably read these twice. Ἀρχέλαος is the only restoration that fits both space and letter traces. Brixhe has pointed out that Mandana is an Iranian name (Brixhe 1995: no. 583; see further Robert 1963: 217–18; Zgusta 1964: 287, n. 68) and that ἠΐθεος cannot carry its usual meaning of 'unmarried youth'. Pleket (*SEG* 1993: 339) is surely correct that it simply means 'young man' here.

PPI.11. Gravestone for Flavia Eide (site PS092a; figs 6.79–6.80)
Location: Against a wall at a crossroad in the upper part of Hamamlı.
Publication: Marek 1993: Kaisareia 90.
Description: Funerary stele with moulding to top and bottom of face and left side only. Broken at upper and lower left and right edges.

Fig. 6.77. PPI.10, site PS092a, inscription, left section

Fig. 6.78. PPI.10, site PS092a, inscription, right section

Dimensions: Height 1.15m; width 0.45m; thickness 0.365m; letters 0.04m.
Text:
 Φλ. Φαίδιος ἔτευξ[ε]
 συνεύνῳ Φλ. Εἴδῃ
 ἠρίον [ἰ]δομένοις
 μνημοσύνης ἕνεκα
  (leaf)
Ligatures: Line 3 HP; line 4 HM.
Translation: Flavios Phaidios fashioned this tomb you behold in memory of his bedfellow Flavia Eide.
Date: Imperial.

Chapter Six

Fig. 6.79. PPI.11, site PS092a, inscription

Fig. 6.80. PPI.11, site PS092a, inscription

PPI.12. Dedication to Demeter and Kore (site PS096; fig. 6.81)

Location: Carved into a vertical rock face on the heights of Asar Tepe.

Publication: Dörner 1963: 138–39; Kaygusuz 1983a: 114, no. 4; *SEG* 1983: 1100; Marek 1993: Kaisareia 12.

Description: A neatly-cut *tabula ansata* containing a ten-line inscription. It has been savagely attacked with a pick-axe.

Dimensions: Height 0.44m; width 0.6m; letters 0.01–0.04m.

Text:

Ἀγαθῇ Τύχῃ· θεα-
[ῖς] Δήμητρι καὶ Κόρῃ
Ἥλιος Ἀλεξάνδρου ἱ-
κέτης κατὰ κέλευ-
5 σιν τῶν θεῶν τόν τε
ναὸν καὶ τὰ ἐν αὐτῷ ἀ-
γάλματα σὺν τῷ προ-
νάῳ ἀνέστησεν ἐκ
τῶν ἰδίων κώμῃ Σεν-
10 δειρῶν. ἔτους σα′

3 [Ἥ]λιος Dörner [Α]ἴλιος Kaygusuz. 11 κώμῃ Σενδειρῶν Schuler (1998: 295. n. 91) κώμης Ἐνδείρων Kaygusuz.

Ligature: Line 2 HMHT.

Translation: With good fortune. The suppliant Helios, son of Alexander, erected the temple and the statues in the temple together with the pronaos for Demeter and Kore according to the order of the goddesses, from his own resources within the village Sendeiron. Year 201.

Date: AD 196.

Comment: The dedicatory nature of this inscription suggests that the temple of Demeter and Kore would have been located in close proximity to it. Two other divinities are recorded as having been worshipped in Kimista: Zeus Kimistenos (see PPI.14 below) and Artemis Kratiane (*SEG* 1983: 1101).

Fig. 6.81. PPI.12, site PS096, inscription

PPI.13. Statue base for Caracalla (site PS096; figs 6.82–6.83)
Location: Close to the summit of Asar Tepe.
Publication: Kaygusuz 1983a: 112, no. 1; *SEG* 1983: 1097; Marek 1993: Kaisareia 6.
Description: Square marble statue base, broken at bottom, with six-line inscription. The first line is inscribed on a raised band; the second line has suffered damage from a pick-axe.
Dimensions: Height 1.5m; width 0.6m; thickness 0.6m; letters 0.015–0.04m.
Text:

Ἀγαθῆι Τύχηι·
[Αὐτοκρά]τορα Καίσαρ[α]
[Μ. Α]ὐρήλιον Ἀντωνεῖνον
[Αὔ]γουστον Σεβαστὸν
5 οἱ γεραιοὶ καὶ ὁ δῆμος
       Κιμιστηνῶν

1 [οἱ] Kaygusuz, Marek.
Ligatures: Line 3 ΝΕ; line 4 ΝΣ; line 5 ΗΜ.
Translation: With good fortune. The councillors and people of Kimista (dedicated this) to the Emperor Caesar M. Aurelius Antoninus Augustus Sebastos.
Date: AD 212–217.
Comment: The ethnic 'Kimistene' is attested in another inscription from this site (PPI.14 below), which must have been called something like Kimista. The similarity that this bears to Strabo's description of a part of Paphlagonia (12.3.41) – ἦν δέ τις καὶ Κινιστηνή, ἐν ᾗ τὰ Κιμίατα, φρούριον ἐρυμνόν, ὑποκείμενον τῇ τοῦ Ὀλγάσσυος ὀρινῇ· – suggests that Asar Tepe was the site of this fortress, and that Strabo's manuscript should be altered to read Κιμιστηνή and Κιμίστα respectively (see above).

Fig. 6.82. PPI.13, site PS096, inscription

Fig. 6.83. PPI.13, site PS096, inscription

PPI.14. Dedication to Zeus Kimistenos (site PS096; fig. 6.84)
Location: Carved into a vertical rock face on the northeast part of the site at Asar Tepe.
Publication: Mendel 1901: 24, no. 161; Kaygusuz 1983a: 113, no. 3; *SEG* 1983: 1099; Marek 1993: Kaisareia 14.
Description: A neatly-cut *tabula ansata* with leaves in the side tabs. The first line of a four-line inscription is carved directly above the upper edge of the box; the remaining three lines are within it.
Dimensions: Height and width not recorded; letters 0.03m.
Text:

Ἀγαθῇ τύχῃ·
Διὶ Κιμιστηνῷ
Ἄλβος Πρόκλου
   ἀνέθηκα

Translation: With good fortune. Albos son of Proklos set this up for Zeus Kimistenos.

Fig. 6.84. PPI.14, site PS096, inscription

Date: Imperial.
Comment: The second epigraphic reference to Kimista (although the earliest discovered).

Fig. 6.85. PPI.15, site PS097, inscription, left section

Fig. 6.86. PPI.15, site PS097, inscription, right section

PPI.15. Gravestone for Archedemos and Markelle (site PS097; figs 6.85–6.86)
Location: Deresemail, just before the mosque on the path from Deresemail to Asar Tepe.
Publication: Kaygusuz 1983a: 121, no. 10; *SEG* 1983: 1106; Kaygusuz 1984: 71, no. 10; Marek 1993: Kaisareia 30.
Description: Round marble funerary column with moulded top and five-line inscription. Placed upside-down with bottom sawn off and hollowed out for use as a mortar.
Dimensions: Height 0.7m; diameter 0.73m; letters 0.04m.
Text:

    Ἀρχέδημος Μόσχου
    ζῶν κ(αὶ) φρονῶν ἑαυτῷ
    ἀνέστησα καὶ τῇ ἀϊμνήσ-
    τῳ συνβίῳ Μαρκέλλῃ, μνή-
5 μης χάριν. ἔτους *(leaf)* σι΄
    (leaf)   *(leaf)*   *(leaf)*

Translation: Archedemos, son of Moschos, while living and conscious, set this up for himself and his lamented wife Markelle, in memory. Year 210.
Date: AD 205.

PPI.16. Inscribed church column (site PS098; figs 6.87–6.88)
Location: Above the first lay-by heading west from Eskipazar on the road to Mengen, amongst what appears to be the debris of a church.
Publication: None.
Description: Large marble column broken into several pieces, one of which has three letters carved into it.
Dimensions: Height and width impossible to determine; letters 0.04m.
Text:
    ΧΑΙ[
Date: Early Byzantine (on the basis of the architectural elements).
Comment: Presumably χαῖρε / χαίρετε 'farewell'.

Fig. 6.87. PPI.16, site PS098, inscribed fragment

Fig. 6.88. PPI.16, site PS098, inscription

PPI.17. Statue base for Constantius (site PS109; fig. 6.89)
Location: In the municipal park of Eskipazar. Moved there from its original find-place 'sur l'acropole d'Hadrianopolis' (Mendel) = Çaylı.
Publication: Mendel 1901: 10, no. 146; Cagnat 1906–1927: 3.150; Marek 1993: Kaisareia 8.
Description: Square limestone statue base with moulding at top and bottom and seven-line inscription, the first line of which is carved on a raised band.
Dimensions: Height 1.45m; width 0.625m; thickness 0.62m; letters 0.03m.
Text:

 Ἀγαθῇ Τύχῃ·
 Τὸν γῆς καὶ θαλάσσης δεσπό-
 την Φλάουιον Οὐαλέριον
 Κωστάντιον τὸν ἐπι-
5 φανέστατον Καίσαρα
 ἡ βουλὴ καὶ ὁ δῆμος Και-
 σαρέων Ἀδριανοπολειτῶν

Translation: With good fortune. The boule and demos of Kaisareia Hadrianopolis (dedicated this) to the lord of the land and sea, Flavius Valerius Constantius, the most renowned Caesar.
Date: AD 292–305.
Comment: Constantius was one of the two Caesars in Diocletian's tetrarchy between AD 292 and 1 May AD 305, when Diocletian and Maximian abdicated and Constantius was elevated to the rank of senior Augustus. Two of the other tetrarchs, Diocletian and Maximian, are also known to have been honoured with an inscription and statue in the territory of Kaisareia Hadrianopolis (*SEG* 1983: 1098 = Marek 1993: Kaisareia 7).

PPI.18. Gravestone for Kyrilla (site PS109; fig. 6.90)
Location: In the municipal park of Eskipazar. Moved there from the Kümbet graveyard in the Çavuşoğlu *mahalle* of Köyceğiz.
Publication: Legrand 1897: 96, no. 11; Peek 1955: 638; Kaygusuz 1984: 67, no. 11; *SEG* 1984: 1281; Marek 1993: Kaisareia 39; Merkelbach, Stauber 2001: 10/02/22.
Description: Triangular-shaped limestone gable with damaged bust (missing its head) in a central niche inset in a pediment. There was a five-line inscription beneath the bust, but only the first three lines are now visible, and it is unclear if the remainder have been buried or sawn off to improve stability for display purposes. Legrand read more of the left of the stone than Kaygusuz: his readings are underlined where not subsequently confirmed.
Dimensions: Height 0.96m; width 1.55m; thickness 0.45m; letters 0.03m.

Fig. 6.89. PPI.17, site PS109, inscription

Fig. 6.90. PPI.18, site PS109, inscription

Text:

 Κυρίλλης τόδε σῆμα νέας κατατεθνηυίης / ἢ καὶ
 νηπιάχους κάλλι-
 πα παῖδας ἑούς· / τοῦτο δὲ μοι τεῦξεν πόσις ὅς
 φίλος, οὔνομα δ' αὐ-
 τῷ / Θεόφιλος, σὺν παισὶ φίλοις εἵνεκεν
 εὐσεβίης. / κάθανα δ' ἐνκύμων
 ἡ δύσμορος, ὡς ἐπὶ τούτῳ / ἄχθος ἔχειν
 γοῶντας ἐμοὺς οἰκῆας
5 ἅπαντας

1 σῶμα Legrand; ΚΑΤΑΤΕΘΝΗΥΙΗΣ stone κατατεθν[η]κυίης Legrand κατατεθνηκυίης Peek and Merkelbach, Stauber. 3 Read φιλ<ί>οις Kaygusuz (metri causa); κά<τ>θανα Legrand and Kaygusuz κά<θ>θανα Peek and Merkelbach, Stauber. 4 Read γο<ό>ωντας Peek and Kaygusuz and Merkelbach, Stauber.
Translation: This is the grave marker of Kyrilla, who died away while young, and left behind infant children. My dear husband, named Theophilos, with my dear children, fashioned this for me, out of piety. Ill-fated, I died while pregnant, thus bringing another burden to all my grieving household.
Date: Imperial.
Comment: An elegiac verse inscription, in which the final verse and the name Theophilos seem to sit out of the meter.

PPI.19. Gravestone for Domitilla (site PS117; fig. 6.91)
Location: In front of a house in the Çavuşoğlu *mahalle* of Köyceğiz.
Publication: Kaygusuz 1984: 61–62; *SEG* 1984: 1271; Lebek 1985: 7–8; Marek 1993: Kaisareia 38; Merkelbach, Stauber 2001: 10/02/12.
Description: Round limestone funerary column with damaged moulding to top and 19-line inscription, the first four lines of which are inscribed on a raised band.
Dimensions: Height 1.65m; diameter 0.5m; letters 0.02–0.04m.
Text:

Τήνδ' ἀρετῆς ἐπίσημον
ὅρα στήλην, παροδεῖτα· /
κεῖται γὰρ Δομιτίλλα κόρη
τῷδ' ἔνδοθι τύμβῳ /
5 τὸν τῆς σωφροσύνης
ἀραμένη στέφανον· /
μούνη γὰρ κουρῶν, ὅσσας ἄγον
εἰς ὕβριν ἄνδρες, /
οὕς ἄγαγ' ἐκ πόντοιο θεῶν
10 χόλος ἠδέ τε μοῖρα, /
τῶν τότε βαρβαρικαῖς
χερσὶν ἀπολλυμένων /
οὐκ ἔτ<ρ>εσεν τὸ θανεῖν
ἀνθ' ὕβρεως στυγερᾶς· /
15 ἑπτὰ μόνων μηνῶν δὲ
φίλον πόσιν εὐφράνασα /
παρθενικὸν λίπε φῶς
τετρὰς καὶ δεκέτης· /
(*leaf*)   χαῖρε   (*leaf*)

9 πόντοιο Peek (1985: 156) Πόντοιο Kaygusuz and Merkelbach, Stauber. 13 ἐτίεσεν stone ἔτ<ρ>εσεν Lebek and Merkelbach, Stauber ἔ<π>εσεν Merkelbach (apud Kaygusuz) if in 7 μούνη. 18 τεττаρακαιδεκέτης Lebek.

Ligatures: Line 5 ΗΣ, ΦΡ; line 6 ΜΕ, ΝΗ; line 7 ΝΗ, ΟΥ, ΩΝ; line 10 ΤΕ; line 11 ΩΝ, ΤΕ; line 13 ΟΥ; line 14 ΩΣ; line 15 ΗΝ; line 16 ΝΠ; line 17 ΩΣ.
Translation: O traveller, look at this stele, this mark of virtue. For within this tomb lies the girl Domitilla, who took up the crown of chastity. For alone of all the girls who were violated by the men that were guided by the wrath of the Gods and fate from overseas, and were destroyed by those barbaric hands, she did not fear death in place of loathsome abuse. She gladdened her dear husband for only seven months and she left her maiden's life at fourteen. Farewell.
Date: Imperial, perhaps AD 262–263 (see comment).
Comment: A metrical inscription. Two points have been raised with regard to this inscription. The first concerns the identity of the barbarians, whom Kaygusuz believed to be the Goths who invaded Asia Minor in AD 262–263, beginning at Herakleia Pontica. Peek (1985: 156) argued that this could instead have been a simple attack by pirates (thus ἐκ πόντοιο rather than Πόντοιο), which is implausible on account of the distance and mountainous terrain that separates this region from the sea. Palumbo Stracca (1996–1997: 19) supports Peek's reading but correctly

Fig. 6.91. PPI.19, site PS117, inscription

points out that this need not refer to pirates, as the Goths too will have come from overseas. The second point regards the age and status of Domitilla, as the phrase παρθενικὸν λίπε φῶς would seem to be incompatible with her married status. Gallavotti (1987: 33–36) suggested that the penultimate line might be understood to indicate that Domitilla was only ten years and four months old at the time of her death (rather than the more conventional 14), and Palumbo Stracca argued that the phrase instead underlined her youth and virginal conduct. However, Tybout in the *SEG* 1987: 1092 summary of Gallavotti's argument pointed out that she had been married for seven months, and that the phrase in question is best interpreted as referring to her status at the time of *marriage*, and not the moment of death, which is surely correct.

PPI.20. Gravestone for Markianos (site PS117; figs 6.92–6.94)
Location: In the garden of the mosque in the Çavuşoğlu *mahalle* of Köyceğiz.
Publication: Kaygusuz 1984: 66, no. 9; *SEG* 1984: 1279; Marek 1993: Kaisareia 45; Merkelbach, Stauber 2001: 10/02/27. Squeeze in collection of the British Institute at Ankara.
Description: Round marble funerary column with moulding at top and five-line inscription. Broken above and below. Now used for laying out the dead.
Dimensions: Height 1.17m; diameter 0.91m; letters 0.035–0.045m.

Fig. 6.93. PPI.20, site PS117, inscription, left section

Fig. 6.94. PPI.20, site PS117, inscription, right section

Text:
Μαρκιανὸς Δόμνης
πατρὸς Δέντου
γονος ἐσθλὸς /
τεῦξεν ζωός ἐών
5 τέρμα φ<ί>λου βιότου /
2 ΛΕΝΤΟΥ Kaygusuz. 4 τεῦξ' ἔτι Herrmann (from ph.) τεῦξε{ξε} Peek (1985: 157) τεῦξ' ἔτι Merkelbach, Stauber. 5 ΦΤΛΟΥ stone, ΤΕΤΡΙΑΦΤΛΟΥ βιότου Kaygusuz, [ἔ]τη τρία φίλου βιότου Marek (from Kaygusuz's copy).
Ligature: Line 1 ΜΝΗΣ.
Translation: Markianos, noble offspring of Domne and his father Dentos, fashioned (this) while alive, at the end of his dear life.
Date: Imperial.

Fig. 6.92. PPI.20, site PS117, inscription

Chapter Six

Fig. 6.95. PPI.21, site PS119, inscription, left section

Fig. 6.96. PPI.21, site PS119, inscription, right section

Comment: An elegiac verse inscription. Kaygusuz read the man's name as ΛΕΝΤΟΥ, which he interpreted as Lent<l>ou = latin Lentulus, but the *delta* is clear on the stone. The name is a hapax. Although the inscription is very worn in the middle of line 4, and there is an unusually large distance between the *epsilon* and *nu* of τεῦξεν, the letters here are clear. The confused final line of Kaygusuz's text led to two attempts at interpretation, of which Peek's suggestion (1985: 157) τέρμα φ<ί>λου βιότου is confirmed by the stone.

PPI.21. Gravestone for Tourigos (site PS119; figs 6.95–6.96)
Location: In the Köle graveyard of the Çavuşoğlu *mahalle* of Köyceğiz.
Publication: Kaygusuz 1984: 65, no. 6; *SEG* 1984: 1276; Marek 1993: Kaisareia 42.
Description: Round marble funerary column with moulding at top and a four-line inscription. Broken above and below.
Dimensions: Height 0.85m; diameter 0.55m; letters 0.05m.
Text:
Ἀπφοῦς καὶ Μαρ-
κιαν[ὸ]ς Τουριγῳ
πατρὶ γλυκυτάτῳ
μνήμης χάριν
Ligature: Line 4 ΜΝΗΜΗ.
Translation: Apphus and Markianos for Tourigos, their dearest father, in memory.
Date: Imperial (late first or second century AD: Kaygusuz).
Comment: The name Tourigos was identified as Celtic by Kaygusuz, but Brixhe (1995: no. 583) has suggested that it could also be Thracian.

PPI.22. Gravestone for Helios (site PS120; fig. 6.97)
Location: In the Kümbet graveyard of the Çavuşoğlu *mahalle* of Köyceğiz.
Publication: Legrand 1897: 96, no. 10; Peek 1955: 1125; Kaygusuz 1984: 67, no. 10; *SEG* 1984: 1280; Marek 1993: Kaisareia 40; Merkelbach, Stauber 2001: 10/02/19.
Description: Round marble funerary column with moulding at top and 12-line inscription. The first four lines of the inscription are carved on a raised band. Broken above and below.

Fig. 6.97. PPI.22, site PS120, inscription

214

Dimensions: Height 1.5m; diameter 0.76–0.86m; letters 0.035–0.04m.
Text:

Ἥλιον ὠκύμορον Κεία
γαμέτην με ποθοῦσα /
καὶ μήτηρ τύμβῳ Ἰούλλα περιπλέκεται· /
ὃν καὶ γανβρὸς ἔκ<λ>αυσε γόοις
5 Πομπηιανὸς ἀπαύστοις /
καὶ κούρη θρήνοις
Ἰούλλα φίλον πατέρα /
Κύριλλός τε νέος καὶ
Ἰουλιανὴ πάνυ βαιοί /
10 σὺν φιλίῳ θείῳ
Ποντικῷ ἀχνύμενοι. /
ἔτους γμσ'

4 ΕΚΑΥΣΕ stone. 5 Πονπηιανὸς Peek and Merkelbach, Stauber. 10 τείῳ Marek.
Ligatures: Line 2 THNM; line 3 MHTHP; line 9 HΠ.
Translation: Keia, yearning for me, her early departed husband Helios, and my mother Ioulla embrace this tomb; and my son-in-law Pompeianos and daughter Ioulla wept in ceaseless grieving for me their dear father, as did young Kyrillos and Iouliane, the little children with my dear uncle Pontikos, in mourning. Year 243.
Date: AD 238.
Comment: An elegiac verse inscription.

PPI.23. Gravestone (site PS124; fig. 6.98)
Location: Dug out of a hillside near a spring above the village of Karaören in 1998. Now lost.
Publication: None.
Description: Triangular-shaped gable, with a flower carved in relief in a sunken pediment above a three-line inscription. Left and right edges broken: the break to the left has resulted in the loss of the beginning of each of the three lines.
Dimensions: Height unknown; length unknown; thickness unknown; letters 0.02–0.03m.
Text:

]ΚΙΓΟΣ τε[ῦ]ξεν Α[.]Ο[..]Ν[..]ΚΕΙΝ
- - - -]Ω[- - - -]ΟΔ[- - - - - -
- - - -]Σ[.]Α[..]ΚΑ[- - - - - -]Ε

Translation: ...] set up [...
Date: Imperial.
Comment: The documentation for this inscription consists of a single photograph taken in 1998, in which only a few letters are visible, and a transcription of the first 12 letters of the first line, which are reproduced above. Only]Κ[- -]Σ τε[ῦ]ξεν can be confirmed from the photograph. It is likely that the traces to the left of the verb hide the name of the dedicant, and the traces to the right that of the deceased.

Fig. 6.98. PPI.23, site PS124, inscription, contrast enhanced

PPI.24. Gravestone of Valens (site PS141; figs 6.99–6.101)
Location: In the garden/fields of the house of the then (2001) *muhtar* of Büyük Tarla Mahallesi, who said that it had been excavated from an adjacent field and dragged to its present location.
Publication: None. Squeeze in collection of the British Institute at Ankara.
Description: Oval limestone funerary column with moulded top and four-line inscription. The base is buried in the ground. Two vertical cracks running through the left and right of the inscribed surface have caused the loss of some of the text.
Dimensions: Height (visible) 1.46m; diameter 0.54m; letters 0.03–0.035m in first three lines, 0.04–0.05m in last.
Text:

(leaf)   [...]ΠΒ Οὐάλεντι στρα-
          [τευσ]αμένῳ ἐντείμως
     Σέκτ[α (le]af) τῷ ἑαυτῆς [ιιατ]ρὶ
          μ[νή]μης   χάρι[ν](leaf)
(leaf)   (leaf)   (leaf)

Translation: [Year ?]77. Sekta, for her own [fath]er Valens, honourably discharged veteran, in memory.
Date: Imperial (AD 177 or 277?).
Comment: The first two extant letters of the inscription must be the remains of a year dating, presumably either [Ρ]ΠΒ' or [Σ]ΠΒ', although there is only sufficient space for an abbreviated version of ἔτους (such as in, for example, Marek 1993: Pompeiopolis 30, line 9 – ἔτ. ρξδ') if this word was included. The word division and restoration in lines 1–2 was kindly suggested to me by Peter Thonemann.

Fig. 6.99. PPI.24, site PS141, inscription, left section

Chapter Six

Fig. 6.100. PPI.24, site PS141, inscription, middle section

Fig. 6.101. PPI.24, site PS141, inscription, right section

Fig. No.	Site No.	Hand	Wheel	Inclusions	Colour	Finish
1	PS003		X	f min	5 YR 7/6	glazed
2	PS004		X	dense f min	10 YR 6/3 surfaces 2.5 Y 7/2	abraded
3	PS007		X	f min, mica	5 YR 7/6	ext grooved decoration
4	PS029		X	f min	7.5 YR 6/4	raised applied rib with impressed notches
5	PS029		X	f min	int 7.5 YR 6/6 core grey/brown	ext brn black
6	PS029		X	min	7.5 YR 6/6 core grey	eroded surfaces
7	PS032			v f min	2.5 YR 6/6 core grey	ext rim red paint
8	PS032		X	f min	5 YR 7/6 core orange	ext upper body finely ribbed band
9	PS032		X	dense f min	int 5 YR 6/6 ext 7.5 YR 7/4 core pale grey	int smoo
10	PS048		X	v f min	5 YR 6/6	ext and upper int brn 2.5 YR 5/6
11	PS064		X	sparse f min	fabric 7.5 YR 8/4	
12	PS064		X	f-m min	10 YR 7/3 core grey	
13	PS064		X	sparse f min	surfaces tan core orange	ext rim and int brn 7.5 YR 6/6
14	PS064		X	f-m min	7.5 YR 6/6 core grey-brown	

Fig. 6.102 (catalogue). Pottery from sites PS003, PS004, PS007, PS029, PS032, PS048, PS064. Abbreviations used in the pottery and object figure catalogues: h = high; m =medium; l = low; min = mineral; veg = vegetal; inc = inclusions; v = very; f = fine; c = coarse; ext = exterior; int = interior; brn = burnished; smoo = smoothed

Landscapes with Figures: Paphlagonia through the Hellenistic, Roman and Byzantine Periods, 330 BC–AD 1453

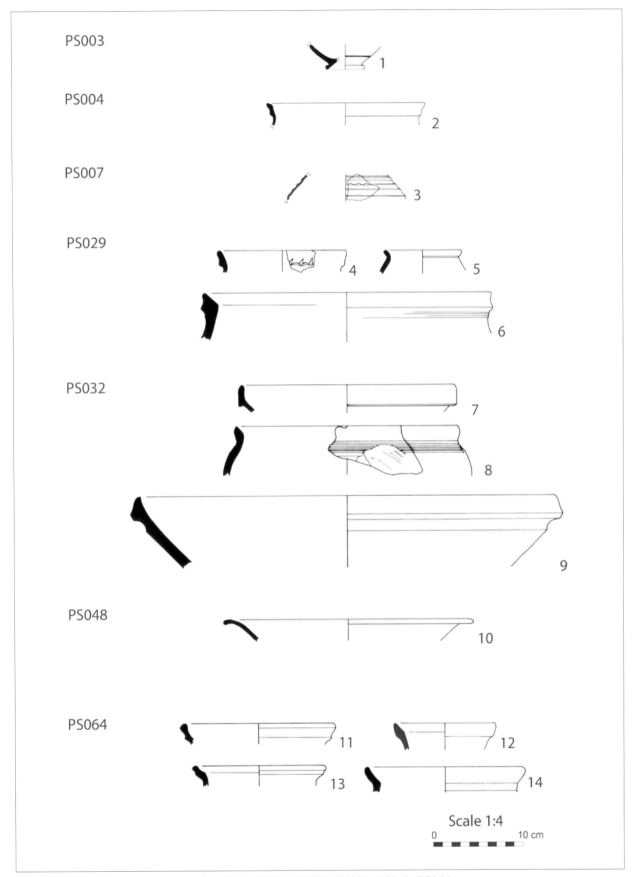

Fig. 6.102. Pottery from sites PS003, PS004, PS007, PS029, PS032, PS048, PS064

Chapter Six

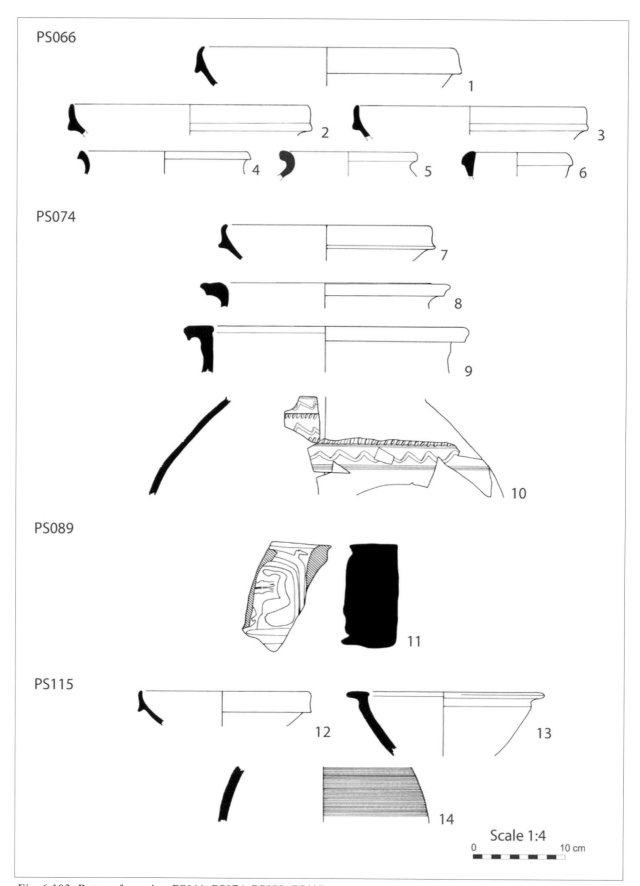

Fig. 6.103. Pottery from sites PS066, PS074, PS089, PS115

Fig. No.	Site No.	Hand	Wheel	Inclusions	Colour	Finish
1	PS066		X	sparse f-m min		ext rim slip very dark red int slip lighter red lower ext brn
2	PS066		X	f min, mica	5 YR 7/6	
3	PS066		X		5 YR 6/6	possible slip or brn
4	PS066		X	min	7.5 YR 6/6 core brown	
5	PS066		X	f	5 YR 7/3 core brownish	
6	PS066		X		5 YR 7/6 core light grey	
7	PS074		X	m min	7.5 YR 7/6	
8	PS074		X	m min	7.5 YR 7/4	
9	PS074		X	m min	5 YR 6/6	ext grooved decoration
10	PS074		X	f min	5 YR 6/8 core pale brown	ext and int slip 2.5 YR 5/6
11	PS089			m min, shell (?)	5 YR 5/6	stamped decoration
12	PS115		X	f min	2.5 YR 5/4	ext and int traces of paint
13	PS115		X	m min	5 YR 6/6 core grey	
14	PS115		X	m mica	5 YR 6/8	ext parallel grooves

Fig. 6.103 (catalogue). Pottery from sites PS066, PS074, PS089, PS115

Chapter Six

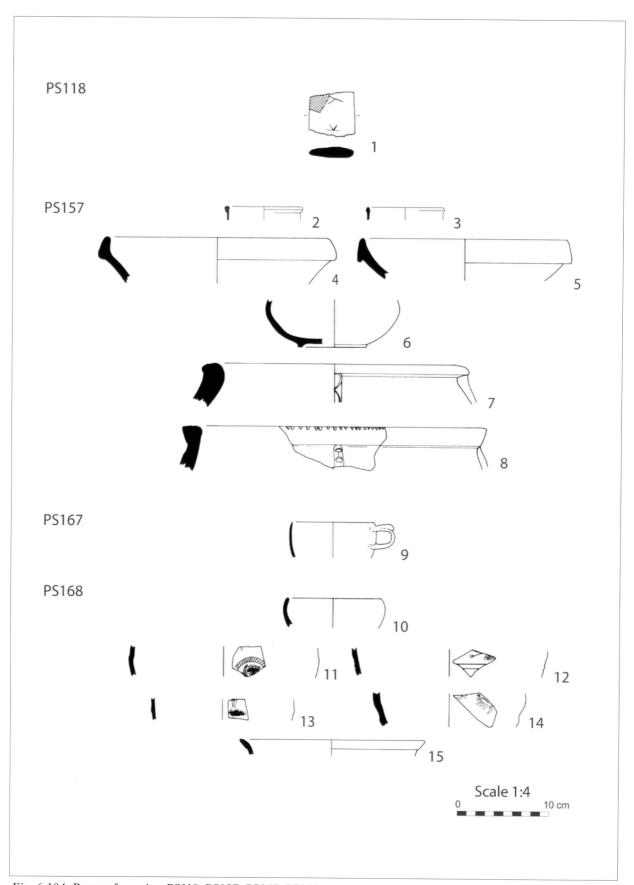

Fig. 6.104. Pottery from sites PS118, PS157, PS167, PS168

Landscapes with Figures: Paphlagonia through the Hellenistic, Roman and Byzantine Periods, 330 BC–AD 1453

Fig. No.	Site No.	Hand	Wheel	Inclusions	Colour	Finish
1	PS118			sparse f min	5 YR 6/4 core grey	ext letters K and Y incised
2	PS157			glass	green/clear	
3	PS157			glass	green/clear	
4	PS157		X	v f min	2.5 YR 5/8	ext and int wash
5	PS157		X	f min	7.5 YR 5/6	ext and int traces of slip/paint
6	PS157		X	v f min	2.5 YR 6/6 surfaces 5 YR 4/2	ext and int glazy wash
7	PS157			m min	2.5 YR 5/6	ext and int brn ext below rim vertical ridge with dents
8	PS157		X	dense min	2.5 YR 5/6	ext rim impressed decoration ext below rim vertical ridge with dents
9	PS167		X	no visible inc	2.5 YR 5/8	
10	PS168		X	v f min	2.5 YR 3/4	ext and int shiny slip, almost glaze
11	PS168		X	f min	int and core 5 YR 6/4 ext 2.5 YR 6.6	ext mould relief
12	PS168		X	no visible inc	2.5 YR 5/8 Samian type fine ware	ext mould relief
13	PS168		X	no visible inc	2.5 YR 5/8 Samian type fine ware	ext mould relief
14	PS168		X	no visible inc	fabric 2.5 YR 5/6 Samian type fine ware	ext mould relief
15	PS168		X	no visible inc	fabric 2.5 YR 5/8 Samian type fine ware	ext and int slipped and shiny

Fig. 6.104 (catalogue). Pottery from sites PS118, PS157, PS167, PS168

Chapter Six

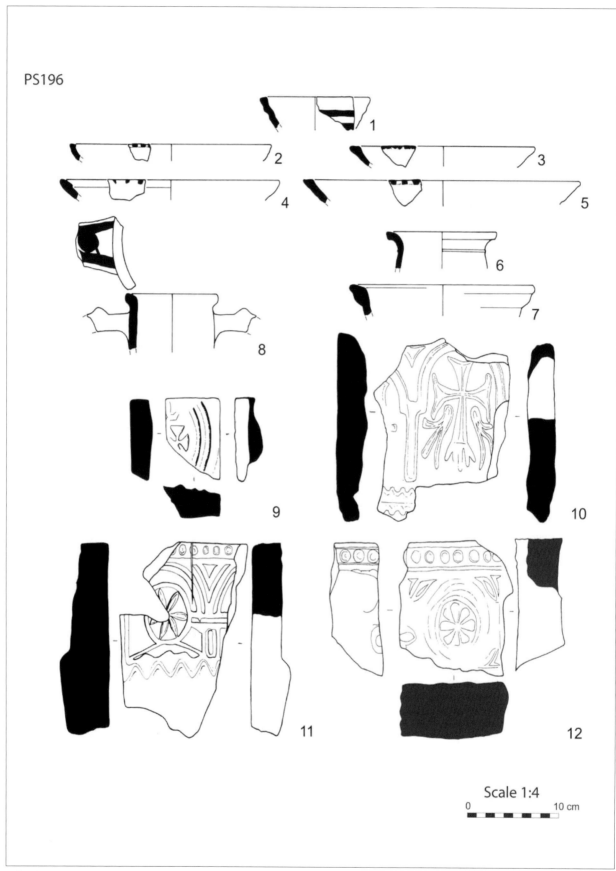

Fig. 6.105. Pottery from site PS196

Fig. No.	Site No.	Hand	Wheel	Inclusions	Colour	Finish
1	PS196		X	m min, mica	5 YR 6/6	ext painted bands 5 YR 4/3
2	PS196		X	m min, mica	2.5 YR 6/6	paint on rim 2.5 YR 5/4
3	PS196		X	m min, mica	2.5 YR 6/6	paint on rim 10 YR 5/4
4	PS196		X	m min, mica	2.5 YR 6/6	paint on rim 2.5 YR 4/4
5	PS196		X	m min, mica	2.5 YR 6/6	paint on rim 5 YR 3/2
6	PS196		X	dense min, mica	7.5 YR 5/4	
7	PS196		X	m min	7.5 YR 6/6	
8	PS196		X	m min, mica	7.5 YR 6/4	paint on handle 7.5 YR 3/2
9	PS196			m min, veg	fabric 2.5 YR 5/6	
10	PS196			f min	2.5 YR 6/6	ext moulded decoration
11	PS196			m min, grog	2.5 YR 6/6	ext moulded decoration
12	PS196			m min, grog	2.5 YR 5/6	ext moulded decoration

Fig. 6.105 (catalogue). Pottery from site PS196

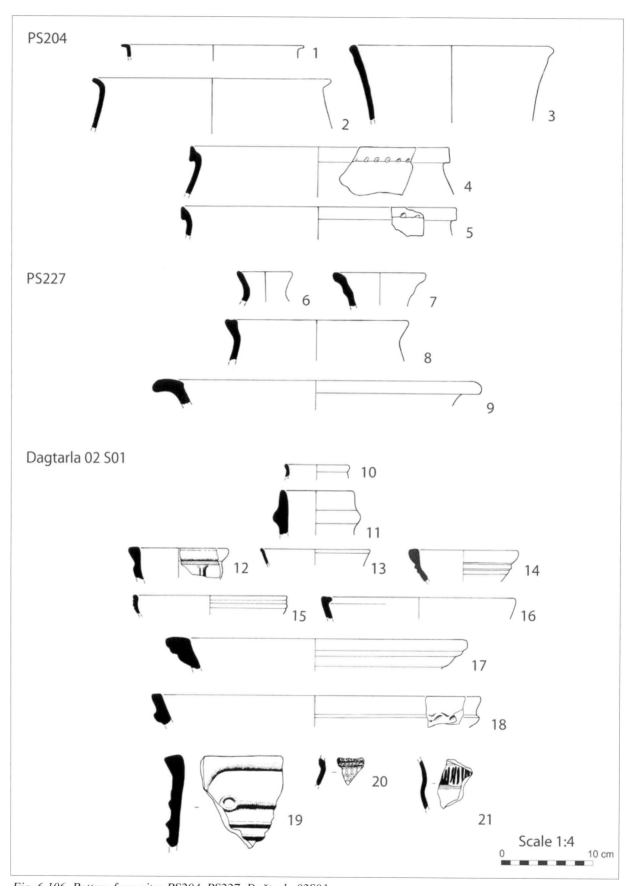

Fig. 6.106. Pottery from sites PS204, PS227, Dağtarla 02S01

Landscapes with Figures: Paphlagonia through the Hellenistic, Roman and Byzantine Periods, 330 BC–AD 1453

Fig. No.	Site No.	Hand	Wheel	Inclusions	Colour	Finish
1	PS204		X	dense min, mica	fabric 5 YR 6/6	
2	PS204		X	dense min, mica	7.5 YR 6/4	
3	PS204		X	dense min, mica	5 YR 6/6	
4	PS204		X	dense min, mica	5 YR 6/6	ext rim dents
5	PS204		X	dense min, mica	5 YR 6/6	ext rim brn; dents
6	PS227		X	m min	5 YR 5/4	
7	PS227		X	m min	5 YR 7/4	
8	PS227		X	m min	2.5 YR 5/4	
9	PS227		X	m min	2.5 YR 6/6	int brn
10	Dağtarla 02S01		X	mica	2.5 YR 5/4	
11	Dağtarla 02S01		X	f-m min	2.5 YR 6/6 core grey	
12	Dağtarla 02S01		X	f min	10 R 6/4	vertical ledge below rim
13	Dağtarla 02S01			f min, mica	2.5 YR 6/6	
14	Dağtarla 02S01		X	f-m min	10 R 6/4	
15	Dağtarla 02S01			f min	2.5 YR 6/4	
16	Dağtarla 02S01		X		2.5 YR 6/4 core grey-brown	
17	Dağtarla 02S01	X?		m min, mica	2.5 YR 6/4	
18	Dağtarla 02S01	X		min	2.5 YR 6/4	ext below rim applied decoration
19	Dağtarla 02S01			dense m inc	2.5 YR 6/4	moulded decoration possible white paint or plaster
20	Dağtarla 02S01			f inc	2.5 YR 5/6	moulded decoration
21	Dağtarla 02S01			f min	5 YR 7/8	ext brn horizontal paint 10 YR 3/6 vertical paint 7.5 YR 3/2

Fig. 6.106 (catalogue). Pottery from sites PS204, PS227, Dağtarla 02S01

Chapter Six

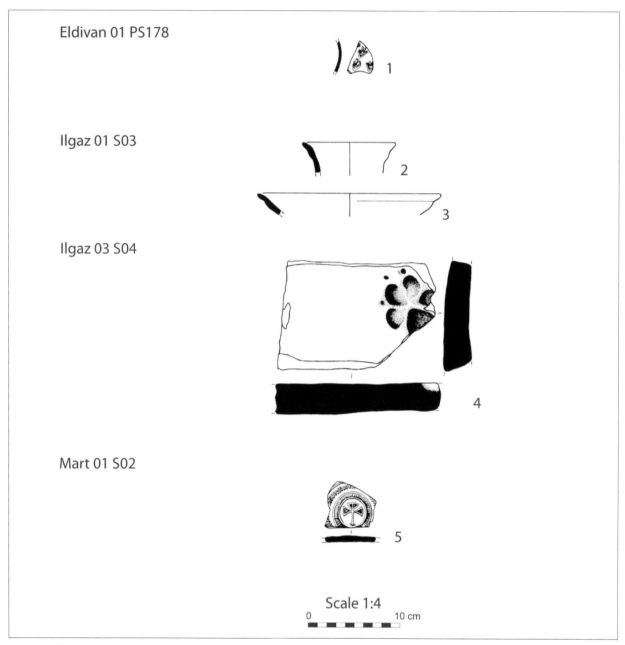

Fig. 6.107. Pottery from sites Eldivan 01 (PS178), Ilgaz 01S03, Ilgaz 03S04, Mart 01S02

Fig. No.	Site No.	Hand	Wheel	Inclusions	Colour	Finish
1	Eldivan 01/PS178		X	no visible inc	ext and core 10 R 5/6 int 10 R 4/1	ext relief decoration
2	Ilgaz 01S03			m min, veg	7.5 YR 6/4	
3	Ilgaz 01S03			m min, veg	7.5 YR 6/4	
4	Ilgaz 03S04					tile with dog paw print
5	Mart 01S02		X		5 YR 7/3	moulded decoration

Fig. 6.107 (catalogue). Pottery from sites Eldivan 01 (PS178), Ilgaz 01S03, Ilgaz 03S04, Mart 01S02

Chapter Seven

Çankırı in History: Insights from Ottoman Documents

M. Mehdi İlhan

Introduction
Recent years have seen an increased exploitation of the extremely rich historical source that takes the form of Ottoman census and tax records (Kiel 1997; 2004; Zarinebaf et al. 2005). Within the remit of Project Paphlagonia I studied a selection of relevant Ottoman documents with the aim of elucidating those periods of the past of the town and province of Çankırı that perhaps do not feature so clearly in the available archaeological record. A study of the development of Çankırı town has already been published (İlhan 2005, partly reworked here) and work is ongoing for a monograph devoted to the socio-economic history of Çankırı province from the early 16th century onwards. The present chapter provides an overview and summary of results relating to research conducted within Project Paphlagonia.

Nature of the sources
The Tapu Tahrir Defters (Ottoman Cadastral Registers) are one of the most important sources of information on the socio-economic history of the Ottoman empire. The Ottoman administrators recorded settlements, heads of households and a host of information potentially of relevance to the taxability of the region in question. The oldest surviving register is dated AH 835/AD 1431–1432 and relates to the province of Albania (İnalcık 1987). In the 16th century, particularly during the reign of Sultan Süleyman, such surveys were carried out for almost all the provinces of the Ottoman empire, and at certain times thereafter.

In total, there are 14 registers relating to the Ottoman province of Çankırı (Kengiri) in the Başbakanlık (Prime Ministerial) Archives (BOA) of Istanbul, five in the Tapu Kadastro Genel Müdürlüğü Kuyud-i Kadime Archives (TKGM) of Ankara and two in Istanbul Belediye (Municipality) Library. There was not time to make an exhaustive study of all these documents and so three of the nine *kaza* or regions were selected for in-depth treatment: Kengiri (Çankırı town and environs), Çerkeş and Koçhisar (today Ilgaz). The focus in this chapter is on the sources firstly as they relate to Çankırı town and secondly as they concern the villages of the three sampled regions.

Of the registers mentioned above as relating to Çankırı province, only two are detailed (cadastral) registers: one in Istanbul (BOA TD 100) dated AH 927/AD 1521 and one in Ankara (TKGM TD 81) dated AH 986/AD 1578. None of the registers carried out prior to AD 1530, namely summary (*icmal*) TD 97 dated AH 926/AD 1520 and detailed (*mufassal*) register TD 100 dated AH 927/AD 1521, include the *vakf* holdings because there are also *vakf* registers of Çankırı province that were maintained separately. These are *vakf* registers of AH 962/AD 1555 (BOA TD 291) and AH 987/AD 1579 (TKGM TD 578). A *vakf* register prior to AD 1530 must also have been carried out since the *vakf* holdings inserted into the *defter* 438, a register which is part of the AD 1530 *Muhasebe-i Vilayet-i Anadolu,* are only summaries. These surveys of the province of Çankırı were carried out at intervals of 25 years.

It is uncertain whether or not a survey was carried out during the reigns of Murad II (AD 1421–1444; 1446–1451) or his son Mehmed II (AD 1444–1446; 1451–1481) since the earliest existing survey of the province is dated AD 1520. This is a summary (*icmal*) register, an indication that an earlier survey must have existed. On the other hand, it is possible, but not certain, that this register is a summary (*icmal*) for BOA TD 100 dated AD 1521; not certain as it is unlikely that a summary of a register would be made before the completion of the detailed (*mufassal*) one. Nevertheless, the incomes recorded in both registers correspond to each other. In either case it is highly probable that an earlier survey was carried out for the province since it could not have been possible for the Ottomans to collect taxes in the province without a survey for a period of at least 70 years. It is also probable that an earlier *vakf* register was made. Had we had an earlier survey it may have been possible to study the impact of the Celali revolts of AD 1519 that had a considerable effect on the city and province of Çankırı (Ayhan 1998: 151). It would have been possible for us at least to establish the difference between the amounts and the kinds of taxes before and after the revolts, as some historians claim that high taxes were one of the causes of the Celali revolts (Uzunçarşılı 1998: 297). My concern for the purpose of research into the province of Çankırı is mainly with the detailed (*mufassal*) and *vakf* surveys. Additionally, comparison will be made with a third survey which is part of *Muhasebe-i Vilayet-i Anadolu* (BOA TD 438). Although this third register is dated AD 1530, it is in fact a synopsis of the *mufassal* register for AD 1521: the *hane* (household) and *mücerred* (bachelor) entries are the same for almost all the quarters, with some minor exceptions. These exceptions were due either to minor changes that were recorded in the later register or to scribal error. The second case is more likely for there is no doubt that the AD 1530 register is a summarised account of the AD 1521 register.

In all three registers there are clear records of tax-exempt persons. In particular, religious personages, particularly *imams* and *müezzins*, appear to be fully recorded. We can classify these tax exemptions in three categories:

> Religious personages such as *imam*, *müezzin*, *hatib* (preacher), *müderris*, *sermahfil* (chorus head), *hafız*, *şeyh*, *kayyum* and *kadı* (judge);
> Non-religious officials such as *kethüda*, *muhassil* (tax collector), *mütevelli* (administrator, trustee of an endowment), *emir*, *mülazım* (lieutenant);
> Disabled personages such as *mecnun* (crazy, mad) *divane* (insane), *a'ma* (blind), *kötürüm* (crippled or paralysed) and *ma'lul* (disabled).

Quite a number of poor (*fakir*, six according to the AD 1521 register) were also recorded as tax-exempt, and two blind and one disabled were recorded as poor. Only one person was recorded as missing (*gayib*). The status of the disabled and poor was determined in court before witnesses (Kaya 2001).

Glossary of terms

akçe	Ottoman silver coin
a'ma	blind, sightless
avarız	a tax collected in extraordinary circumstances such as during campaigns or war
avarız hane	a division of the population of a district liable to *avarız* tax into a varying number of household units depending on the financial capacity of the inhabitants of the district
bennak	a peasant holding little or no land
bey	military commander of a *sancak*
caba	landless peasant; landless bachelor subject to feudal taxation
cema'at	tribe
çift	a unit of land ploughed by a pair of oxen, literally a pair of oxen yoked to a plough; a peasant (*ra'aya*) who holds a *çift*; a plot of land of 20–30 acres, that can be cultivated with a single plough; the surface of 60–150 *dönüms* depending on the fertility of land
çingan	gypsy
defter	tax register
divane	insane
emir (pl. *ümera*)	commander, chief, leader, ruler, same as bey
fakir	poor
gayib	missing
hafız (pl. *huffaz*)	one who can recite by heart the full text of the Kur'an
hali	empty, uninhabited
hamam	bathhouse
hane	household, as a taxable unit
hatib	preacher
icmal defter	summary tax register (as opposed to *mufassal defter*)
ihtisab	market dues
imam	leader of prayer
'imaret	soup kitchen for the poor
kadı	Islamic judge
karbansaray	caravanserai
kayyum	a sweeper or caretaker of a mosque
kaza	district, next level below *sancak*
kethüda	steward, head of a guild
kötürüm	paralysed, crippled
kurbet	intimacy, nearness to God, thus may mean a hermit who has devoted himself to God; a mystic or a *sufi*
ma'a şüreka	with shareholders
ma'lul	disabled
mecnun	mad
medrese	Islamic school
mevkufat	arrested, detained
mezra'a	arable land
mir-i liva	district governor
mu'allimhane	a teacher's house, school
mufassal defter	detailed tax register (as opposed to

	icmal defter)
muhassıl	tax collector
mücerred	unmarried man, bachelor
müderris	teacher
mufti	Muslim priest, expounder of Islamic law
mülazım	lieutenant
mütevelli	administrator, trustee
nahiye	administrative sub-district, usually of a *kaza*
nam-ı diger	alternative name, also known as
nim	a peasant who holds half of a *çift*
ra'aya (sing. *ra'iyyet*)	subject, tax-paying inhabitants of the Ottoman empire, the peasantry
ra'iyyet	a subject
resm-i çift	land tax
salname	a year book; a semi-official year book of the Ottoman empire or of a province of the empire
sancak	sub-province
sekban	mercenary military unit
sermahfil	assistant to the chief *muezzin*, usually in a big mosque
sipahi	fief-holding cavalry soldier
suhte	a term used for a *medrese* student
şeyh	sheikh, head of a religious order
tahrir heyeti	registration committee
timar	fief, taxes granted to *sipahis*, but also to civilian officials
vakf	Islamic charitable foundation and associated property usually exempt from state taxes
yaylak	summer pastures
zaviye	cell (of a recluse); lodge (of dervishes)
zekât	alms
zemin	land, place
zevle/zivle/züvle	a unit of land equivalent to a quarter of a *çift*; literally a side rod in an ox-yoke to keep the oxen under control; a person who holds a quarter of a *çift*

Çankırı town in Ottoman history

Çankırı, Roman Germanikopolis, was known as Khanjara in Arabic sources (Al-Tabari VI: 12; Ibn Al-Athir IV: 578) and as Kengiri in Selçuk and Ottoman sources, this latter version more closely approximating its Iron Age name of Gangra (see Chapter Six). During the eighth century AD the town gained the name of Hısnu'l-Hadid (Iron Fortress) due to its successful resistance to attack by Arab armies (Al-Tabari VI: 469; Al-Ya'kubi II: 292, 300). The region passed into Turkish hands after the battle of Manzikert in AD 1071. Karatekin, a Selçuk emir, conquered the city in AD 1082 during the reign of Süleyman Shah (Ayhan 1998: 101). Soon after, in AD 1084, he went on to conquer Sinop and Kastamonu, and establish a principality of his own that lasted until the Crusaders' invasion (Ayhan 1998: 101–04). Karatekin died during one of the battles against the Crusaders, perhaps in AD 1106, and is buried in the citadel of Çankırı in a mausoleum bearing his name. Crusaders attacked the city in AD 1101 and, failing to take it, sacked its environs. Following the death of Emir Gazi in AD 1134 the city alternated rapidly between Byzantine and Danishmendid suzerainty before its Selçuk conquest. The Candarids, rulers of Kastamonu, took over rule of the city upon the demise of the Selçuks, and later it fell under the Ottomans during the reign of Murad I (AD 1362–1389).

Ottoman rule, however, did not last long as Timur handed over the city to İsfendiyaroğulları following the battle of Ankara in AD 1402. Çankırı passed into Ottoman hands once more when İsfendiyaroğlu Kasım Bey took refuge with Mehmed Çelebi, and it remained under Ottoman control apart from a short interlude when İsfendiyar Bey reconquered it during the reign of Murad II (AD 1438–1451). Merely to list this rather dizzying sequence of conquests and reconquests of the city over these few centuries gives some idea of both its significance and its vulnerability within a system of strategic control of the landscape in this part of Turkey and movement across it. As discussed in Chapter Six, this fraught historical environment doubtless provides the context for the construction and use of the many hilltop fortified sites still evident on the landscape today.

Demography

Town quarters

There are 24 quarters of Çankırı town recorded in AD 1521 and AD 1530, and 23 in AD 1578 (table 7.1). There is no record of Tohte quarter in AD 1578 and Şeyh Hünkar Hacı Bahaeddin quarter is noted as being empty (*hali*). It is possible that its inhabitants had moved to other quarters. Over this 57-year period some quarters enjoyed an increase in the number of inhabitants whereas others, almost half, suffered a decrease (fig. 7.1). Karataş quarter had the highest increase while Cami' quarter had the most noticeable decrease, most probably due to the construction in Cami' quarter of the Sultan Süleyman mosque between AD 1552 and 1558, having been commissioned by the Sultan during his AD 1548 Persian campaign. It is probable that this mosque was constructed to replace an old Selçuk mosque built over the ruins of a church. There are still two Byzantine columns at the sides of the entrance to the mosque's garden.

Chapter Seven

Quarter	Population in AD 1521	Population in AD 1578
Mescid-i Hatib	101	108
Karataş-ı Kayser	202	252
Şeyh 'Osman	93	76
Haci Musa	115	205
'Imaret	127	169
Mescid-i Halil Ağa	152	179
Mescid-i Havace Kasım	103	47
Pürdedar Gazi	80	93
Cami' (Sultan Süleyman)	62	42
Tohte	31	-
Küçük Menare	155	104
Alaca Mescid	139	137
Emir-i Ahur	111	123
Hıdırlık	29	64
Mescid-i Haci Mü'minin	123	112
Havace Bahşayiş	46	108
Şeyh Hankah-i Haci Bahaeddin	30	0
Kadi	94	53
Bimarhane	83	112
Çukur	22	64
Umur Fakih (Havace Elvan)	141	125
Çetince	114	40
Havace İbrahim	60	98
Kara Taş	148	216
Total	**2,361**	**2,527**

Table 7.1. The quarters of Çankırı town in AD 1521 and AD 1578

The quarters of Çankırı, as in other towns, were named after a mosque or a distinguished man. All the names are of Turkish or Islamic origin. Apart from perhaps Karataş-ı Kayser, there is no quarter whose name has its origin prior to the Turkish conquest. The quarters named after Şeyh Hünkar Hacı Bahaeddin, Umur Fakih and Şeyh 'Osman, the companions of Karatekin in the conquest of Çankırı, most probably originate from the Selçuk period. The quarter of Mescid-i Havace Kasım may have had its roots in the period of the İsfendiyarid principality since Kasım Bey, son of İsfendiyar Bey, had a mosque, 'imaret, zaviye and a medrese built in the town. The Candarid Kasım Bey also had a mosque called 'Imaret built in AD 1397 on the present-day 'Imaret Street and it is possible therefore that 'Imaret quarter originated from the Candarid period.

Partly due to the lack of suitable maps, it is difficult to estimate the boundaries of the 16th-century quarters as they relate to the existing town. Most of the names have changed and the modern municipal map has the names of only a few quarters and the new streets. A close study of this map, however, shows that the boundaries of the old town have been largely preserved since Ottoman days. Many houses were certainly built from the 17th century up to the 20th century, but the quarter boundaries remained relatively constant. In other words, the old town stretched along the foot of the hill on the northern side of what has grown up very recently as the modern town (fig. 1.2). The castle was built on this hill, where the tomb of Karatekin, the conqueror of Çankırı in AD 1082, also stands. The Karatekin quarter that stretches immediately from the foot of the hill below the cemetery is recorded in both registers under the name Emir-i Ahur. Taş Mescid (figs 7.2–7.3), the hospital section of which was built by Çankırı Atabeyi Cemaleddin Ferruh in AD 1235 during the reign of the Selçuk Sultan Alaaddin Keykubad I, son of Keyhüsrev, is recorded in both registers as Bimarhane. A medrese was added to the hospital in AD 1242. I have established in an unpublished article on Amasya that the Selçuks built their own quarters rather than settling in existing Christian quarters. Thus Torumtay Medrese, Gök Medrese and Bimarhane are on the outskirts of the ancient town of Amasya. Likewise, Taş Mescid is on the outskirts of the ancient town of Çankırı and Karatekin, also a Selçuk quarter, is at the northern periphery.

The quarter of Cami' (Cami'-i Sultan Süleyman), originally a Selçuk quarter, is also called Mimar Sinan, although the mosque was built by Sadık Kalfa, Mimar Sinan's assistant master. The boundaries of present-day Mimar Sinan quarter reach as far as the upper boundaries of the foot of the hill. The lower boundaries of the Ottoman quarters excluding Taş Mescid were most probably the present-day Orgeneral Haluk Karadayı Street stretching from the northwest and continuing with Atatürk Bulvarı in the south, while the northwestern boundary was probably the cemetery.

The 24 quarters of Çankırı town were contained within a small area that stretched 0.5km from south to north and 1.5km from west to east. They were thus very small quarters both in AD 1521 and AD 1578, with an average of only nine to ten households. Dividing the town into small quarters was perhaps a matter of convenience for both registrars and administrators. The number and the names of the quarters continue only slightly changed by the end of the 17th century when there are 17 quarters recorded in the court registers of Çankırı with only the Yoğurtçu quarter as an addition (Kaya 2001). The quarter of Cami' is recorded in one place as Cami'-i

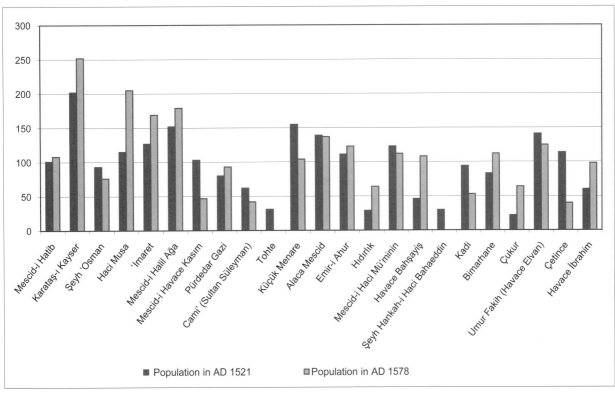

Fig. 7.1. Population shifts by quarter AD 1521–1578

Fig. 7.2. View of Taş Mescid

Fig. 7.3. View of Taş Mescid

Kebir and as the Hıdırlık quarter in another. There is mention of a Şeyh 'Osman quarter on a gravestone inscription dated AH 1277/AD 1860–1861 (fig. 7.4). The inscription runs as follows:

Huve'l-Baki
Dem çeker ez durr [ezder?] misali
Yeniçerinin erleri
Dilerim Bari Huda'dan
Cennet olsun yerleri
Şeyh 'Osman mahallesinden
El-Seyyidi [?] Kul Muhammed Ağa
Fatiha Sene 1277

He [God] is everlasting.
Warbles like a wild bird [?]
The janissary's men
I beg God, the Creator
Let their abode be paradise
From the quarter of Şeyh Osman
El-Seyyid Kul Muhammed Ağa
Fatiha, the year 1277 [AD 1860]

Population

A close study of the quarters and comparison of the registers invites some observations. There are no major differences between the AD 1521 and AD 1530 registers, although there are slight discrepancies that were probably due to the carelessness of the scribe, as discussed above. Both in AD 1521 and AD 1530 there were 409 households and 215 (214 in AD 1530) bachelors. It is difficult to believe that the number of households went up from 409 in AD 1521 to only 417 in AD 1578 and the number of bachelors from 215 to 217, an increase of only eight and two respectively over a period of 57 years. The number of bachelors is unusually high when compared with the registers of other provinces such as Amid (İlhan 2000: 142) and Şehrizol. The numbers of blind (five) and crippled (one) were the same in AD 1521 and AD 1578.

The rather low population of Çankırı in both AD 1521 and AD 1578 and the very low rate of increase over 57 years might be due to certain events that took place in the region in the 16th century. An earthquake lasting 45 days shook Anatolia in AD 1509. Çankırı was one of the towns affected and many lives were lost. A number of revolts took place that had negative effects on both the AD 1521 and AD 1578 surveys. Shortly before the AD 1521 survey of Çankırı started, a *timar* holder called Kızılbaş Celal of Bozok, a Turcoman from the town of Turhal near Amasya, declared himself as Mahdi and started a revolt, backed by Shah Isma'il, with 20,000 followers. Şehsuvar Ali Bey, the governor of Elbistan, defeated the rebels in AD 1518. Although Kızılbaş Celal

Fig. 7.4. Gravestone inscription dated AH 1277/AD 1860–1861

managed to escape, he was caught near Erzincan and beheaded (Uzunçarşılı 1998: 297). A famine broke out in Çankırı in AD 1574 and lasted three years (Ayhan 1998: 159) coinciding with the time, or soon after the start, of a survey for the province of Çankırı that was completed in AD 1578.

Perhaps most important of all, about a decade before the start of the survey a series of *suhte*, *kurbet* and *çingan* movements took place, and according to the Mühimme documents lasted at least two decades. These movements may have played a significant role not only in the depopulation of the province of Çankırı and its surroundings, but also in hampering the process of conducting official survey. A Mühimme decree of AD 1564 (MD 6: 206), addressed to the *beys* and *kadıs* of all the *sancaks* in the provinces of Anadolu, Karaman, Dhu'l-Kadirlu, Aleppo and Diyarbekir, orders them to suppress the highly mobile *kurbet* and *çingan* groups who were causing havoc throughout Asia Minor by means of highway robbery and other illegal activities. In AD 1566, according to other Mühimme documents (MD 5: 1224), the brigands called

Kara Kader, Cafer, Kirmani and Şah with 15 horsemen were holding-up people and robbing them in the mountain passes of Çorum and Çankırı provinces. Likewise, some *kurbet* and *suhte* groups were killing and robbing people in Çankırı, Bolu and Kastamonu provinces in the same year (MD 5: 1301; MD 5: 1582). These *suhte* and *kurbet* movements appear to have continued for at least two decades. Ayhan (1998: 149–50, 159) mentions another *suhte* and *kurbet* movement that took place in AD 1576, about the same time that officials started to carry out the survey in the province of Çankırı that was concluded in AD 1578. There are also Mühimme documents ranging from AD 1581 to AD 1588 that give many details on the *suhte* and *kurbet* movements. According to these decrees addressed to the *beys* and *kadıs* of Çankırı, Kastamonu and Bolu certain groups of *suhte*, *kurbet* and other bandits under the leadership of rebels such as Çalık Veliyuddin, Ekmekoğlu, Arpacıoğlu, Kılıçoğlu and Fakihoğlu were raiding towns and villages and waylaying travellers on highways. They were collecting 'alms' (*zekât*) from people in excessive amounts and injuring those who did not comply. They were carrying away with them 'smooth-faced young boys' and young girls. They beat and robbed people. Most important of all, these criminals were sheltered by some officials and inhabitants in the provinces (MD 46: 64; MD 52: 617; MD 53: 700; MD 60: 586; MD 61: 43; MD 64: 382). The Ottoman government issued decrees ordering officials to catch these criminals, imprison them and send them to the Porte. But there were cases where they deceived officials such as *sekbans* and janissaries sent to investigate and catch them (MD 53: 730). Some even managed to escape after they were arrested and brought to Istanbul (MD 62: 59). The *suhte* and *kurbet* movements usually took place whenever there were military campaigns and, in fact, in one of the Mühimme decrees it is specifically mentioned that the *suhte* movements had been going on since the start of the Eastern Campaign (MD 60: 640; MD 64: 382).

The population of Çankırı appears to have grown rapidly in the 17th century. According to one of the Court register documents there were 242 and a quarter *avarız hanes* in Çankırı in 1698 (Kaya 2001). I multiplied this figure by an estimated actual *hane* of four which gives us at least 968 actual households, a figure more than double that recorded in both the AD 1521 and AD 1578 registers. This figure of actual *hane* multiplied by five gives us 5,324 as the population of Çankırı at the end of the 17th century. According to Evliya Çelebi (died ca. AH 1095/AD 1684), however, there were 4,000 houses in Çankırı (Ayhan 1998: 202), which means a population of about 20,000, which is most probably an exaggeration, for, according to the sources, the population of Çankırı was 12,000 in AD 1831 and 15,000 at the end of the 19th century. Both these figures as well as the figure that I calculate from *avarız hanes* for the end of the 17th century are below that of Evliya Çelebi but more closely fit a pattern of expected growth.

The total number of households recorded by the scribe did not always correspond to the actual household entries. I therefore did my own calculation and included such tax-exempts as *imams*, *müezzins* and *a'mas* assuming that they also had families. The population of the quarters and that of the town was then calculated. The 10% military as suggested by Barkan (1970) was excluded, as my purpose was to work out the distribution of population within the quarters. The quarter with the highest population both in AD 1521 and AD 1578 was Karataş-ı Kayser, perhaps one of the oldest quarters of the town. The quarter with the lowest population in AD 1521 was Çukur with only four households and two bachelors, and in AD 1578 was Cami'-i Sultan Süleyman which was simply called Cami' in AD 1521. The quarter of Tohte with six households and one bachelor in AD 1521 was not recorded in AD 1578. Another quarter with low population was Şeyh Hünkar Bahaeddin with five households and five bachelors in AD 1521. This quarter is recorded as empty (*hali*) in AD 1578. There are virtually no traces of Christian quarters. It is believed that shortly after the Turkish conquest in AD 1082 most of the inhabitants, perhaps almost all, converted to Islam and the chief-bishopric was moved from Çankırı to Amasra (Ayhan 1998: 100). It is also possible that those who did not convert emigrated to Amasra and other neighbouring towns.

The population of the town of Çankırı was 2,361 in AD 1521 and 2,527 in AD 1578 (fig. 7.5). There was an increase of only about 7% in 57 years, a very insignificant growth each year (about 10 per 10,000 in one year). The population of the town grew to an estimated 5,324 by AD 1698 (see above) and its population was 12,203 in AD 1831 according to the census carried out by Silahşoran-ı Hassa Süleyman Bey (Ayhan 1998: 188). Charles Texier, French archaeologist and traveller, estimated Çankırı's population as 16,000 with only 40 Greek families at the end of the first half of the 19th century (Ayhan 1998: 177), but then it is not possible to explain the figures given by Tshichatsheff in AD 1839, who estimates that there were 1,800 households (which multiplied by five gives us a population of 9,000 persons) in Çankırı, of which 40 were non-Muslims (Ayhan 1998: 193). On the other hand, the population of the town according to the AD 1869 *salname* was 16,605 Muslims, 207 Greeks and 70 Armenians (Ayhan 1998: 196). Here at least the non-Muslim population can be verified with figures for AD 1882 quoted by Ayhan (who gives no

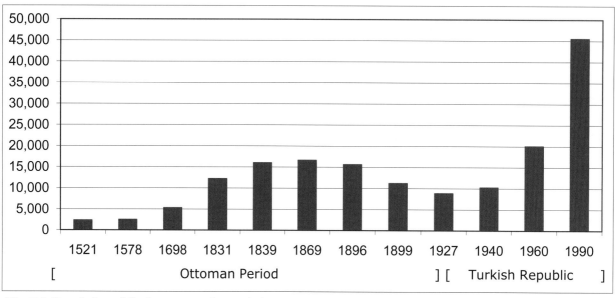

Fig. 7.5. *Population of Çankırı town at intervals from AD 1521–1990*

source): the non-Muslim population of Çankırı was 758 Greeks and 298 Armenians. According to Ali Cevad's census in 1898 there were 969 Greeks and 959 Armenians in Çankırı (Ayhan 1998: 199, 203). Furthermore, Cuinet's (1894: 551) figure is 15,632 for the population of Çankırı, of which 780 were Greeks and 472 were Armenians. These figures may sound reasonable, but it is difficult to understand why the town's population should fall to 11,200 according to the AD 1899 *salname* of Kastamonu (Mordtmann 1960). Out of this population 476 were Greek men, 415 Greek women, 186 Armenian men and 179 Armenian women, while in AD 1913 there were 1,337 Greeks and 482 Armenians in Çankırı (Ayhan 1998: 202, 204, 209). During the First World War and the War of Independence the population of the town fell drastically, for in AD 1927 it was down to 8,847 and in AD 1940 it was 10,235. By 1960 the town's population had doubled, to 20,047, and by AD 1990 more than doubled again to 45,496 (Şahin 1993), despite massive emigration from the province as a whole over most of this period (Aydın 1990). The population figures for the Republican period are probably reliable, and can be explained by natural growth and by the centripetal attraction of Çankırı town at the expense of rural settlement: the rural population of Ilgaz *ilçe*, for example, fell from 34,592 in AD 1927 to 23,281 in AD 1990 (Alexandre 1994: 38). But the figures for the Ottoman period show considerable variation and are at times no doubt unreliable. A study of the graphics, however, at least gives us an idea of what the population of the town was for each century starting from AD 1521. The sources on the non-Muslim population figures are also inconsistent and at times exaggerated, but it appears that there was a steady rise perhaps due as much to immigration as to natural growth.

Education
The personal names recorded in the AD 1521 register reflect a town with a strong religious inclination. Most of the names used by the inhabitants are either the names of the Prophet and his companions or of the other prophets. The most common of these names are Muhammed, Ahmed, Mahmud, Mustafa, Hamza, 'Ali and Hüseyin on the one hand, and Musa, 'Isa and Yusuf on the other. Such names are not an indication of ethnic groups, but rather point to an Islamic religious community, which had its own system of education.

The basic units of education in the Ottoman empire were *medreses* and schools, but at the same time the mosques and other religious foundations such as *zaviyes* served equally as bases of both religious and secular education. Many learned men such as *müderrises*, *imams*, *müezzins* and *huffaz* employed in these institutions were not only highly educated, but also served as educators to the broader community. In an earlier study I calculated that about 2% of adult males in the Ottoman province of Anatolia were educators in one way or another (İlhan 1996: 128), a very high percentage considering that the whole population, including the inhabitants of villages, was taken into account. The proportion in towns was most probably higher. Nevertheless, we cannot say the same for the town of Çankırı, for my calculation here shows that only 1% of the population were educators. There were 24 quarters in the town of

Çankırı according to the AD 1521 and AD 1530 registers (see above) and 22 according to the AD 1578 register. There was almost one *imam* in every quarter and perhaps an equal number of *muezzins*, although five in the AD 1521 and 12 in the AD 1578 register were recorded. Adding to these numbers *hatibs* (preachers), *sermahfil*, *huffaz* and *şeyhs* we arrive at a figure of 1% of the population of the town as educators. A *müderris* and a *kadı* are registered only in the AD 1578 register. We know that Ebu'su'ud Mehmed Efendi was offered the post of *müderris* at the *medrese* of Çankırı in AD 1516, but it is uncertain whether or not he accepted the post (Ayhan 1998: 156). Furthermore, according to the Ottoman administration there was a *kadı* and a *müfti* in Çankırı as well as *kadıs* in its *kazas* and *nahiyes* such as Çerkeş, Kurşunlu, Tosya and Toht (MD 6: 537; MD 6: 890; MD 6: 1347; MD 71: 55; MD 82: 48). There were 35 men of religion in AD 1521 and 36 in AD 1578, namely one man of religion per 12 or 13 households.

Economy of Çankırı town

Information on economic activities in the town of Çankırı is derived from several registers. The information is scattered. The basic income of the town was from the *mumhane* (candle factory), the *bozahane* (*boza*-factory, beverage made of fermented millet) and salt. The income for the first two cannot be calculated because it is cited along with the taxes such as sheep tax and oxen tax as well as taxes taken from fruit, pastures, *mezra'as* (arable fields), vineyards and orchards. The total income from all was 15,000 *akçes* in AD 1521 and 16,000 *akçes* in AD 1578 which went to the *mir-i liva* (BOA TD 100: 88; TKGM KK TD 81). The income from salt according to both the AD 1521 and AD 1578 registers was considerably higher. In AD 1521 income from salt was 55,000 *akçes* plus an income of 5,000 *akçes* from base (a chemical substance capable of combining with an acid to form salt). This income from salt increased to 71,667 *akçes* in AD 1578 (BOA TD 100: 87; TKGM KK TD 81), all of which income went to the Imperial Hass. According to the AD 1530 *icmal* (synopsis) register the total income of the Imperial Hass from the *nahiye* of Kengiri was 225,000 *akçes*. Of this, 60,000 *akçes* was from rice, 80,000 *akçes* from ….?, 55,000 *akçes* from salt work and 30,000 *akçes* from *mevkufat* (perhaps taxes taken from runaways and arrested persons). The total income for *mir-i liva* was 216,000 *akçes*. This income was from the *bozahane* and the candle factory mentioned above as well as from some villages and *yaylaks* (summer pastures) (BOA TD 100: 375; TKGM KK TD 81).

The AD 1521 register also has valuable information on agriculture, husbandry and stockbreeding, but the income from these is low. Çift tax (*resm-i çift*) is only 112 *akçes* and the income from wheat, barley, orchards and beehives is equally low. The income from all amounted to only 924 *akçes*. There are quite a number of orchards and pastures around the town but the income from them varies between four and 25 *akçes*. The description given of these orchards and pastures gives us a good idea of where they are distributed: around places such as Karataş, Acı Su, Bimarhane and Tabbağlar (TKGM KK TD 81).

The income from casual taxes (*bad-i hava ve cürm ve cinayet ve resm-i arusane*) in AD 1578 was 60,775 *akçes*. The income from sheep tax (excluding that of Yörügan) according to the AD 1578 register was 150,000 *akçes*, from *mevkufat-i yava* (capturing of runaways) 30,000 *akçes*, capitation tax (*cizye-i nefs-i* Kengiri), perhaps from some Christians living near or in town, was 5,000 *akçes* and *ihtisab* 4,300 *akçes* (TKGM KK TD 81).

Villages and agriculture in Çankırı province

According to register TD 81 in TKGM in Ankara the *sancak* of Çankırı in AD 1578 was divided into ten *nahiyes* including that of Kengiri itself. As explained above, for reasons of time and limited resources, documentary research was restricted to three *nahiyes*, that is Kengiri, Çerkeş and Koçhisar. The study here focuses on evidence from the registers of AD 1521 (TD 100), AD 1555 (TD 291) and AD 1578 (TD 81). Of these, the data pertaining to the AD 1578 register were assembled in alphabetical order, the AD 1521 data were studied in their original order as recorded in the register, since it appeared that the registrar and his retinue had visited all the villages for the purpose of registration, and the data of the AD 1555 register, a *vakf* register, were organised according to the status of the *vakf* holders.

The AD 1521 (TD 100) register was of particular interest. By locating the villages on a map it is possible to demonstrate that the registrar and his retinue (*tahrir heyeti*: registration committee) followed a certain route in order to register the *ra'aya* in the villages. It appears that the committee selected either a remote or a nearby village as their starting point, making a circuit back to the centre each time and registering villages on their way. These circuits continued until they had registered all the villages within a *nahiye*. Below are some examples of the routes the committee followed in the *nahiye* of Çerkeş:

> Yalak Özi, Yamaklu, Yoncalu, Kasaç, Hacılar;
> Kara Mustafa, Dikenli, Çömlekçi, Yukarı Çukurca, Yakuplar, Çukur Viran, (Pü)türbaşı
> Şeyh Toğan, Aşağı Kadı Özi, Ahur, Bedil, Bazman, Kızıllar, Kara Kınık, Çamluca, Berçin, Orman, Ali Özi, Ovacık.

Villages and population

According to the AD 1521 *timar* (fief) register (TD 100) there were 104 *timar* entries and a total of 77 villages in the *sancak* of Çankırı, with a total population of 12,388 (fig. 7.6). Some villages were shared between more than one fief-holder. Villages with high populations include those of Akyazı, Yonca and Baydekin, recorded as one village probably due to the fact they were adjacent to each other, with a total population of 884. Other villages with relatively high populations are Kazak (population 409) Dikenlu (397), Kermişki (376), Biğalu (370) and Söğüt Özi (359). The villages with the lowest populations are those of Renin (ten) and 'Alemdar (ten) as well as the *mezra'a* of Kuduz Çiftliği (five).

In the AD 1578 register (TD 81) we find that the population of the villages had increased. The villages of Akyazı (437) and Baydekin (three in number with a population of 189+500+444), recorded separately this time, almost doubled in population to a total of 1,570, and the population of the villages of Kazak (771) and Kermişki (679) also almost doubled. The population of the village of Dikenlu, however, dropped from 397 to 329, and that of the village of 'Alemdar increased only from ten to 13. The number of villages registered in Çankırı in AD 1578 increased to 100, whose total population almost doubled to 23,404. Villages such as Paşa (684), Beş Tut (553) and Belid Özi (447) feature in the AD 1578 register as the villages with the highest population, while those such as Bikenç (21), a *mezra'a* in the AD 1521 register, lie at the other end of the scale.

There were 14 *cema'ats* (tribes) recorded in Kengiri *nahiye* in the AD 1521 register and 11 in the AD 1578 register, their combined population increasing over this period from 2,366 to 3,778. According to the AD 1555 *vakf* register there were 57 *vakf* villages with a total population of 15,159. The total population of the villages of Çerkeş went up from 10,035 in AD 1521 to 17,619 in AD 1578, and the total population of the villages of Koçhisar almost doubled for the same period, increasing from 6,526 to 12,529. The total population of *vakf* villages of Çerkeş was 1,287 in AD 1555 while no *vakf* villages were recorded in Koçhisar for the same year.

Kırk (population rise from 562 in AD 1521 to 566 in AD 1578), Ilısoluk (from 642 to 1,147) and Yiva (from 415 to 790) were the villages with the highest population in the *nahiye* of Koçhisar, and Kara Kınık (from 432 to 478), Viran (from 414 to 494) and Saray (Sancak) (from 307 to 471) were the most populated villages in Çerkeş. These villages with high populations were generally situated on hill slopes with abundant water supplies and close to town centres and highways. The smaller and less dynamic villages, by contrast, were generally situated in remote locations, with little arable land and away from town centres and highways.

Land units, ownership, taxes

The Çankırı registers utilise divisions of *ra'aya* into *çift*, *nim*, *bennak*, *caba* and *mücerred*. Occasionally there occurs the word *zivle*, which is clearly part of this system of classification. In Şemseddin Sami's *Kamus-i*

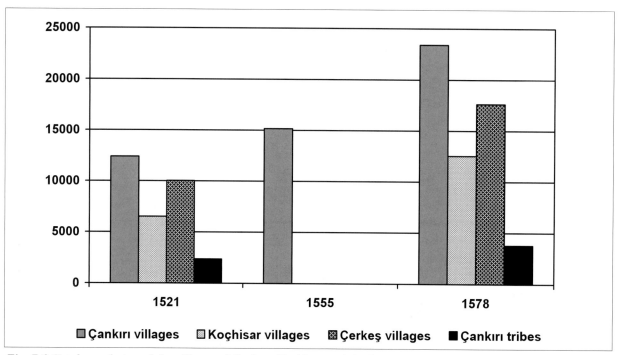

Fig. 7.6. Total population of the villages of Çankırı, Koçhisar and Çerkeş through the 16th century AD

Türki this word is spelt as *zilve*, while in the Redhouse dictionary it appears as *zevle* and *zavle*, and in one place in the AD 1578 register it is spelt as *züvle* (TD 291: 40). The word *zevle* means 'a side rod in an ox-yoke to keep the oxen under control'. Thus, there is no doubt that the word, just like *çift*, *nim*, *bennak* and *caba* refers to a unit of land registered in the name of a *ra'aya*. In fact, when we calculate the tax taken from a *zevle* in comparison to that taken from a *çift* it works out as equal to a quarter of a *çift*. In any case, for whatever reason only one *zevle* was recorded under a *zemin*, and very often a *ra'aya* had three *zevles* recorded in his name. Since one *zevle* was a quarter of a *çift* and had a value of 14.25 *akçes*, then a *ra'aya* with three *zevles* paid 42.75 akçes as *resm-i çift*. According to the Çankırı register, particularly with regard to the calculations based on TD 291, a *ra'aya* with a *çift* paid 57 *akçes*, with a *nim* 28.5 *akçes*, with a *bennak* 18 and at times 17 *akçes*, and with a *caba* 13 *akçes* as land tax. We may conclude that the *mücerreds* (bachelors) were not paying this tax since they were recorded within almost every village yet with no tax recorded against their names. In fact a clause in the *kanunname* of Bolu register clearly demonstrates that the *mücerreds* did not pay tax:

> No tax is recorded in the name of those registered as *mücerreds* in the *defter*. But those registered as *mücerreds* who get married or become bread-owners shall pay *resm-i bennak* and if they come to hold a piece of land they shall pay tax according to the size they hold.
>
> (TD 438: 418)

The note 'all the people in the village attest to the fact that he has no land in his possession' written above the name of 'Ali veled-i Mahmud, also recorded as *bennak* under the village of Kulasi in the AD 1555 register, confirms the clause in the *kanunname* (TD 291: 20).

In the Çankiri registers, particularly the AD 1555 *vakf* register we find that *çift* and its lesser units (*nim*, *bennak*, *caba* and *zevle*) were on occasion shared by more than one person. Such persons, for whom the term *ma'a şüreka*, 'with shareholders', is used, were generally brothers but not always so. In cases where they were not brothers the phrase *ma'a X* is used instead of *ma'a biraderan* or *ma'a biradereş* or even *ma'a biradereş ve ebna-i X* (TD 291: 223). These shareholders are not included in the population figures employed in this study, since that would be a repetition, as it is clear that they were recorded before and after the notes in the register. In the *kanunname* of Bolu the position of the land shareholders is clearly explained:

> And if the sons of a *ra'iyyet* [subject], some of whom are recorded as *resm-i çift* and some others as *resm-i bennak*, are holding their father's land in shares then they shall participate in paying *resm-i çift* and *resm-i bennak*. And if one of the sons of the deceased *ra'iyyet* dies and leaves behind a son while they are holding this land as *müşa'* [undivided] and *müşterek* [joint] then this share goes to his son, but if he does not have a son his share does not go to his brother. Also, the share of such a deceased person should not be given to a stranger. If the brothers pay what a stranger would pay then the land must be given to the brothers. If the brothers have no interest in the land then the *timar* holder can give it to whomever he wishes. The *sipahi* in giving the brother's share to the [other] brother must act in the way of experienced [and just] people; they must be in mutual agreement and must not take extra *akçe*.
>
> (TD 438: 418)

Occasionally we obtain informative glimpses of some of the difficulties met by the *defter* registrars, working in trying circumstances in rural districts a long way from a sophisticated urban environment. We encounter notes made by the scribe in the *defter* stating that the *ra'aya* of the village of Viranlı in Çerkeş did not show up for the registration and that therefore the details of this village were copied from the old register. In such cases, if a village, and in particular a tribe, did not show up and there is not an old register then the scribe put down an approximate figure (İlhan 1987: 789). Likewise, according to a note in the AD 1555 register, the officials in Istanbul noticed that the scribe had forgotten to record sheep tax (*resm-i ğanem* or *ğanem vergisi*) for the *vakf* village of Kedend and the *mülk* village of Kati (*nam-ı diger* Küvaz), in the *timar* holding of Paşa Çelebi bin Muhammed, a descendant of Mahmud Çelebi, in the new register. Thereupon the Grand Vizier and the other viziers were asked for permission to record them in the register. A note was added to the register explaining the case:

> The *resm-i ğanem* of this *vakf* village was mentioned and written in the old register, but mistakenly was not recorded in the new register. Therefore, as it is imperative to record it in the new register, permission for inscribing was granted by his highness the Exalted [*Hazret-i*] Rüstem Paşa, the Exalted 'Ali Paşa, the Exalted Muhammed Paşa and the Exalted Pertev Paşa, may it prolong their lives. Written in mid-Cemaziye'l-ahir 963 [26 April AD 1556] by Mustafa bin Celal Tevki'i, the most humble servant of Glorious and Supreme God who may forgive them.
>
> (TD 291: 48-50)

Village names and locations
In addition to the central *sancak* that is *kaza-i* Kengiri, the province of Çankırı (Kengiri) had another eight *kazas*, namely: Koçhisar (Ilgaz), Milan, Kurşunlu, Çerkeş, Tosya, Korgu, Kal'acik and Kari-Bazarı, each of which had *vakf* holdings. The *vakf* holdings in productive areas such as the *kazas* of Kengiri (195,365 *akçes*), Tosya (29,797 *akçes*) and Kari-Bazarı (18,178 *akçes*) generated higher incomes than other less productive *kazas* such as Koçhisar (Ilgaz) (2,051 *akçes*) and Milan (2,093). Overall, according to the *Muhasebe-ı Vilayet-i Anadolu* (*defter* 438 dated AH 937/AD 1530), the province was rather poor with regard to its religious and civil foundations in the light of the number of its *kazas* and villages. Thus the province consisted of nine *kazas* and 550 villages yet had only two '*imarets*, seven Friday mosques, 36 mosques, three *medreses*, two *mu'allimhanes*, eight *hamams* and six *karbansarays*.

There are 108 villages recorded within the *kaza* of Kengiri in the 16th century. The population and income of these villages vary greatly. Muslims inhabited all villages and there was only one village, Alur, where 71 Christian households are recorded along with 31 Muslim households. The names of these villages are mostly Turkish. There are cases where a reference is made to the ancient (older, *nam-ı diger*) name, for example, Karye-i Akören *nam-ı diger* Çadik: the village of Akören, also known as Çadik. Other names give a hint as to the origin of the inhabitants, such as the villages called Özbek, Bayındır, Kıbçak, Kazak and Yörük. Still others provide a description of the location of the settlement, such as Acı Kuyu, İnce Su, Bozca Yer, Karaca Kaya, while some derive their names from important buildings such as Hisarcık and Saraycık. It seems certain that the detailed (*mufassal*) cadastral registers give an accurate picture of the villages of the province. If a village had become derelict it is recorded as such, as are villages that have shifted location. Such information, if systematically deployed in the field, might aid in the identification of now abandoned Ottoman settlements. Pasture lands are also recorded in the registers, including Aydos, Tokruk, Aldus and Korucuk, which were used by tribes such as Aytaç, Şarkli, Kuçekli, Mikayillu and Gençlu.

The cadastral registers contain much detailed information on agricultural lands, and produce such as wheat and barley, while orchards, gardens and vineyards are also recorded. It is possible to draw the boundaries of villages by calculating the amount of agricultural produce and the number of farms. All types of husbanded animals are recorded in the registers. There has not been time within the remit of this project to pursue all these research avenues to their doubtless highly-productive conclusions but work continues to proceed in these and other directions. Future work might also attempt more fully to associate the rich Ottoman written texts with contemporary archaeological evidence on the ground. A major issue here is that many of the settlements attested in the Ottoman tax and census records have continued in existence until the present-day and it has not proven possible within the scope of Project Paphlagonia to detect and characterise an archaeological signature that distinguishes Ottoman settlements from their modern successors on the same spot. Very few abandoned Ottoman villages were located in the survey. Comparison of Ottoman evidence with the census records of the early Turkish Republic is also likely to be a highly fruitful avenue for future exploration.

Chapter Eight

People and Place in Paphlagonia: Trends and Patterns in Settlement through Time

Roger Matthews and Claudia Glatz

Diachronic settlement trends and patterns in Project Paphlagonia

Of the 337 archaeological sites recorded by Project Paphlagonia, 134 can be characterised as settlements. A summary view of settlement in Inner Paphlagonia from Chalcolithic to Ottoman times is shown in fig. 8.1, which includes both settlement count per period as well as aggregate site area in hectares per period. Site counts have also been weighted by taking into account the length of each chronological period in order to provide some control over differential time-spans of cultural and historical phases and the lack of subdivisions within them. The weighted settlement count thus gives an estimate of how many settlements may have been occupied at any one point in time during each period.

Some major issues can be underlined on the basis of this diagram. Most notably, up to the end of the Byzantine period the overall trend is for increasing numbers and areas of settlement from the Chalcolithic period onwards. Site sizes throughout the entire span of settlement in Inner Paphlagonia remain relatively small in comparison to average site sizes in other areas of Anatolia. Of the 134 settlements sites in our sample, only 11 (8%) are larger than 5ha, while the vast majority (80%) are smaller than 2ha. At the same time, period-specific settlement systems show considerable variation with respect to site-size distributions (fig. 8.2).

Within the broad trend of increasing settlement, especially notable is a major episode of expansion in the Early Bronze Age, the earliest period of significant settlement across Paphlagonia, as we saw in Chapter Three. Levels of settlement through the second and first millennia BC remain relatively constant. A decline in site numbers in the Hellenistic period is countered by a sizable increase in aggregate site area, which hints towards the consolidation of, and agglomeration on, the major sites. The apparent collapse of settlement numbers in the Hellenistic and early Roman periods is to be viewed with caution, in view of the problems in ceramic chronology and identification as outlined in Chapter Six. Beyond question are the massive upturns of the Roman and Roman–Byzantine eras, characterised firstly in the Roman period by a great increase in aggregate settlement area, a product of concentration and expansion of settlement in key nodes or towns, and secondly by an explosive spread of settlement across the landscape in the Roman–Byzantine centuries. These developments are doubtless a direct consequence of the establishment of relative peace and security throughout the region for a few hundred years in the first half of the first millennium AD. We employ the term 'relative peace and security' advisedly in this context, given the vivid textual evidence for incursions of violent intruders, perhaps pirates, attested in inscriptions of the third century AD (Chapter Six, PPI.19).

Patterns of continuity and abandonment of sites offer an alternative perspective on the history of occupation in Paphlagonia (fig. 8.3). Following the Middle Palaeolithic, for which there is evidence in Inner Paphlagonia in the form of lithic scatters and three sites which may or may not date to the Neolithic (see also Düring 2008), the earliest settlement sites in this part of north-central Anatolia that can be dated confidently are assigned to the Early Chalcolithic period, between about 6000 and 5500 cal BC. Project Paphlagonia identified a total of five Chalcolithic settlements, all of which are mounds that continue to be occupied during the Early Bronze Age. As is the case in other parts of Anatolia and the Near East, Paphlagonia also experienced a significant surge in settlement numbers during the Early Bronze Age to a total of 21 sites. A change in settlement preferences is notable for the ensuing Middle Bronze Age, in which about one third of settlements are new establishments. Among those Chalcolithic and Early Bronze Age sites

Chapter Eight

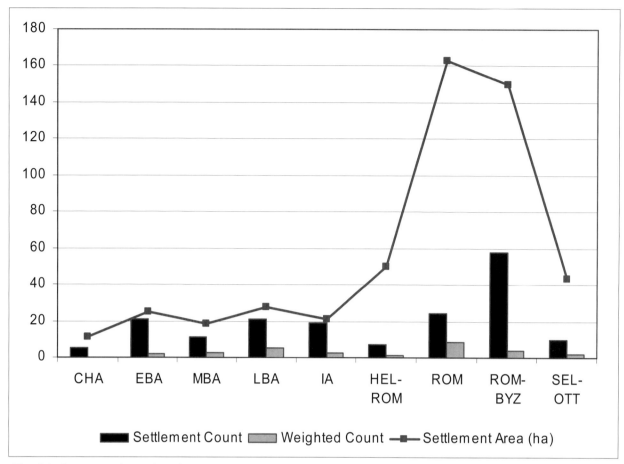

Fig. 8.1. Summary chart of settlement count, weighted count (sites per century) and aggregate settlement areas, in hectares, per period

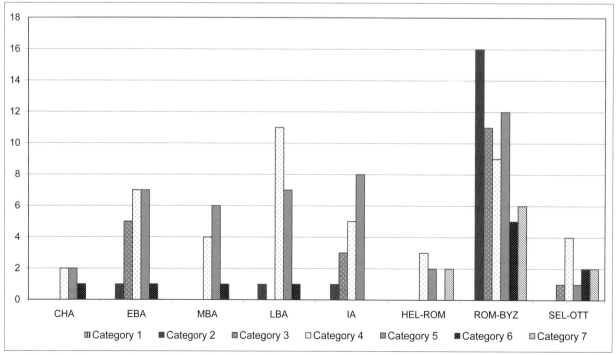

Fig. 8.2. Site-size distributions period by period

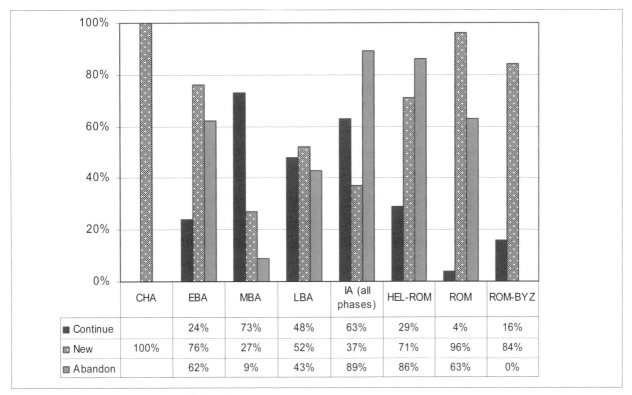

Fig. 8.3. Settlement continuity and abandonment

continuing into the Middle Bronze Age are large mounds (Maltepe PS183) that are also occupied in the following Late Bronze Age. The Late Bronze Age settlement pattern is characterised by strong continuity in site location on the one hand – only one Middle Bronze Age site appears to have been abandoned in the Late Bronze Age – and an almost doubling of site numbers on the other. Aggregate settlement area increased by about 10ha or 33% in the Late Bronze Age. The sites carrying this increase in settled area are settlements ranging between 1ha and 2ha in size.

Overall, and despite period-specific idiosyncrasies in settlement organisation, fluctuations in site numbers and the locations of particularly smaller and special purpose sites, there is a pronounced continuity in settlement from the Chalcolithic until the end of the Bronze Age. This stability in site locations was anchored in the relatively continuous occupation of large, multi-period mound settlements. The first signs of the break-up of this long-term settlement continuity start to appear in the course of the second millennium BC, although *höyüks* are not entirely abandoned until after the Hellenistic period.

Notwithstanding settlement continuity from the Late Bronze Age at two thirds of sites with evidence for Iron Age occupation, Iron Age settlement strategies appear to have differed from those of preceding periods. While settlement numbers (19 sites) differ only insignificantly from those of the Late Bronze Age, the total settled area decreased by a quarter from 28ha to 21ha during the latter phase. With the largest Bronze Age mound, Maltepe (PS183), abandoned, three 3ha sites, two of them new establishments, appear to have headed the Iron Age settlement hierarchy in Inner Paphlagonia. Small, sub-hectare sites also tend to be new foundations. There is however continuity at several Late Bronze Age mound settlements that may reflect an ongoing concern with security (see Chapter Five).

Another period during which a fundamental restructuring of the settlement system occurred is the phase following the Iron Age. First, almost all Iron Age settlements were abandoned during the subsequent Hellenistic and later periods. Second, keeping in mind the already mentioned difficulties of distinguishing between material from the Hellenistic and Roman periods, our assessments suggest a marked decrease in settlement numbers from 19 to seven sites from the Iron Age to the Hellenistic period. Third, this decrease in site numbers is offset by an increase in aggregate site area from 21ha to 50ha, which is carried by two Hellenistic sites of about 20ha each (PS121, PS040). Sites with diagnostic materials for the Roman period also appear at novel locations in the landscape. Settlement numbers in this period triple and aggregate settlement area reaches an absolute peak of about 163ha.

Wrought by difficulties of ceramic differentiation, the strong discontinuity between sites with Roman and late Roman/Byzantine materials has to be treated with caution. Similarly, the large number of settlements (58 in total) dated to the Roman/Byzantine period has to be viewed in the light of the chronological span of this phase. With the exception of nine, for the most part, very large sites, the vast majority (84%) of late Roman/Byzantine settlements did not yield evidence for Roman occupation. During the late Roman/Byzantine periods the aggregate settlement area is mainly constituted by small sites measuring less than 1ha, rather than the large towns that were typical for the Hellenistic and Roman periods. Thus, although more settlement sites have been dated to the late Roman/Byzantine phase than to any other, aggregate site area drops below that of the Roman period, which again points to a rather different mode of settlement.

The apparent serious decline in settlement density and spread in Turkish times should not be taken at face value as it is certain that numerous early Turkish settlements lie under and within existing villages and towns of the region, which we did not systematically explore. Indeed, we require a dedicated project specifically to investigate the many interesting issues of post-Byzantine settlement and society in this region of Turkey, which might fully integrate the documentary and archaeological sources in ways hinted at in Chapter Seven.

To sum up, against the overall background of increasing site numbers and demographic densities through time, each phase in the Paphlagonian past had its own characteristic settlement developments, some of which were rooted more deeply in preceding periods than others. Despite different spatial manifestations in each of the periods, the interplay of Inner Paphlagonia's environmental conditions, topography, resource distribution and geographical situation resulted in recurrent settlement themes.

First, although resource exploitation and exchange were important in all periods, the extraction and exchange of natural resources were especially important during the Chalcolithic and Early–Middle Bronze Age phases of settlement in Paphlagonia, and structured settlement patterns during these periods. These resources probably included salt, obsidian and silver-lead, which are all present in the region.

Second, 'at the edge of empires' sums up the region's geo-political position from the Late Bronze Age until the end of the Byzantine period. The large-scale political entities aiming to control the region faced the challenge of bringing the small-scale and mobile communities that operated in the region under their dominion. In the end, all successive attempts at urbanisation by empires proved short-lived experiments, falling apart when these empires crumbled. Further, the region's geography was instrumental in the development of a number of frontier zones, which for short periods of time lifted it from its quiet existence into the limelight of history (Matthews 2004b).

Comparison with diachronic settlement patterns in Turkey

The specific settlement trends and patterns in Project Paphlagonia may best be appreciated when set against the results from other surveys conducted in Turkey, but, first, two reservations must be expressed. Firstly, as discussed by Erciyas (2006a: 4–5), very few multi-period survey projects in Turkey pay proper attention to post-Iron Age periods, just as very few Classical-Roman-Byzantine surveys reciprocate that attention to pre-Classical times. Secondly, even where a full range of materials is collected it is rarely published in a manner adequate for our purposes here. Nevertheless there are useful indicators from several regions, which enable comparisons to be made. Many of these points have been made *en passant* in the preceding chapters of this volume, so that here the aim is to summarise the more egregious, and therefore probably significant, of these gross-scale trends and patterns across much of Anatolia at varying stages in its past.

Adjacent regions of north and central Turkey show broadly similar patterns of settlement development through long time periods, where evidence is available (Erciyas 2006a: 53–61 provides a convenient graphic summary of gross settlement trends for the regions of Amasya, Sivas, Çorum, Tokat and Samsun). In particular, all regions host a major increase in settlement numbers with the onset and through the course of the Early Bronze Age, followed by a decline in numbers in the second millennium BC and often steady continuity of, and increase in, settlement numbers, if not of settlement location, into the Iron Age. The major distinction from Inner Paphlagonia is that the Late Bronze Age settlement in our survey region increases while elsewhere it trends downwards. To the north of our survey region there is considerable evidence for settlement disruption through the second and into the first millennium BC, as attested in Sinop province for example, where a thriving early second-millennium BC settlement structure is severely disrupted and dissipated for the best part of an entire millennium from about 1700 BC (Işın 1998; Dönmez 2002). Eastwards, survey in the province of Bayburt has delineated a settlement history remarkably similar to that of Inner Paphlagonia, including a distinct lack of Neolithic sites, scant Chalcolithic presence, major increase in the Early Bronze Age, decline in the second millennium and resurgence in the

Iron Age (Sagona 2004). Broadly similar trends can be discerned in long-term settlement trajectories around the Salt Lake in central Turkey (Kashima 2001), as well as on the Konya plain (Baird 2001; 2004) and in the Gordion region (Kealhofer 2005).

Settlement patterns of the later first millennium BC and into the first millennium AD are much harder to descry, principally because of problems in ceramic definition, as outlined throughout this volume, as well as the tendency of survey projects not to treat this long period in an integrated and appropriate manner. But indications from multi-period surveys that have attempted to span this traditional divide unquestionably reveal a significant expansion and intensification of settlement through the imperial Roman and early Byzantine centuries, as attested in the regions of Alişar (Branting 1996), Gordion (Kealhofer 2005), the Konya plain (Baird 2004) and beyond. In the following section, we summarise the findings of preceding chapters and examine in more detail settlement trends in Inner Paphlagonia through time and within their regional context.

The Chalcolithic Age (6000–3000 BC)
Project Paphlagonia has identified a total of five Chalcolithic settlement sites, all of them *höyüks* (fig. 3.7). Two of these fall into the sub-hectare Category 4 and two range around 1.5ha (Category 5). The largest identified Chalcolithic site is Maltepe at 6.3ha. Notwithstanding the fact that these five sites are only a sample of the Chalcolithic settlement in the region, population levels were evidently low during this period, with a total aggregate site area of about 11ha. The location of Chalcolithic settlement is mainly structured by two factors. The first is a concern with the extraction of resources. Second, sites are also situated along the major north-south and east-west thoroughfares leading from the central plateau to the Marmara region and the Black Sea coast.

The earliest hint for the region's participation in inter-regional exchange networks of raw materials is provided by the presence of obsidian from the Sakaeli sources in Inner Paphlagonia in Late Neolithic/Early Chalcolithic levels at Ilıpınar in northwest Anatolia (Bigazzi et al. 1995: 148). Salur Höyük (PS050), which was settled from at least the Early Chalcolithic, is located close to the Sakaeli obsidian sources as well as to nearby chert deposits. It is very likely that inhabitants of Salur Höyük were involved in the extraction, working and exchange of these materials. Another site with evidence for occupation from the Early Chalcolithic period is Sarıçı Höyük (Çivi 05S01), which is located directly beside massive rock-salt deposits. The remainder of Chalcolithic sites in Inner Paphlagonia are situated along natural passes and other communication routes.

The Chalcolithic evidence in Inner Paphlagonia, on the whole, resonates with the results of other surveys across north-central Anatolia, which report scant traces of Chalcolithic presence (Branting 1996; Işın 1998; Marro 2000; Yıldırım, Sipahi 2004; Dönmez 2006a). From the limited information available, it seems that settlement in northern Anatolia in this period was dispersed and heterogeneous with respect to site location, function and cultural affiliation.

The Early Bronze Age (3000–2000 BC)
Surveys and excavations across Anatolia and in the wider Near East indicate a sharp rise in site numbers during the Early Bronze Age (Wilkinson 2003). In Inner Paphlagonia, settlement numbers rose from five to 21, with the majority of settlements falling into sub-hectare categories, but they also include five new sites between 1.5ha and 3.3ha in size. Maltepe (6.3ha) remained the largest site in the region. The phenomenon of urban agglomeration did not take root in the region, however (Çevik 2007), much as in later periods. In terms of both settlement and material culture, continuities with the preceding Chalcolithic can be established. Early Bronze Age settlement continued on the mounds established during the Chalcolithic, with new sites scattered in their vicinity (fig. 3.14).

An aspect of Anatolia's significance within the Early Bronze Age was its role as a supplier of metal ores (Yener 2000). It is argued that Early Bronze Age settlement in Inner Paphlagonia was significantly structured by the exploitation of metal ores, as well as by a desire to tap into other natural resources, most notably the mining of rock-salt deposits near the site of Sarıçı Höyük (Çivi 05S01) and the extraction of obsidian and flint at Salur Höyük (PS050). Evidence for wide-ranging exchange networks that were central to the emergent Anatolian élite culture in this period can be found in the ceramic tradition of Yazıboy (PS111), a small site located in the western part of the survey region with distinctive ceramic connections well to the west of Anatolia.

Despite Inner Paphlagonia's riches in natural resources and the opportunities they offer for participation in large-scale exchange networks, emergent complex communities may have encountered the limits of a more restricted resource, namely that of arable land, during the Early Bronze Age. At least this is one possible explanation for increasing evidence of the demarcation of territory through cemeteries, such as Salur North (PS219) (Matthews 2004a) and Balıbağı (Süel 1989), and a concern with security in the form of fortification walls.

Of the 21 Early Bronze Age settlements recorded by Project Paphlagonia, seven have evidence of dry-stone enclosure or fortification walls (Çivi 05S01, Dumanlı 03S04, PS016, PS050, PS057, PS122, PS218), while many of the remaining sites occupied protected positions in the landscape. The majority of fortification walls may likely belong to later occupation phases at many of the Early Bronze Age sites, but the fortified settlement of Dumanlı 03S04 appears to date exclusively to the Early Bronze Age. Comparable walled Early Bronze Age sites are found across Anatolia at Karaoğlan Mevkii near Afyon (Topbaş et al. 1998), Demircihüyük (Seeher 1987) and Elmalı-Karataş north of Antalya (Warner 1994). Recent survey in nearby Çorum province has revealed further small Early Bronze Age fortified settlements (Yıldırım, Sipahi 2004: 310), while a major fortified Early Bronze Age settlement appears to lie buried underneath Classical Tavium in Çorum province (Gerber 2005: 87).

The Early Bronze Age settlement evidence from Inner Paphlagonia broadly corresponds to trends observed by surveys in northern Anatolia and beyond (Burney 1956; Parzinger 1993; Wilkinson 2003). To the north of Project Paphlagonia, increases in settlement numbers have been noted in Kastamonu (Marro 2000), Sinop (Işın 1998) and Samsun (Dönmez 1999), similar patterns occur to the east in Amasya, Tokat (Özsait 1994; Özsait, Koçak 1996) and Çorum (Yıldırım, Sipahi 2004), as well as to the south, in Ankara and Konya provinces (Baird 2001; Omura 2002). Early Bronze Age settlement systems in all these regions were centred on multi-period mounds, while smaller new sites were established in their vicinities and in previously uninhabited regions at an unparalleled scale.

Early Bronze Age settlement in Inner Paphlagonia, while showing a dramatic increase from the Chalcolithic period, however, does not mirror the overwhelming peak in site numbers we find elsewhere. A similar situation is found at another relatively peripheral location, the Gordion survey area. At Gordion settlement numbers peak for the first time during the Middle Bronze Age (Kealhofer 2005: table 11-2; see also Çevik 2007 for an overview) while the number of second millennium BC sites in Inner Paphlagonia at least matches those of the Early Bronze Age.

The Middle and Late Bronze Ages (2000–1200 BC)

With the second millennium BC we enter one of the most significant episodes of the Paphlagonian past. During the Middle Bronze Age (2000–1600 BC), northern Anatolia was increasingly drawn into large-scale trade networks within the organisational structures of the Old Assyrian trading network and against the background of competing Anatolian principalities. These trade networks intensified the inter-regional exchange systems that were already operating in earlier periods. In the subsequent Late Bronze Age (1600–1200 BC), this economic incorporation of Inner Paphlagonia was followed up by an effort to incorporate the region into a larger political framework, and in this period the region was the arena for the drama of Hittite imperial struggle and ultimate demise.

Middle Bronze Age texts point to commercial and political interchange between the central Anatolian plateau and the Black Sea coast, with the site of İkiztepe, possibly ancient Zalpa (Alkım et al. 1988), as a major regional player. Archaeological evidence also suggests close cultural links between the inhabitants of İkiztepe and central Anatolia during the Middle Bronze Age (Müller-Karpe 2001). Sometime during the 16th and 15th centuries BC, however, the northernmost regions of Anatolia underwent a major transformation that is archaeologically manifested as a hiatus in permanent settlement. Arguably, this retreat of recognisable Late Bronze Age settlement from the Black Sea region may have been caused by the incursion of Kaska tribes and their settlement in the mountainous northern fringes of the central plateau during the course of the Late Bronze Age (Klinger 2002; *contra* von Schuler 1965; Singer 2007). Former Hittite territories, including important cult centres, are reported to have been destroyed and plundered by this new enemy (von Schuler 1965). Throughout the remaining part of the Late Bronze Age, Hittite sources report on Kaska raids in the Hittite heartland, and the northern fringes of the central plateau were turned into a perpetual war-zone. Neither Hittite military force nor diplomacy were ultimately able to contain the Kaska effectively, due to the latter's flexible political structure and mobile way of life.

The results of Project Paphlagonia suggest that for once we may be able to marry textual and archaeological evidence rather well (Glatz, Matthews 2005; also Matthews, Glatz forthcoming). A total of 21 substantive second-millennium BC settlements, 16 of them *höyüks*, were recorded by Project Paphlagonia. Eleven of these sites have material of the Middle Bronze Age and eight yielded transitional Middle to Late Bronze Age pottery. Four of the Middle Bronze Age sites fall into the sub-hectare Category 4, seven range between 1ha and 3.3ha in size, while Maltepe continues as the largest site in Inner Paphlagonia. All of the 21 settlements were occupied during the early and middle part of the Late Bronze Age (fig. 8.4). Twelve settlements may have endured until the end of the Late Bronze Age. Against the background of strong settlement continuity between the Middle to the Late Bronze Age, Inner Paphlagonia thus experienced a 38% increase in settlement numbers

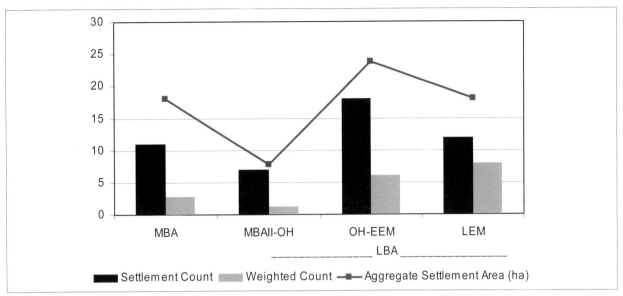

Fig. 8.4. Settlement count, weighted count (sites per century) and aggregate settlement areas, in hectares, for the second millennium BC. OH = Old Hittite; EEM = Early Empire; LEM = Late Empire

carried mostly by sub-hectare sites. This makes the Late Bronze Age the most prominent pre-Roman settlement phase in the region.

The spatial arrangement of these sites is striking (fig. 4.1). Looking at the northwestern half of the region we find a number of strategically located and often fortified sites lining the Devrez Çay and, with the exception of İnceboğaz (PS122), little else beyond to the north. To the south of this line of fortified sites, we find a more widespread scatter of settlement centred around Maltepe (PS183) and taking advantage of communication routes, natural resources and pockets of arable land. Surveys in Kastamonu and further north (Marro et al. 1996; Kuzucuoğlu et al. 1997; Marro et al. 1998) report an ephemeral scatter of early to mid second-millennium BC materials, but do not seem to have encountered any definite Late Bronze Age pottery either. To the northeast of Paphlagonia, Middle Bronze Age communities appear to have thrived in Sinop (Işın 1998), Samsun and northern Amasya (Dönmez 2002). Archaeologically recognisable permanent settlement, however, appears to cease in the central Black Sea region at the start of the Late Bronze Age (Dönmez 2002; *contra* Yakar, Dinçol 1974; Yakar 1980). This apparent settlement retreat came to a halt in inner Samsun and the northern part of Amasya with a more widespread settlement pattern to the south (Özsait 1988; 1989; 1990; 1991; 1992; 1993; 1994; 1995; 1998; 1999; 2000a; 2000b; 2003a; 2003b; 2004; 2005; Özsait, Koçak 1996; Özsait, Dündar 1997; Özsait, Özsait 2001; Dönmez 2002). Second millennium BC settlement dynamics in other parts of Anatolia point to rather different developments.

The Iron Age (1200–330 BC)

The period following the collapse of the Hittite empire around 1200–1180 BC is an archaeological and historical dark age. Settlement numbers drop after a Late Bronze Age peak, suggesting a sparse Iron Age occupation of Inner Paphlagonia (figs 5.1, 8.5). The material culture of the Early Iron Age has only recently begun to be identified at excavated sites in central and southern Anatolia (Genz 2000a; 2000b; 2003; 2004a; 2004b; 2005; Özsait 2003b; Ünlü 2005; Hansen, Postgate 2007). Seven of the 19 Iron Age settlement sites in Inner Paphlagonia yielded material similar to that of the middle part of the Early Iron Age at Boğazköy-Büyükkaya (Seeher 2000b; Genz 2004a; 2005). This suggests an initial hiatus of permanent or recognisable settlements after the end of the Late Bronze Age, a trend which is matched by excavation and survey results from some parts of north Anatolia (Henrickson 1994; Muscarella 1995: 94; Genz 2003: 185; but see Voigt 1994: 276; Dönmez 2003: 214; 2005: 68). The choice of Early and also later Iron Age settlement locations, however, suggests a degree of continuity from the previous period, with the majority of sites falling into size Categories 3, 4 and 5.

In the context of surface collections, Middle to Late Iron Age sites are usually identified by Phrygian grey wares. These assemblages are often interpreted not only as indicators of strong cultural links with Phrygia proper, but have further been seen as implicating political links as well (Summers 1994: 244; Dönmez 2006b; Postgate 2007). Altogether nine sites in the Project Paphlagonia survey area have yielded Phrygian grey wares. As with

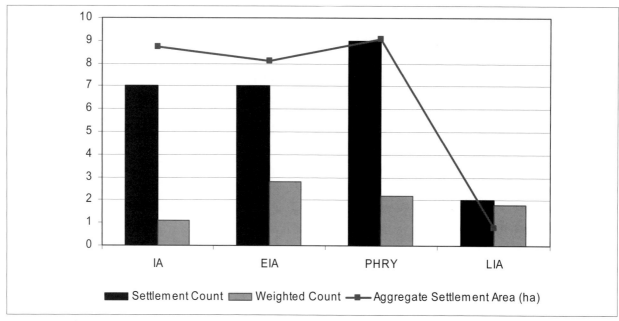

Fig. 8.5. Settlement count, weighted count (sites per century) and aggregate settlement areas, in hectares, for the Iron Age

the Early Iron Age sites, Middle to Late Iron Age settlement locations are broadly distributed across the territory in Inner Paphlagonia. Few sites with Phrygian grey wares, however, have been detected to the north and northeast. Surveys in Kastamonu province have found a few sites with Phrygian grey ware north of the Ilgaz range (Marro et al. 1996: 284; Kuzucuoğlu et al. 1997: 288; see also Dönmez 2006b: 17) and one site on the Gökırmak (Marro et al. 1998: 322). 'Late Phrygian' pottery is known from a few sites in Sinop province, but apparently none have yielded grey ware (Işın 1998: 98, table 1). Samsun, like Sinop, apparently lacks traces of human occupation for the entire period between the 18th and eighth centuries BC (Işın 1998: 110). In contrast, surveys in regions to the east and south of Project Paphlagonia have noted an increasing occurrence of grey wares and painted Iron Age pottery (Yıldırım, Sipahi 2004: 310). Settlement around Gordion peaks in the Middle Phrygian period (Kealhofer 2005).

It thus appears that Inner Paphlagonia may have formed part of the border zone between a Phrygian state in the south and its neighbour to the north. More than half of Middle to Late Iron Age settlements are located on top of Late Bronze Age predecessors, which may mean that the concerns of defence and control that structured the Late Bronze Age landscape continued to be important.

The Late Iron Age is difficult to define on the basis of survey data due to ceramic continuities from preceding periods as well as the almost total invisibility of Achaemenid presence in northern Anatolia (Erciyas 2006a). Rare occurrences of Achaemenid-style carinated bowls, however, do allow us to assign a Late Iron Age date to two sites (PS015 and PS172), both of which fall into the sub-hectare category.

In contrast to Paphlagonia, where settlement numbers drop after the Late Bronze Age, the Iron Age constitutes a second peak in site numbers after the Early Bronze rise in settlement numbers in most other parts of Anatolia (Mikami, Omura 1988; 1990; Özsait 1988; 1989; 1990; 1991; 1992; 1993; 1994; 1995; 1998; 1999; 2000b; 2002; 2003a; 2003b; 2004; 2005; Omura 1989; 1991; 1992; 1993; 1994; 1995; 1996; 1997; 1998; 2000; 2001; 2002; 2003; 2005; Özsait, Koçak 1996; Özsait, Dündar 1997; Ökse 1998; Sipahi, Yıldırım 1998; 1999; 2000; 2001; 2005; Sipahi 2003; Bahar, Koçak 2004; Yıldırım, Sipahi 2004; Kealhofer 2005) as well as in the wider region of the Near East. This includes a diversification in settlement types and locations, which Inner Paphlagonia's inhabitants again seem to forgo in favour of reoccupying older settlement locations.

The Hellenistic period (330–6 BC)

Project Paphlagonia detected only two Hellenistic settlements and a further seven which were assigned a Hellenistic–Roman date (figs 6.6, 8.6). Of these, three fall into the sub-hectare Category 4, two into Category 5 and a further two range around 20ha. Although this may be a highly-selective sample, influenced no doubt to some degree by the difficulties of detecting Hellenistic occupation through surface pottery, the apparent rarity of sites of this period in our survey fits with broader patterns observed along the north Anatolian fringe (Erciyas 2006a) and in other parts of the Hellenistic and early Roman world (Alcock 1994: 188; 2001: 332). In northern Anatolia, survey results indicate a 50% decline in settlement numbers from the preceding Iron Age, which may be associated with increasing urbanisation and settlement agglomeration typical of this phase (Erciyas 2006a: 53–62). By contrast, the south-central plateau experiences a steady rise in both numbers of settlements and aggregate site area from the end of the Iron Age (Baird 2004: 232). As in preceding periods, warfare, this time the Mithridatic wars, was a major factor in structuring settlement preferences in Hellenistic Paphlagonia. This may in part explain the apparent retreat of small-scale rural settlement during the Hellenistic period. Rather, remote hilltop sites such as Asar Tepe (PS096) appear to have been the defining settlement type. For the last time also some of the *höyüks* were reoccupied.

The Roman period (6/5 BC–AD 285)
With the region's incorporation into the Roman world from 63 BC (Mitchell 1993a: 92–93), Inner Paphlagonia experienced a steady increase in the density and intensity of settlement and an ever-expanding agricultural exploitation (fig. 8.6). For the first time, Paphlagonia hosted centres of urban dimensions, integrated into the Roman road network (Leonhard 1915; Wilson 1960; French 1988a; 1988b; 1989; Belke 1996). The distribution of the 24 Roman settlement sites in Inner Paphlagonia differs dramatically from all earlier patterns (fig. 6.29). For the first time, we see a settlement spread over almost the entire survey region, particularly in the northwest. There is also for the first time a true hierarchy of settlement with sites ranging from tiny hamlets and farmsteads, through villages to sizeable towns, covering all except for the smallest of the size categories as defined in Chapter One. Administrative centres of this period include Gangra/Germanikopolis, Kaisareia Hadrianopolis and Antoninopolis at Çerkeş/Kızıllar.

Broadly similar settlement and associated demographic developments have been detected in survey projects throughout Anatolia, including Phrygia (Kealhofer 2005: 148), Lydia (Pleket 2003: 89), the Konya plain (Baird 2004: 232), around Sagalassos (Vanhaverbeke et al. 2004: 255) and in Cilicia (Blanton 2000: 60). The thriving of urban and rural settlement in the Roman period across Anatolia can have been supported only by demographic growth and economic prosperity. Especially distinctive to the region of Inner Paphlagonia within this overall pattern is the extensification and stratification of human settlement with only minimal input from communities of truly urban scale and proportions.

The Byzantine period (AD 285–1453)
Through the fifth and sixth centuries AD across Asia Minor major changes occurred in which Roman towns lost their role as the foci of civic life, with local élites turning to their landed estates as sources of power. This

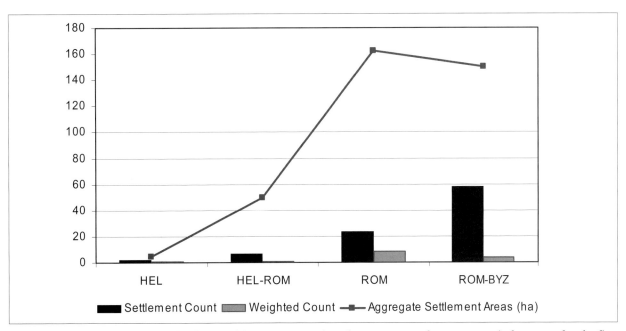

Fig. 8.6. Settlement count, weighted count (sites per century) and aggregate settlement areas, in hectares, for the first millennium AD

process gradually replaced the Classical city with the medieval castle (Crow 1996: 23). By the 11th century at the latest urbanism in Inner Paphlagonia, to the degree that it had existed at all, had totally collapsed. One of the most significant features of the later Byzantine period in Inner Paphlagonia is the Arab and Turkish incursions over a period of some 500 years. Inner Paphlagonia once more found itself at the edge of empire and once more hosted a drawn-out episode of cross-border conflict (Vryonis 1971), which manifested itself clearly in the ways in which the landscape was settled. At least a dozen fortified hilltop sites were discovered or newly recorded during our survey (fig. 6.46). Almost all of these sites date to the centuries from AD 700, about the time of the first incursions of Arab forces, to around AD 1200, when the final absorption of the region into the Turkish world took place.

We can document a fall in settlement distribution and hierarchy occurring through the Byzantine era in Inner Paphlagonia. After around AD 700 the trend appears to be one of steady rural collapse across northern Anatolia (Kealhofer 2005: 148; Erciyas 2006a: 59) and in regions beyond, such as Cilicia (Blanton 2000: 60), the Konya plain (Baird 2004: 245) and the territory of Sagalassos (Vanhaverbeke et al. 2004: 272). With the onset of the Ottoman period until the present day, Paphlagonia reverted once again from imperial frontier zone to rural remoteness.

Project Paphlagonia: concluding thoughts

Where in this narrative do we situate the people of old Paphlagonia? We have walked over their abandoned villages, farmsteads and hilltop refuges, collected a few scraps of their material culture, measured the width and length of the fortifications they laboured to construct against dangers now long forgotten, photographed, recorded, documented, analysed and interpreted the scant traces of lives long gone. From this what can we say about the spirit of life in the uplands and valleys of Inner Paphlagonia? A major structuring factor, stressed in the title of this volume, is the location of the region at the edge of empires or other large-scale political entities. The indigenous peoples of Paphlagonia played their part in a series of imperial dramas acted out over millennia (Matthews 2004b) but the specifics of each drama need to be teased out of the material and written evidence, illustrating the historical contingency of the region's participation in each successive episode of its past, as we have tried to summarise from the settlement point of view in the pages above.

Even in the Early Bronze Age, with the construction of small fortified sites in Inner Paphlagonia, paralleled in the contemporary scene across much of Anatolia and beyond, as we discussed in Chapter Three, there appears to be an element of contestation, a staking of territory manifest in fortifications as well as discrete cemeteries, and a concern with defence that adumbrate an era of tension and conflict.

In the Late Bronze Age, and in particular during the Hittite imperial period, Inner Paphlagonia was a militarised frontier zone, an arena for chronic conflict between a major imperial power and its Kaska neighbours to the north. Recent studies (Glatz, Matthews 2005; Singer 2007; Zimansky 2007) have striven to approach the Kaska more sympathetically than the purely Hittite-derived textual sources might at first encourage, for example, by situating them within long-term trajectories of settlement rather than seeing them as disruptive and recent incomers to the region who set out repeatedly to spoil the Hittite imperial project. The Hittite origin of the textual sources through which we approach the Kaska inevitably shapes and restricts our view of them, to the degree that it may be claimed, 'The Kaska themselves may have been, to a certain extent, the creation of the Hittite Empire' (Zimansky 2007: 157). The proximity of the Hittites' capital city of Hattusa to the Kaska border, only some 120km distant, meant that systematic and persistent defence of their northern frontier was an essential component of the very survival of empire. The archaeological and historical evidence agree in demonstrating the major imperial input into the construction and maintenance of a landscape of control within an ideology of imperial might and divine justification.

During the Iron Age the picture is less clear, not only because of the dearth of written documents from this time but also because of difficulties in interpreting the material evidence of the Phrygian state on the one hand, which in its settlement location and distribution resembles the Hittite imperial pattern, as we saw above, and of the archaeologically obscure, at least in terms of its provincial manifestations, Achaemenid empire. At least the distribution of Phrygian settlements allows us to postulate an ongoing Iron Age concern with border protection, as had so engaged the Hittites in the Late Bronze Age.

The case of the Roman empire and its interaction with the same region is completely different from all preceding imperial or quasi-imperial episodes. Through the course of the Mithridatic Wars the Romans, unlike the Hittites, did succeed in militarily subduing the region and were able to replace a militarised landscape with one of peace and stability, where a few cities could flourish and where the rural landscape of Inner Paphlagonia hosted a blooming of settlement and agricultural productivity not equalled till modern times. Within the environment of the *pax Romana* the indigenous peoples of Inner Paphlagonia ultimately bought into the Roman imperial project, farmed the land, paid their taxes and inscribed their tombstones in Greek, until the arrival from the later first millennium AD of new invaders, Arabs, Crusaders and Turks, brought this episode of relative calm and security to a close. For Byzantium, Inner Paphlagonia had a yet different significance as a rather remote backwater, a source of eunuchs and good bacon (Magdalino 1998), and the people of the region were largely left to look after their own defences over a period of some 500 years. Their response was to build hilltop refuge sites and take to the hills whenever danger threatened, as it frequently did. By AD 1350 the absorption of the area into the Turkish world was complete and a new era of peace and stability steadily enabled the return of communities to their farms, fields and villages, where they remained till taking their place in the demographic trend of rural emigration that has so severely affected the region in the past few decades.

Five years of extensive and intensive field survey in Inner Paphlagonia have generated a wealth of information on the archaeology and history of this previously poorly-researched region. It has been the aim in this volume, and the associated web resource (http://www.ucl.ac.uk/paphlagonia/), both to present that information, in at least summary form, and to provide an interpretive narrative of long-term settlement history in a coherent and readable manner. It may be felt that at some points this aim has been realised, if at all, only through too brusque treatment of the frequently patchy and difficult evidence. As director of the fieldwork and co-editors of the publication we have felt obliged to maximise the interpretive potential of the collected evidence – after all amounting to no more than a few dozen plastic crates of fragmentary sherds, tiles and stone chips, all now stored in Çankırı Museum – by attempting to situate it in a context of broad historical narrative, while striving to remain acutely aware of the limitations of the evidence itself. Not the least reason for doing so is our belief that only by articulating explicit interpretations will we advance the study of the region through the time-honoured procedure of the proposal, testing and reformulation of specific hypotheses.

As discussed in Chapter One, Project Paphlagonia was from the start designed as a multi-period survey with the overarching aim of investigating long-term settlement trends and patterns across a very large area. The project's spatial and chronological parameters are immense, and some may wonder about the validity of taking on a project of such a scale within a five-year remit. Justification for this decision is outlined in Chapter One, but readers here will doubtless detect considerable variability in the depth of detail and analysis across the successive chapters of the volume, which may be seen as a short-coming. A major issue, which we prefer not to dwell on, is the problems in securing expert input on every relevant aspect of a project that covers such a broad chronological scope. Ideally such input should be available and exercised at every stage of the project, from field collection through processing to final interpretation and publication, but the exigencies of modern academic life have meant that such has not wholly been the case here, notwithstanding that we are more than pleased with the input that we have enjoyed from our colleagues on the project. For the future, we note that already in the few years since completion of fieldwork in Project Paphlagonia, new field and research initiatives are well underway in the area, now focusing on the Bronze Age (Sipahi, Yıldırım 2005) and Roman–Byzantine periods (Laflı, Zäh 2008) of its past. We look forward to seeing how these and doubtless other researches in the quiet valleys and austere uplands of Inner Paphlagonia continue to enrich our understanding of its distinctive history.

Project Paphlagonia: Site Catalogue

Site number	Site no.	Site ID	X	Y	Type of site	Dating	Site area (ha)	Size category	Class. category
PS001	PS97.001	PS-001	561517.6899	4542730.936	cemetery	BYZ	0.08	2	G
PS002	PS97.002	PS-002	563232.0438	4543050.644	settlement	BYZ	0.27	4	C
PS003	PS97.003	PS-003	560532.1039	4537915.668	settlement	IA (EIA), HEL, ROM	19.63	7	A, I
PS003a	PS97.003a	PS-003a	560694.1988	4537904.363	stones, not *in situ*	ROM/BYZ	0.00	1	K
PS004	PS97.004	PS-004	565002.0549	4539435.688	settlement	LROM/EBYZ	2.36	5	B
PS005	PS97.005	PS-005	557226.3239	4536212.037	cemetery	CHA, EBA, MBA-LBA, LBA (OH-EEM), ROM	0.16	3	G
PS006	PS97.006	PS-006	557262.9861	4539802.968	cemetery	LROM/BYZ	0.13	3	G
PS007	PS97.007	PS-007	556164.7536	4535291.319	cemetery?	LROM/BYZ	0.14	3	G
PS008	PS97.008	PS-008	556551.4273	4534214.773	han	TRK	0.02	2	N
PS009	PS97.009	PS-009	554582.8936	4531001.676	cemetery	HEL, ROM	0.22	3	G
PS010	PS97.010	PS-010	554950.2841	4527521.206	rock-cut chapel and tombs	BYZ	0.12	3	F
PS011	PS97.011	PS-011	567247.1095	4529240.791	tumulus	IA?	0.13	3	H
PS011a	PS97.011a	PS-011a	567350.5103	4529243.993	settlement	EBA?, ROM/BYZ	0.13	3	C
PS012	PS97.012	PS-012	566990.1322	4529697.545	cemetery	LROM/EBYZ	0.39	4	G
PS013	PS97.013	PS-013	550917.2937	4523010.725	*höyük*	EBA, MBA-LBA (MBA II-OH), LBA (OH-EEM, LEM), TRK	0.79	4	M
PS014	PS97.014	PS-014	556639.8059	4522027.975	tumulus	ROM?	0.02	2	H
PS015	PS97.015	PS-015	554772.5622	4529454.615	*höyük*	EBA, MBA-LBA (MBA II-OH), LBA (OH-EEM), IA (EIA, MIA, LIA), HEL, ROM	0.61	4	M
PS016	PS97.016	PS-016	554502.3322	4529386.96	fortified lowland	EBA, MBA, MBA-LBA (MBA II-OH), LBA (OH-EEM, LEM?), IA?, ROM, BYZ	1.40	5	D
PS017	PS97.017	PS-017	547397.2307	4535785.591	tumulus	IA?	0.01	2	H
PS017a	PS97.017a	PS-017a	547525.2055	4535784.649	settlement	?	0.07	2	C
PS018	PS97.018	PS-018	554789.057	4534989.987	settlement	LROM and BYZ	0.79	4	C
PS019	PS97.019	PS-019	553370.1676	4535068.397	cemetery	LROM/BYZ?	0.07	2	G

Project Paphlagonia

Site number	Site no.	Site ID	X	Y	Type of site	Dating	Site area (ha)	Size category	Class. category
PS020	PS97.020	PS-020	553670.9096	4530129.754	tumulus	IA?	0.07	2	H
PS021	PS97.021	PS-021	553521.558	4530509.833	tumulus	IA?	0.28	4	H
PS022	PS97.022	PS-022	552902.5041	4531054.33	stones, not *in situ*	HEL/ROM	0.00	1	T
PS023	PS97.023	PS-023	544332.3122	4528135.634	settlement	ROM/BYZ	0.79	4	C
PS024	PS97.024	PS-024	539679.1529	4532838.876	rock-cut tomb	?	0.01	2	F
PS025	PS97.025	PS-025	537097.2833	4540525.477	settlement	ROM	0.19	3	C
PS026	PS97.026	PS-026	541172.2405	4541680.496	settlement	LROM/BYZ	0.09	2	C
PS027	PS97.027	PS-027	534669.1901	4537104.785	tumulus	IA?	0.21	3	H
PS028	PS97.028	PS-028	503575.703	4489010.367	stones, not *in situ*	ROM/BYZ	0.00	1	T, K
PS029	PS97.029	PS-029	502564.8563	4489666.072	fortified hilltop	LROM/BYZ	0.08	2	E
PS030	PS97.030	PS-030	501242.9812	4486660.668	settlement	BYZ	0.05	2	C
PS031	PS97.031	PS-031	501255.0332	4485854.256	cemetery	BYZ	0.07	2	G
PS032	PS97.032	PS-032	503312.9563	4487665.675	settlement	ROM	1.18	5	B
PS033	PS97.033	PS-033	512302.8453	4492400.701	rock-cut cistern	?	0.01	2	F
PS033a	PS97.033a	PS-033a	512288.3796	4492439.618	settlement	MBA, MBA-LBA, LBA (OH-EEM), IA?	0.03	2	Q
PS034	PS97.034	PS-034	509980.7519	4494440.734	stones, not *in situ*	ROM/BYZ	0.00	1	T
PS035	PS97.035	PS-035	507752.9088	4501681.224	stones, not *in situ*	ROM/BYZ	0.00	1	T
PS036	PS97.036	PS-036	509748.685	4498200.219	pithos, not *in situ*	BYZ	0.00	1	T
PS037	PS97.037	PS-037	518023.5315	4491988.539	rock-cut chambers	ROM/BYZ	0.01	2	F
PS038	PS97.038	PS-038	517959.0916	4492826.257	stones, not *in situ*	ROM/BYZ	0.00	1	T
PS039	PS97.039	PS-039	518023.5315	4498174.77	rock-cut tombs	ROM/BYZ, TRK	0.02	2	F
PS040	PS97.040	PS-040	523114.2842	4500365.727	settlement	LBA (OH-EEM), ROM	19.63	7	A
PS040a	PS97.040a	PS-040a	523114.2842	4500494.606	rock-cut tombs	ROM	0.25	3	F
PS041	PS97.041	PS-041	513127.4685	4501748.236	stones, not *in situ*	ROM/BYZ	0.00	1	T
PS042	PS97.042	PS-042	514269.4586	4503327.132	rock-cut tombs and cistern	?	0.04	2	F
PS042a	PS97.042a	PS-042a	514315.2049	4503327.132	stones, not *in situ*	ROM/BYZ	0.00	1	T, K
PS043	PS97.043	PS-043	516134.3126	4505183.337	fortified hilltop	BYZ?	0.18	3	E
PS044	PS97.044	PS-044	502229.7145	4497086.298	stones, not *in situ*	ROM/BYZ	0.00	1	T
PS045	PS97.045	PS-045	499955.458	4495276.175	stones, not *in situ*	ROM/BYZ	0.00	1	T
PS046	PS97.046	PS-046	494310.7931	4492457.998	stones, not *in situ*	ROM/BYZ	0.00	1	T
PS047	PS97.047	PS-047	494337.9872	4493660.557	tumulus	IA?	0.02	2	H
PS047a	PS97.047a	PS-047a	494310.7931	4493646.822	settlement	LROM/BYZ	0.06	2	C
PS048	PS97.048	PS-048	499997.8883	4500590.541	settlement	HEL, ROM	0.16	3	C
PS049	PS97.049	PS-049	499858.6363	4501515.702	cemetery	ROM	0.47	4	G
PS050	PS97.050	PS-050	505155.3028	4500320.263	*höyük*	CHA, EBA, MBA-LBA (MBA II-OH), LBA (OH-EEM, LEM), IA (EIA, M-LIA)	0.96	4	M
PS051	PS97.051	PS-051	521739.0814	4521844.335	fortified hilltop	BYZ?	1.80	5	E
PS052	PS97.052	PS-052	533312.4574	4521010.614	*höyük*	LBA (OH-EEM), IA (M-LIA)	0.08	2	M
PS052a	PS97.052a	PS-052a	533439.6955	4521005.423	tumulus	IA?	0.02	2	H

Site Catalogue

Site number	Site no.	Site ID	X	Y	Type of site	Dating	Site area (ha)	Size category	Class. category
PS053	PS97.053	PS-053	528897.4718	4524140.555	settlement	HEL, LROM/BYZ	0.87	4	C
PS054	PS97.054	PS-054	529951.5879	4524140.304	stones, not *in situ*	ROM/BYZ	0.00	1	T
PS055	PS97.055	PS-055	535249.9792	4521093.729	cemetery	TRK	0.05	2	C
PS056	PS97.056	PS-056	520186.5943	4504477.896	stones, not *in situ*	ROM/BYZ	0.00	1	T
PS057	PS97.057	PS-057	519297.8907	4505287.757	fortified lowland	EBA, MBA, LBA (OH-EEM), IA?	3.30	5	D
PS058	PS97.058	PS-058	522320.6406	4514328.581	natural cave	PAL?	0.02	2	O
PS059	PS97.059	PS-059	521998.2564	4512448.007	mill	TRK	0.02	2	N
PS060	PS97.060	PS-060	521675.8723	4513039.045	rock-cut tombs	ROM/BYZ?	0.12	3	F
PS061	PS97.061	PS-061	516986.9419	4525395.072	tumulus	HEL, IA?	0.03	2	H
PS062	PS97.062	PS-062	490284.5786	4519378.911	stones, not *in situ*	ROM/BYZ	0.00	1	T, K
PS063	PS97.063	PS-063	486167.3997	4520679.257	stones, not *in situ*	ROM/BYZ	0.00	1	T
PS064	PS97.064	PS-064	486845.6469	4521750.872	settlement	HEL, ROM, LROM/BYZ	28.26	7	A
PS065	PS97.065	PS-065	487400.8602	4522046.582	stones, not *in situ*	ROM/BYZ	0.00	1	T
PS066	PS97.066	PS-066	487903.708	4521399.788	cemetery?	HEL, ROM, LROM/BYZ, BYZ	0.20	3	G
PS067	PS97.067	PS-067	487456.4367	4521385.36	stone in field	LROM/BYZ	0.00	1	K
PS068	PS97.068	PS-068	486617.7837	4529925.197	settlement?	ROM	0.68	4	C
PS069	PS97.069	PS-069	485920.5686	4534419.844	stones, not *in situ*	ROM/BYZ	0.00	1	T
PS070	PS97.070	PS-070	483956.82	4532975.911	stones, not *in situ*	ROM/BYZ	0.00	1	T, K
PS071	PS97.071	PS-071	486221.8672	4527690.831	stones, not *in situ*	ROM/BYZ	0.00	1	T, K
PS072	PS97.072	PS-072	489254.5441	4520103.751	stones, not *in situ*	ROM/BYZ	0.00	1	T
PS073	PS97.073	PS-073	491763.3141	4513856.822	tumulus	IA?	0.01	2	H
PS074	PS97.074	PS-074	492329.4205	4514649.371	fortified hilltop	ROM, LROM/BYZ	0.72	4	E
PS075	PS97.075	PS-075	493348.4121	4514705.982	stones, not *in situ*	ROM/BYZ	0.00	1	T
PS076	PS97.076	PS-076	482365.9471	4509271.36	tumulus	IA?	0.02	2	H
PS077	PS97.077	PS-077	484800.2048	4512441.556	stones, not *in situ*	ROM/BYZ	0.00	1	T
PS078	PS97.078	PS-078	486555.1348	4509441.192	stones, not *in situ*	ROM/BYZ	0.00	1	T
PS079	PS97.079	PS-079	486252.9317	4510270.358	rock-cut ?well	ROM?	0.02	2	F
PS079a	PS97.079a	PS-079a	486272.0816	4510346.962	settlement	ROM?	0.24	3	C
PS080	PS97.080	PS-080	489838.5522	4513517.158	stones, not *in situ*	ROM/BYZ	0.00	1	T
PS081	PS97.081	PS-081	489046.0031	4509384.581	stones, not *in situ*	ROM/BYZ	0.00	1	T
PS082	PS97.082	PS-082	491140.597	4508535.422	rock-cut habitation	?	0.01	2	F
PS083	PS97.083	PS-083	499027.1901	4515373.177	rock-cut tomb	?	0.02	2	F
PS084	PS97.084	PS-084	499392.7787	4516110.406	settlement	?	0.06	2	C
PS085	PS97.085	PS-085	504364.7308	4510546.183	fortified hilltop	LROM/ BYZ	0.20	3	E
PS086	PS97.086	PS-086	467556.5459	4520790.85	stones, not *in situ*	ROM/BYZ	0.00	1	T
PS087	PS97.087	PS-087	470026.9971	4521460.803	stones, not *in situ*	ROM/BYZ	0.00	1	T
PS088	PS97.088	PS-088	501997.6475	4516394.271	stones, not *in situ*	ROM/BYZ	0.00	1	T
PS089	PS97.089	PS-089	553305.2455	4532188.929	settlement	ROM, BYZ, TRK	0.25	3	C
PS089a	PS97.089a	PS-089a	553335.7823	4532184.336	stones, not *in situ*	ROM, BYZ, TRK	0.00	1	T
PS090	PS98.090	PS-090	459069.7856	4533421.502	hamam	TRK	0.02	2	N
PS091	PS98.091	PS-091	459011.8632	4534406.183	hamam	TRK	0.02	2	N

Project Paphlagonia

Site number	Site no.	Site ID	X	Y	Type of site	Dating	Site area (ha)	Size category	Class. category
PS092	PS98.092	PS-092	470738.822	4525564.264	hamams and old bridge	TRK	0.04	2	N
PS092a	PS98.092a	PS-092a	470780.694	4525564.264	stone, not *in situ*	ROM/BYZ	0.00	1	T, K
PS093	PS98.093	PS-093	461547.9531	4535139.969	hamam	TRK	0.02	2	N
PS094	PS98.094	PS-094	461827.5185	4535129.953	hamam	TRK	0.02	2	N
PS095	PS98.095	PS-095	464830.7609	4539037.965	hamam	TRK	0.02	2	N
PS096	PS98.096	PS-096	467608.6033	4537519.411	fortified hilltop	HEL, ROM	50.00	7	E, K, L
PS097	PS98.097	PS-097	466904.8832	4537352.74	stones, not *in situ*	ROM/BYZ	0.00	1	T, K
PS098	PS98.098	PS-098	458353.0036	4531869.972	settlement	ROM/BYZ	5.00	6	A
PS099	PS98.099	PS-099	457016.6013	4531509.521	rock-cut tombs	ROM/BYZ	0.02	2	F
PS100	PS98.100	PS-100	456378.3243	4531393.471	rock-cut tombs	ROM/BYZ	0.10	3	F
PS101	PS98.101	PS-101	453167.5972	4531045.32	stones, not *in situ*	ROM/BYZ	0.00	1	T
PS102	PS98.102	PS-102	457113.31	4531973.723	stones, not *in situ*	ROM/BYZ	0.00	1	T
PS103	PS98.103	PS-103	455843.389	4530883.319	stones, not *in situ*	ROM/BYZ	0.00	1	T
PS104	PS98.104	PS-104	458736.1273	4529977.02	stones, not *in situ*	ROM/BYZ	0.00	1	T
PS105	PS98.105	PS-105	457973.0275	4529059.993	settlement	ROM/BYZ	0.06	2	C
PS106	PS98.106	PS-106	460968.1212	4533975.138	tumulus	IA?	0.07	2	H
PS107	PS98.107	PS-107	459996.5439	4534406.183	tumulus	IA?	0.07	2	H
PS108	PS98.108	PS-108	461791.5955	4538334.588	stones, not *in situ*	ROM/BYZ	0.00	1	T
PS109	PS98.109	PS-109	460307.1459	4532058.201	stones, not *in situ*	ROM/BYZ	0.00	1	T, K
PS110	PS98.110	PS-110	453979.9499	4531857.673	rock-cut tomb	ROM/BYZ	0.02	2	F
PS111	PS98.111	PS-111	453913.0414	4531704.941	settlement	EBA	0.12	3	C
PS112	PS98.112	PS-112	466384.1284	4525354.904	stones, not *in situ*	ROM/BYZ	0.00	1	T
PS113	PS98.113	PS-113	464558.0224	4522395.097	settlement	MBA II-OH, LBA, ROM/BYZ, TRK	0.16	3	C
PS114	PS98.114	PS-114	464416.1418	4522884.452	natural cave	ROM/BYZ	0.02	2	O
PS115	PS98.115	PS-115	466873.003	4522420.113	settlement	ROM/BYZ	0.03	2	C
PS116	PS98.116	PS-116	473778.4584	4529862.268	stones, not *in situ*	ROM/BYZ	0.00	1	T
PS117	PS98.117	PS-117	461855.0002	4538614.71	stones, not *in situ*	ROM/BYZ	0.00	1	T, K
PS118	PS98.118	PS-118	461632.9254	4538804.939	church?	ROM/BYZ	0.02	2	U, T
PS119	PS98.119	PS-119	461904.7668	4538519.434	stones, not *in situ*	ROM/BYZ	0.00	1	T, K
PS120	PS98.120	PS-120	462238.1079	4538612.029	stones, not *in situ*	ROM/BYZ	0.01	2	T, K
PS121	PS98.121	PS-121	476602.0893	4531901.087	settlement	ROM/BYZ	22.50	7	A
PS122	PS98.122	PS-122	476686.005	4531618.659	fortified lowland	CHA, EBA, MBA, LBA (OH-EEM, LEM), IA (EIA)	1.50	5	D
PS123	PS98.123	PS-123	476684.9454	4531446.619	tumulus	IA?	0.03	2	H
PS124	PS98.124	PS-124	472129.0192	4540734.639	stones, not *in situ*	ROM/BYZ	0.00	1	T, K
PS125	PS98.125	PS-125	471334.987	4541438.212	cemetery	ROM/BYZ	0.20	3	G
PS126	PS98.126	PS-126	471319.0396	4542015.654	settlement	TRK	1.50	5	B
PS127	PS98.127	PS-127	468852.3801	4540051.168	stones, not *in situ*	ROM/BYZ	0.00	1	T
PS128	PS98.128	PS-128	472999.9129	4527071.658	tumulus	IA?	0.26	4	H
PS129	PS98.129	PS-129	474339.8186	4528034.715	tumulus	IA?	0.28	4	H
PS130	PS98.130	PS-130	476606.6199	4528908.096	stones, not *in situ*	ROM/BYZ	0.00	1	T

Site Catalogue

Site number	Site no.	Site ID	X	Y	Type of site	Dating	Site area (ha)	Size category	Class. category
PS131	PS98.131	PS-131	478294.8318	4527450.751	cemetery and stones	ROM/BYZ	0.25	3	G
PS132	PS98.132	PS-132	476570.8575	4529525.871	tumulus	IA?	0.03	2	H
PS132a	PS98.132a	PS-132a	476579.7808	4529525.871	settlement	ROM/BYZ?	0.02	2	C
PS133	PS98.133	PS-133	481748.5502	4531605.926	stones, not *in situ*	ROM/BYZ	0.00	1	T
PS134	PS98.134	PS-134	453615.5956	4531765.479	stones, not *in situ*	ROM/BYZ	0.00	1	T
PS135	PS98.135	PS-135	451053.0363	4535589.888	settlement	TRK	1.50	5	B
PS136	PS98.136	PS-136	473796.7858	4540562.51	settlement	ROM/BYZ	1.50	5	B
PS137	PS98.137	PS-137	472420.4994	4540563.771	stones, not *in situ*	ROM/BYZ	0.00	1	T
PS138	PS98.138	PS-138	472209.4275	4540995.966	stones, not *in situ*	ROM/BYZ	0.00	1	T
PS139	PS98.139	PS-139	471662.8314	4540310	settlement	BYZ	1.50	5	B
PS140	PS98.140	PS-140	471737.8258	4540984.995	settlement	?	1.50	5	B
PS141	PS98.141	PS-141	469988.1476	4542332.755	stone, allegedly close to *in situ*	ROM	0.00	1	T, K
PS142	PS98.142	PS-142	492042.8435	4554692.66	rock-cut tomb	IA?	0.02	2	F
PS142a	PS98.142a	PS-142a	492216.1155	4554750.418	settlement	EBA?, ROM/BYZ	0.02	2	C
PS143	PS98.143	PS-143	491465.2704	4554346.116	stones, not *in situ*	ROM/BYZ	0.00	1	T
PS144	PS98.144	PS-144	494930.7091	4547299.724	stones, not *in situ*	ROM/BYZ	0.00	1	T
PS145	PS98.145	PS-145	490483.3962	4537076.68	tumulus	IA?	0.02	2	H
PS145a	PS98.145a	PS-145a	490598.9108	4537076.68	tumulus	IA?	0.02	2	H
PS146	PS98.146	PS-146	490367.8815	4536614.622	tumulus	IA?	0.07	2	H
PS147	PS98.147	PS-147	490867.7094	4535215.184	settlement	ROM/BYZ	2.50	5	B
PS148	PS98.148	PS-148	490712.71	4535315.182	settlement	ROM/BYZ	2.50	5	B
PS149	PS98.149	PS-149	500302.139	4544007.558	*höyük*	EBA, ROM/BYZ, IA?	0.05	2	H
PS150	PS98.150	PS-150	500302.139	4543487.742	stones, not *in situ*	ROM/BYZ	0.00	1	T
PS151	PS98.151	PS-151	501515.0426	4542332.596	stone, not *in situ*	HEL?	0.00	1	T
PS152	PS98.152	PS-152	499551.294	4539675.759	stones, not *in situ*	ROM/BYZ	0.00	1	T
PS153	PS98.153	PS-153	564040.1546	4493492.535	settlement?	EBA?	0.20	3	C
PS154	PS98.154	PS-154	563928.5279	4496245.219	*höyük*	MBA, IA (M-LIA)	1.18	5	M
PS155	PS98.155	PS-155	563714.0066	4487935.636	cemetery	EBA, MBA?, LBA (OH-EEM)	4.00	5	G
PS156	PS98.156	PS-156	585635.7288	4493863.283	*höyük*	EBA, LBA (OH-EEM, LEM?), IA (M-LIA), ROM/BYZ	0.79	4	M
PS157	PS98.157	PS-157	585682.2136	4493211.234	settlement	ROM/BYZ	15.00	7	A
PS158	PS98.158	PS-158	585185.8798	4493552.762	rock-cut tombs	ROM/BYZ	0.25	3	F
PS159	PS98.159	PS-159	585102.3624	4493803.314	stones, not *in situ*	ROM/BYZ	0.00	1	T
PS160	PS98.160	PS-160	588562.1831	4493986.248	settlement	ROM/BYZ	1.50	5	B
PS161	PS98.161	PS-161	592066.3741	4493891.76	rock-cut tomb	ROM/BYZ	0.10	2	F
PS162	PS98.162	PS-162	590417.2243	4486161.33	*höyük*	EBA, MBA, LBA (OH-EEM)	0.80	4	M
PS163	PS98.163	PS-163	551127.4629	4499610.926	*höyük*	?	0.60	4	M
PS164	PS98.164	PS-164	549370.54	4499032.474	tumulus	IA?	0.03	2	H
PS164a	PS98.164a	PS-164a	549443.3072	4499032.474	tumulus	IA?	0.03	2	H
PS165	PS98.165	PS-165	551237.3971	4508460.852	church?	BYZ	0.02	2	U

Site number	Site no.	Site ID	X	Y	Type of site	Dating	Site area (ha)	Size category	Class. category
PS166	PS98.166	PS-166	551527.397	4508135.856	settlement	?	0.50	4	C
PS167	PS98.167	PS-167	551651.01	4506954.696	cemetery	ROM/BYZ	1.00	4	G
PS168	PS98.168	PS-168	552463.1432	4496049.021	fortified hilltop	ROM/BYZ, TRK	4.00	5	A, E
PS169	PS98.169	PS-169	553872.6511	4470886.192	höyük	LBA (OH-EEM, LEM)	1.00	4	M
PS170	PS98.170	PS-170	545442.7285	4470181.136	höyük	MBA-LBA, LBA (OH-EEM, LEM), IA (EIA), ROM/BYZ	1.00	4	M
PS171	PS98.171	PS-171	561797.5485	4476151.874	höyük	LBA (OH-EEM, LEM)	1.00	4	M
PS172	PS98.172	PS-172	579532.5054	4460711.47	höyük	IA (LIA), HEL	0.20	3	M
PS173	PS98.173	PS-173	579877.4956	4461636.464	settlement	ROM/BYZ, TRK	0.12	3	C
PS174	PS98.174	PS-174	567872.5792	4464341.352	höyük	EBA, ROM/BYZ	0.24	3	M
PS175	PS98.175	PS-175	584829.2288	4472529.141	tumulus	IA?	0.02	2	H
PS176	PS98.176	PS-176	584927.3696	4472811.405	höyük	EBA, MBA II-OH, LBA (OH-EEM, LEM?)	0.50	4	M
PS177	PS98.177	PS-177	541751.9841	4488929.506	cemetery	ROM/BYZ	0.20	3	G
PS178	PS98.178	PS-178	541926.8378	4488998.2	höyük	MBA, LBA (OH-EEM), IA?	0.79	4	M
PS179	PS98.179	PS-179	539616.2467	4491371.204	cemetery	ROM/BYZ	0.50	4	G
PS180	PS98.180	PS-180	539765.2785	4492810.884	cemetery	ROM/BYZ	0.50	4	G
PS181	PS98.181	PS-181	539759.8895	4489672.622	cemetery	ROM/BYZ	0.50	4	G
PS182	PS98.182	PS-182	546750.9232	4482732.636	cemetery	ROM/BYZ	0.20	3	G
PS183	PS98.183	PS-183	548842.6245	4480301.074	höyük	CHA, EBA, MBA, LBA (OH-EEM, LEM)	6.30	6	M
PS184	PS98.184	PS-184	544349.6079	4477748.088	cemetery	ROM/BYZ	0.02	2	G
PS185	PS98.185	PS-185	544852.6793	4477501.069	settlement	ROM/BYZ	2.00	5	B
PS186	PS98.186	PS-186	542566.8131	4487608.034	stones, not in situ	ROM/BYZ	0.00	1	T
PS187	PS98.187	PS-187	553518.2666	4496558.391	tumulus?, cemetery?	EBA	1.50	5	H
PS188	PS98.188	PS-188	554064.0201	4497504.364	cemetery	ROM/BYZ	0.25	3	G
PS189	PS98.189	PS-189	574056.6416	4509044.649	cemetery	?	0.25	3	G
PS190	PS98.190	PS-190	577030.5873	4507982.526	rock-cut tombs	ROM/BYZ, TRK	0.25	3	F
PS191	PS98.191	PS-191	575224.9774	4504371.306	rock-cut tomb	ROM/BYZ	0.25	3	F
PS192	PS98.192	PS-192	573419.3675	4504530.625	tumulus	IA?	0.02	2	H
PS193	PS98.193	PS-193	567467.2985	4503001.017	höyük	EBA	1.18	5	M
PS194	PS98.194	PS-194	574162.854	4500282.131	cemetery	ROM/BYZ	0.25	3	G
PS195	PS98.195	PS-195	576977.4811	4503521.607	cemetery?	ROM/BYZ?	0.02	2	G
PS196	PS98.196	PS-196	569157.1865	4516385.915	monastery?	BYZ	0.36	4	C, U
PS197	PS98.197	PS-197	539728.8949	4506381.954	cemetery	ROM/BYZ	0.25	3	G
PS198	PS98.198	PS-198	540117.5157	4505170.798	höyük	CHA, EBA, LBA (LEM)	1.77	5	M
PS199	PS98.199	PS-199	538855.6893	4506345.571	stones, not in situ	ROM/BYZ	0.00	1	T
PS200	PS98.200	PS-200	550527.0073	4514426.587	tumulus	IA?	0.03	2	H
PS201	PS98.201	PS-201	550791.9269	4513587.675	rock-cut tomb	ROM/BYZ	0.02	2	F

Site Catalogue

Site number	Site no.	Site ID	X	Y	Type of site	Dating	Site area (ha)	Size category	Class. category
PS202	PS98.202	PS-202	535680.0663	4501912.284	rock-cut tomb	ROM/BYZ	0.02	2	F
PS203	PS98.203	PS-203	536775.5448	4499205.808	stones, not *in situ*	ROM/BYZ	0.00	1	T
PS204	PS98.204	PS-204	516437.4709	4482090.44	natural caves with sherds all around	BYZ	0.10	2	O
PS205	PS98.205	PS-205	517054.8283	4482090.44	cemetery	ROM/BYZ?	0.25	3	G
PS206	PS98.206	PS-206	518015.1622	4482707.797	cemetery/rock-cut tombs	ROM/BYZ?	0.50	4	F, G
PS207	PS98.207	PS-207	519318.4723	4483942.512	cemetery	ROM/BYZ?	0.25	3	G
PS208	PS98.208	PS-208	527037.759	4487215.854	lithic scatter	PAL?	0.25	3	J
PS209	PS98.209	PS-209	527882.8374	4489539.822	stones, not *in situ*	ROM/BYZ	0.00	1	T
PS210	PS98.210	PS-210	549561.1897	4504500.017	settlement	BYZ?	0.20	3	C
PS211	PS98.211	PS-211	549552.4579	4503289.351	rock-cut tomb	ROM/BYZ	0.01	2	F
PS211a	PS98.211a	PS-211a	549625.225	4503362.118	settlement	IA?, ROM/BYZ	0.25	3	C
PS212	PS98.212	PS-212	523681.8248	4514514.894	bridge	OTT?	0.01	2	N
PS213	PS98.213	PS-213	522666.2999	4536017.532	tumulus	IA?	0.02	2	H
PS213a	PS98.213a	PS-213a	522975.3727	4536061.685	settlement	ROM/BYZ	0.20	3	C
PS214	PS98.214	PS-214	526419.327	4536988.903	cemetery	ROM/BYZ	0.25	3	G
PS215	PS98.215	PS-215	519928.7977	4533412.489	natural cave/rock shelter	?	0.01	2	F
PS216	PS98.216	PS-216	503854.1834	4515558.83	fortified hilltop	BYZ?	0.10	3	E
PS217	PS99.217	PS-217	516203.9763	4501161.401	stones, not *in situ*	ROM/BYZ	0.00	1	T
PS218	PS99.218	PS-218	540334.5692	4509110.887	fortified lowland	EBA, MBA (MB II-OH), LBA (OH-EEM), IA (M-LIA), BYZ?	1.50	5	D
PS219	PS99.219	PS-219	505165.0067	4500458.809	cemetery	EBA, LBA (OH-EEM)	0.10	2	G
PS220	PS99.220	PS-220	503558.7113	4501015.31	tumulus	IA?	0.02	2	H
PS221	PS99.221	PS-221	557021.7922	4493474.621	sherd scatter	OTT?	1.00	4	C
PS222	PS99.222	PS-222	564074.5088	4492390.953	sherd scatter	?	0.02	2	Q
PS223	PS99.223	PS-223	564427.8612	4490629.191	tumulus	IA?	0.02	2	H
PS224	PS99.224	PS-224	533949.2449	4505447.912	settlement	TRK	1.00	4	C
PS225	PS99.225	PS-225	531266.2987	4535613.37	tumulus	IA?	0.02	2	H
PS226	PS99.226	PS-226	557984.3499	4493056.117	settlement	MPAL, ROM?	0.06	2	C
PS227	PS99.227	PS-227	558193.6016	4493725.723	settlement	ROM	3.75	5	B
PS228	PS99.228	PS-228	460995.2009	4533137.725	rock-cut quarry?	?	0.36	4	I
PS229	PS99.229	PS-229	474017.095	4529387.396	sherd scatter	OTT?	0.25	3	Q
PS230	PS99.230	PS-230	540593.1071	4508748.934	lithic scatter	NEO?	0.25	3	J
PS231	PS99.231	PS-231	506409.4546	4500321.631	flint outcrops	PAL?, TRK	2.50	5	I
PS232	PS99.232	PS-232	506930.9467	4499964.312	flint outcrops	PAL?, TRK	2.50	5	I
PS233	PS99.233	PS-233	552353.9925	4495466.884	church	BYZ	0.25	3	U
PS234	PS00.234	PS-234	562120.6321	4493796.819	tumulus	IA?	0.02	2	H
PS235	PS00.235	PS-235	542547.5968	4487696.05	stone, not *in situ*	ROM/BYZ	0.00	1	T
PS236	PS00.236	PS-236	538510.9423	4488111.414	tumulus	IA?	0.02	2	H
PS237	PS00.237	PS-237	476825.4819	4530454.09	tumulus	IA?	0.02	2	H
PS238	PS00.238	PS-238	540108.4389	4489162.369	lithic scatter	?	0.25	3	J
PS239	PS00.239	PS-239	487937.4807	4517721.807	stones, not *in situ*	ROM, BYZ	0.00	1	T

Project Paphlagonia

Site number	Site no.	Site ID	X	Y	Type of site	Dating	Site area (ha)	Size category	Class. category
PS240	PS00.240	PS-240	483783.3101	4517884.179	stones, not *in situ*	PHRY, ROM, BYZ	0.00	1	T
PS241	PS00.241	PS-241	483570.9573	4531625.908	tumulus	IA?	0.02	2	H
PS242	PS00.242	PS-242	483783.3101	4518517.282	tumulus	IA?	0.07	2	H
PS243	PS00.243	PS-243	524684.8337	4472616.147	fortified hilltop	BYZ?	0.08	2	E
PS244	PS00.244	PS-244	535938.1355	4479269.281	settlement	BYZ	0.25	3	C
Bölükören 01 S01	Inceboğaz 01 S01	BKR1-01	475760.7533	4531925.722	church	LROM, BYZ	0.04	2	U
Bölükören 02 S01	Inceboğaz 02 S01	BKR2-01	476282.9522	4529851.772	settlement	LROM, BYZ	1.50	5	B
Bölükören 02 S02	Inceboğaz 02 S02	BKR2-02	476612.1921	4529795.262	settlement	?	0.01	2	C
Bölükören 03 S01	Inceboğaz 03 S01	BKR3-01	476977.0029	4533123.433	settlement	LROM, BYZ	1.00	4	C
Çerkeş 01 S01	Çerkeş 01 S01	CRK1-01	487325.9431	4520220.432	settlement	ROM/BYZ	0.38	4	C
Çerkeş 03 S01	Çerkeş 03 S01	CRK3-01	485539.9809	4516960.281	settlement	ROM/BYZ	4.10	6	A
Çivi 01 S01	Çivi 01 S01	CIV1-01	564060.7066	4496453.271	lithic scatter, sherd scatter	BYZ	0.07	2	J, Q
Çivi 03 S01	Çivi 03 S01	CIV3-01	564085.319	4490390.088	tumulus	IA?	0.02	2	H
Çivi 03 S02	Çivi 03 S02	CIV3-02	564077.6055	4490450.776	tumulus	IA?	0.05	2	H
Çivi 03 S03	Çivi 03 S03	CIV3-03	564103.8201	4490336.578	tumulus	IA?	0.01	2	H
Çivi 03 S04	Çivi 03 S04	CIV3-04	564095.9556	4490366.002	tumulus	IA?	0.01	2	H
Çivi 03 S05	Çivi 03 S05	CIV3-05	564106.2491	4490290.144	tumulus	IA?	0.01	2	H
Çivi 03 S06	Çivi 03 S06	CIV3-06	562452.2128	4490330.397	settlement	LROM, BYZ	0.35	4	C
Çivi 04 S01	Çivi 04 S01	CIV4-01	561696.0251	4494839.291	cemetery	LROM, BYZ	0.80	4	G
Çivi 04 S02	Çivi 04 S02	CIV4-02	561647.5348	4494729.007	settlement	BYZ	4.10	6	A
Çivi 04 S03	Çivi 04 S03	CIV4-03	561651.7127	4494891.474	tumulus	IA?	0.02	2	H
Çivi 04 S04	Çivi 04 S04	CIV4-04	564124.6816	4494800.048	settlement	BYZ	0.50	4	C
Çivi 05 S01	Çivi 05 S01	CIV5-01	563422.7573	4487765.877	höyük	CHA, EBA, MBA, LBA (OH-EEM)	0.50	4	M
Çivi 05 S02	Çivi 05 S02	CIV5-02	562779.7925	4488405.084	settlement	ROM, BYZ, ETRK	0.31	4	C
Dağtarla 01 S01	Dağtarla 01 S01	DAG1-01	517206.5634	4520592.677	tumulus	IA?	0.01	2	H
Dağtarla 01 S02	Dağtarla 01 S02	DAG1-02	516139.3121	4520490.264	tumulus	IA?	0.06	2	H
Dağtarla 01 S03	Dağtarla 01 S03	DAG1-03	517107.5228	4520510.034	tumulus	IA?	0.02	2	H
Dağtarla 02 S01	Dağtarla 02 S01	DAG2-01	516988.0148	4522443.371	settlement	ROM?, BYZ, ETRK	14.00	7	A
Dağtarla 03 S01	Dağtarla 03 S01	DAG3-01	518523.6132	4519556.134	tumulus	IA?	0.01	2	H
Dağtarla 03 S02	Dağtarla 03 S02	DAG3-02	518552.3204	4519554.57	fortified lowland	?	2.10	5	D
Dumanlı 02 S01	Dumanlı 02 S01	DUM2-01	519528.695	4507246.601	tumulus	IA?	0.02	2	H
Dumanlı 02 S02	Dumanlı 02 S02	DUM2-02	519485.9047	4507246.601	tumulus	IA?	0.02	2	H

Site Catalogue

Site number	Site no.	Site ID	X	Y	Type of site	Dating	Site area (ha)	Size category	Class. category
Dumanlı 02 S03	Dumanlı 02 S03	DUM2-03	519384.28	4508299.234	rock-cut tombs	?	0.50	4	F
Dumanlı 02 S04	Dumanlı 02 S04	DUM2-04	519448.0991	4505361.389	track	?	0.02	2	R
Dumanlı 02 S05	Dumanlı 02 S05	DUM2-05	519465.2396	4504850.517	settlement	EBA, MBA II-OH, LBA	2.25	5	B
Dumanlı 03 S01	Dumanlı 03 S01	DUM3-01	521900.8716	4507457.736	tumulus	IA?	0.02	2	H
Dumanlı 03 S02	Dumanlı 03 S02	DUM3-02	521890.3023	4507475.836	lithic scatter	LPAL-MPAL	0.04	2	J
Dumanlı 03 S03	Dumanlı 03 S03	DUM3-03	521830.5316	4507812.565	lithic scatter	LPAL-MPAL	0.04	2	J
Dumanlı 03 S04	Dumanlı 03 S04	DUM3-04	521677.4105	4506708.08	fortified lowland	EBA	0.16	3	D
Eldivan 02 S01	Eldivan 02 S01	EDV2-01	539891.028	4489966.128	settlement	LROM, BYZ	0.72	4	C
Eldivan 02 S02	Eldivan 02 S02	EDV2-02	539856.5311	4489067.724	road	ROM?	0.02	2	R
Eldivan 02 S03	Eldivan 02 S03	EDV2-03	539878.5458	4488966.961	lithic scatter	MPAL	0.36	4	J
Eldivan 02 S04	Eldivan 02 S04	EDV2-04	539990.9506	4489166.795	lithic scatter	MPAL	1.77	5	J
Eldivan 03 S01	Eldivan 03 S01	EDV3-01	543256.9578	4491845.836	settlement	IA (EIA), ROM	3.00	5	B
Eldivan 04 S01	Eldivan 04 S01	EDV4-01	544805.6842	4489460.336	stone pile	LBA (OH-EEM)	0.01	2	S
Eldivan 04 S02	Eldivan 04 S02	EDV4-02	544837.879	4488213.418	embankment	?	0.01	2	S
Eldivan 05 S01	Eldivan 05 S01	EDV5-01	537805.2641	4490353.29	tumulus	IA?	0.02	2	H
Eldivan 05 S02	Eldivan 05 S02	EDV5-02	538070.7509	4491122.937	road	ROM?	0.02	2	R
Eldivan 05 S03	Eldivan 05 S03	EDV5-03	538735.7365	4490596.844	settlement	IA (M-LIA), BYZ	0.16	3	C
Ilgaz 01 S01	Ilgaz 01 S01	ILG1-01	557330.3134	4532466.461	settlement	BYZ	0.20	3	C
Ilgaz 01 S02	Ilgaz 01 S02	ILG1-02	553822.3875	4532290.751	settlement	LROM, BYZ	0.07	2	C
Ilgaz 01 S03	Ilgaz 01 S03	ILG1-03	553526.2104	4532339.709	settlement	LROM, BYZ	14.00	7	A
Ilgaz 01 S04	Ilgaz 01 S04	ILG1-04	553808.9962	4532441.079	tumulus	IA?	0.01	2	H
Ilgaz 02 S01	Ilgaz 02 S01	ILG2-01	554648.8121	4529882.095	settlement	IA (M-LIA), LROM, BYZ	3.00	5	B
Ilgaz 02 S02	Ilgaz 02 S02	ILG2-02	556480.5299	4529636.313	settlement	LROM, BYZ	0.07	2	C
Ilgaz 03 S01	Ilgaz 03 S01	ILG3-01	555587.3939	4534951.543	settlement	LROM, BYZ	0.07	2	C
Ilgaz 03 S02	Ilgaz 03 S02	ILG3-02	555586.4086	4535137.196	fortified hilltop	?	1.44	5	E
Ilgaz 03 S03	Ilgaz 03 S03	ILG3-03	555385.8458	4534929.149	track	?	0.01	2	R
Ilgaz 03 S04	Ilgaz 03 S04	ILG3-04	554883.7196	4535026.197	settlement	LROM, BYZ	4.10	6	A
Ilgaz 03 S05	Ilgaz 03 S05	ILG3-05	554386.6369	4535045.512	settlement	LROM, BYZ	0.07	2	C
Ilgaz 03 S06	Ilgaz 03 S06	ILG3-06	556242.0316	4535026.471	settlement	LROM, BYZ	0.20	3	C
Ilgaz 03 S07	Ilgaz 03 S07	ILG3-07	556490.969	4534907.278	settlement	LROM, BYZ	3.14	5	B
Ilgaz 04 S01	Ilgaz 04 S01	ILG4-01	554736.4923	4527547.08	fortified hilltop	?	0.42	4	E
Ilgaz 04 S02	Ilgaz 04 S02	ILG4-02	554564.0389	4527542.435	fortified hilltop	?	0.02	2	E

Project Paphlagonia

Site number	Site no.	Site ID	X	Y	Type of site	Dating	Site area (ha)	Size category	Class. category
Ilgaz 04 S03	Ilgaz 04 S03	ILG4-03	554504.9578	4527646.79	settlement	LROM, BYZ	8.00	6	A
Ilgaz 04 S04	Ilgaz 04 S04	ILG4-04	556248.0551	4527520.054	embankment	?	0.01	2	S
Ilgaz 05 S01	Ilgaz 05 S01	ILG5-01	555425.7889	4535739.765	settlement	?	0.04	2	C
Ilgaz 05 S02	Ilgaz 05 S02	ILG5-02	555265.4156	4535662.097	tumulus	IA?	0.05	2	H
Ilgaz 05 S03	Ilgaz 05 S03	ILG5-03	555260.9397	4535659.809	settlement	LROM, BYZ	0.09	2	C
Mart 01 S01	Mart 01 S01	MRT1-01	530392.5326	4472636.573	*höyük*	MBA-LBA, MBA (MBA II-OH), LBA (OH-EEM, LEM), IA (EIA)	1.02	5	M
Mart 01 S02	Mart 01 S02	MRT1-02	530374.1767	4472875.2	settlement	LBA, BYZ	16.38	7	A
Salur 01 S01	Salur 01 S01	SLR1-01	505612.2241	4500407.421	settlement	OTT	5.00	6	A
Salur 01 S02	Salur 01 S02	SLR1-02	505494.4826	4500345.929	lithic scatter	?	0.25	3	J
Salur 02 S01	Salur 02 S01	SLR2-01	505721.8556	4497898.93	lithic scatter	?	1.00	4	J
Salur 02 S02	Salur 02 S02	SLR2-02	505989.2695	4497948.371	lithic scatter	?	0.04	2	J
Salur 02 S03	Salur 02 S03	SLR2-03	506022.8627	4497920.679	lithic scatter	?	0.04	2	J
Salur 02 S04	Salur 02 S04	SLR2-04	506484.2485	4497933.51	rock-cut cemetery	LROM, BYZ	0.60	4	F
Salur 02 S05	Salur 02 S05	SLR2-05	503816.7315	4497857.603	tumulus	IA?	0.02	2	H
Salur 02 S06	Salur 02 S06	SLR2-06	503363.0484	4497819.211	road	ROM?, BYZ	0.02	2	R
Salur 03 S01	Salur 03 S01	SLR3-01	505313.4835	4502668.146	rock-cut tombs, chapel	BYZ	0.25	3	F
Salur 03 S02	Salur 03 S02	SLR3-02	503806.5239	4502812.11	lithic scatter	MPAL	1.00	4	J

Key to dating terms:

BYZ	Byzantine		LPAL	Late Palaeolithic
CHA	Chalcolithic		LROM	Late Roman
EBA	Early Bronze Age		MBA	Middle Bronze Age
EBYZ	Early Byzantine		MIA	Middle Iron Age
EEM	Early Hittite Empire		MPAL	Middle Palaeolithic
EIA	Early Iron Age		NEO	Neolithic
ETRK	Early Turkish		OH	Old Hittite
HEL	Hellenistic		OTT	Ottoman
IA	Iron Age		PAL	Palaeolithic
LBA	Late Bronze Age		PHRY	Phrygian
LEM	Late Hittite Empire		ROM	Roman
LIA	Late Iron Age		TRK	Turkish

Bibliography

Ainsworth, W.F. 1842: *Travels and Researches in Asia Minor, Mesopotamia, Chaldea and Armenia, I–II*. London

Akman, Y., Yurdakulol, E., Demirörs, M. 1983: 'The vegetation of the Ilgaz mountains' *Ecologia Mediterranea* 9/2: 137–65

Alcock, S.E. 1994: 'Breaking up the Hellenistic world: survey and society' in I. Morris (ed.) *Classical Greece: Ancient Histories and Modern Archaeologies*. Cambridge: 171–90

— 2001: 'The reconfiguration of memory in the eastern Roman empire' in S.E. Alcock, T.N. D'Altroy, K.D. Morrison, C.M. Sinopoli (eds) *Empires. Perspectives from Archaeology and History*. Cambridge: 323–50

Alcock, S.E., Cherry, J.F. (eds) 2004: *Side-by-Side Survey. Comparative Regional Studies in the Mediterranean World*. Oxford

Alex, M. 1985: *Klimatdaten ausgewählter Stationen des Vorderen Orients* (Beihefte zum Tübinger Atlas des Vorderen Orients Reihe A: 14). Wiesbaden

Alexandre, G. 1994: *Bassin et montagnes dans le district d'Ilgaz*. Unpublished MA thesis, Université de Paris IV Sorbonne

Alkım, U.B. 1973: 'Tilmen Hüyük and the Samsun region' *Anatolian Studies* 23: 62–65

Alkım, U.B., Alkım, H., Bilgi, Ö. 1988: *İkiztepe I. The First and Second Seasons' Excavations (1974–1975)*. Ankara

Alp, S. 1991: *Hethitische Briefe aus Maşat-Höyük*. Ankara

Alpagut, B., Andrews, P., Martin, L. 1990: 'New hominoid specimens from the Middle Miocene site at Paşalar, Turkey' *Journal of Human Evolution* 19: 397–422

Ambraseys, N.N. 1970: 'Some characteristic features of the North Anatolian Fault zone' *Tectonophysics* 9: 143–65

Arpat, E., Şaroğlu, F. 1972: 'East Anatolian fault system: thoughts on its development' *Bulletin of the Mineral Research and Exploration Institute of Turkey* (foreign edition) 78: 33–39

— 1975: 'Some recent tectonic events in Turkey' *Bulletin of the Geological Society of Turkey* 18/1: 91–100 (in Turkish with English abstract)

Aydın, Z. 1990: 'The World Bank and the Çorum-Çankırı rural development project in Turkey' in M. Salem-Murdock, M.M. Horowitz, M. Sella (eds) *Anthropology and Development in North Africa and the Middle East*. Boulder: 312–35

Ayhan, B. 1998: *Çankırı Tarihi*. Ankara

Bahar, H., Koçak, Ö. 2004: *Eskiçağ Konya Araştırmaları 2*. Konya

Bailey, D.W. 1999: 'What is a tell? Settlement in fifth millennium Bulgaria' in J. Brück, M. Goodman (eds) *Making Places in the Prehistoric World*. London: 94–111

Baird, D. 2001: 'Konya plain survey' *Anatolian Archaeology* 7: 16

— 2002: 'Early Holocene settlement in central Anatolia: problems and prospects as seen from the Konya plain' in F. Gérard, L. Thissen (eds) *The Neolithic of Central Anatolia*. Istanbul: 139–52

— 2004: 'Settlement expansion on the Konya plain, Anatolia: 5th–7th centuries AD' in W. Bowden, L. Lavan, C. Machado (eds) *Recent Research on the Late Antique Countryside*. Leiden: 219–46

Balkan, K. 1973: *İnandık'ta 1966 yılında bulunan eski hitit çağında ait bir bağış belgesi. Eine Schenkungsurkunde aus der althethitischen Zeit, gefunden in İnandık 1966*. Ankara

Barka, A.A. 1984: 'Kuzey Anadolu Fay Zonundaki bazı Neojen-Kuvaterner havzaların jeolojisi ve tektonik evrimi' in *Proceedings of Ketin Symposium*. Ankara: 209–27

Barkan, Ö.L. 1970: 'Research on the Ottoman fiscal survey' in M.A. Cook (ed.) *Studies in Economic History of the Middle East*. Oxford: 167–71

Başaran, S. 1999: 'Enez çevresinde yapılan arkeolojik araştırmalar' in N. Başgelen, G. Çelgin, A.V. Çelgin (eds) *Anatolian and Thracian Studies in Honour of Zafer Taşlıklıoğlu*. Istanbul: 169–97

Becker Bertau, F. 1986: *Die Inschriften von Klaudiupolis*. Bonn

Beckman, G. 2000: 'Hittite chronology' *Akkadica* 119–20: 19–32

Belke, K. 1996: *Tabula Imperii Byzantini 9. Paphlagonien und Honōrias*. Vienna

Beug, J. 1967: 'Contributions to the post-glacial vegetational history of northern Turkey' in E.J. Cushing, H.E. Wright Jr (eds) *Quaternary Palaeoecology*. New Haven: 349–56

Bigazzi, G., Oddone, M., Yegingil, Z. 1995: 'A provenance study of obsidian artifacts from Ilıpınar' in J. Roodenberg (ed.) *The Ilıpınar Excavations I*. Istanbul: 143–50

Bilgi, Ö. 1999: 'İkiztepe in the Late Iron Age' in A. Çilingiroğlu, R. Matthews (eds) *Anatolian Iron Ages 4* (*Anatolian Studies* 49). London: 27–54

— 2001: *Protohistoric Age Metallurgists of the Central Black Sea Region. A New Perspective on the Question of the Indo-Europeans' Original Homeland*. Istanbul

Bingöl, E. 1989: *Turkiye Jeoloji Haritası* (map at scale 1:2,000,000). Ankara

Bittel, K., Otto, H. 1939: *Demirci-Hüyük. Eine vorgeschichtliche Siedlung an der phrygisch-bithynischen Grenze*. Berlin

Blanton, R.E. 2000: *Hellenistic, Roman and Byzantine Settlement Patterns of the Coast Lands of Western Rough Cilicia*. Oxford

Bommeljé, S., Doorn, P., Deylius, M., Vroom, J., Bommeljé, Y., Fagel, R., van Wijngaarden, H. 1987: *Aetolia and Aetolians*. Utrecht

Bossert, E.-M. 2000: *Die Keramik phrygischer Zeit von Boğazköy* (Boğazköy-Hattusa Ergebnisse der Ausgrabungen 18). Mainz

Bosworth, A.B., Wheatley, P.V. 1998: 'The origins of the Pontic house' *The Journal of Hellenic Studies* 118: 155–64

Bottema, S., Woldring, H. 1990: 'Anthropogenic indicators in the pollen record of the eastern Mediterranean' in S. Bottema, G. Entjes-Nieborg, W. van Zeist (eds) *Man's Role in Shaping of the Eastern Mediterranean Landscape*. Rotterdam: 231–64

Bottema, S., Woldring H., Aytuğ, B. 1993/1994: 'Late Quaternary vegetation history of northern Turkey' *Palaeohistoria* 35/36: 13–72

Bottema, S., Woldring, H., Kayan, I. 2001: 'The Late Quaternary vegetation history of western Turkey', in J.J. Roodenberg, L.C. Thissen (eds) *The Ilıpınar Excavations II*. Leiden: 327–54

Brandes, W. 1989: *Die Städte Kleinasiens im 7. und 8. Jahrhundert*. Amsterdam

Branting, S. 1996: 'The Alişar regional survey 1993–1994: a preliminary report' *Anatolica* 22: 145–58

Brinkmann, R. 1976: *Geology of Turkey*. Amsterdam

Brixhe, C. 1995: 'Bulletin épigraphique: Asie Mineure' *Revue des études grecques* 108: 507–43

Bryce, T. 1998: *The Kingdom of the Hittites*. Oxford

Burney, C. 1956: 'Northern Anatolia before Classical times' *Anatolian Studies* 6: 179–203

Cagnat, R. 1906–1927: *Inscriptiones Graecae ad res Romanas pertinentes*. Paris

Carruba, O. 1993: 'Zur Datierung der ältesten Schenkungsurkunden und anonymen Tabarna-Siegel' *Istanbuler Mitteilungen* 43: 71–85

Cavruc, V. 1997: 'The final stage of the Early Bronze Age in southeastern Transylvania (in the light of new excavations at Zoltan)' *Thraco-Dacica* 18: 97–133

Corsten, T. 1991–1993: *Die Inschriften von Prusa ad Olympum*. Bonn

Coulton, J.J. 2005: 'Pedestals as "altars" in Roman Asia Minor' *Anatolian Studies* 55: 127–57

Crow, J. 1996: 'Alexios Komnenos and Kastamon: castles and settlement in middle Byzantine Paphlagonia' in M. Mullett, D. Smythe (eds) *Alexios I Komnenos* (Belfast Byzantine Texts and Translations 4.1). Belfast: 12–36

Cuinet, V. 1894: *La Turquie d'Asie*. Paris

Cunningham, T., Driessen, J. 2004: 'Site by site: combining survey and excavation data to chart patterns of socio-political change in Bronze Age Crete' in S.E. Alcock, J.F. Cherry (eds) *Side-by-Side Survey. Comparative Regional Studies in the Mediterranean World*. Oxford: 101–13

Czichon, R.M., Flender, M., Klinger, J. 2006: 'Interdisziplinäre Geländebegehungen im Gebeit von Oymaağaç-Vezirköprü/Provinz Samsun' *Mitteilungen der Deutschen Orient-Gesellschaft* 138: 157–76

Czichon, R.M., Klinger, J. 2005: 'Auf der Suche nach der hethitischen Kultstadt Nerik' *Alter Orient* 6: 18–19

Çevik, Ö. 2007: 'The emergence of different social systems in Early Bronze Age Anatolia: urbanisation versus centralisation' *Anatolian Studies* 57: 131–40

Çınaroğlu, A., Genç, E. 2004: 'Kastamonu-Kınık 2002 yılı kazısı' *Kazı Sonuçları Toplantısı* 25/1: 355–66

— 2005: '2003 yılı Kastamonu-Kınık kazısı' *Kazı Sonuçları Toplantısı* 26/1: 277–90

Darbyshire, G., Mitchell, S., Vardar, L. 2000: 'The Galatian settlement in Asia Minor' *Anatolian Studies* 50: 75–97

Dercksen, J.G. 2001: '"When we met in Hattuš" Trade according to Old Assyrian texts from Alishar and Boğazköy' in W.H. van Soldt (ed.) *Veenhof Anniversary Volume*. Leiden: 39–66

De Vincenzi, T. 2008: 'Fortification walls. Development and conformation of Anatolian "saw-tooth wall", "Kastenmauer", "Casematte" defence systems, and their building techniques in the Bronze Age' in H. Kühne, R.M. Czichon, F.J. Kreppner (eds)

Proceedings of the 4th International Congress of the Archaeology of the Ancient Near East 29 March –3 April 2004, Freie Universität Berlin. Volume 1. Wiesbaden: 309–20

DeVries, K., Sams, G.K., Voigt, M.M. 2005: 'Gordion re-dating' in A. Çilingiroğlu, G. Darbyshire (eds) *Anatolian Iron Ages 5* (British Institute at Ankara Monograph 31). London: 45–46

Dolukhanov, P.M. 2007: 'Environment and early human migrations in the eastern Black Sea area' in G. Erkut, S. Mitchell (eds) *The Black Sea: Past, Present and Future* (British Institute at Ankara Monograph 42). London: 21–26

Dönmez, Ş. 1999: 'Sinop-Samsun-Amasya illeri yüzey araştırması, 1997' *Araştırma Sonuçları Toplantısı* 16/2: 513–36

— 2002: 'The 2nd millennium BC settlements in Samsun and Amasya provinces, central Black Sea region, Turkey' *Ancient West and East* 1: 243–93

— 2003: 'The Early Iron Age problem in the central Black Sea region' in B. Fischer, H. Genz, É. Jean, K. Köroğlu (eds) *Identifying Changes: the Transition from Bronze to Iron Ages in Anatolia and its Neighbouring Regions.* Istanbul: 213–28

— 2005: 'Amasya province in the Iron Age' in A. Çilingiroğlu, G. Darbyshire (eds) *Anatolian Iron Ages 5* (British Institute at Ankara Monograph 31). London: 65–74

— 2006a: 'Recent observations on the cultural development of the central Black Sea region before the Early Bronze Age II' in D.B. Erciyas, E. Koparal (eds) *Black Sea Studies Symposium Proceedings.* Istanbul: 89–98

— 2006b: 'Some observations on the socio-economic structure and ethnic make-up of the central Black Sea region of Turkey during the Iron Age in the light of new evidence' *Ancient West and East* 5: 13–43

Dörner, F.K. 1963: 'Vorbericht über eine Reise in Bithynien und im bithynisch-paphlagonischen Grenzgebiet 1962' *Anzeiger Österreichische Akademie der Wissenschaften* 100: 132–39

Durbin, G.E.S. 1971: 'Iron Age pottery from the provinces of Tokat and Sivas' *Anatolian Studies* 21: 99–124

Düring, B. 2008: 'The Early Holocene occupation of north-central Anatolia between 10,000 and 6,000 BC cal: investigating an archaeological *terra incognita*' *Anatolian Studies* 58: 15–46

Durugönül, S. 1994: 'The sculpture of a lion in the Amasya museum' *Anatolian Studies* 44: 149–52

Dyson, R.H. Jr 1999: 'The Achaemenid painted pottery of Hasanlu IIIA' in A. Çilingiroğlu, R. Matthews (eds) *Anatolian Iron Ages 4* (*Anatolian Studies* 49). London: 101–10

Easton, D.F. 1981: 'Hittite land donations and Tabarna seals' *Journal of Cuneiform Studies* 33: 3–43

Eastwood, W.J., Roberts, N., Lamb, H.F. 1998: 'Palaeoecological and archaeological evidence for human occupance in southwest Turkey: the Beyşehir Occupation Phase' *Anatolian Studies* 48: 69–86

Efe, T. 1988: *Demircihüyük. Die Ergebnisse der Ausgrabungen 1975–1978 Band III,2. Die Keramik 2.* Mainz am Rhein

— 1989–1990: 'Three early sites in the vicinity of Eskişehir: Asmainler, Kanlıtaş, and Kes Kaya' *Anatolica* 16: 31–60

— (ed.) 2001: *The Salvage Excavations at Orman Fidanlığı a Chalcolithic Site in Inland Northwestern Anatolia.* Istanbul

— 2003: 'Küllüoba and the initial stages of urbanism in western Anatolia' in M. Özdoğan, H. Hauptmann, N. Başgelen (eds) *From Village to Cities. Studies Presented to Ufuk Esin.* Istanbul: 265–82

Emre, K. 1966: 'The pottery from Acemhöyük' *Anadolu* 10: 99–151

— 1979: 'Maşat Höyük'de Eski Tunç Çağı – the Early Bronze Age at Maşat Höyük' *Belleten* 169: 21–48

Emre, K. Çinaroğlu, A. 1993: 'A group of metal Hittite vessels from Kınık-Kastamonu' in M.J. Mellink, E. Porada, T. Özgüç (eds) *Aspects of Art and Iconography: Anatolia and its Neighbors: Studies in Honour of Nimet Özgüç.* Ankara: 675–717

England, A. 2006: *Late Holocene Palaeoecology of Cappadocia (Central Turkey).* Unpublished PhD thesis, University of Birmingham

Erciyas, D.B. 2006a: *Wealth, Aristocracy and Royal Propaganda under the Hellenistic Kingdom of the Mithradatids in the Central Black Sea Region of Turkey* (Colloquia Pontica 12). Leiden

— 2006b: 'The Black Sea region in the Hellenistic period: the Pontic kingdom, its settlements, monuments and coins' in D.B. Erciyas, E. Koparal (eds) *Black Sea Studies Symposium Proceedings.* Istanbul: 219–30

Esin, U. 1993: 'Gelveri – ein Beispiel für die kulturellen Beziehungen zwischen Zentralanatolien und Südosteuropa während des Chalkolithikums' *Anatolica* 19: 47–56

Faegri, K., Iversen, J. 1989: *Textbook of Pollen Analysis.* Chichester

Fergar, F.K. (ed.) 1992: *Modern Turkish Poetry.* Ware

Finkelstein, I., Lederman, Z. 1997: 'Introduction' in I. Finkelstein, Z. Lederman (eds) *Highlands of Many Cultures. The Southern Samaria Survey. The Sites.* Tel Aviv: 1–8

Fischer, F. 1963: *Die Hethitische Keramik von Boğazköy-Hattusa*. Berlin

Forlanini, M. 1977: 'L'Anatolia nordoccidentale nell'impero eteo' *Studi Micenei ed Egeo-Anatolici* 18: 197–225

Forrer, E. 1932: 'Balâ' in E. Ebeling, B. Meissner (eds) *Reallexikon der Assyriologie* 1: 392–93

Foss, C. 2000: 'Map 86 Paphlagonia' in R.J.A. Talbert (ed.) *Barrington Atlas of the Greek and Roman World*. Princeton: 1217–25

French, D.H. 1967: 'Prehistoric sites in northwest Anatolia I. The İznik area' *Anatolian Studies* 17: 49–100

— 1969: 'Prehistoric sites in northwest Anatolia II. The Balıkesir and Akhisar/Manisa areas' *Anatolian Studies* 19: 41–98

— 1980: 'The Roman road-system of Asia Minor' *Aufstieg und Niedergang der Römischen Welt* 7/2: 698–729

— 1988a: 'Roman roads and milestones of Asia Minor 1987' *Anatolian Studies* 38: 8–10

— 1988b: *Roman Roads and Milestones of Asia Minor. Fascicle 2: An Interim Catalogue of Milestones Part 2* (British Institute of Archaeology at Ankara Monograph 9, BAR International Series 392:ii). Oxford

— 1989: '1987 yılı Roma yolları ve miltaşları çalışması' *Araştırma Sonuçları Toplantısı* 6: 273–81

— 1991: 'New milestones from Pontus and Galatia' *Pontica* 1: 77–96

— 2003: *Roman, Late Roman and Byzantine Inscriptions of Ankara. A Selection*. Ankara

Fuat, M. 1985: *Çağdaş Türk Şiiri Antolojisi*. Istanbul

Gallavotti, C. 1987: 'Revisione di testi epigrafici' *Bollettino dei classici* 8: 33–36

Garrard, A. 1998: 'Palaeolithic and Neolithic survey at a southeastern "gateway" to Turkey' in R. Matthews (ed.) *Ancient Anatolia. Fifty Years' Work by the British Institute of Archaeology at Ankara*. London: 7–16

Genz, H. 2000a: 'The Early Iron Age in central Anatolia in light of recent research' *Near Eastern Archaeology* 63: 111

— 2000b: 'Die Eisenzeit in Zentralanatolien im Lichte der keramischen Funde vom Büyükkaya in Boğazköy/Hattuša' *Tüba-Ar* 3: 35–54

— 2003: 'The Early Iron Age in central Anatolia' in B. Fischer, H. Genz, É. Jean, K. Köroğlu (eds) *Identifying Changes: the Transition from Bronze to Iron Ages in Anatolia and its Neighbouring Regions*. Istanbul: 179–91

— 2004a: *Büyükkaya I. Die Keramik der Eisenzeit. Funde aus den Grabungskampagnen 1993 bis 1998* (Boğazköy-Hattuša 21). Mainz am Rhein

— 2004b: 'Erste Ansätze zu einer Chronologie der frühen Eisenzeit in Zentralanatolien' in M. Novák, F. Prayon, A.-M. Wittke (eds) *Die Außenwirkung des späthethitischen Kulturraumes. Güteraustausch – Kulturkontakt – Kulturtransfer. Akten der zweiten Forschungstagung des Graduiertenkollegs 'Anatolien und seine Nachbarn' der Eberhard-Karls-Universität Tübingen (20. bis 22. November 2003)* (Alter Orient und Altes Testament 323). Münster: 219–36

— 2005: 'Thoughts on the origin of the Iron Age pottery traditions in central Anatolia' in A. Çilingiroğlu, G. Darbyshire (eds) *Anatolian Iron Ages 5* (British Institute at Ankara Monograph 31). London: 75–84

Georgiev, G.I., Merpert, N., Katincharov, R., Dimitrov, D. 1979: *Ezero. Eine Siedlung aus der Frühbronzezeit*. Sofia

Gerber, C. 2005: 'Tavium in the first millennium BC: first survey results' in A. Çilingiroğlu, G. Darbyshire (eds) *Anatolian Iron Ages 5* (British Institute at Ankara Monograph 31). London: 85–90

Glatz, C., Matthews, R. 2005: 'Anthropology of a frontier zone: Hittite-Kaska relations in Late Bronze Age north-central Anatolia' *Bulletin of the American Schools of Oriental Research* 339: 21–39

Glendinning, M.R. 1996: 'A mid-sixth century tile roof system at Gordion' *Hesperia* 65: 99–119

— 2005: 'A decorated roof at Gordion. What tiles are revealing about the Phrygian past' in L. Kealhofer (ed.) *The Archaeology of Midas and the Phrygians. Recent Work at Gordion*. Philadelphia: 82–100

Goetze, A. 1960: 'The beginning of the Hittite instructions for the commander of the border guards' *Journal of Cuneiform Studies* 14: 69–73

Gorny, R.L. 1989: 'Environment, archaeology, and history in Hittite Anatolia' *Biblical Archaeologist* 52: 78–96

— 1995 'Hittite imperialism and anti-Hittite resistance as viewed from Alishar Höyük' *Bulletin of the American School of Oriental Research* 299/300: 65–90

Gropp, G. 2001: 'Sassen die Skudra wirklich in Thrakien? Ein Problem der Satrapienverteilung in Kleinasien' in T. Bakır (ed.) *Achaemenid Anatolia*. Leiden: 37–42

Gürkan, G., Seeher, J. 1991: 'Die frühbronzezeitliche Nekropole von Küçükhöyük bei Bozüyük' *Istanbuler Mitteilungen* 41: 39–96

Güterbock, H.G. 1961: 'The north-central area of Hittite Anatolia' *Journal of Near Eastern Studies* 20: 85–97

Hancock, P.L., Barka, A.A. 1983: 'Tectonic interpretations of enigmatic structures in the North Anatolian Fault Zone' *Journal of Structural Geology* 5: 217–20

Hansen, C.K., Postgate, J.N. 2007: 'Chapter 26: Pottery from Level II' in J.N. Postgate, D.C. Thomas (eds) *Excavations at Kilise Tepe, 1994–1998: From Bronze Age to Byzantine in Western Cilicia.* Cambridge: 343–70

Hardie, L.A., Smoot, J.P., Eugster, H.P. 1978: 'Saline lakes and their deposits: a sedimentological approach' in A. Matter, M.E. Tucker (eds) *Modern and Ancient Lake Sediments* (International Association of Sedimentologists, Special Publication 2). Oxford: 7–41

Harmankaya, S., Erdoğu, B. 2002: *Türkiye Arkeolojik Yerleşmeleri 4 İlk Tunç.* Istanbul

Harmankaya, S., Tanındı, O. 1996: *Türkiye Arkeolojik Yerleşmeleri 1 Paleolitik/Epipaleolitik.* Istanbul

Harmankaya, S., Tanındı, O., Özbaşaran, M. 1997: *Türkiye Arkeolojik Yerleşmeleri 2 Neolitik.* Istanbul

— 1998: *Türkiye Arkeolojik Yerleşmeleri 3 Kalkolitik.* Istanbul

Hauptmann, H. 1969: 'Die Grabungen in der prähistorischen Siedlung auf Yarıkkaya' in K. Bittel, H.G. Güterbock, H. Hauptmann, H. Kühne, P. Neve, W. Schirmer *Boğazköy IV. Funde aus den Grabungen 1967 und 1968.* Berlin: 66–69

—1975: 'Die Felsspalte D' in K. Bittel (ed.) *Das hethitische Felsheiligtum Yazılıkaya.* Berlin: 62–75

Henrickson, R.C. 1993: 'Politics, economics, and ceramic continuity at Gordion in the late second and first millennia BC' in W.D. Kingery (ed.) *The Social and Cultural Contexts of New Ceramic Technology* (Ceramics and Civilization 6). Westerville: 89–176

— 1994: 'Continuity and discontinuity in the ceramic tradition of Gordion during the Iron Age' in A. Çilingiroğlu, D.H. French (eds) *Anatolian Iron Ages 3* (British Institute at Ankara Monograph 16). London: 95–129

— 1995: 'Hittite potters and pottery: the view from Late Bronze Age Gordion' *Biblical Archaeology* 58: 82–90

Hiller, S., Nikolov, V. 1997: *Karanovo. Die Ausgrabungen im Südsektor 1984–1992.* Salzburg, Sofia

Houwink ten Cate, P.H.J. 1966: 'Mursili's northwestern campaigns – additional fragments of his comprehensive annals' *Journal of Near Eastern Studies* 25: 162–91

— 1967: 'Mursili's northwestern campaigns – a commentary' *Anatolica* 1: 44–61

İlhan, M.M. 1987: 'The Katif district (Liva) during the first few years of Ottoman rule: a study of 1551 Ottoman cadastral survey' *Belleten* 51: 781–800

— 1996: 'Introducing *438 Numaralı Muhasebe-i Vilayet-i Anadolu Defteri (937/2530) I, Kütahya, Karahisar-ı Sahib, Sultan-önü, Hamid ve Ankara Livaları,* Ankara 1993' *Al-Manarah* 1/1: 121–43

— 2000: *Amid (Diyarbakır).* Ankara

— 2005: 'The town of Çankırı: its population and development' in C. Imber, K. Kiyotaki (eds) *Frontiers of Ottoman Studies.* London: 127–38

İnalcık, H. 1987: *Hicri 835 Tarihli Suret-i Defter-i Sancak-i Arvanid* (second edition). Ankara

Işık, A. 2001: *Antik Kaynaklarda Karadeniz Bölgesi.* Ankara

Işın, M.A. 1998: 'Sinop regional field survey' *Anatolia Antiqua* 6: 95–139

Jameson, M.H., Runnels, C.N., van Andel, T.H. 1994: *A Greek Countryside: the Southern Argolid from Prehistory to the Present Day.* Stanford

Jones, A.H.M. 1971: *The Cities of the Eastern Roman Provinces* (second edition). Oxford

Jones, M.D., Roberts, N., Leng, M.J., Türkeş, M. 2006: 'A high-resolution late Holocene lake isotope record from Turkey and links to North Atlantic and monsoon climate' *Geology* 34/5: 361–64

Kansu, Ş.A. 1940: *Etiyokuşu Hafriyatı Raporu (1937).* Ankara

Kashima, K. 2001: 'The relationship between the distribution of archaeological sites and their geomorphologic conditions in the Lake Tuz basin, central Turkey' in *Kaman-Kalehöyük 10* (Anatolian Archaeological Studies 10). Tokyo: 129–39

Kaya, K. 2001: *5 Numaralı Şer'iyye Sicillerine Göre XVII. Yüzyıl Sonlarında (H. 1109–1110/M. 1697–1698) Çankırı Sancağı.* Unpublished MA thesis, Ankara University

Kaygusuz, İ. 1982: 'Deux inscriptions de Gangra-Germanicopolis' *Zeitschrift für Papyrologie und Epigraphik* 49: 177–83

— 1983a: 'Kimistene'den yazıtlar' *Türk Arkeoloji Dergisi* 26: 111–43

— 1983b: 'Zwei neue Inschriften aus Ilgaz (Olgassys) und Kimiatene' *Epigraphica Anatolica* 1: 59–61

— 1983c: 'Ilgaz (Olgassys) dan iki yazıt ve Kimiatene' *Belleten* 47: 47–66

— 1984: 'Inscriptions of Kimistene (Paphlagonia)' *Epigraphica Anatolica* 4: 69–72

Kealhofer, L. 2005: 'The Gordion regional survey. Settlement and land use' in L. Kealhofer (ed.) *The Archaeology of Midas and the Phrygians. Recent Work at Gordion.* Philadelphia: 137–48

Keleş, V. 2006: 'Persian influence at Sinope based on the evidence of coins' in D.B. Erciyas, E. Koparal (eds) *Black Sea Studies Symposium Proceedings.* Istanbul: 111–18

Keller, J., Seifried, C. 1990: 'The present status of obsidian source identification in Anatolia and the Near East' *Pact* 25: 57–87

Kiel, M. 1997: 'The rise and decline of Turkish Boeotia, 15th–19th century' in J. Bintliff (ed.) *Recent Developments in the History and Archaeology of Central Greece. Proceedings of the 6th International Boeotian Conference* (BAR International Series 666). Oxford: 315–58

— 2004: 'Anatolian-Balkan connections. The central Greek district of Vitrinitsa (Tolophon) and the north Anatolian town of Amasya in the 15th–17th centuries according to unknown and rarely-used Ottoman Turkish sources' *Anatolica* 30: 219–37

Kimball Armayor, O. 1978: 'Herodotus' catalogues of the Persian empire in the light of the monuments and the Greek literary tradition' *Transactions of the American Philological Association* 108: 1–9

Kitov, G. 1999: 'Royal insignia, tombs and temples in the valley of the Thracian rulers' *Archaeologia Bulgarica* 3/1: 1–20

Klinger, J. 1995: 'Das Corpus der Maşat-Briefe und seine Beziehungen zu den Texten aus Hattuša' *Zeitschrift für Assyriologie* 85: 74–108

— 2002: 'Die hethitisch-kaškäische Geschichte bis zum Beginn der Großreichszeit' in S. de Martino, F. Pecchioli Daddi (eds) *Anatolia Antica: Studi in memoria di Fiorella Imparati* (Tomo I). Firenze: 437–51

Koçak, Ö. 2006: 'Mining at the central Black Sea region in the ancient period' in D.B. Erciyas, E. Koparal (eds) *Black Sea Studies Symposium Proceedings*. Istanbul: 39–62

Koçyiğit, A., Rojay, B., Cihan, M., Özacar, A. 2001: 'The June 6, 2000, Orta (Çankırı, Turkey) earthquake: sourced from a new antithetic sinistral strike-slip structure of the North Anatolian Fault System, the Dodurga fault zone' *Turkish Journal of Earth Sciences* 10: 69–82

Koşay, H.Z. 1941: *Pazarlı Hafriyatı Raporu*. Ankara

Koşay, H.Z., Akok, M. 1957: *Ausgrabungen von Büyük Güllücek, 1947 und 1949*. Ankara

Kökten, İ.K. 1944: 'Orta, doğu ve kuzey Anadolu'da yapılan tarih öncesi araştırmaları' *Belleten* 8: 659–80

Kowalewski, S.A. 2008: 'Regional settlement pattern studies' *Journal of Archaeological Research* 16: 225–85

Kuhn, S.L. 2002: 'Paleolithic archeology in Turkey' *Evolutionary Anthropology* 11: 198–210

Kühne, H. 1987: 'Politische Szenerie und internationale Beziehungen Vorderasiens um die Mitte des 2. Jahrtausends vor Chr. (Zugleich ein Konzept der Kurzchronologie)' in H. Kühne, H.J. Nissen, J. Renger (eds) *Mesopotamien und seine Nachbarn: politische und kulturelle Wechselbeziehungen im alten Vorderasien vom 4. bis 1. Jahrtausend v. Chr.* (Berliner Beitrage zum Vorderen Orient, Band 1). Berlin: 203–64

Kull, B. 1988: *Demircihüyük: Die mittelbronzezeitliche Siedlung. Die Ergebnisse der Ausgrabungen 1975–1978*. Mainz

Kümmerly, Frey 1985: *Road Map* (Turkey at scale 1:1,000,000). Bern

Kunst- und Ausstellungshalle der Bundesrepublik Deutschland (ed.) 2002: *Die Hethiter und ihr Reich. Das Volk der 1000 Götter*. Stuttgart

Kuzucuoğlu, C., Marro, C., Özdoğan, A., Tibet, A. 1997: 'Prospection archéologique Franco-Turque dans la région de Kastamonu (Mer Noire). Deuxième rapport préliminaire' *Anatolia Antiqua* 5: 275–306

Laflı, E. 2007: 'A Roman rock-cut cult niche at Paphlagonian Hadrianoupolis' *Araştırma Sonuçları Toplantısı* 24: 43–66

Laflı, E., Zäh, A. 2008: 'Archäologische Forschungen im byzantinischen Hadrianoúpolis in Paphlagonien' *Byzantinische Zeitschrift* 101

Lattimore, O. 1962: *Studies in Frontier History. Collected Papers 1928–1958*. London

Lebek, W.D. 1985: 'Das Grabepigramm auf Domitilla' *Zeitschrift für Papyrologie und Epigraphik* 59: 7–8

Legrand, M.E. 1897: 'Inscriptions de Paphlagonie' *Bulletin de Correspondance Hellénique* 21: 92–101

Leonhard, R. 1915: *Paphlagonia. Reisen und Forschungen im nördlichen Kleinasien*. Berlin

Leschhorn, W. 1993: *Antike Ären: Zeitrechnung, Politik und Geschichte im Schwarzmeerraum und in Kleinasien nördlich des Tauros*. Stuttgart

Leshtakov, K. 1996: 'Trade centres from Early Bronze Age III and Middle Bronze Age in Upper Thrace' in L. Nikolova (ed.) *Early Bronze Age Settlement Patterns in the Balkans (ca. 3500–2000 BC, Calibrated Dates). Part 2*. Sofia: 239–87

Levick, B.M. 1996: 'Greece (including Crete and Cyprus) and Asia Minor from 43 BC to 69 AD' in A.K. Bowman, E. Champlin, A. Lintott (eds) *The Cambridge Ancient History. Volume X. The Augustan Empire, 43 BC–69 AD*. Cambridge: 641–75

Lichter, C. 2005: 'Introduction to the workshop' in C. Lichter (ed.) *How Did Farming Reach Europe?* (BYZAS 2). Istanbul: 1–11

Lightfoot, K.G., Martinez, A. 1995: 'Frontiers and boundaries in archaeological perspective' *Annual Review of Anthropology* 24: 471–92

Lloyd, S. 1956: *Early Anatolia*. Harmondsworth

Lloyd, S., Mellaart, J. 1962: *The Chalcolithic and Early Bronze Age Levels* (Beycesultan I). London

L'vov-Basirov, O.P.V. 2001: 'Achaemenian funerary practices in western Asia Minor' in T. Bakır (ed.) *Achaemenid Anatolia*. Leiden: 101–07

MTA n.d.: *Geologic Map Series* (Bolu-G29, Çankırı-G30, Çankırı-G31, at scale 1:100,000). Ankara

Macqueen, J.G. 1980: 'Nerik and its "Weather-God"' *Anatolian Studies* 30: 179–87

Magdalino, P. 1998: 'Paphlagonians in Byzantine high society' in S. Lampakis (ed.) *Byzantine Asia Minor, 6th–12th Centuries*. Athens: 141–50

Magie, D. 1950: *Roman Rule in Asia Minor to the End of the Third Century after Christ*. Princeton

Mango, C., Scott, R. 1997: *The Chronicle of Theophanes Confessor*. Oxford

Marek, C. 1993: *Stadt, Ära und Territorium in Pontus-Bithynia und Nord-Galatia* (Istanbuler Forschungen 39). Tübingen

— 2003: *Pontus et Bithynia. Die römischen Provinzen im Norden Kleinasiens*. Mainz am Rhein

Marro, C. 2000: 'Archaeological survey in the Kastamonu region, Turkey: remarks on the pre-classical cultural geography of the southern Black Sea' in P. Matthiae, A. Enea, L. Peyronel, F. Pinnock (eds) *Proceedings of the First International Congress on the Archaeology of the Ancient Near East. Rome, May 18th–23rd 1998*. Rome: 945–65

Marro, C., Özdoğan, A., Tibet, A. 1996: 'Prospection archéologique Franco-Turque dans la région de Kastamonu (Mer Noire). Premier rapport préliminaire' *Anatolia Antiqua* 4: 273–90

— 1998: 'Prospection archéologique Franco-Turque dans la région de Kastamonu (Mer Noire). Troisième rapport préliminaire' *Anatolia Antiqua* 6: 317–35

Marsh, B. 1999: 'Sakarya river history and the alluvial burial of Gordion' *Journal of Field Archaeology* 26: 163–75

— 2005: 'Physical geography, land use, and human impact at Gordion' in L. Kealhofer (ed.) *The Archaeology of Midas and the Phrygians: Recent Work at Gordion*. Philadelphia: 161–71

Mason, K. 1942: *Turkey. Volume I* (Geographical Handbook Series BR 507). London

— 1943: *Turkey. Volume II* (Geographical Handbook Series BR 507A). London

Matsumura, K. 2000: 'On the manufacturing techniques of Iron Age ceramics from Kaman-Kalehöyük' in *Kaman-Kalehöyük 9* (Anatolian Archaeological Studies 9). Tokyo: 119–35

— 2001: 'On the manufacturing techniques of Iron Age ceramics from Kaman-Kalehöyük (II): the cultural influence of Phrygia at Kaman-Kalehöyük' in *Kaman-Kalehöyük 10* (Anatolian Archaeological Studies 10). Tokyo: 101–10

Matsunaga, M., Nakai, I. 2000: 'Study on the origin of the silver luster on gray Iron Age pottery' in *Kaman-Kalehöyük 9* (Anatolian Archaeological Studies 9). Tokyo: 207–11

Matthews, R. 1997: 'Project Paphlagonia' *Anatolian Archaeology* 3: 20–21

— 1998: 'Project Paphlagonia' *Anatolian Archaeology* 4: 21–22

— 1999a: 'Regional survey in Paphlagonia' *Anadolu Medeniyetleri Müzesi 1998 Konferansları*: 66–75

— 1999b: 'Project Paphlagonia: regional survey in Çankırı province, 1997' *Araştırma Sonuçları Toplantısı* 16: 245–54

— 1999c: 'Project Paphlagonia: landscapes with figures' *Anatolian Archaeology* 5: 16–18

— 2000a: 'Project Paphlagonia: regional survey in Çankırı and Karabük provinces, 1998' *Araştırma Sonuçları Toplantısı* 17: 175–80

— 2000b: 'Hittites and "barbarians" in the Late Bronze Age: regional survey in northern Turkey' *Archaeology International* 3: 32–35

— 2000c: 'A long walk in the park: Project Paphlagonia 2000' *Anatolian Archaeology* 6: 19–20

— 2000d: 'Time with the past in Paphlagonia' in P. Matthiae, A. Enea, L. Peyronel, F. Pinnock (eds) *Proceedings of the First International Congress on the Archaeology of the Ancient Near East. Rome, May 18th–23rd 1998*. Rome: 1013–27

— 2000e: *The Early Prehistory of Mesopotamia 500,000 to 4,500 bc* (Subartu V). Turnhout

— 2001a: 'Project Paphlagonia: regional survey in Çankırı and Karabük provinces, 1999' *Araştırma Sonuçları Toplantısı* 18: 249–56

— 2001b: 'Project Paphlagonia 2001' *Anatolian Archaeology* 7: 20–21

— 2002: 'Project Paphlagonia: regional survey in Çankırı and Karabük provinces, 2000' *Araştırma Sonuçları Toplantısı* 19: 9–14

— 2003: 'Project Paphlagonia: regional survey in Çankırı and Karabük provinces, 2001' *Araştırma Sonuçları Toplantısı* 20: 219–22

— 2004a: 'Salur North: an Early Bronze Age cemetery in north-central Anatolia' in A. Sagona (ed.) *A View from the Highlands. Archaeological Studies in Honour of Charles Burney*. Leuven: 55–66

— 2004b: 'Landscapes of terror and control. Imperial impacts in Paphlagonia' *Near Eastern Archaeology* 67: 200–11

— 2007: 'An arena for cultural contact: Paphlagonia (north-central Turkey) through prehistory' *Anatolian Studies* 57: 25–34

— 2008: 'Social and cultural transformation: the archaeology of transitional periods and dark ages' in H. Kühne, R.M. Czichon, F.J. Kreppner (eds) *Proceedings of the 4th International Congress of the Archaeology of the Ancient Near East 29 March–3 April 2004, Freie Universität Berlin. Volume 2*. Wiesbaden: 3–8

Matthews, R., Glatz, C. Forthcoming: 'The historical geography of north-central Anatolia in the Hittite period: texts and archaeology in concert' *Anatolian Studies* 59

Matthews, R., Pollard, T., Ramage, M. 1998: 'Project Paphlagonia: regional survey in northern Anatolia' in R. Matthews (ed.) *Ancient Anatolia. Fifty Years' Work by the British Institute of Archaeology at Ankara*. London: 195–206

Mattingly, D. 2000: 'Methods of collection, recording and quantification' in R. Francovich, H. Patterson (eds) *Extracting Meaning from Ploughsoil Assemblages*. Oxford: 5–15

McGing, B.C. 1986: *The Foreign Policy of Mithridates VI Eupator King of Pontus*. Leiden

Mendel, G. 1901: 'Inscriptions de Bithynie' *Bulletin de Correspondance Hellénique* 25: 5–92

Menkova, M. 2000: 'Time and space in Ezero culture interrelations: the Early Bronze Age' *Archaeologia Bulgarica* 4/2: 1–17

Merkelbach, R., Stauber, J. 2001: *Steinepigramme aus dem griechischen Osten 2. Die Nordküste Kleinasiens (Marmarameer und Pontos)*. Stuttgart

Mielke, D.P. 1998: 'Die Nachuntersuchungen am Westhang' in A. Müller-Karpe 'Untersuchungen in Kuşaklı 1997' *Mitteilungen der Deutschen Orient-Gesellschaft* 130: 120–29

— 2006: 'İnandıktepe und Sarissa. Ein Beitrag zur Datierung althethitischer Fundkomplexe' in D.P. Mielke, U.-D. Schoop, J. Seeher (eds) *Strukturierung und Datierung der hethitischen Archäologie: Voraussetzungen – Probleme – Neue Ansätze. Internationaler Workshop Istanbul, 26–27. November 2004* (BYZAS 4). Istanbul: 251–76

Mikami, T., Omura, S. 1988: '1986 Kırşehir ili sınırları içinde yapılan yüzey araştırmaları' *Araştırma Sonuçları Toplantısı* 5: 123–56

— 1990: '1988 Kırşehir, Yozgat ve Nevşehir illeri yüzey araştırmaları' *Araştırma Sonuçları Toplantısı* 7: 295–305

Mitchell, S. 1993a: *Anatolia. Land, Men, and Gods in Asia Minor. Volume I The Celts in Anatolia and the Impact of Roman Rule*. Oxford

— 1993b: *Anatolia. Land, Men, and Gods in Asia Minor. Volume II The Rise of the Church*. Oxford

— 2002: 'In search of the Pontic community in antiquity' *Proceedings of the British Academy* 114: 35–64

— 2003: 'Recent archaeology and the development of cities in Hellenistic and Roman Asia Minor' in E. Schwertheim, E. Winter (eds) *Stadt und Stadtentwicklung in Kleinasien* (Asia Minor Studien 50). Bonn: 21–34

— Forthcoming: 'The Ionians of Paphlagonia'

Mordtmann, A.D. 1925: *Anatolien. Skizzen und Reisebriefe aus Kleinasien*. Hannover

Mordtmann, J.H. 1960: 'Çankırı' in *Encyclopedia of Islam* (second edition). Leiden

Müller-Karpe, A. 1988: *Hethitische Töpferei der Oberstadt von Hattuša. Ein Beitrag zur Kenntnis spät-großreichszeitlicher Keramik und Töpferbetriebe unter Zugrundelegung der Grabungsergebnisse von 1978–82 in Boğazköy*. Marburg

— 2003. 'Remarks on the central Anatolian chronology of the Middle Hittite Period' in M. Bietak (ed.) *SCIEM 2000: The Synchronisation of Civilisations in the Eastern Mediterranean in the Second Millennium BC II, Proceedings of the SCIEM 2000 – EuroConference Haindforf, 2nd of May–7th of May 2001*. Vienna: 383–94

Müller-Karpe, V. 1998: 'Keramikfunde aus dem Gebäude C der Akropolis von Kuşaklı' in A. Müller-Karpe 'Untersuchungen in Kuşaklı 1997' *Mitteilungen der Deutschen Orient-Gesellschaft* 130: 112–19

— 2001: 'Zur frühhethitischen Kultur im Mündungsgebiet des Maraššantija' in G. Wilhelm (ed.) *Akten des IV. Internationalen Kongresses für Hethitologie. Würzburg 4.–8. Oktober 1999* (StBoT 45). Wiesbaden: 430–42

Muscarella, O.W. 1995: 'The Iron Age background to the formation of the Phrygian state' *Bulletin of the American Schools of Oriental Research* 299/300: 91–101

Neve, P. 1984: 'Ein althethitischer Sammelfund aus der Unterstadt' in K. Bittel (ed.) *Boğazköy VI. Funde aus den Grabungen bis 1979*. Berlin: 63–89

Nikolova, L. 1999: *The Balkans in Later Prehistory. Periodization, Chronology and Cultural Development in the Final Copper and Early Bronze Age (Fourth and Third Millennia BC)*. Oxford

Ökse, A.T. 1998: 'Siedlungsgeschichte des oberen Kızılırmak-Gebietes von der Frühbronze- bis zur Eisenzeit' *Belleten* 62: 337–90

— 1999: 'Orta Anadolu'nun doğusunun Demirçağ kültür ve yerleşim dokusu' in *1998 Yılı Anadolu Medeniyetleri Müzesi Konferansları*. Ankara: 85–116

— 2000: 'Neue hethitische Siedlungen zwischen Maşat Höyük und Kuşaklı' *Istanbuler Mitteilungen* 50: 87–111

— 2001: 'Hethitisches Territorium am oberen Maraššantia. Ein Rekonstruktionsversuch' in G. Wilhelm (ed.) *Akten des IV. Internationalen Kongresses für Hethitologie. Würzburg 4.–8. Oktober 1999* (StBoT 45). Wiesbaden: 499–510

Omura, S. 1989: '1987 Kırşehir ili sınırları içinde yapılan yüzey araştırmaları' *Araştırma Sonuçları Toplantısı* 6: 555–70

— 1991: '1989 yılı Kırşehir, Yozgat, Nevşehir, Aksaray illeri sınırları içinde yürütülen yüzey araştırmaları' *Araştırma Sonuçları Toplantısı* 8: 69–81

— 1992: '1990 yılı orta Anadolu'da yürütülen yüzey araştırmaları' *Araştırma Sonuçları Toplantısı* 9: 541–60

— 1993: '1991 yılı iç Anadolu'da yürütülen yüzey araştırmaları' *Araştırma Sonuçları Toplantısı* 10: 365–86

— 1994: '1992 yılında iç Anadolu'da yürütülen yüzey araştırmaları' *Araştırma Sonuçları Toplantısı* 11: 311–36

— 1995: '1993 yılında iç Anadolu'da yürütülen yüzey araştırmaları' *Araştırma Sonuçları Toplantısı* 12: 215–44

— 1996: '1994 yılı iç Anadolu'da yürütülen yüzey araştırmaları' *Araştırma Sonuçları Toplantısı* 13: 243–72

— 1997: '1995 yılı iç Anadolu'da yürütülen yüzey araştırmaları' *Araştırma Sonuçları Toplantısı* 14: 283–302

— 1998: '1996 yılı iç Anadolu'da yürütülen yüzey araştırmaları' *Araştırma Sonuçları Toplantısı* 15: 41–50

— 2000: 'Preliminary report of the general survey in central Anatolia (1999)' in *Kaman-Kalehöyük 9* (Anatolian Archaeological Studies 9). Tokyo: 37–96

— 2001: 'Preliminary report of the general survey in central Anatolia (2000)' in *Kaman-Kalehöyük 10* (Anatolian Archaeological Studies 10). Tokyo: 37–86

— 2002: 'Preliminary report of the general survey in central Anatolia (2001)' in *Kaman-Kalehöyük 11* (Anatolian Archaeological Studies 11). Tokyo: 45–112

— 2003: 'Preliminary report of the general survey in central Anatolia (2002)' in *Kaman-Kalehöyük 12* (Anatolian Archaeological Studies 12). Tokyo: 37–88

— 2005: 'Preliminary report of the 2004 general survey in central Anatolia' in *Kaman-Kalehöyük 14* (Anatolian Archaeological Studies 14). Tokyo: 55–96

Orthmann, W. 1963a: *Frühe Keramik von Boğazköy-Hattusa aus den Ausgrabungen am Nordwesthang von Büyükkale*. Berlin

— 1963b: *Die Keramik der frühen Bronzezeit aus Inneranatolien*. Berlin

— 1984: 'Keramik aus den ältesten Schichten von Büyükkale' in K. Bittel (ed.) *Boğazköy VI. Funde aus den Grabungen bis 1979*. Berlin: 9–62

Özdoğan, M. 1982: 'Doğu Marmara ve Trakya araştırmaları' *Türk Arkeoloji Dergisi* 26/1: 37–61

— 1996: 'Pre-Bronze Age sequence of central Anatolia: an alternative approach' in U. Magen, M. Rashad (eds) *Vom Halys zum Euphrat. Thomas Beran zu Ehren* (Altertumskunde des Vorderen Orients 7). Münster: 185–202

— 1998: 'Tarihöncesi dönemlerde Anadolu ile Balkanlar arasındaki kültür ilişkileri ve Trakya'da yapılan yeni kazı calışmaları' *Tüba-Ar* 1: 63–93

— 2001: 'Kırklareli excavations: Aşağı Pınar and Kanlıgeçit' in O. Belli (ed.) *Istanbul University's Contributions to Archaeology in Turkey*. Istanbul: 56–63

Özdoğan, M., Parsinger, H., Karul, N. 1999: 'Kırklareli Höyüğü 1997 yılı kazısı' *Kazı Sonuçları Toplantısı* 20/1: 139–64

Özgüç, T. 1978: *Excavations at Maşat Höyük and Investigations in its Vicinity*. Ankara

— 1988: *İnandıktepe. An Important Cult Center in the Old Hittite Period*. Ankara

Özgüç, T., Akok, M. 1958: *Horoztepe. An Early Bronze Age Settlement and Cemetery*. Ankara

Özsait, M. 1988: '1986 yılı Amasya – Lâdik çevresi tarihöncesi araştırmaları' *Araştırma Sonuçları Toplantısı* 5: 239–56

— 1989: '1987 yılı Amasya – Suluova tarihöncesi araştırmaları' *Araştırma Sonuçları Toplantısı* 6: 287–300

— 1990: '1988 yılı Gümüşhacıköy çevresi tarihöncesi araştırmaları' *Araştırma Sonuçları Toplantısı* 7: 367–79

— 1991: '1989 yılı Göynücek çevresi tarihöncesi araştırmaları' *Araştırma Sonuçları Toplantısı* 8: 239–56

— 1992: '1990 yılı Ordu – Mesudiye çevresinde yapılan yüzey araştırmaları' *Araştırma Sonuçları Toplantısı* 9: 357–76

— 1993: '1991 yılı Ordu – Çeltikçi ve Yeşilova yüzey araştırmaları' *Araştırma Sonuçları Toplantısı* 10: 331–44

— 1994: '1988 yılı Tokat-Erbaa çevresi tarih öncesi araştırmaları' *Türk Tarih Kongresi* 11: 113–29

— 1995: '1993 yılı Ordu – Mesudiye ve Sivas-Koyulhisar yüzey araştırmaları' *Araştırma Sonuçları Toplantısı* 12: 459–82

— 1998: '1995 ve 1996 yıllarında Amasya – Merzifon ve Gümüşhacıköy yüzey araştırmaları' *Araştırma Sonuçları Toplantısı* 15: 143–61

— 1999: '1997 yılı Tokat ve Çevresi yüzey araştırmaları' *Araştırma Sonuçları Toplantısı* 16: 89–107

— 2000a: 'Göller bölgesi yüzey araştırması ve Harmanören kazısı' in O. Belli (ed.) *Türkiye Arkeolojisi ve İstanbul Üniversitesi (1932–1999).* Istanbul: 147–53

— 2000b: '1997 ve 1998 yılı Tokat-Zile ve çevresi yüzey araştırmaları' *Araştırma Sonuçları Toplantısı* 17: 73–88

— 2002: '1999–2000 yılı Amasya-Merzifon ve Ordu-Kumru yüzey araştırması' *Araştırma Sonuçları Toplantısı* 19: 191–216

— 2003a: '2001 yılı Samsun ve Amasya yüzey araştırmaları' *Araştırma Sonuçları Toplantısı* 20: 127–50

— 2003b: 'Les céramiques du Fer Ancien dans les régions d'Amasya et de Samsun' in B. Fischer, H. Genz, É. Jean, K. Köroğlu (eds) *Identifying Changes: The Transition from Bronze to Iron Ages in Anatolia and its Neighbouring Regions.* Istanbul: 199–212

— 2004: '2002 yılı Samsun-Amasya yüzey araştırmalarının ilk sonuçları' *Araştırma Sonuçları Toplantısı* 21: 273–84

— 2005: '2003 yılı Amasya, Samsun ve Ordu illeri yüzey araştırmaları' *Araştırma Sonuçları Toplantısı* 22: 263–74

Özsait, M., Dündar, A. 1997: '1995 yılı Amasya – Gümüşhaciköy ve Hamamözü yüzey araştırmaları' *Araştırma Sonuçları Toplantısı* 14: 171–92

Özsait, M., Koçak, Ö. 1996: '1994 yılı Amasya-Taşova yüzey araştırmaları' *Araştırma Sonuçları Toplantısı* 13: 273–91

Özsait, M., Özsait, N. 2001: 'Les sites archéologiques du IIe millénaire avant J.-C. à Tokat' in G. Wilhelm (ed.) *Akten des IV. Internationalen Kongresses für Hethitologie. Würzburg 4.–8. Oktober 1999* (StBoT 45). Wiesbaden: 541–51

Palumbo Stracca, B.M. 1996–1997: 'Hybris barbarica e sophrosyne greca. L'epitafio per Domitilla' *Romanobarbarica* 14: 15–32

Parzinger, H. 1993: *Studien zur Chronologie und Kulturgeschichte der Jungstein-, Kupfer- und Frühbronzezeit zwischen Karpaten und mittlerem Taurus.* Mainz am Rhein

Parzinger, H., Sanz, R. 1992: *Die Oberstadt Keramik von Hattuša. Hethitische Keramik aus dem zentralen Tempelviertel.* Berlin

Peek, W. 1955: *Griechische Vers-Inschriften I. Die Grabepigramme.* Berlin

— 1985: 'Zu neugefunden Epigrammen aus Kleinasien' *Epigraphica Anatolica* 5: 156–58

Pleket, H.W. 2003: 'Economy and urbanization: was there an impact of empire in Asia Minor?' in E. Schwertheim, E. Winter (eds) *Stadt und Stadtentwicklung in Kleinasien* (Asia Minor Studien 50). Bonn: 85–95

Postgate, J.N. 2007: 'The ceramics of centralisation and dissolution: a case study from Rough Cilicia' *Anatolian Studies* 57: 141–50

Prayon, F., Wittke, A.-M. 1994: *Kleinasien vom 12. bis 6. Jh. v. Chr.* (Beihefte zum Tübinger Atlas des Vorderen Orients Reihe B 82). Wiesbaden

Ramsay, W.M. 1890: *The Historical Geography of Asia Minor* (Royal Geographical Society Supplementary Papers). London

Robert, L. 1963: *Noms indigènes dans l'Asie Mineure gréco-romaine.* Paris

— 1980: *A Travers L'Asie Mineure.* Athens

Roberts, N. 1982: 'Forest re-advance and the Anatolian Neolithic' in M. Bell, S. Limbrey (eds) *Archaeological Aspects of Woodland Ecology.* Oxford: 231–46

Roberts, N., Reed, J., Leng, M.J., Kuzucuoğlu, C., Fontugne, M., Bertaux, J., Woldring, H., Bottema, S., Black, S., Hunt, E., Karabıyıkoğlu, M. 2001: 'The tempo of Holocene climatic change in the eastern Mediterranean region: new high-resolution crater-lake sediment data from central Turkey' *The Holocene* 11: 719–34

Roodenberg, J. 2003: 'Note on the Early Bronze Age pithos burials from Ilıpınar-Hacılartepe' in M. Özdoğan, H. Hauptmann, N. Başgelen (eds) *From Village to Cities. Studies Presented to Ufuk Esin.* Istanbul: 297–306

Root, M.C. 1991: 'From the heart: powerful Persianisms in the art of the western empire' in H. Sancisi-Weerdenburg, A. Kuhrt (eds) *Achaemenid History VI. Asia Minor and Egypt: Old Cultures in a New Empire.* Leiden: 1–29

Ryan, W.B.F., Pitman III, W.C. 1998: *Noah's Flood: The New Scientific Discoveries about the Event that Changed History.* New York

Sagona, A. 2004: 'Settlement patterns' in A. Sagona, C. Sagona (eds) *Archaeology at the North-East Anatolian Frontier, I. An Historical Geography and a Field Survey of the Bayburt Province* (Ancient Near Eastern Studies Supplement 14). Louvain: 235–43

Sams, G.K. 1994: *The Early Phrygian Pottery* (Gordion Excavations, 1950–1973: Final Reports 4). Philadelphia

Schoop, U.-D. 2003a: 'Pottery traditions of the later Hittite empire: problems of definition' in B. Fischer, H. Genz, É. Jean, K. Köroğlu (eds) *Identifying Changes: the Transition from Bronze to Iron Ages in Anatolia and its Neighbouring Regions.* Istanbul: 167–78

— 2003b: 'Erste Beobachtungen zum Keramikinventar aus dem Tal vor Sarıkale' *Archäologischer Anzeiger* 2003/1: 14–20

— 2005a: 'Early Chalcolithic in north-central Anatolia: the evidence from Boğazköy-Büyükkaya' *Tüba-Ar* 8: 15–37

— 2005b: 'The late escape of the Neolithic from the central Anatolian plain' in C. Lichter (ed.) *How Did Farming Reach Europe?* (BYZAS 2). Istanbul: 41–58

— 2005c: *Das anatolische Chalkolithikum* (Urgeschichtliche Studien 1). Remshalden

— 2006: 'Dating the Hittites with statistics. Ten pottery assemblages from Boğazköy-Hattuša' in D.P. Mielke, U.-D. Schoop, J. Seeher (eds) *Strukturierung und Datierung der hethitischen Archäologie: Voraussetzungen – Probleme – Neue Ansätze. Internationaler Workshop Istanbul, 26–27. November 2004* (BYZAS 4). Istanbul: 215–39

— Forthcoming: 'Hittite pottery – a summary' *Ancient West and East*

Schuler, C. 1998: *Ländliche Siedlungen und Gemeinden im hellenistischen und römischen Kleinasien*. Munich

Seeher, J. 1987: *Demircihüyük. Die Ergebnisse der Ausgrabungen 1975–1978 Band III,1. Die Keramik 1*. Mainz am Rhein

— 2000a: *Die bronzezeitliche Nekropole von Demircihüyük-Sarıket. Ausgrabungen des Deutschen Archäologischen Instituts in Zusammenarbeit mit dem Museum Bursa, 1990–1991* (Istanbuler Forschungen 44). Tübingen

— 2000b: 'Hattuša/Boğazköy'ün yerleşim tarihine yeni katkılar: Büyükkaya kazılarına toplu bir bakış' *Tüba-Ar* 3: 15–34

— 2001: 'Die Zerstörung der Stadt Hattuša' in G. Wilhelm (ed.) *Akten des IV. Internationalen Kongresses für Hethitologie. Würzburg 4.–8. Oktober 1999* (StBoT 45). Wiesbaden: 623–34

SEG = *Supplementum Epigraphicum Graecum*. Leiden 1923–

Séfériadès. M. 1996: 'Deshayes' excavations at Dikili Tash: the Early Bronze Age levels' in L. Nikolova (ed.) *Early Bronze Age Settlement Patterns in the Balkans (ca. 3500–2000 BC, Calibrated Dates). Part 2*. Sofia: 95–128

Sherratt, A. 1986: 'The pottery of phases IV and V: the Early Bronze Age' in C. Renfrew, M. Gimbutas, E.S. Elster (eds) *Excavations at Sitagroi. A Prehistoric Village in Northeast Greece*. Los Angeles: 429–76

Singer, I. 2007: 'Who were the Kaška?' *Phasis* 10: 166–81

Sipahi, T. 2000: 'Eine althethitische Reliefvase vom Hüseyindede Tepesi' *Istanbuler Mitteilungen* 50: 63–85

— 2001: 'New evidence from Anatolia regarding bull-leaping scenes in the art of the Aegean and the Near East' *Anatolica* 27: 107–25

— 2003: '2001 yılı Çorum ve Çankırı bölgeleri yüzey araştırması' *Araştırma Sonuçları Toplantısı* 20/2: 275–84

Sipahi, T., Yıldırım, T. 1998: '1996 yılı Çorum bölgesi yüzey araştırmaları' *Araştırma Sonuçları Toplantısı* 15: 19–39

— 1999: '1997 yılı Çorum bölgesi yüzey araştırmaları' *Araştırma Sonuçları Toplantısı* 16: 433–50

— 2000: '1998 yılı Çorum bölgesi yüzey araştırması' *Araştırma Sonuçları Toplantısı* 17: 31–40

— 2001: '1999 yılı Çorum yöresi yüzey araştırması' *Araştırma Sonuçları Toplantısı* 18/2: 101–12

— 2005: '2003 yılı Çorum ve Çankırı illeri yüzey araştırması' *Araştırma Sonuçları Toplantısı* 22: 353–64

Steadman, S.R. 1995: 'Prehistoric interregional interaction in Anatolia and the Balkans: an overview' *Bulletin of the American Schools of Oriental Research* 299/300: 13–32

Strobel, K. 2002: 'State formation by the Galatians of Asia Minor. Politico-historical and cultural processes in Hellenistic central Anatolia' *Anatolica* 28: 1–46

Süel, M. 1989: 'Balıbağı/1988 kurtarma kazısı' *Türk Arkeoloji Dergisi* 28: 145–63

Summerer, L. 2007: 'Greeks and natives on the southern Black Sea coast in antiquity' in G. Erkut, S. Mitchell (eds) *The Black Sea: Past, Present and Future* (British Institute at Ankara Monograph 42). London: 27–36

Summers, G.D. 1994: 'Grey ware and the eastern limits of Phrygia' in A. Çilingiroğlu, D.H. French (eds) *Anatolian Iron Ages 3* (British Institute of Archaeology at Ankara Monograph 16). London: 241–52

— 2002: 'Concerning the identification, location and distribution of the Neolithic and Chalcolithic settlements in central Anatolia' in F. Gérard, L. Thissen (eds) *The Neolithic of Central Anatolia*. Istanbul: 131–37

Şahin, İ. 1993: 'Çankırı' in *TDV İslam Ansiklopedisi*. Istanbul

Şengör, A.M.C. 1979: 'The North Anatolian Fault: its age, offset and tectonic significance' *Journal of Geological Society of London* 136: 269–82

Şengör, A.M.C., Yılmaz, Y. 1981: 'Tethyan evolution of Turkey: a plate tectonic approach' *Tectonophysics* 75: 181–241

Talbert, R.J.A. 2000: *Barrington Atlas of the Greek and Roman World*. Princeton

Talbot, M.R., Kelts, K. 1986: 'Primary and diagenetic carbonates in the anoxic sediments of Lake Bosumtwi, Ghana' *Geology* 14: 912–16

Teller, J.T., Last, W.M. 1990: 'Paleohydrological indicators in playas and salt lakes, with examples from Canada, Australia and Africa' *Palaeogeography, Palaeoclimatology, Palaeoecology* 76: 215–40

Thissen, L.C. 1993: 'New insights in Balkan-Anatolian connections in the Late Chalcolithic: old evidence from the Turkish Black Sea littoral' *Anatolian Studies* 43: 207–37

— 1995: 'A synopsis of pottery shapes from phases X–VI' in J. Roodenberg (ed.) *The Ilıpınar Excavations I*. Istanbul: 109–19

— 2001: 'The pottery of Ilıpınar, phases X to VA' in J. Roodenberg, L.C. Thissen (eds) *The Ilıpınar Excavations II*. Istanbul: 3–154

Thompson, J.B., Ferris, F.G. 1990: 'Cyanobacterial precipitation of gypsum, calcite and magnesite from natural alkaline lake water' *Geology* 18: 995–98

Todd, I.A. 1998: 'Central Anatolian survey' in R. Matthews (ed.) *Ancient Anatolia. Fifty Years' Work by the British Institute of Archaeology at Ankara*. London: 17–26

Tokay, M. 1973: 'Kuzey Anadolu fay zonunun Gerede ile Ilgaz arasındaki kısmında jeolojik gözlemler' in *Symposium on the North Anatolian Fault and Earthquake Belt*. Ankara: 12–29

— 1982: 'Recently active breaks along the North Anatolian Fault zone between Gerede and Ilgaz' in A.M. Işıkara, A. Vogel (eds) *Multidisciplinary Approach to Earthquake Prediction*. Braunschweig: 173–84

Topbaş, A., Efe, T., İlaslı, A. 1998: 'Salvage excavations of the Afyon Archaeological Museum, part 2: the settlement of Karaoğlan Mevkii and the Early Bronze Age cemetery of Kaklık Mevkii' *Anatolia Antiqua* 6: 21–94

Treadgold, W. 1997: *A History of the Byzantine State and Society*. Stanford

Ünlü, E. 2005: 'Locally produced and painted Late Bronze Age to Iron Age transitional period pottery of Tarsus-Gözlükule' in A. Özyar (ed.) *Field Seasons 2001–2003 of the Tarsus-Gözlükule Project*. Istanbul: 145–68

Uzunçarşılı, I.H. 1998: *Osmanli Tarihi*. Ankara

Vanhaverbeke, H., Martens, F., Waelkens M., Poblome, J. 2004: 'Late antiquity in the territory of Sagalassos' in W. Bowden, L. Lavan, C. Machado (eds) *Recent Research on the Late Antique Countryside*. Leiden: 247–79

Vanhaverbeke, H., Waelkens, M. 1998: 'Lower, Middle and Upper Palaeolithic in the territory of Sagalassos (SW Turkey): problems and prospects' *Anatolia Antiqua* 6: 1–19

Vardar, L.E., Vardar, N.A. 2001: 'Galatia bölgesi kaleleri/yerleşmeleri yüzey araştırması: Ankara ve Kırıkkale illeri, 1999' *Araştırma Sonuçları Toplantısı* 18/2: 237–48

Veenhof, K.R. 1995: 'Kanesh: an Assyrian colony in Anatolia' in J.M. Sasson (ed.) *Civilizations of the Ancient Near East*. New York: 859–71

Voigt, M.M. 1994: 'Excavations at Gordion 1988–89; the Yassıhöyük stratigraphic sequence' in A. Çilingiroğlu, D.H. French (eds) *Anatolian Iron Ages 3* (British Institute of Archaeology at Ankara Monograph 16). London: 265–93

— 2002: 'Gordion: the rise and fall of an Iron Age capital' in D.C. Hopkins (ed.) *Across the Anatolian Plateau. Readings in the Archaeology of Ancient Turkey* (*Annual of the American Schools of Oriental Research* 57). Boston: 187–96

— 2005: 'Old problems and new solutions. Recent excavations at Gordion' in L. Kealhofer (ed.) *The Archaeology of Midas and the Phrygians. Recent Work at Gordion*. Philadelphia: 22–35

Voigt, M.M., DeVries, K., Henrickson, R.C., Lawall, M., Marsh, B., Gürsan-Salzman, A., Young Jr, T.C. 1997: 'Fieldwork at Gordion: 1993–1995' *Anatolica* 23: 1–59

Voigt, M.M., Henrickson, R.C. 2000: 'Formation of the Phrygian state: the Early Iron Age at Gordion' *Anatolian Studies* 50: 37–54

Voigt, M.M., Young Jr, T.C. 1999: 'From Phrygian capital to Achaemenid entrepot: Middle and Late Phrygian Gordion' *Iranica Antiqua* 34: 191–241

Von der Osten, H.H. 1937: *The Alishar Hüyük. Seasons of 1930–1932. Part 1* (Oriental Institute Publications 28). Chicago

von Flottwell, V. 1895: 'Aus dem Stromgebiet des Qyzyl-Yrmaq (Halys)' *Petermanns Mitteilungen Ergänzungsheft* 114: 1–56

von Gall, H. 1966: *Die paphlagonischen Felsgräber* (Istanbuler Mitteilungen Beiheft 1). Tübingen

— 1967: 'Felsgräber der Perserzeit im pontischen Kleinasien' *Archäologischer Anzeiger* 1: 585–95

von Schuler, E. 1965: *Die Kaskäer: Ein Beitrag zur Ethnographie des alten Kleinasien* (Archiv für Orientforschung Beiheft 10). Berlin

Vryonis, S. Jr 1971: *The Decline of Medieval Hellenism in Asia Minor and the Process of Islamization from the Eleventh through the Fifteenth Century*. Berkeley

Warner, J.L. 1994: *Elmalı-Karataş II. The Early Bronze Age Village of Karataş*. Bryn Mawr

Wilhelm, G. 2005: 'Zur Datierung der älteren hethitischen Landschenkungsurkunden' *Altorientalische Forschungen* 32/2: 272–79

Wilhelm, G., Boese, J. 1987: 'Absolut Chronology und die hethitische Geschichte des 15. und 14. Jahrtausends v. Chr.' in P. Åström (ed.) *High, Middle or Low?* Gotenburg: 74–117

Wilkinson, T.J. 1989: 'Extensive sherd scatters and land-use intensity: some recent results' *Journal of Field Archaeology* 16: 31–46

— 2003: *Archaeological Landscapes of the Near East.* Tucson

Wilson, D.R. 1960: *The Historical Geography of Bithynia, Paphlagonia and Pontus in the Greek and Roman periods: A New Survey with Particular Reference to Surface Remains Still Visible.* Unpublished BLitt thesis, Oxford University

Yakar, J. 1980: 'Recent contributions to the historical geography of the Hittite empire' *Mitteilungen der Deutschen Orient-Gesellschaft* 112: 75–93

— 1985: *The Later Prehistory of Anatolia. The Late Chalcolithic and Early Bronze Age.* Oxford

— 1994: *Prehistoric Anatolia. The Neolithic Transition and the Early Chalcolithic Period. Supplement No. 1.* Tel Aviv

Yakar, J., Dinçol, A.M. 1974: 'Remarks on the Historical Geography of north central Anatolia during the pre-Hittite and Hittite periods' *Tel Aviv* 1: 85–99

Yanko-Hombach, V. 2007: 'Late Quaternary history of the Black Sea: an overview with respect to the Noah's Flood hypothesis' in G. Erkut, S. Mitchell (eds) *The Black Sea: Past, Present and Future* (British Institute at Ankara Monograph 42). London: 5–20

Yegül, F.K. 2000: 'Memory, metaphor and meaning in the cities of Asia Minor' in E. Fentress (ed.) *Romanization and the City. Creation, Transformations, and Failures* (Journal of Roman Archaeology, Supplementary Series 38). Portsmouth: 133–53

Yener, K.A. 2000: *The Domestication of Metals. The Rise of Complex Metal Industries in Anatolia.* Leiden

Yerasimos, S. 1991: *Les Voyageurs dans l'Empire Ottoman (XIVe–XVIe siècles).* Ankara

Yıldırım, T. 2000: 'Yörüklü/Hüseyindede: Eine neue hethitische Siedlung im Südwesten vom Çorum' *Istanbuler Mitteilungen* 50: 43–62

Yıldırım, T., Sipahi, T. 2004: '2002 yılı Çorum ve Çankırı illeri yüzey araştırmaları' *Araştırma Sonuçları Toplantısı* 21/2: 305–13

Zarinebaf, F., Bennet, J., Davis, J.L. 2005: *A Historical and Economic Geography of Ottoman Greece. The Southwestern Morea in the 18th Century* (Hesperia Supplement 34). Princeton

Zgusta, L. 1964: *Kleinasiatische Personennamen.* Prague

Zimansky, P. 2007: 'The Lattimore model and Hatti's Kaska frontier' in E.C. Stone (ed.) *Settlement and Society. Essays Dedicated to Robert McCormick Adams.* Los Angeles: 157–72